P9-CBK-984

DISCARDED

379.151
M28

133687

DATE DUE			

Other titles in the Policy Analysis and Education Series

POLICY DECISION-MAKING IN EDUCATION
An Introduction to Calculation and Control
Dale Mann

IMPACT AND RESPONSE
Federal Aid and State Education Agencies
Mike M. Milstein

DELIVERING EDUCATIONAL SERVICE
Urban Schools and Schooling Policy
David Goodwin

IMPLEMENTATION, CHANGE, AND THE FEDERAL BUREAUCRACY
School Desegration Policy in H.E.W., 1964-1968
Beryl A. Radin

EDUCATION, SOCIAL SCIENCE, AND THE JUDICIAL PROCESS
Ray C. Rist and Ronald J. Anson (editors)

MAKING CHANGE HAPPEN?

DALE MANN, Editor

CARL A. RUDISILL LIBRARY
LENOIR RHYNE COLLEGE

Teachers College, Columbia University
New York and London

iv

Copyright © 1978 by Teachers College, Columbia University. Published by Teachers College Press, 1234 Amsterdam Avenue, New York, N.Y. 10027. All rights reserved.

Chapters 1, 2, 3, 6, 8, and 9 copyright © 1976 by Teachers College, Columbia University; Chapter 8 copyright © 1978 by Teachers College, Columbia University—all these chapters originally appeared in *Teachers College Record*.

We wish to acknowledge permission to reprint the following:

Richard F. Elmore, "Organizational Models of Social Program Implementation," *Public Policy*, vol. 26, no. 1, Spring 1978. Copyright © by the President and Fellows of Harvard College. Reprinted by permission of John Wiley & Sons, Inc.

Willis D. Hawley, "Horses Before Carts: Developing Adaptive Schools and the Limits of Innovation." Reprinted by permission of the publisher, from Sam K. Gove and Frederick M. Wirt, eds., *Political Science and School Politics* (Lexington, Mass.: Lexington Books, D. C. Heath and Company, 1976).

Sar A. Levitan and Robert Taggart, "The Great Society Did Succeed," *Political Science Quarterly*, vol. 91, no. 4, Winter 1976–77, pp. 601–618. Reprinted with permission from the Academy of Political Science and the authors.

Richard Weatherley and Michael Lipsky, "Street-Level Bureaucrats and Institutional Innovation: Implementing Special Education Reform," *Harvard Educational Review*, vol. 47, no. 2, May 1977, pp. 171–197. Copyright © by the President and Fellows of Harvard College.

Cover design and illustrations opposite Parts I, II, and III by Ner Beck.

379.151
M28
133687
Oct. 1985

Library of Congress Cataloging in Publication Data

Main entry under title:

Making change happen?

(Policy analysis and education series)
Includes bibliographical references and index.
1. Educational innovations—United States—
Addresses, essays, lectures.   2. Education and
state—United States—Addresses, essays, lectures.
I. Mann, Dale.   II. Series.
LA210.M16   379'.151'0973   78-21849
ISBN 0-8077-2548-X
Manufactured in the U.S.A.

8 7 6 5 4 3 2 1   78 80 81 82 83 84

To Edith and Ben

Contents

PART III   WHAT NEXT?

Contributors

R. Gary Bridge is associate professor of psychology and education at Teachers College, Columbia University.

Wayne J. Doyle was director of the Northwest Regional Educational Laboratory's external evaluation team and is the executive director of the Organization and Leadership Programs at the University of San Francisco.

Richard F. Elmore is an assistant professor at the Graduate School of Public Affairs, University of Washington.

Ralph A. Hanson is a senior member of the professional staff at SWRL Educational Research and Development, Los Alamitos, California.

Willis D. Hawley is the director of the Center for Education Policy, Institute for Policy Sciences and Public Affairs, Duke University.

Paul T. Hill is a social scientist with the Rand Corporation, Washington, D.C.

Sar A. Levitan is professor of economics and director of the Center for Social Policy Studies at George Washington University in Washington, D.C.

Michael Lipsky is a professor in the Department of Political Science, Massachusetts Institute of Technology.

Dale Mann is professor and chairperson of the Department of Educational Administration at Teachers College, Columbia University.

Milbrey Wallin McLaughlin is a social scientist with the Rand Corporation, Santa Monica, California.

Edward W. Pauly is an assistant professor at the Institution for Social and Policy Studies, Yale University.

Richard E. Schutz is the executive director of SWRL Educational Research and Development, Los Alamitos, California.

Robert Taggart is the administrator of the Office of Youth Programs, U.S. Department of Labor, Washington, D.C.

Constancia Warren is a project associate with the Institute for Urban and Minority Education, Teachers College, Columbia University.

Richard Weatherley is a professor with the School of Social Work and the Center for Social Welfare Research, University of Washington.

John G. Wirt is an operations research specialist with the Rand Corporation, Washington, D.C.

Introduction

In the last decade, federal and state education agencies have invested heavily in attempting to stimulate and sometimes force improvements in schooling. These efforts have used different theories of educational change and a variety of program strategies. The federal government has built labs and R&D centers, developed curriculum packages, sponsored workshops and staff development activities, and otherwise attempted to promote innovation in education. Those efforts at changing local schools have been evaluated through progress reports, contract audits, and a galaxy of formative and summative procedures. They have provided some interesting answers, but the question persists: ''What happened?''

Most of the studies reported here do not relieve the generally melancholy picture of how little of the reform agenda of the recent past has been achieved. Most educators realize that the amount and pace of change has fallen far short of initial expectations. The problem is more profound than simply pointing at the unrealistic impatience of the sixties. Programs were planned, curriculum was developed, teaching/learning units were packaged, teachers were trained, and the results were frustrating, uneven, unexpected, and temporary. With hindsight it is easy to see that designing and disseminating change is not *implementing* change. What happens inside the school, at the service delivery level, is absolutely related to our success or failure, yet the gap in our knowledge about implementing change in the schools is formidable.

The authors represented in this book have a variety of explanations for generally similar (and generally disappointing) results of change in schools. An additional conjecture may be in order. It is possible to argue that change agents in education were peculiarly disadvantaged precisely because they were educators working in educational institutions. Think of a number of very common, and very deeply rooted, assumptions held by most of us who work in and with schools.

First, we believe that people can be changed—that they are malleable, even that they may be perfectable. Since education is held to be one of the principal ways through which people are changed, the assumption that they can be changed is not very exceptional.

Second, we tend to assume that people are rational, that they orient them-selves toward goals, that they use information and calculation to govern their actions. We assume that if people are provided with more information about something, or if they are "educated," then they will modify their behavior accordingly.

Third, we assume that people in education share social purposes at some lofty or abstract level. We tend to think that there is a unitary set of values or goals, at some level of conceptualization, on which school people agree. Or, as an alternative to this third assumption, if people are held not to agree about values, then since they are malleable and since they are rational, we assume that they can be encouraged or influenced to agree about values. Either way there is a kind of expectation about consensual goals that guides our efforts at change in schools.

A number of questions can be raised about these assumptions—how malle-able are people, how rational are they—and while it might be interesting to debate them, these assumptions are not the focus of this essay. Instead, the point here is that the values of professionals and quasi-professionals in schools have not been sufficiently consensual to allow change-agent strategies, grounded in these assumptions, to work as they were supposed to work. Thus, the peculiar disadvantage of change agents in education lies in·applying methods which are largely educational to situations which are fundamentally political. The two modes are not necessarily incompatible, but neither the individuals in schools nor the schools as organizations represent pure enough concentrations of the assumed properties to allow strategies based almost ex-clusively on those assumptions to work.

Most diffusion/adoption/dissemination people in education have treated in-novation as a matter of organizational learning. For organizations, as well as individuals, who would not wish to learn more? Is not life-long learning and continual renewal the kind of goal which we should all rush to embrace? How can anyone be against improvement? But even in an "educational" mode, change raises fundamental questions of values and of power. The goals of change in education which were so fervently held at the policy formation level of the education system in the 60s turned out to have a very different meaning at the delivery level. Federal policy makers believed in change although they usually talked about the more neutral "innovation" or the more desirable "im-provement." But the people whose behavior was to change or be changed disagreed about the necessity for change. As generally dedicated professionals whose current practices represented their best effort, they were unlikely to agree on the need for change. Where two people agree on what is to be done, there is cooperation. Most change-agent efforts correctly assumed that cooper-ation would not be pandemic. Where two people initially disagree, but the second can be persuaded to adopt the goals or objectives of the first, that is influence. It was this influence model (which is very close to an educational model) that characterized most change-agent attempts. Yet, the model assumes that the party to be influenced will abandon his or her goals and adopt a new set, and that expectation says something about the relative illegitimacy of the abandoned goals and the relative superiority of the adopted goals. People at the delivery level, those who were to be the targets of the change-agent efforts, were generally unwilling to agree that their goals for students were morally or ethically inferior to anyone else's or that their pedagogy was worse than someone else's. Thus, models of change rooted in cooperation and/or influence fell short in situations where there were legitimate differences among the parties. Where two parties persist in their disagreement, yet one is somehow to do what he or she would not do otherwise, we have a situation of power. Power was not a common way to look at the change-agent experience, yet it may help to explain some otherwise puzzling outcomes.

It might, for example, help understand the salience of mutual adaptation. Virtually everyone assumed that change-agent projects would effect what was done in schools; that was, after all, their *raison d'être*. Policy makers were enthusiastic about potential change and people at the delivery level were apprehensive about it, but not many doubted that it would happen. Yet those expectations were not confirmed by the evaluations or studies that hunted for program—or project—effects on schooling sites. When only very faint and intermittent project-to-site effects appeared, people asked, "Why not?" What was wrong with the projects or programs? Only recently have we had reliable evidence about the other side of the coin, the site-to-project effects. It now seems clear that projects and sites are locked in a kind of arm wrestle to change the other before they are changed by the other. Thus, the melancholy history of change-agent programs needs to be explained not only by the weakness of the projects but also by the power inherent in the various sites. Evaluations which focused only on the intended project-to-site direction concluded, incorrectly, that not much was happening. The site was changing *project* features faster and more thoroughly than the project could change the site. These events are captured in the phrase "mutual adaptation" but the real flavor comes through best with the addition of the adjective "partisan." As Boss Plunkett once said of "politics," changing schools "ain't bean bag." The values at stake (and the consequences of the new behaviors) are significant and go to the heart of the professional's work in schools and the society's benefits from that work.

This book spells out some of the evidence and some of the ramifications of this current level of understanding about the implementation of change.

The three chapters in Part I, "Change Agent One," report on some of the results from the first year of one of the most extensive examinations of the change process in recent time. The chapters are secondary analyses of the Rand Corporation's study of federal programs supporting educational change which was undertaken on behalf of the United States Office of Education.

The Rand research strategy had two phases: an extensive survey-data-based exploration of 293 change-agent projects, followed by an intensive case analysis-based exploration of twenty-nine projects. The three chapters examine some of the results from the field analysis stage of that project.[1] Anyone who has seriously investigated the business of change in education knows what a thicket it is. Although some things work better than others, and although some options are clearly preferable to others, there are no easy answers. Worse, there are many wrong questions. The Rand project staff invested a great deal of effort in conceptualizing and reconceptualizing the field of planned change in education and the subfield of federally supported attempts to create planned change in education.

The change-agent strategy was designed to improve schools; individual projects temporarily supported by the government were to be the vehicle of that change. The central question addressed in the fieldwork was, quite simply, what happens when an innovative project is implemented in a school. The school as a unit of analysis for implementation was one distinguishing feature of this project. Another was its focus on the process of implementation. The project sought answers to two major questions:

1. Do projects with various characteristics change what parts of school?
2. Do schools with various characteristics change what parts of federally supported projects?

The field data collection, analysis, and interpretation was organized by a process schemata that asked key questions about each stage in the career of a change-agent project:

1. *Initiation Stage*: Why and how did the school initiate the project? What were the original characteristics of the project?
2. *Implementation Stage:* What were the early characteristics of the project and of the site?
3. *Adaptation:* Did the school affect the project and, if so, how?
4. *Near Term Behaviorial Change*: Did the project affect the school and, if so, how?
5. *Continuation:* What characteristics of the project were likely to be continued after the termination of federal support?
6. *Dissemination/Diffusion*: Was the project disseminated to other schools and school districts?

The number and complexity of the fascinating, important, and at least potentially testable hypotheses which could be generated from the Rand field data

---

1   The chapters represent essentially secondary analyses of those data and do not necessarily reflect the policies of either the Rand Corporation or the United States Office of Education.

were limited only by the boggling threshold of one's imagination. Sites were selected by each team by a preliminary analysis of the 293 places from an earlier, survey effort. Basic information about the project's purposes, size, duration, methods, and relative success was already available. Sites were chosen to represent a stratification of variables thought to be of interest to each of the teams. The project leadership reviewed the initial selection in order to insure a representation of fieldwork case sites on such variables as geography, level of schooling, type of intervention, etc. Projects which appeared, *prima facie*, to be successful were overrepresented on the grounds that those places which had changed would be more fruitful sites for the investigation of the process of innovation than those which had not changed.

The fieldwork was conducted in the course of a three- to five-day visit at each site by the two-person teams (more than 700 man-days of field work). Each team sought to conduct interviews with the district's superintendent, the relevant state and federal program officers, the project director, the principal of the school or schools affected, the classroom teachers, and others as appropriate. Information developed over the course of the interviews was often cross-checked with prior information. The teams were encouraged to return their case analyses, in draft form, to the responsible site personnel for comments and corrections.[2]

The first chapter, "The Politics of Training Teachers in Schools," is based on a field analysis of those change-agent projects which had staff development, or in-service training, as their focus. In that chapter, I discuss how partisan mutual adaptation developed when efforts were made to change the existing authority system in the "teacher's classroom" and the "principal's school." The chapter examines the consequences of the volunteer focus (projects that were unable to require participation and instead relied on volunteers for their trainees) and the phenomenon of project decay (the simplification of treatments, the diminution of goals, etc.).

The innovations examined in Milbrey Wallin McLaughlin's chapter, "Implementation as Mutual Adaptation: Change in Classroom Organization,"

2 Additional information on the field methodology is available in Peter W. Greenwood. Dale Mann, and Milbrey Wallin McLaughlin. *Federal Programs Supporting Educational Change. Vol. III: The Process of Change*. Santa Monica, Calif.: Rand Corporation, R-1589/3-HEW. April 1975. Other volumes relevant to the first year of this project are: Paul Berman and Milbrey Wallin McLaughlin. *Federal Programs Supporting Educational Change, Vol. I: A Model of Educational Change*. Santa Monica, Calif.: Rand Corporation, R-1589/1-HEW, April 1975: Paul Berman and Edward W. Pauly. *Federal Programs Supporting Educational Change, Vol. II: Factors Affecting Change Agent Projects*. Santa Monica, Calif.: Rand Corporation, R-1589/2-HEW, April 1975: Paul Berman and Milbrey Wallin McLaughlin. *Federal Programs Supporting Educational Change, Vol. IV: The Findings in Review:* Santa Monica, Calif.: Rand Corporation, R-1589/4-HEW, April 1975: and Paul Berman, Peter W. Greenwood, Milbrey Wallin McLaughlin, and John Pincus. *Federal Programs Supporting Educational Change, Vol. V: Executive Summary,* Santa Monica, Calif.: Rand Corporation, R-1589/5-HEW, April 1975.

went beyond techological change to organizational change. These innovations shared a belief that humanistic, individualized, and child-centered education requires more than incremental or marginal change in the behavior of the classroom teacher. McLaughlin makes the fundamental point that the demands of implementation itself dominate the innovation process and its outcomes regardless of the educational treatment being attempted, the level of resources applied, or the type of federal funding used.

McLaughlin describes the process of implementation in three different patterns: *Mutual adaptation* describes the successful projects in which the site and the technology shaped each other. *Cooptation* occurred when the site captured the project but then remained unchanged by the project. *Nonimplementation* occurred where the projects broke down or were ignored by the site. McLaughlin argues persuasively that exactly because of the generally amorphous but highly complex nature of the pedagogy employed in open education classroom innovations, the only reasonable strategy of change was one that counted on mutual adaptation.

Reading and the teaching of reading is a perennial topic of concern. John G. Wirt's chapter, "Implementing Diagnostic/Prescriptive Reading Innovations," is the third piece drawn from the Rand change-agent study. Wirt notes that the diagnostic/prescriptive approach is an organizational, not an instructional, innovation since it specifies only how teachers should organize their classroom activities and leaves them theoretically free to use whatever instructional techniques they prefer. The projects examined by Wirt were especially illuminating since they involved a "total approach" rather than isolated, single changes in techniques for teaching reading.

"Change Agent One" has been an extraordinarily provocative study and widely discussed. But a few additional implications may be in order. First, all change in schools is not paid for by federal programs. Neither is the corollary true that if it wasn't paid for by a federal grant, it didn't happen. That attitude has excluded far too many of the good things that school people have done spontaneously, autochthonously. Moreover, the attitude leads teachers and principals to believe that if they can't get a grant, they can't try anything new, different, or better. Second, it is not the case that all change is intentional. The expectation that innovation is a rational, logico-deductive process, carefully and analytically pursued, damps a lot of otherwise useful enthusiasm. The process of discovery is often not very clear to those in the middle of the act of uncovering something new. Expecting clarity frequently means waiting forever. Third, it is not true that all change is packaged. In the world of educational R&D, there has been enormous stress on the development "D" and quite properly so. But just as evaluators have had to learn not to measure improvement by the dichotomous presence or absence of programmed lumps, so practitioners should not believe that buying boxes of materials is buying improvement or that they can avoid the imperative of betterment until it can be boxed. Finally, it is not the case that all change is good. Although innovation has been devoutly wished for in Washington, in many state capitals, and in some district offices, that fervor dissipates rapidly in the ranks of the organization where the services are delivered. The people who are to change or be changed get quite heated when it is suggested that their current best efforts are lousy and that therefore they should leap enthusiastically on the great bandwagon of change. Obviously, they need to be convinced wherever possible. But just as obviously, there are situations where inaction in the absence of consensus is less defensible than action pursued with consent.

Part II, "Big Shocks, Big Programs, Big Money," extends the book's focus to experiences with large-scale, intense, or comprehensive efforts to change schooling practices. The first chapter is a welcome extension of some recent political science insights to the field of education.

Historically, political science and public administration had treated "policy" as something that happened at the upper reaches of organizations. Policy was handed down to the workers who then faithfully implemented what others had determined. But, as political science became more behavioral, it also started to pay less attention to the actor's location on an organization chart and more to what the person did. If by "policy" we mean the determination of the values an organization serves, and if lower-level employees can reinterpret guidelines, make exceptions, ignore directions, selectively enforce rules and so on, then the question arises, Who makes policy? It was in this context that Michael Lipsky began developing a theory of "street-level bureaucrats" (the people who interact with an organization's clients) and their role in policy development and implementation. In their chapter, "Street-Level Bureaucrats and Institutional Innovation: Implementing Special Education Reform," Professors Lipsky and Richard Weatherley use the street-level bureaucrat theory to explain how the reform of Massachusetts' special education programs has been fundamentally constrained by the responsibilities, roles, and decisions of the people—at the district and school level—who had to do the work. The chapter weaves together a number of concerns familiar to educators (the stigmatizing effect of labels, the consequences of teaching, etc.) with a number of political concerns about the values that are served by state policies and local schools. The Weatherley-Lipsky analysis sharpens a persistent dilemma between the professional educators' legitimate claim to determine their own conditions of practice and the state's equally legitimate claim to guarantee public outcomes.

Wayne J. Doyle's chapter, "A Solution in Search of a Problem: Comprehensive Change and the Jefferson Experimental Schools," deals with one of the most intense efforts to bring fundamental change to American schooling. Stung by criticisms that reforms had been too slow and too little, the federally sponsored Experimental Schools Program set out to support a small number of highly innovative alternative schools. The programs and procedures of the experimental schools were designed to depart substantially from more traditional schools. In order to gain the maximum amount of insight from the experiences of its experimental schools, the National Institute of Education supplemented its usual contract evaluation procedures with documentation and analysis efforts. Because evaluations deal with the life and death of a project, they are also subject to a great deal of distortion. The documentation and analysis contractors were to be rather more neutral, disinterested, dispassionate observers (they often, for example, worked in an ethnographic or anthropological mode). Wayne Doyle led the documentation and analysis team from the Northwest Regional Educational Laboratory as that group recorded the progress of the Jefferson School District. Professor Doyle's chapter records the major events in Jefferson's experience and allows him to comment on several key management practices in the federal government's support of local school improvement.

For the last decade, schools were supposed to be "closed systems," responsive only to their own bureaucratic imperatives, impervious to outside forces, especially those associated with clientele demands that are different from the values held by the insider professionals. In seeking to protect their own autonomy and to preserve their world from intrusions by those unlike themselves, the professionals have put up high barriers around the public school as an institution. The "closed system" allegation about schooling seems questionable (schools are more or less closed than what other areas—social welfare? medicine? public safety?), but the conserving tendency of educators seems an accurate characterization. Thus, many students of the educational reform have concluded that schools, especially urban schools, change most from outside, "exogenous" shock. And parents are outsiders.

R. Gary Bridge's chapter, "Parent Participation in School Innovations," develops several aspects of the pivotal role parents play in accepting or rejecting innovations at the local school level. Drawing on his own extensive experience with the Rand Corporation's study of the Alum Rock (California) Education Voucher Demonstration, Professor Bridge asks three central questions: (1) What kinds of schooling decisions do normative models suggest parents should make? (2) What kinds of schooling decisions do parents want to make? and (3) Who seems to be competent to participate effectively? Professor Bridge examines different procedures for parent/administrator decision making based on the need for group acceptance of the decision and the importance attached to the quality of the decision. In a concluding section outlining some guidelines for parent involvement, he describes situations in which parent participation is likely to be most effective.

It has frequently been observed that small changes, timidly advanced, have not made much difference in school reform. A similar charge has been laid against the government's support of research and development efforts that have been so meagerly financed that they cannot afford the risk of exploration, the talents of multidisciplinary teams, or the long-term concentration of experts. Not much ventured, not much gained. In their chapter, Ralph A. Hanson and Richard E. Schutz discuss the results of one departure from that pattern. Over the last several years the Southwest Regional Educational Laboratory (SWRL) has been able to devote a substantial part of its budget to a series of closely linked programs designed to improve reading skills in the early grades. In cooperation with a publisher (Ginn and Company) the lab has gathered data on two years' experience on the part of 20 percent of the nation's kindergarten children. The results are, literally, remarkable.

1. Learned achievement increased as a function of the number of curriculum units completed (i.e., when taught more, children learned more).
2. The achievement results are more closely related to the number of units completed than to what Hanson and Schutz refer to as "biosocial" characteristics. That is, black children and poor children (both were overrepresented in the sample) learn as well as do other children.
3. The implementation of the program on the school level has been faithful. The program's requirements and the school's ability and willingness to use the program appear to be nicely matched.
4. Contrary to the charge that schools can't teach and that they don't make as much of a difference in children's achievement as do nonschool factors such as ethnic group and family income, Hanson and Schutz argue that the variables related to student achievement are well within the school's reach. By spending more time teaching some kinds of carefully developed curriculum, the school can affect student achievement.

A lack of funds sufficient to effect anything more than marginal change has been a common lament among innovators. But in New York City's Experimental Elementary Programs which Constancia Warren examines in her chapter, each of the participating elementary schools had about three-quarters of a million *extra* dollars added to its yearly budget. The EEP schools also had the benefits of a program design that featured a concentrated provision of resources in a range of alternative models: teacher-intensive, technology-intensive, home/school linkage-intensive, and so on.

In examining why "all that money [went] for business as usual," Warren focuses on the discrepancy between a role change model of implementation and the power (political or otherwise) necessary to overcome barriers to such change. Warren points out that it is disastrous to conceive of policy making and policy implementation as separate problems. Clearly, they must go on together, but the question remains how can the two be merged.

In "Implementation of ESEA Title I: A Problem of Compliance." Milbrey Wallin McLaughlin returns to comment on the experience of the federal government's large-scale attempt to improve the education of the disadvantaged through Title I of ESEA. McLaughlin's discussion concentrates clearly on the dilemma of making policy about implementation, that is, on the difficulty of forming judgments and actions at an overall level that will in fact have an impact at the discrete, delivery, or implementation level. She indicates that "the failure of Title I . . . is not so much a failure of special programs, but a failure of a federal policy to bring about these programs on the local level." Her analysis turns around the interaction of four related factors at the different levels of policy formation and implementation—goals, knowledge, incentives, and authority. The absence of clearly understood and operational amounts of all of those things at the delivery level meant that Title I was virtually never implemented. Thus, for good reason, there was no local compliance.

With the single exception of the Hanson-Schutz analysis, Parts I and II demonstrate how difficult and arduous a business it is to try to make change happen.

Schools have not been improved at a level that we might have expected. The bulk of previous explantions for that have focused on the technological inadequacy of what was tried; we are arguing here for attention to the power of sites as well. It turns out, in a sense, that all those school people who have been saying "you don't know *my* teachers, or *my* school, or *my* district" were right. But what are the consequences? What for example does that say about a system of public intervention based on project grants, on special activities, on services provided through very particular processes and carriers? Is the message of the gathering storm of implementation studies that we should abandon our relatively singular efforts to bring change/improvement to an array of wildly differing situations? The consequences of this implementation dilemma will become apparent during the course of public debate, private negotiation, conflict and compromise. While an eventual resolution may be difficult to foresee, the question is nonetheless significant to anyone responsible for public institutions since it is likely to influence how much they try to achieve in public affairs.

These findings may strike a responsive chord with many people. In the recent past, we have aspired to many things and achieved only a little bit of a few of them and that temporarily. As a people, we have diminished our sense of ourselves, and that may be measured by the phenomenal popularity ratings (89 percent approval) of the people of California for a nominally liberal Democrat governor who argued that "sometimes non-action is better." Voters are fond of decrying the Tweedledum-Tweedledee choice between the political parties, but the 1976 presidential election was the first in a long time in which both parties campaigned for less government.

Now if changing schools is as difficult as it seems to be, and if public sentiment seems to counsel a tactical retreat from activist ambitions and strategies, what, in fact, can be concluded about attempts to change the schools? Alice Rivlin and Michael Timpane looked at a number of carefully constructed social/educational experiments in education that had been designed so that those methods with superior outcomes would be dramatically apparent. When there were no such outcomes, they edited a book with the apt subtitle, "Should We Give Up or Try Harder?" A former Secretary of the Department of Health, Education, and Welfare, F. David Matthews, remarked that the 70s may be remembered as "The Age When Things Did Not Work Out Like They Thought They Would." Moreover, this new evidence about the obduracy of schools moves in the same direction as the earlier criticisms of the public schools for being ineffectual, especially with respect to social mobility. It is entirely possible that many school people will conclude that they should give up, or at least that they should retreat to much smaller arenas, where personal influence and intimate contact can yield a more hopeful prospect of effect. Thus we may see a withdrawal from public into private pursuits.

But there are some alternate interpretations. For one, the implementation studies point clearly to the intended effects of a federal political system. Planning change, legislating change, promulgating change, packaging change, training for change all fall short of the mark of actually changing. People at the site or delivery level may have compared what they were being asked to do with what they were already doing and agreed with the famous dictum of Averch et al., "Research has not identified a variant of the existing system that is consistently related to students' educational outcomes."[3] Does that mean that there are no techniques which are preferable to others under specified conditions? Not at all. But the message from the delivery level is that the people who do the teaching remain unconvinced either about the purposes or the production function sufficiency of most innovations to which they are exposed. And in the absence of convincing proof to the contrary, they have refused to surrender themselves to change. Since we have been unable to persuade school people generally of the desirability of (any particular set of) changes, then the fact that we lack the technology to force change may be salutary. Some, even many, of the resistances to change documented in this book may be misguided—but that is not how they are seen by teachers and other professionals who share responsibility for the system. Rather, those people have sets of individual interests which they are reluctant to relinquish. The values from other levels in the system lack a clarity and a comprehensiveness necessary to inform a more effective policy about change. In the absence of that clearly superior (or clearly consensual) set of values, forced change cannot be legitimated.

3 Harvey A. Averch et al., "How Effective Is Schooling? A Critical Review/and Synthesis of Research Findings." Santa Monica: Calif.: Rand Corporation, R-956-PCSF/RC March 1972, p x.

Still, an essential test of public policy is its regularity. The task of responsible policy makers is not simply to deliver change to suburban ''lighthouse'' districts or to inner-city ''magnet'' schools. Virtually anyone can do some good in such felicitous circumstances. But the policy question is how can the achievement of public purposes be insured, or systematized, or maximized over a variety of circumstances so as to include those most hostile places which are often the most in need of change. And in order for that to happen we will have to know more than we do at present about the conditions of successful innovation. Part III turns to the task of interpreting the evidence about change in education and discusses its implications for future practice.

Professor Richard F. Elmore of the University of Washington begins his chapter with the observation that failures of implementation are failures of organization since bureaucracies and formal organizations are the so-far almost inevitable channels through which we have tried to pursue solutions to social welfare problems. Elmore thus uses a comparative organizational analysis method to examine the assumptions that underlie four models of social program implementation and the consequences which flow from those assumptions. Elmore first asks what can be learned about the process of implementation if we assume that it is a problem of *systems management* where the key principle is that behavior is value maximizing. Routinized behavior, not value maximization, is the pivotal element in Elmore's second model, that of *bureaucratic process*. The third model used to illuminate recent experience with implementation is *organizational development* where the problem of implementation is seen as the search for a way to integrate differing personal-individual and corporate-organizational demands. Elmore's final model is one that is most consonant with the perspective of most of this book's authors—*conflict and bargaining*. In that model, there are no assumptions about shared interest or behavior determined either by calculation or by organizational constraint. Instead, movements toward a new future are the result of differing interests, vigorously pursued. Anyone who has tried to lead an organization will recognize the dilemmas immanent in choosing among these models. Which works better, carrots or sticks? reorganizing or exhorting? and so on. Elmore's first-rate synthesis of four diverse literatures and his use of those schools of thought to illuminate the problems of implementation will be useful to both scholars and practitioners.

In a book about change and innovation, it is useful to have someone who has mounted an exceptionally thoughtful challenge to the whole notion of innovation as a goal of public policy. In ''Horses Before Carts: Developing Adaptive Schools and the Limits of Innovation,'' Willis D. Hawley argues for a redirection of our attention from innovation to adaptiveness. The trouble with innovation, Hawley maintains, is that it assumes that there is a one-best-way to teach (that best way being what's inside the innovative project's package). Hawley observes what is amply documented elsewhere in this book, that adopting an innovation is not the same thing as implementing one. And implementing an innovation too often makes no difference in student outcomes. By contrast, adaptiveness, the capacity over time to solve problems—to be flexible and creative—is a more desirable goal than innovativeness. Since attention to the learning needs of individual students is the in-school variable most clearly associated with success, Hawley focuses on how adaptiveness can be facilitated in teachers. After a discussion of the costs and benefits that might accrue to teachers from a more adaptive stance, Hawley points out the implications of his argument for the organization and administration of schools.

Paul T. Hill, who directed the National Institute of Education's study of compensatory education, provides a kind of a rejoinder to Hawley's analysis. Hill argues that teachers and principals are so hedged about with constraints from local and national demands that they cannot be expected to achieve adaptiveness on their own. Hill's first point is directly counter to an emerging consensus about the quintessentiality of the delivery level. Hill outlines some changes in accountability and in incentives that would contribute to local level adaptive capacity.

Hawley has called for more attention to creating educational environments that encourage school people to be adaptive; he wants us to set up the conditions that would support problem-solving behavior. Edward W. Pauly's chapter deals with a central part of that concern. Pauly, a political scientist at Yale, was also involved in Rand's "Change Agent One." From those data, he began to ask about the sources of educational innovation, about what is known about the decision to innovate. Pauly notes that the risks involved push administrators away from innovation (e.g., innovation creates uncertainty, multiplies complexity, and may result in unfavorable publicity). Why then does an innovation occur at all? Pauly's data indicate that the pursuit of career advancement is a powerful drive, more powerful than wide variations school district characteristics. The analysis also discriminates among three different types of advancement variables: those available to executives, those available to administrative staff, and those available to all school officials. Each administrator makes the go/no-go innovation decision based not on an analysis of the students' needs, but on an assessment of particular local circumstances that will affect the perceived successfulness of the innovation and thus the administrator's career (e.g., Will there be conflict? Will there be recognition? What effect will there be on comparative assessments for a promotion?). Pauly finds that his career pursuit theory explains 65–90 percent of the district level decisions about innovating with a federal program. Moreover, he points out that districts that do not innovate do not do so because their administrators are reading environmental signals that discourage them from doing anything other than a cautious, but not necessarily child-centered, job. By changing the organizational environment for their administrators, those districts, too, could increase the amount of innovation.

If "Change Agent One" is a correct diagnosis, then what can be done? "The User-Driven System and Modest Proposal" begins with a dilemma that is basic to federal policies in support of school improvement. How can a system be both user-driven and federally supported? On the one hand, if better practices are to be successfully adopted, the autonomy of the adopters, or users, has to be maximized. But, if they are already satisfied with what they are doing, and if the federal government retains a responsibility to require that certain values be realized—whether or not other officials at other levels agree—then the autonomy of many users cannot be maximized. This chapter outlines a series of design specifications for the user-driven system, features which to the extent that they can be represented in federally sponsored programs should increase their effectiveness. The design specifications include a stress on self-interest, the use of natural entry points, the incorporation of insights from learning theory, and "overdesigning." A final feature of the system—disjointed incrementalism—is intended to orient users to the fragmented and marginal world of change.

The chapter ends with a modest proposal offered as an alternative to the built-in limitations associated with supporting school improvement through discrete projects. The proposal outlines a form of merit pay that would pay teachers for each point of "overachievement" (i.e., achievement above a predicted level of gain) scored by students with a variety of learning-related social and/or personal characteristics. This incentive grant plan would allow the federal government to continue to direct the emphasis of improvement but would also allow *all* pedagogical decisions to be made closest to individual students, that is, by individual teachers.

Politics is usually specific to a given policy area: there is a politics of oil, a politics of defense, and so on. One consequence of this is that educators seldom have the opportunity to compare their performance with that of other social welfare areas. The final chapter of this book provides some comparative insights. In "The Great Society Did Succeed," Sar A. Levitan and Robert Taggart make exactly that point. For example, in 1963 there were 36 million poor people in the U.S. By 1969, largely through federal efforts, the number was 24 million. People who deny the federal government's ability to ameliorate problems have overlooked these and other massive, beneficial, and intended effects. Levitan and Taggart point out that it is not possible to lessen problems of health care, housing, income maintenance, civil rights—or education—without active intervention and without causing some additional problems. The critics have focused on the additional problems and have treated the goals of the Great Society as absolutes which, not having been achieved, must now be regarded as failures. Instead, Levitan and Taggart remind us of President

Johnson's words about his domestic hopes: ''The Great Society is not a safe harbor, a resting place, a final objective, a finished work. It is a challenge constantly renewed, beckoning us toward a destiny where the meaning of our lives matches the marvelous products of our labors.''

This introduction may be concluded with three observations. First, our current technologies of change are inadequate to the demands of the delivery level of schooling. Second, the values which inform our technologies are insufficiently persuasive. And, third, it now seems clear that there are situations or areas of public policy which are beyond the reach, beyond the capability, of government action. Historically, we have tended to assume that almost any social problem could be ameliorated—if not solved—with a corresponding social program. On the basis of what is now known about available technologies, available values, and the characteristics of many sociopolitical problems, that assumption is incorrect.

Where do we go from here? Recognizing the current limits of government action may allow us to develop new ways to overcome those limits. As part of that effort, the prevailing paradigm of planned change in education certainly needs closer scrutiny if not sledgehammer blows. Omelettes and scientific progress are both made by breaking things. The need for new technologies is always important but both scholars and practitioners are habitually in search of new technologies, and thus hardly need encouragement to do more of what they are already doing.

What would be most useful in that exercise of design or invention would be better information about the sites where technologies are to be employed. It now appears that site characteristics are extraordinarily powerful, yet we remain uncertain about how and why. In reading the implementation literature, one gets the sense that policy makers are sending plays to their change-agent team members, but the other side, the site team, is already in possession of their opponent's game plan and are thus able to defend themselves against every possible maneuver. It seems clear that sites are far more complex than we have assumed, but it is doubtful that every school in the United States is literally idiosyncratic. Although the regularities are more subtle, more limited, and more finely grained than we had hoped, we still need to discern them. Or more accurately, we need to learn how to discern them.

There is a second implication to this finding about the power of the sites. We know that the impact of partisan mutual adaptation pushed project techniques and goals away from their original conceptualization. McLaughlin argues that mutual adaptation is *how* projects were to be implemented if they were to be implemented at all. In a sense, mutual adaptation represents the price charged by the site for accepting any of the project's means or goals. But if that is the case. then it should, somehow, be reflected in the original activities of policy formation and project or program design. The original configuration of projects should take account of their eventual mutual adaptation fate, or in my own terms, of the project's inevitable decay. Yet that is clearly beyond our current design capabilities. McLaughlin puts the dilemma squarely before us when she says: "... project implementers cannot know what it is they need to know until project operations are well underway."

Better technology and better information about the sites for change may certainly help, but the problem of values will remain. The pursuit of change in American schools must take place in the context of a pluralistic society. A plural democracy ultimately grounds its values in the differences among individual members. The clash of values which is so clearly present in site resistance to change is the clash of legitimately differing interests. Many of our most interesting public situations involve such rights-in-conflict. They are intriguing and demanding exactly because they are the context of leadership. Hopefully the results presented in this volume will equip leaders and followers to deal better with the persistent agenda of improvement in schools.

As Curriculum Study Requested It

As Administration Implemented It

PART I

Change Agent One

If to do were as easy as to know what to do,
chapels had been churches, and poor men's
cottages princes' palaces.
> SHAKESPEARE, *The Merchant of Venice*

CHAPTER 1

The Politics of Training
Teachers in Schools

DALE MANN

In the recent past, it has been relatively easy to effect school reform through teacher turnover and recruitment. As long as teacher mobility remained high, a principal could count on replacing perhaps as much as one-fifth of the staff in a year. But now and for the foreseeable future, mobility will be greatly constricted by the teacher surplus, the availability of maternity leaves, the need for multiple incomes per family, and the effects of unionization. School reform must now be accomplished through existing personnel. More than ever before, those who seek to change schools must change teachers while they are working in the schools. The euphemism for that is staff development.

The results reported here were developed as part of the Rand Corporation's study of United States Office of Education-supported change-agent programs. The analysis and the conclusions in the current paper are the result of a secondary analysis of the data and are the author's sole responsibility.[1] The field sites selected for study were located in all parts of the country and in communities ranging from a rural hamlet to a megalopolis. The field team conducted 50 to 100 interviews in each place visited. The number of schools visited in each place varied from five to twenty. Interviews began at the top of the system and followed the project down through the administrative hierarchy to the teachers in the various schools. This chapter concentrates on describing a process of (1) initiation, (2) implementation, (3) partisan mutual adaptation, (4) continuation, and (5) dissemination/diffusion which has been generalized from the data. It uses illustrations as often as possible but necessarily concentrates on a process description, not on the description of multiple contexts. The reader is invited to compare this analysis with his or her own experience and with the case materials available from The Rand Corporation.[2]

---

1   See footnote 2, "Introduction," page XV.
2   The complete staff development cases are available in "Appendix A" of Peter W. Greenwood, Dale Mann, and Milbrey Wallin McLaughlin. *Federal Programs Supporting Educational Change: Vol. III: The Process of Change*. Santa Monica, Calif.: Rand Corporation, R-1589-3-HEW, April 1975.

THE INITIATION PHASE

Why and how did the projects begin? Where did the idea come from? How much support was necessary from how many people?

The literature on planned change stresses the importance of a high level of felt need for change. The idea occurs in two different forms: (1) the "goal seeking" or "rational" model in which the impetus for change comes from a desire to move to a preferred future; and (2) a "problem solving" orientation in which dissatisfaction with current situations prompts a definitive remedy. *None* of these projects were initiated in response to a significantly felt need to change among school staff. In fact, it was always assumed that the objects of the project's efforts, those people who were to be "developed" (changed) would resist that effort, deny the project's utility, and otherwise be obstacles to change. Most projects came into being because of a small cell of persons who operated independently of or in opposition to the wishes of district superordinates and the trainee group as well.

Most school districts store their needs in a bottomless pit. When outside money appears, the district fishes around the pit until it finds a need that matches the announced purposes of the soft money. That need is then elevated to the status of a priority in order to demonstrate the district's commitment, and not incidentally in order to capture the bucks. The process is exactly why so many districts object to having their programs jerked around by program-specific, rather than general or bloc, assistance. The point here is that the process invalidates the central tenet of a district-based goal-seeking model of change. From the federal government's viewpoint, the opportunism evident in this process is probably useful since it demonstrates district responsiveness (at least initially) to a federal agenda. Because it is less grand, "problem solving" seems to be a slightly more accurate characterization of the motives for initiation. But the "problem solving" approach was one in which districts moved not so much toward any carefully conceptualized future, as away from whatever problems were most pressing and which could be ameliorated (note, not "solved") by someone else's money.[3]

The planning activity is a noticeable departure from the synoptic rational model. If the practice of searching for alternatives implies a conscious search for the different options available in some universe of potential solutions prior to initiating the project, then there simply was no such search. The alternatives considered were those that were immanent in the experience or education of the small group of project initiators. Planning in the sense of programming or

---

3 Since we were looking only at places with federally supported projects, it is obvious that those places were using someone else's money. Clearly there are other, indigenous problem-solving efforts—reorganizing, program redirection, new program starts, and so on.

scheduling might have been provoked by the requirements of federal grants. We did find a relationship between extensive planning and the success of the projects, but the explanation for that lay not in intrinsic value of the planning activity but in the fact that the most successful projects were also the most ambitious, complicated and thus demanding of good planning.

Since most districts now recognize that they can take virtually any amount of someone else's money to attempt almost any task, they regard the proposal process fatalistically. But it is impossible to predict the development and results of an untested intervention in a complex and unknown behavioral system. Only in trivial (and uninteresting) circumstances can there be a behaviorally adequate prior specification of the sort necessary to support detailed planning (and the subsequent accountability for the realization of that plan). Two important consequences follow. First, in most districts the possibility of good planning is prematurely deprecated; second, the resulting cynicism causes people to fall far short of the achievements they might otherwise realize.

Widespread participation in planning is supposed to be a *sine qua non* of successful projects. But since the projects were designed to improve purportedly deficient behavior, asking those needy people to become involved would have been embarrassing. In no case did target groups select themselves as the focus of change. In general, they were unaware of what was to happen to them, or if they knew of the projects' existence, its goals were stated in such softy-lofty terms that no one could object. Opposition increased as the specific identification of the trainee group (e.g., high school math teachers, special ed curriculum developers, etc.) increased. Precise purposes, although good from a planning standpoint, increased conflict.

The best summary characterization of the initiation process in these cases was (a) the recognition of some outside resources which might (b) be applied to an emergent generalized need for change in someone else's behavior as determined by a small group of middle-level people, who then (c) plunged into the first project treatment that satisficed them and the funding agency.

THE IMPLEMENTATION PHASE

Project Characteristics   Implementation begins when the project settles down to the hard work of trying to influence teacher behavior. But the vast majority of teachers believed in what they were already doing, not in what some newly arrived change-agent project wanted them to do. The teachers' convictions may not be firmly held or clearly displayed, but their own professional behavior remained a basic point of orientation. That situation created a dilemma for all projects. The more in need of change was the group, the more important it was that they not be invidiously labeled.[4] Thus, most projects used public goals that were more than usually amorphous.

We also considered how far the project's goals diverged from those of the district. On the face of it, a set of operational goals at odds with those of the larger district is not too much to expect from a change-oriented activity. We found instead a strong need for protective coloration. To survive, it was necessary for the teachers to believe that the project represented only a relatively small change in their existing practices. Schools are continuing organizations and their preproject methods are a sort of distribution of benefits and power and are thus the objects of fierce loyalty. Although to the outsider, preexisting goals may seem to be meaningless generalities, they have frequently been the focus of bitter conflict, and only painfully resolved. A direct challenge to those goals might stop the change-agent challenger by destroying access and by mobilizing the opposition. The notion of change as an organizational *summum bonum* which is held in such esteem by various levels above the local school is, in fact, a kiss-of-death handicap in the testing ground for innovation. Since many of these same schools and districts are the most in need of change, the committed change agent is presented with an interesting choice between candor and effectiveness. Where the goals of the project included attention to strongly held cultural values (attitudes about race, ethnic pluralism, student responsibilities), the projects tended to concentrate on the supposedly more neutral and technical aspects of pedagogy and consistently avoided engaging in controversies. Thus, projects that started out to deal with race ended up working on instructional techniques.

The amount of change attempted is another goal-related characteristic. Even though they could not broadcast their intentions, the best projects set out to make a big difference, to help people to depart substantially and radically from their previous patterns. Less successful projects contributed more to organizational maintenance than to organizational change. Big change aspirations seemed to be functional because they provided their participants with early motivation and commitment and because when the inevitable compromises came (see ''Adaptation'' below), ambitious projects could still salvage a significant portion of their purpose. A second measure of the ambition of a project is the extent or ''critical mass'' of its intended changes. Here the strong social sanctions of the schools as a small band of professionals exerted itself very

---

4 This holds only for models of cooperative and semicooperative change. Where conflict is to be the engine of change, prior labeling may very well be a good tactic to get the target group's attention. Many people deny the possibility of any change in education except through the cooperative route. On the basis of these cases, that attitude seems as much a description of the problem as a valid conclusion. The purpose of public policy remains the regular achievement of public goods—under many circumstances but especially in instances of conflict or disagreement which are after all the most significant environment for public policy.

strongly. An occasional maverick could buck those sanctions and implement the changed behavior in isolation. But mostly schools singled out these rate-busters and deprecated or ostracized them until they regressed to the mean. Change is frequently an indictment of existing practice and of existing practitioners; in its field reality, it is not a state devoutly to be sought, nor is it a clinical, bloodless, consensual process. It was resisted by teachers who were threatened by it. For these reasons, it was important to succeed with enough of a school building's staff to provide a potentially self-contained unit. Allowing for defections, backsliding, and partial implementation, that usually meant not fewer than 20–25 percent of the school's staff had to be thoroughly indoctrinated in project techniques.

Considering project treatments, the first aspect is the complexity of the design. Complexity was not related to size. We saw very simple projects that were enormously costly; on the other hand, one of the most successful projects was fabulously and endlessly complicated—a sort of educational Gaudi design. This is a curious finding since the probability of successful implementation would seem to go down as the number of necessary precursor contingencies goes up. Yet the most successful projects relied on various inputs, the availability of different sorts of actor attitudes, long chains of changes and events, and so on. The message may be that no lesser sort of effort will suffice and the risks of complexity are a necessary condition for success.

The most successful projects tailor-made and prepackaged their own materials. Locally developed curriculum counteracted the parochiality of teachers, most of whom believed that no one else could possibly know anything of *their* situations. When the trainers wrote their own guides and curricula, they knew them better and believed in them more than if they had simply adopted pre-existing materials. Successful materials were those which offered early successes and a number of alternate points of entry (e.g., classroom physical organization, child self-concept, diagnostic procedure, etc.) so that teachers could begin wherever they felt they needed help. The availability of material rewards was not a significant incentive for teachers to start the training, but it was a useful reinforcement to continue it. In an area where graduate training is notorious for the level of its standards, it is interesting to note that three of the projects incorporated tough-minded evaluation of what the trainees had or had not acquired. One project was especially active in that regard. Failure to pass a component competence examination was a relatively frequent experience, but rather than being discouraged, the trainees seemed to feel that it contributed credibility to the training experience and distinguished it from many of the demeaning "Mickey Mouse" institutes and workshops to which they had been subjected.

The most powerful programs had the following characteristics:

1. The simple availability, over time, of the training staff as a source of help on

the trainees' demand and on the trainees' problems. This reduced the teachers' apprehension that change projects meant more unrealistic work for them.

2. The provision of a demonstration lesson done by the trainer with the trainees' classes but with no participation or responsibility on the part of the trainee. That helped establish the trainer's credibility and the treatment's feasibility.
3. Provision of multimedia, multitopic, self-paced, auto-instructional teaching packages for the trainees' independent use. It should be kept in mind that many teachers do not like to read.
4. The credible, non-individious, independent evaluation of individual progress at relatively frequent intervals by people outside the teacher's school-based chain of command and unrelated to the teacher's "official," permanent-record performance evaluation. Only one project was able with impunity to incorporate the principal's participation in the teacher's evaluation. Needless to say, that place did not have a union or even a strong teachers' association.

Projects that aspire to teacher change must deal with the teacher's boss—the principal. The projects which achieved the least of their own change-oriented agendas did so in large part because building principals redirected or subverted project efforts at the school building level. Most building principals did not favor staff development efforts that challenged their traditional role as the instructional leader, master teacher, or chief teacher trainer in the school. Also, the project was almost bound to try to move teachers away from practices that had already been sanctioned by the responsible head of the school, the principal. Few principals opposed the district's initiation of projects, but many opposed project efforts once they had crossed the school's threshold. Two projects tried to do an end-run around the principals to the teachers. One case succeeded because of the passivity and unsophistication of that group of principals. In the other case, the principals lost a few of the early battles and then won the war with a sort of "scorched earth" strategy directed against project personnel. Project goals did not completely govern resource allocation but did so in combination with other criteria such as (a) the prior social access of the training staff to trainees, (b) the accessibility of grade levels to treatment, (c) the demands of a particular treatment, and (d) idiosyncratic, largely uncontrolled, and largely unanticipated factors. Resource allocation patterns attested to the power of the principals. Where principals controlled, they used resources largely to maintain and buttress the status quo (cover ordinary classes, act as substitutes, etc.). Where project people controlled, project purposes were better served, and where, because of political opposition from the principals, they could not be served at least the project staff was in a stronger position to negotiate terms of the compromises.

Evaluation in the sense of *informal* but serious stock taking by project staff and district clientele was an important activity in the most successful projects. They paid attention to it and they changed because of it. Evaluation in the sense of *formal* project assessment for the state and federal grantors was done to continue to qualify for money, not for its utility to project management.

Trainee Characteristics The people to be developed strongly influenced the success or failure of the projects. The higher the grade level, the more resistant to training was the teacher. No project was able to have any impact on a high school. A number of things about high schools seemed to be at work here.

1. High school teachers relate to their topical fields more than to an overall schooling mission. While most change projects emphasized process, high school teachers consistently subordinated process considerations to topic coverage.

2. Topic specialization provides an organizing base which makes high school teachers believe themselves to be superior to their lower grade colleagues. That specialization strengthens defenses against outsiders and makes resistance to change easier and more effective.

3. Many high school faculties are often already split into antagonistic groups of "core," "solids" or "academic" teachers and "electives" teachers. The lack of cooperation among those factions makes things like scheduling changes and team teaching very difficult to realize. Norms of local unanimity further freeze this situation. (One group's cohesively expressed desires will not be interfered with by another group.)

4. The baby boom has not yet ebbed in the high schools which remain relatively overcrowded, thus affording teachers there less free time and organizational slack than is currently available in lower grades.

5. High school teachers deal more briefly with many more and older students and thus tend to blame the anonymous mass of threatening students more than themselves for the failure of schooling. Students who fail or who are failed by the high school simply go away and are not persistent problems within the same organization. These factors diminish the sense of personal responsibility and thus the felt need to change.

6. Because high schools are large and more specialized with more intermediate organizational layers, high school teachers are less dependent on their principals than are elementary school teachers and thus are more insulated by the chain of command.

7. High school faculties are usually more unionized than their elementary colleagues and thus less malleable with respect to "extra" demands of training programs.

8. There is less exogenous pressure on high schools.

The other strong relationship in the area of trainee characteristics had to do with the way in which teachers joined the project. Most projects devoted the bulk of their resources to and had greatest impact on volunteers. The volunteers tended to be "friends and neighbors" of the project staff members; as a more congenial group sharing many assumptions, the initial training was easier to conduct and moved faster. Since most projects had been designed for work with a more difficult population, the early successes with the volunteers were gratifying, especially so for the people who were uncertain about the sufficiency and reception of their techniques and who needed early successes to justify their further efforts. In addition, special projects which were untried and struggling for credibility and support seldom had the political clout to require participation. Often the premises of the training techniques (organizational development, for example) made it inappropriate to force participation. The teachers' organizations, their regular responsibilities, and their professional status usually were sufficient protection from such mandates anyway. Thus, the focus was placed on a training population of volunteers.

Unfortunately, that early concentration on volunteers had some deleterious effects. It misled trainers about what to expect. It encouraged them to modify their training agenda based on experiences with volunteers which then would not work at all when (or if) the project took on a nonvolunteer audience. Third, it created obligations and expectations for continued service which subtly steered the project's resources back toward the most receptive audiences—the volunteers. But, since most volunteers already agreed with the project's premises and were eager for its treatment (why else volunteer?) the result was to allocate the most resources where they were least needed. The whole sequence is as understandable as it is serious in its impact on program direction and success.

The extent to which trainees perceived a need for their own (further) development is an important but complicated characteristic. Where would the support for development come from? Where projects were initiated because of a particular crisis (e.g., racial outbursts, rampant drug abuse), the perceived need often related only to that crisis and not to underlying causes. When the crisis was resolved the impetus for change disappeared. What should be done in the absence of a perceived need to change? Once the project had exhausted its pool of volunteers, the rest of the potential population was likely to feel that they were doing well without the project. The vivid shift that occurred in this single behavioral characteristic—from those who wanted the project's treatment to those who didn't—would seem to dictate two distinctly different training techniques, yet *no* projects made an adequate response to that shift.

The defensive characteristics of the nonvolunteer audience need some explanation. As a whole, teachers must try to perform virtually impossible tasks with a technology that is inadequate or simply wrong. Defensiveness and secretiveness are understandable attitudes where the circumstances demand a professional, pedagogical role performance even though there is no sufficient knowledge about what causes good teaching and learning. Also, because teachers recognize that they are supposed to perform intellectual tasks, and because their intellect is clearly on display in most kinds of professional interaction (especially in training sessions), the safest performance is the least performance. Thus, to guard themselves from negative evaluation, they simply clammed up. It is hard to train clams.

There is a lot of debate in the literature about the heterophilous/homophilous nature of the trainers in relation to the trainees. The most successful trainers we encountered were those who had paid their dues in the instant client system but who were at some emotional, professional, and tactical distance from it. The most effective trainers seemed naively enthusiastic and maintained that enthusiasm in the face of reality.

Many projects used outside consultants in an attempt to get critical attitudes and the freedom to act on them. All of the projects which employed outside consultants as trainers dropped them after the first year. They were simply not credible enough, responsive enough, or available enough to succeed.

Organizational and Personal Characteristics The project's location in relation to the bureaucracy of the schools was an important characteristic. Teachers depend on their principals for many critical things (desirable teaching assignments, free time, scheduling cooperation, materials and supplies, promotions, protection from parents and other "outsiders," approbation, and exemption from scores of harrassing, petty regulations). Where the principal refused to allow carpet squares in a teacher's classroom (they were alleged to "breed vermin") or where the principal could reduce a teacher to tears in front of her colleagues for allowing "noise" (children talking to children) or where a principal could dump *all* of the school's behavior problems on a teacher as a reward for her newly acquired teaching skills in the area of learning disabilities—then teachers thought *very* carefully about their principal's reaction. The training project and staff were temporary phenomena; soon enough the teacher would be left to make peace with the school's permanent authority figure. This anticipated reaction among the training population was central to the success or failure of projects and it gave every principal a built-in lever to influence the teachers' responses to the development effort.

Thus, every project identified the system's principals as a critical force.

Only one project even attempted to buck the principals, entering schools and conducting a training session on the authority of the superintendent—a practice that lasted until the principals' association forced the board to rescind the superintendent's authority! More commonly, the project announced the district-wide availability of its services in tones of muted assertiveness, but when the trainers crossed the school's threshold they worked with teachers chosen by the principal, on problems identified by the principal, and with success determined by the principal. More happily, principals sometimes exercised plenary power to reinforce the project. But, since change is almost necessarily a challenge to authority, that was rare. In those few cases where principals did support the projects, the changes were as swift and dramatic as a proposal writer's fondest dream.

Few effects came through more clearly than the salutary consequences of personal commitment on these projects. Where the staff believed in what they were doing, the projects had a much greater chance to flourish. Could project features themselves encourage that commitment? The most useful incentive seems to have been the visibility or mobility of project personnel. The more successful projects were run by people who reported changes in their career prospects while the less successful projects were run by people who were comfortably resigned to falling back to classroom teaching at the project's conclusion. The explanation for this is probably related to the animosity which vigorous change attempts engendered. Successful people needed a way to escape from the district and were glad to have it; less successful people could easily sink back into the organizations which they had never challenged. A number of factors of personal demography (age, training, sex, etc.) were checked but found to be unrelated to success.

PARTISAN MUTUAL ADAPTATION

Adaptation deals with the impact of the school on the project. We had hypothesized that a great deal of the reported outcomes (and especially shortfalls) of change-agent projects could be attributed to the school's transmogrification of the projects which were supposed to have changed the school. All projects displayed a clear and similar pattern of adaptation. With the passage of time they: (a) became less ambitious about the system-wide effects they sought; (b) simplified their treatments; (c) slowed the pace of their activities; (d) decreased the amount of changed behavior expected from any individual; and (e) decreased their expectations about how many people within a site could be changed.

Three of the projects examined initially intended to retrain teachers at all levels of their systems, K–12. All three began with a focus on the elementary school teacher population but never succeeded in coming to grips with the high schools. Ordinarily, a project starts out with a very ambitious agenda of change, in part in order to capture funds. But after the original funding has been secured, there is a need to justify continued funding and that means demonstrating success with much more discrete, measurable phenomena than those in the original agenda. Unfortunately, although superficially precise, the measured phenomena are only a small and usually not very important fragment of the project's goals. One project that began as a total curriculum revolution had its most successful and widespread implementation in the teaching of spelling.

A similar phenomenon operated to reduce the risk involved in a project. Broad and sincere attempts to change organizations and people encountered vivid resistance. Resisting the resistance burned up the project's capital. When the staff began to appreciate how slow and costly change is, they often scaled down their goals to match the available resources. Thus projects which started out to end illiteracy ended up trying to teach any kids just a little bit about anything. Projects that had tried for individualized instruction satisfied themselves with having achieved differentiated small(er) group interaction. Problem solving gave way to remediation. Revolution gave way to reform.

Similar processes operated to simplify the project treatment. The panoply of services and activities and the sequences of phases and events which characterized the early stages were diluted as they were transferred from the project leadership to the training staff to the trainees. In one project, for example, a consulting firm which specialized in organizational development tried to teach that technology in capsule form to a group of teachers who were then actually to conduct the OD interventions in their home schools. The result was that one group (the consultants) had all the technology and no responsibility while the teachers had only a little technology and all the responsibility. Predictably, the teachers only employed the simplest and "safest" of the techniques. The training audience also acted to prune the treatment. The real world knocks a lot of the edges off the ivory tower original conceptualizations. (Parenthetically we wish to report the discovery of quite a few ivory towers located not in universities but in district headquarters.) Thus, some project materials were cut by half, the amount of collateral reading was reduced, the length of training exposure was shortened, etc. Treatments also were simplified by being captured. Trainers arriving at the school with an elaborate training routine often discovered that the principal or the teacher-clients had other ideas about how the project staff should be used. A related phenomenon has to do with the fact that sufficient behavioral intervention is a time-consuming process which, because it is so costly, can only be made available to a relatively small group of people. But where the project was viewed as a benefit or "goodie" to be distributed, there was often pressure to make that benefit available to as many people as possible. Thus, in order to spread the benefit to more people (and, not incidentally, to build a base of political support), the treatment was thinned and applied to more people, but with less effect on any given person.

Another phenomenon probably accounts for even more of these projects' actual outcomes. That phenomenon deals with the tiny changes made at the margins of the instructional behavior of a great many teachers. Although the bulk of their practice might still appall the project staff, it remains a significant achievement if, after the project, "trained" teachers hit *fewer* students, allowed *slightly* more interaction, praised *slightly* more often, and so on. Not only are such changes barely visible and usually barely conscious, many teachers strain to deny them or at least deny that the project introduced them. The defensiveness of quasi-professionals is such that many teachers with whom we talked deprecated project techniques and praised traditional instruction. But their classrooms sometimes featured wall charts of student behavior, interest centers, and the paraphernalia of differentiated instruction. When asked to explain those features, they would claim to have been doing those things all along or to have invented them themselves, although in fact that was not the case. In assessing the total impact of these projects, the contribution of these two groups—the isolated "loners" and the "denying doers"—needs to be added to the more dramatic and rare instances of schoolwide transformation.

In only one instance was the fate of the project of extreme interest to the district's superordinates. In that case, the project constituted 90 percent of their attempts at reforming the district, and thus they regarded it very highly. In another case, the project's resources were the only leverage available to a superordinate although he simply could not get a handle on them fast enough to turn a floundering activity to his own advantage. In most cases, superordinates were mildly pleased to have the projects as symbols of their modernity but indifferent to the outcomes.

Table 1.1 summarizes the features of the most and least successful cases along with one "mixed case."

CONTINUATION

The key question here is, what characteristics of the project were likely to be continued after the end of federal support? Because of our one-time data collection exigencies, this judgment was in large part an informed guesstimate. The continuation of project efforts in the most successful district appeared assured if only because the materials and procedures produced remained intact and the training activities were never dependent on pacing or guidance by the teachers themselves. Thus the project's dissolution left a stock of materials with which many of the district's teachers already had a favorable experience. To add to that happy prospect, the project staff had lobbied hard to have completion of parts of the training materials accepted as qualification for a higher step on the district's pay scale. Then, when the state education department required all districts to come up with a new set of performance competencies for recertification of their faculties, the project staff successfully

TABLE 1.1

SUMMARIZED PROJECT CHARACTERISTICS RELATED TO AMOUNT OF SUCCESS

The Least Successful Cases

Case #4

- Interrupted leadership. Some commitment but also uncertainty about content of techniques.

- No real goals. Search for problems which might be helped.

- Change from bottom up.

- Simple project treatment.

- Consultant provision of materials with little on-site development. No trainee progress evaluation. Relevance only to one part of the teacher's role (participation in management).

- Strong theoretical base but among consulting group, not project staff.

- Limited availability of staff to project treatment.

- No rewards, only risks.

- Low felt need among a knowledgeable but complacent and suspicious population.

- Superordinate opposition; opposition from principals.

- No peer group support. No critical mass.

Case #5

- Changing leadership. No confidence in techniques. Status quo orientation.

- Goals of organizational maintenance.

- No change intended.

- Laissez-faire, situationally determined project treatments.

- No materials. High role relevance.

- No theoretical base.

- High availability of staff to project treatment.

- No rewards.

- No felt need among a veteran and extremely resistant population.

- Superordinate support; subversion by principals.

- Same as #4.

The Two Most Successful Cases

Case #1

- An integral, highly committed management group that stayed with the project from its initiation on. The group provided itself with social and material support against opposition.

- A goal of substantial transformation in the most important areas of the district's teaching practices.

- Change initiated from the central office middle management level down.

- A relatively complicated project treatment with several components and sequences.

- Strong emphasis on on-site development of materials and written curriculum. Material to allow multiple entry points, teacher pacing, and independent but non-invidious evaluation. Highly role-relevant training.

Case #2

- Same as #1 plus overtones of true-believer, messianic and revolutionary spirit.

- A goal of revolutionary change in all parts of the system.

- Change initiated from the higher reaches of the central office down.

- An extremely complicated and comprehensive treatment.

- Same as #1.

- Strong theoretical base.

- Availability of some staff assistance on site.

- Some material rewards as reinforcement for continuation not as incentive to begin.

- Very high felt need among an innocent and trusting training population.

- No opposition; some principal support.

- Peer group support in the schools and several critical masses.

- Limited on-site staff assistance. Some demonstration lessons.

- Same as #1.

- High felt need among an innocent but xenophobic training population. Some teacher motion in a direction the project could reinforce.

- Opposition and very little limited support from principals.

- More limited supported and fewer critical masses.

The Mixed Case

Case #3

This case is different from the others in that the project leadership refused to force the pace of the training activities until they felt that the majority of the school's faculty wanted to change and had assimilated an OD truth/trust attitude. Thus, in the first two years of what was nominally a project to differentiate instruction, there had been no attempt to communicate the technology or content of staff development.

- A single leader through the project but a management group which was elected by the teachers and thus fluctuated. Some cohesion against opposition.

- A goal of substantial change in several areas but patience about the rate of progress.

- Top support and several superordinate moves that paralleled and reinforced the project's moves.

- A persistent stress on a single theme (truth-trust) to date.

- A fetish about bootstraps. Total on-site determination of project activities but few materials. Independent, non-invidious evaluation. Focus to date not perceived as being very role relevant.

- Material but not staff assistance to trainees. No demonstration lessons.

- High felt need among a frustrated and suspicious population.

- No opposition; support from principal.

- Very strong peer group support and critical mass, but at only one grade level.

inserted their project's own list of desired teacher outcomes. All teachers must now pay more attention to those standards. Since the project never had to face any significant opposition and since a high proportion of the district's teachers have had a favorable experience with the training, the prospects for the continuation of the project's activities (but not of the project itself) seem good.

Similar points may be made with respect to the other of the clearly successful project sites. There, the staff anticipated from the beginning that the reemergence of the conservative forces would inevitably overwhelm the project. Part of the staff's drive to produce a great many materials and to infiltrate all parts of the bureaucracy was in preparation for that contingency. The hope was that out of a "blanket" or "cascade" of services, some would survive. In addition to that fishegg strategy, in order to guard against backsliding on the part of project personnel who were returning to their former (unreconstructed) environs, all such personnel were required to undergo the complete training cycle a second time. The project's enemies have moved vigorously against it, but the project has "gone underground" and thus many activities should survive.

In the mixed case school, where enactment of many of the project's goals and technology has been substantially delayed, it is very hard to predict continuation. The theoretical justification for emphasizing interpersonal communications is to ensure that the ensuing changes will be more profound and more lasting. So one hopes.

For the other schools, the most that can be hoped for is that those relatively fewer teachers whose behavior was affected will not return to their old patterns of behavior. There is evidence to support that expectation. Most of the teachers whose instructional practices were changed as a result of these projects were already somewhat dissatisfied with their performance or became persuaded of its inadequacy. There was agreement that it would be impossible to move back to large group, teacher-talk instruction and, to a person, our respondents denied that they ever would. Thus, at the atomistic but still important level of the individual, continuation seems to have a reasonable prospect.

DISSEMINATION/DIFFUSION

The key question here was whether the project was disseminated to other schools or districts. Only two projects demonstrated any real impact on schools other than the original target schools. In both cases that effort was linked to the personal drive of the project's leadership. In one case, the leader was a former professor who had a habit of publication and a need for career-enhancing publicity. In the other case, the project director had set up a statewide organization of project directors as a defense against what he felt was SEA interference. He did a lot of speaking, inevitably about his own experiences, and therefore received a lot of publicity, visitors, and requests for information from his colleagues.

All projects felt hampered by SEA and federal regulations putting stringent conditions on their dissemination activities. In the absence of any broader audience, the only people to whom the project might be diffused were the other schools in each district. That did not happen either.

It was a universal experience of these projects that, regardless of their degree of success, they were studiously ignored by their district colleagues. Although the school may have been a virtual Walden III, visitors were still more likely to come from 200 miles away than from two miles away. The educator's insecurity is probably the chief explanation for this. Someone working in the same environment with roughly the same resources who does a demonstrably better job is seen as a threat, a show-off, and probably a cheat. The same phenomenon applies among faculties. Teacher trainers are much more acceptable when they travel to neighboring schools than when they try to ply their trade in their own schools. The educator's response is to ignore the lighthouse school if it is close to home and instead go far enough away so that (a) asking for help can be a more anonymous and "safer" experience; (b) it won't be necessary to acknowledge the superiority of someone with whom you are in competition; and (c) the ideas can be changed with impunity and then (d) credited to one's self.

CHAPTER 2

Implementation as Mutual Adaptation: Change in Classroom Organization

MILBREY WALLIN McLAUGHLIN

Most observers believe that the educational innovations undertaken as part of the curriculum reform movement of the 1950s and early 1960s, as well as the innovations that comprised the initiatives of the "Education Decade," generally have failed to meet their objectives.[1] One explanation for these disappointments focuses on the *type* of innovations undertaken and points out that until recently few educators have elected to initiate innovations that require change in the traditional roles, behavior, and structures that exist within the school organization or the classroom. Instead, most innovative efforts have focused primarily on *technological* change, not *organizational* change. Many argue that without changes in the structure of the institutional setting, or the culture of the school, new practices are simply "more of the same" and are unlikely to lead to much significant change in what happens to students.

Since 1970, however, a number of educators have begun to express interest in practices that redefine the assumptions about children and learning that underlie traditional methods—new classroom practices that attempt to change the ways that students, teachers, parents, and administrators relate to each other. Encouraged and stimulated by the work of such writers as Joseph Featherstone, Charles Silberman, and William Glasser, some local schoolmen have undertaken innovations in classroom organization such as open education, multiage grouping, integrated day, differentiated staffing, and team teaching.

---

1 This chapter is a revision of a paper presented at the March 1975 American Educational Research Association meeting in Washington, D.C. It is based on the data collected for the Rand Corporation study of federal programs supporting educational change. However, the interpretation and speculations offered in this paper are my sole responsibility and do not necessarily represent the views of the Rand Corporation, or the study's sponsor, the United States Office of Education, or my colleague Paul Berman, who has been so helpful in formulating this chapter.

These practices are not based on a "model" of classroom organization change to be strictly followed, but on a common set of convictions about the nature of learning and the purpose of teaching. These philosophical similarities, which can be traced to the work of the Swiss psychologist Piaget, are based on a belief that humanistic, individualized, and child-centered education requires more than incremental or marginal change in classroom organization, educational technology, or teacher behavior.

Because classroom organization projects require teachers to work out their own styles and classroom techniques within a broad philosophical framework, innovations of this type cannot be specified or packaged in advance. Thus, the very nature of these projects requires that implementation be a *mutually adaptive process* between the user and the institutional setting—that specific project goals and methods be made concrete over time by the participants themselves.

Classroom organization projects were among the local innovations examined as part of Rand's Change-Agent Study. Of the 293 projects surveyed, eighty-five could be classified as classroom organization projects; five of our thirty field sites were undertaking innovation of this nature. The findings of the change-agent study suggest that the experience of these projects should be examined in some detail. At the most general level, the change study concluded that implementation—rather than educational treatment, level of resources, or type of federal funding strategy—dominates the innovative process and its outcomes. The study found that the mere adoption of a "better" practice did not automatically or invariably lead to "better" student outcomes. Initially similar technologies undergo unique alterations during the process of implementation and thus their outcomes cannot be predicted on the basis of treatment alone. Further, the process of implementation that is inherent in classroom organization projects was found to describe effective implementation generally. Specifically, the change-agent study concluded that *successful implementation is characterized by a process of mutual adaptation.*

Contrary to the assumptions underlying many change strategies and federal change policies, we found that implementation did not merely involve the direct and straightforward application of an educational technology or plan. Implementation was a dynamic organizational process that was shaped over time by interactions between project goals and methods, and the institutional setting. As such, it was neither automatic nor certain. Three different interactions characterized this highly variable process.

One, *mutual adaptation*, described successfully implemented projects. It involved modification of both the project design and changes in the institutional setting and individual participants during the course of implementation.

A second implementation process, *cooptation*, signified adaptation of the project design, but no change on the part of participants or the institutional setting. When implementation of this nature occurred, project strategies were simply modified to conform in a pro forma fashion to the traditional practices the innovation was expected to replace—either because of resistance to change or inadequate help for implementers.

The third implementation process, *nonimplementation*, described the experience of projects that either broke down during the course of implementation or were simply ignored by project participants.

Where implementation was successful, and where significant change in participant attitudes, skills and behavior occurred, implementation was characterized by a process of mutual adaptation in which project goals and methods were modified to suit the needs and interests of participants and in which participants changed to meet the requirements of the project. This finding was true even for highly technological and initially well specified projects; unless adaptations were made in the original plans or technologies, implementation tended to be superficial or symbolic and significant change in participants did not occur.

Classroom organization projects provided particularly clear illustration of the conditions and strategies that support mutual adaptation and thus successful implementation. They are especially relevant to understanding the operational implications of this change-agent study finding for policy and practice not only because mutual adaptation is intrinsic to change in classroom organization, but also because the question of institutional receptivity does not cloud the view of effective implementation strategies afforded by these projects.

The receptivity of the institutional setting to a proposed innovation varied greatly among the projects we examined—from active support to indifference to hostility. The amount of interest, commitment, and support evidenced by principal actors had a major influence on the prospects for successful project implementation. In particular, the attitudes and interest of central administrators in effect provided a "signal" to project participants as to how seriously they should take project goals and how hard they should work to achieve them. Unless participants perceived that change-agent projects represented a school and district educational priority, teachers were often unwilling to put in the extra time and emotional investment necessary for successful implementation. Similarly, the attitudes of teachers were critical. Unless teachers were motivated by professional concerns (as opposed to more tangible incentives such as extra pay or credit on the district salary scale, for example), they did not expend the extra time and energy requisite to the usually painful process of implementing an innovation.

Classroom organization projects were almost always characterized by high levels of commitment and support for their initiation, both at the district and at the building level. This is not surprising when we consider the risk and difficulty associated with these projects; it is unlikely that a district would elect to undertake a project of this nature unless they believed strongly in the educational approach and were committed to attempting the changes necessary to implement it.

In fact, classroom organization projects possess none of the features traditionally thought to encourage local decision makers to adopt a given innovation:

1. Ease of explanation and communication to others.

2. Possibility of a trial on a partial or limited basis.

3. Ease of use.

4. Congruence with existing values.

5. Obvious superiority over practices that existed previously.[2]

Innovations that focus on classroom organization are at odds with all five of these criteria. First, since there is no specific "model" to be followed, it is difficult to tell people how these approaches operate. Advocates can only offer general advice and communicate the philosophy or attitudes that underlie innovation in classroom organization and activities.

Second, although open classroom or team-teaching strategies can be implemented slowly, and can be installed in just one or two classrooms in a school, it is generally not possible to be "just a little bit" open or just a "sometime" part of a team-teaching situation. The method is based on fundamental changes which are hard to accomplish piecemeal.

Third, change in classroom organization is inherently very complex. Innovations of this nature require the learning of new attitudes, roles and behavior on the part of teachers and administrators—changes far more difficult to bring about than the learning of a new skill or gaining familiarity with a new educational technology. Classroom organization changes also typically require new arrangements of classroom space, the provision of new instructional materials, and usually new school scheduling and reporting practices.

Fourth, strategies of open education or team teaching are a radical departure from the traditional or standard practices of a school, district, or teacher. Change in classroom organization means changing deeply held attitudes and customary behavior. These projects, by attempting to change organizational structure and goals, attempt to affect the fundamental nature of the organization and are therefore basically incongruent with existing values.

Fifth, although proponents argue that humanistic, child-centered education represents a big advance, the objective evidence is ambiguous. Most evaluations of informal classrooms conclude that participating children do better on affective measures, but there is little evidence of significant cognitive differ-

---

2 E. Rogers and F. Shoemaker. *Communications of Innovation.* New York, N.Y.: Free Press, 1962.

ences that could confidently be attributed to open classrooms themselves. An administrator contemplating a change in classroom organization is confronted with a complicated innovation that shows no clear advantage over existing practices—at least in the ways that often matter most to school boards, voters, and anxious parents.

Thus, given the complex, unspecified, and inherently difficult nature of these projects, they were rarely initiated without the active support and commitment of district officials and participants. Consequently, the insufficient institutional support that negatively influenced implementation in other projects and so made it difficult to obtain a clear picture of the strategic factors affecting project implementation (i.e., did disappointing implementation result from a lack of enthusiasm or from inadequate training?) generally was not a problem for classroom organization projects. Variance in the implementation outcome of classroom organization projects, consequently, can be attributed in large measure to the project's particular implementation strategy.

For classroom organization projects, as for other change-agent projects, *institutional receptivity was a necessary but not a sufficient condition for successful implementation.* Unless project implementation strategies were chosen that allowed institutional support to be engaged and mutual adaptation to occur, project implementation foundered. A project's particular implementation strategy is the result of many local choices about how best to implement project goals and methods. What seems to be the most effective thing to do? What is possible given project constraints? What process fits best with local needs and conditions? Decisions about the type and amount of training, the planning necessary, and project participants are examples of such choices. They effectively define how a proposed innovation is put into practice. Implementation strategies are distinguishable from project treatment. That is, the educational method chosen for a project (i.e., team teaching, diagnostic/prescriptive reading) is different from the strategies selected for implementing the method. No two reading projects, for example, employ quite the same process or strategy for achieving their almost identical goals.

IMPLEMENTATION STRATEGY

Each project employs its own combination of strategies that effectively defines its *implementation strategy*. Thus, in addition to identifying especially effective component strategies, it is meaningful to examine how and why the various individual strategies interact with each other to form a "successful" implementation strategy and to promote mutual adaptation. The experience of classroom organization projects suggests at least three specific strategies that are particularly critical and that work together to form an adaptive implementation strategy: local materials development; ongoing and concrete staff training; iterative, on-line planning combined with regular and frequent staff meetings.

Local Material Development   In almost all of the classroom organization projects, the staff spent a substantial amount of time developing materials to use in the project classrooms. These materials either were developed from scratch or put together from bits of commercially developed materials. Although these activities were sometimes undertaken because the staff felt they couldn't locate appropriate commercial materials, the real contribution lay not so much in "better pedagogical products" but in providing the staff with a sense of involvement and an opportunity to "learn-by-doing." Working together to develop materials for the project gave the staff a sense of pride in its own accomplishments, a sense of "ownership" in the project. It also broke down the traditional isolation of the classroom teacher and provided a sense of "professionalism" and cooperation not usually available in the school setting. But even more important, materials development provided an opportunity for users to think through the concepts which underlay the project, in practical, operational terms—an opportunity to engage in experience-based learning. Although such "reinvention of the wheel" may not appear efficient in the short run, it appears to be a critical part of the individual learning and development necessary for significant change.

Staff Training   All the classroom organization projects we visited included both formal and informal, preservice and inservice staff training. For example, one project's formal training took place in a two-week summer session before the project began; its informal development activities had been extensive, providing for almost constant interaction among project staff. Almost all of these projects provided preservice training that included observations in operating classrooms. One open classroom project staff even participated in a trip to observe British infant schools. All projects also conducted regular workshops throughout the first three years of project implementation.

One-shot training, or training heavily concentrated at the beginning of the project, was not effective. Although such training designs have the virtues of efficiency and lower cost, they ignore the critical fact that project implementers cannot know what it is they need to know until project operations are well underway. This is generally true for all innovative efforts, but particularly salient in the case of amorphous classroom organization projects. There is just so much that a would-be implementer can be taught or can understand until problems have arisen in the course of project implementation, and solutions must be devised. Training programs that attempt to be comprehensive and cover all contingencies at the outset are bound to miss their mark and also to be less than meaningful to project participants.

Project staffs agreed that staff development and training activities were a critical part of successful implementation. They also agreed that some kinds of training activities were more useful than others. With few exceptions, visits by outside consultants and other outside "experts" were not considered particularly helpful. Teachers in all the change-agent projects we examined complained that most visiting consultants could not relate to the particular problems they were experiencing in their classrooms, or that their advice was too abstract to be helpful. Where outside experts were considered useful, their participation was concrete and involved working closely with project teachers in their classrooms or in "hands-on" workshops. However, it was unusual for outside consultants to have either the time or the inclination to provide assistance in other than a lecture format. Such expert delivery of "truth and knowledge," however, was seldom meaningful to participants, and foreclosed more powerful learning opportunities.

The sessions participants thought most useful were regular meetings of the project staff with local resource personnel in which ideas were shared, problems discussed, and support given. Materials development often provided the focus for these concrete, how-to-do-it training sessions. Visits to other schools implementing similar projects were also considered helpful; the teachers felt that seeing a similar program in operation for just a few hours was worth much more than several days of consultants delivering talks on philosophy.

Some commentators on the outcomes of planned change contend that where innovations fail, particularly innovations in classroom organization, they fail because their planners overlooked the "resocialization" of teachers. Even willing teachers have to go through such a *learning (and unlearning) process* in order to develop new attitudes, behaviors, and skills for a radically new role. Concrete, inquiry-based training activities scheduled regularly over the course of project implementation provide a means for this developmental process to occur.

Adaptive Planning and Staff Meetings Because of their lack of prior specification, almost all classroom organization projects engaged in adaptive or on-line planning. Planning of this nature is a continuous process that establishes channels of communication and solicits input from a representative group of project participants. It provides a forum for reassessing project goals and activities, monitoring project activities, and modifying practices in light of institutional and project demands. Planning of this nature has a firm base in project and institutional reality; thus issues can be identified and solutions determined before problems become crises. Just as one-shot training activities can neither anticipate the information needs of implementers over time nor be comprehensible to trainees in the absence of direct experience with particular problems, neither can highly structured planning activities that attempt extensive prior specification of operational procedures and objectives effectively address all contingencies in advance or foresee intervening local conditions. Often problems arise and events occur during the course of implementation that are unexpected and unpredictable. As a result, project plans drawn up at one point in time may or may not be relevant to project operations at a later date. Planning activities that are on-going, adaptive, and congruent with the nature of the project and the changing institutional setting are better able to respond to these factors.

Frequent and regular staff meetings were often used as a way to carry out project planning on a continuous basis. Projects that made a point of scheduling staff meetings on a frequent and regular basis had fewer serious implementation problems and greater staff cohesiveness. Staff meetings not only provided a vehicle for articulating and working out problems, but they also gave staff a chance to communicate project information, share ideas, and provide each other with encouragement and support.

Finding time for these meetings or planning activities was a problem that some districts were able to solve and others were not. One classroom organization project, for example, arranged time off one afternoon a week for meetings. Project participants almost universally singled out these meetings as one of the most important factors contributing to project success. Such time to share ideas and problems was, in the view of all classroom organization respondents, especially important in the rough and exhausting first year of the project. Where meetings were infrequent or irregular, morale was noticeably lower and reports of friction within the project were higher.

Past research on implementation is almost unanimous in citing "unanticipated events" and "lack of feedback networks" as serious problems during project implementation.[3] Routinized and frequent staff meetings combined with ongoing, iterative planning can serve to institutionalize an effective project feedback structure, as well as provide mechanisms that can deal with the unanticipated events that are certain to occur.

TWO OPEN CLASSROOM PROJECTS[4]

The critical role that such elements of an adaptive implementation strategy play in project implementation and outcomes is best illustrated by describing the

3 See for example, W. W. Charters et al. *Contrasts in the Process of Planning Change of the School's Institutional Organization, Program 20.* Eugene, Ore.: Center for the Advanced Study of Educational Administration, 1973; O. Carlson et al. *Change Processes in the Public Schools.* Eugene, Ore.: Center for the Advanced Study of Educational Administration, 1971; M. Fullan and A. Pomfret. *Review of Research on Curriculum Implementation.* Toronto, Ont.: The Ontario Institute for Studies in Education, April 1975; M. Shipman. *Inside a Curriculum Project.* London, Eng.: Methuen, 1974; N.C. Gross et al. *Implementing Organizational Innovations.* New York, N.Y.: Basic Books, 1971; and L.M. Smith and P.M. Keith. *Anatomy of Educational Innovations: An Organizational Analysis of an Elementary School.* New York, N.Y.: John Wiley, 1971.

4 Project and site names are fictitious.

experiences of two open classroom projects that were similar in almost every respect—resources, support and interest, target group background characteristics—but differed significantly in implementation strategy and in implementation outcome. The Eastown open education project had extensive and ongoing staff training, spent a lot of staff time and energy on materials development, arranged for staff to meet regularly, and engaged in regular formative evaluation. This project was also well implemented, ran smoothly, and met its objectives. In fact, this project received validation as a national exemplary project in its second year—a year before it was theoretically eligible.

The very similar Seaside project, in contrast, did not employ such an implementation strategy. Because of late funding notification, there was little time for advance planning or preservice training; project teachers were asked to implement a concept that they supported but that few had actually seen in operation. The planning that was done subsequently was mainly administrative in nature. The inservice training was spotty and was offered almost totally by "outside experts." The Seaside project did no materials development but instead tried to convert traditional materials to the goals of open education. This project has not only been less successful than hoped, but in our judgment, its central percepts and objectives are yet to be fully implemented. Teacher classroom behavior exhibits only a very superficial understanding of the rhetoric of open education; our observations led to the conclusion that teachers have yet to understand the practical implications of the tenets of open education, and have made only symbolic use of the more standard methods. For example, in many of the classrooms we visited, although the teacher had set up interest centers, these centers had not been changed in six or seven months. Thus they failed to serve their purpose of providing a continually changing menu of material for students. Teachers in the Seaside project had dutifully rearranged their classroom furniture and acquired rugs—as befits the open classroom—but even in this changed physical space, they continued to conduct their classes in a traditional manner. A student teacher commented that many of the teachers in this school conducted their class in the small groups or individualized manner appropriate to this educational philosophy only on visitors' day. In our judgment, many of the teachers in the school honestly wanted to implement open education, and many sincerely believed that they had accomplished that goal. But, in our view, implementation in this project was only *pro forma*—largely because of the absence of implementation strategies that would allow learning, growth, and development or mutual adaptation to take place.

SUMMARY

In summary, overcoming the challenges and problems inherent to innovations in classroom organization contributes positively and significantly to their effective implementation. The amorphous yet highly complex nature of classroom organization projects tends to *require* or *dictate* an adaptive implementation strategy that permits goals and methods to be reassessed, refined and made explicit during the course of implementation, and that fosters "learning-by-doing."

The adaptive implementation strategies defined by effectively implemented local projects were comprised of three common and critical components—local materials development; concrete, on-going training; on-line or adaptive planning and regular, frequent staff meetings. These elements worked together in concert to promote effective implementation. Where any one component was missing or weak, other elements of the overall implementation strategy were less effective than they might be. A most important characteristic these component strategies hold in common is their support of individual learning and development—development most appropriate to the user and to the institutional setting. The experience of classroom organization projects underlines the fact that the process of mutual adaptation is fundamentally a learning process.

General Implications   It is useful to consider the implications of the classroom organization projects and the general change-agent study findings in the context of the on-going debate about the "implementation problem."

The change-agent study is not the first research to point to the primary importance of implementation in determining special project outcomes.[5] A number of researchers and theoreticians have come to recognize what many practitioners have been saying all along: Educational technology is not self-winding. Adoption of a promising educational technology is only the beginning of a variable, uncertain, and inherently local process. It is the unpredictability and inconsistency of this process that have generated what has come to be called the "implementation problem."

There is general agreement that a major component of the "implementation problem" has to do with inadequate operational specificity.[6] There is debate concerning *who* should make project operations more specific, *how* it can be done, and *when* specificity should be introduced.

One approach prescribes more specificity prior to local initiation. Adherents of this solution ask that project planners and developers spell out concrete and detailed steps or procedures that they believe will lead to successful project

---

5   See especially the analysis of this debate in Fullan and Pomfret, *op. cit.* See also E.C. Hargrove. *The Missing Link: The Study of the Implementation of Social Policy.* Washington, D.C.: The Urban Institute, 1975, paper 797–1; and W. Williams, "Implementation Analysis and Assessment," Public Policy Paper No. 8, Institute of Governmental Research, University of Washington, February 1975.

6   See Fullan and Pomfret, *op. cit.*

implementation. It is hoped that increased prior operational specificity will minimize the necessity for individual users to make decisions or choices about appropriate project strategies or resources as the project is implemented. This essentially technological approach to the "implementation problem"—exemplified at the extreme by "teacher-proof" packages—aims at standardizing project implementation across project sites. It is expected that user adherence to such standardized and well-specified implementation procedures will reduce local variability as project plans are translated into practice and so lead to predictable and consistent project outcomes, regardless of the institutional setting in which the project is implemented.

A second approach takes an organizational rather than a technological perspective and focuses primarily on the development of the user, rather than on the prior development of the educational treatment or product. This approach assumes that local variability is not only inevitable, but a good thing if a proposed innovation is to result in significant and sustained change in the local setting. This approach also assumes that the individual learning requisite to successful implementation can only occur through user involvement and direct experience in working through project precepts. Instead of providing packages which foreclose the necessity for individuals to make decisions and choices during the course of project implementation, proponents of this perspective maintain that implementation strategies should be devised that give users the skills, information, and learning opportunities necessary to make these choices effectively. This approach assumes that specificity of project methods and goals should evolve over time in response to local conditions and individual needs. This second solution to the "implementation problem," in short, assumes that mutual adaptation is the key to effective implementation.

The findings of the change-agent study strongly support this second perspective and its general approach to the "implementation problem." We found that *all* successfully implemented projects in our study went through a process of mutual adaptation to some extent. Even fairly straightforward, essentially technological projects were either adapted in some way to the institutional setting—or they were only superficially implemented and were not expected to remain in place after the withdrawal of federal funds. Where attempts were made to take short cuts in this process—out of concern for efficiency, for example—such efforts to speed up project implementation usually led to project breakdown or to only *pro forma* installation of project methods.

Viewed in the context of the debate over the "implementation problem," these findings have a number of implications for change-agent policies and practice. At the most general level, they suggest that adaptation, rather than standardization, is a more realistic and fruitful objective for policy makers and practitioners hoping to bring about significant change in local educational practice. Such an objective would imply change-agent policies that focused on implementation, not simply on adoption—policies that were concerned primarily with the development of users and support of adaptive implementation strategies. Specifically, the classroom organization projects suggest answers to the strategic issues of "who, how, and when" innovative efforts should be made operationally explicit, and how user development can be promoted.

Furthermore, the classroom organization projects, as well as other innovative efforts examined as part of the change-agent study, imply that the would-be innovator also must be willing to learn and be motivated by professional concerns and interests if development is to take place. Thus, change-agent policies would be well advised not only to address the user needs that are part of the implementation process *per se*, but also to consider the developmental needs of local educational personnel that are requisite to the initial interest and support necessary for change-agent efforts. It is not surprising that teachers or administrators who have not been outside their district for a number of years are less eager to change—or confident in their abilities to do so—than planners would hope. Internships and training grants for administrators, or travel money and released time for teachers to participate in innovative practices in other districts, are examples of strategies that may enable educational personnel to expand their horizons and generate enthusiasm for change.

The findings of the change-agent study and the experience of the classroom organization projects also have implications for the dissemination and expansion of "successful" change-agent projects. They suggest, for example, that an effective dissemination strategy should have more to do with people who could provide concrete "hands-on" assistance than with the transcription and transferral of specific successful project operations. It is somewhat ironic that staff of the "developer-demonstrator" projects who last year pointed to the central importance of local materials development are, in their dissemination year, packaging their project strategies and materials without a backward glance. Indeed, the change-agent findings concerning the importance of mutual adaptation and "learning by doing" raise a number of critical questions for educational planners and disseminators. For example, to what extent can this developmental process be telescoped as project accomplishments are replicated in a new setting? What kinds of "learning" or advice can be transferred? If adaptation is characteristic of effective implementation and significant change, what constitutes the "core" or essential ingredients of a successful project?

District administrators hoping to expand successful project operations face similar issues. Our findings suggest that—even within the same district— replication and expansion of "success" will require that new adopters replicate, in large measure, the developmental process of the original site. While there are, of course, general "lessons" that original participants can transfer to would-be innovators, there is much that the new user will have to learn for himself.

In summary, the experience of classroom organization projects together with the general change-agent study findings suggest that adaptation should be seen as an appropriate goal for practice and policy—not an undesirable aberration. These findings suggest a shift in change-agent policies from a primary focus on the *delivery system* to an emphasis on the *deliverer*. An important lesson that can be derived from the change-agent study is that unless the developmental needs of the users are addressed, and unless project methods are modified to suit the needs of the user and the institutional setting, the promises of new technologies are likely to be unfulfilled. Although the implementation strategies that classroom organization projects suggest will be effective represent "reinvention of the wheel" to a great extent—an unpalatable prospect for program developers, fiscal planners, and impatient educational policy makers—the experience of these projects counsels us that a most important aspect of significant change is not so much the "wheel" or the educational technology but the process of "reinvention" or individual development. Though new educational technologies are undoubtedly important to improved practices, they cannot be effective unless they are thoroughly understood and integrated by the user. The evidence we have seen strongly suggests that the developmental process of mutual adaptation is the best way to ensure that change efforts are not superficial, trivial, or transitory.

CHAPTER 3

Implementing Diagnostic/Prescriptive Reading Innovations

JOHN G. WIRT

The diagnostic/prescriptive approach to reading instruction is currently being advanced as an effective means of improving reading achievement in schools across the country.[1] The basic idea of this approach is to rationalize the teaching of reading by providing teachers with a hierarchical sequence of well-defined reading skills around which to organize their reading instructional program. Reading experts differ on what this sequence of reading skills should be, but, in general, the skill hierarchies that have been developed specify that teachers should begin with simple reading readiness skills and build progressively up to more advanced vocabulary, word analysis, and comprehension tasks. Once some hierarchy of skills is selected, the diagnostic/prescriptive approach involves specifying diagnostic tests for each skill in the hierarchy, administering these tests to children to diagnose their reading skill deficiencies, and finally prescribing specific reading activities to children on an individual basis based on the results of these tests. Theoretically, the diagnostic/prescriptive approach leads to reading improvement through logical ordering and individualization of the sequence of reading activities presented to students.

Although the effects of the diagnostic/prescriptive approach on student achievement have been studied to some extent, there are far fewer analyses of school district experiences in implementing this innovation. More knowledge of past experiences in implementing diagnostic/prescriptive reading innovations could be useful in developing improved implementation strategies. This chapter summarizes the results of fieldwork designed to examine the implementation

1 The work upon which this chapter is based was performed pursuant to Contract No. HEW OS-73216 with the United States Office of Education, Department of Health, Education, and Welfare. Views or conclusions contained in this publication should not be interpreted as representing the official opinion or policy of either the United States Office of Education or the Rand Corporation.

process in six diagnostic/prescriptive reading projects in local school districts.[2] The purpose of this chapter is to present the findings of this research and to indicate some of the major barriers to implementation that were observed. These barriers have implications for the appropriate implementation strategy to use.

The fieldwork was done as part of a large Rand study of innovative projects in four federal programs: Title III of the Elementary and Secondary Education Act; Title VII (the Bilingual Program) of that same Act; the Vocational Education Act, Part D; and the Right-to-Read Program. Two of the reading projects examined in the fieldwork were in the Title IV program and four in the Right-to-Read program. Fieldwork data were collected through semistructured interviews with superintendents, project directors, principals, teachers, and others with a knowledge of the project, such as district office personnel or parents. Up to a week was spent in each project by two Rand staff members conducting these interviews.

PROJECT CHARACTERISTICS

The six fieldwork projects were selected from among the sample of 293 included in the entire Rand study. The criteria for choosing them were that they should have involved the implementation of:

1. A hierarchical sequence of well-defined *basic reading skills* as a guide for teachers in planning classroom reading activities;
2. *Diagnostic testing* of student achievement with respect to these basic reading skills;
3. *Individualization* of reading activities in the classroom to provide each student with learning experiences designed to strengthen performance in skill areas of weakness detected through testing; and
4. Several other changes in conjunction with diagnostic/prescriptive reading— i.e., a *total approach* to reading improvement.

The first three of these criteria comprise the basic components of a diagnostic/ prescriptive approach to reading.

The diagnostic/prescriptive approach to reading is an organizational, as distinct from an instructional, innovation in reading because the approach specifies only how teachers should organize their classroom activities for reading and leaves them theoretically free to use whatever instructional techniques (e.g., phonics or language experience) and reading materials they prefer and

---

2   A more detailed description and analysis of the implementation of these six projects is available in John Wirt et al., "Appendix B: Innovations in Reading," in Peter Greenwood, Dale Mann, and Milbrey Wallin McLaughlin. *Federal Programs Supporting Educational Change: Vol. III: The Process of Change*. Santa Monica, Calif.: Rand Corporation, R-1589/3-HEW, April 1975.

have available. The organizational implications of the diagnostic/prescriptive approach are that teachers must: (1) diagnose students' reading needs on an individual basis, (2) assign students to separate groups organized according to skill areas of reading need, (3) select appropriate instructional activities for each of these groups, and (4) reform these groups as the children progress in their reading abilities. The diagnostic/prescriptive approach allows grouping within a single classroom or, at a higher level of complexity, among several classrooms at any one grade level, or across several grade levels, with all teachers involved cooperating by specializing in the teaching of certain reading skills.

The diagnostic/prescriptive approach constrasts greatly with the traditional approach to the teaching of reading where students proceed lockstep through an instructional program decided upon by the teacher, perhaps early in the school year, with little or no periodic testing, and little adjustment of the curriculum to meet individual needs. Most teachers adjust their reading curriculum to individual students to some extent by giving some students extra help and by testing through interpreting informal cues; but with the diagnostic/prescriptive approach, instructional activities should be much more highly differentiated among students and much more frequently modified during the course of instruction.

For the purposes of our fieldwork, a *total approach* to reading improvement—the fourth selection criterion—was defined to be that the project:

1. Was aimed at changing the behavior of the *regular classroom teachers* in the project schools;
2. Included *other components* such as the introduction of learning centers into classrooms, reading resource centers, peer tutoring, or parent involvement; and
3. Involved *all the students* in the project schools, or at least all the students in several grades.

In practical terms, these criteria eliminated reading projects that were strictly tutorial or remedial in intent or did not have a sizable in-service training component. Perhaps the key feature of the projects that were selected was that they were going directly to the classroom teachers instead of bypassing them by setting up auxiliary instructional components.

To give a better idea of what a "total approach" to reading improvement can involve, the most complex (and the most successful) of the reading projects included:

1. Removal of individual desks from classrooms and replacement with tables.
2. Media and learning centers in classrooms.

3. Use of gymnasiums, spare rooms, and other areas for specific learning activities.
4. Multiple and well-defined instructional components, two related to reading and others related to reading readiness.
5. A grouping strategy where students moved from room to room throughout the parts of the school day devoted to reading and reading-readiness activities.
6. A wealth of commercial materials (over twenty different programs) matched to each component and selected for specific purposes.
7. Instructional materials stored in the classroom and catalogued for use.
8. A separate reading center for intensive student drill in reading skills and staffed by a reading specialist and an aide.
9. Required participation of all teachers at each grade level included in the project, plus a specialist teacher to handle some of the learning tasks.
10. Classroom aides trained in the instructional materials used and assigned to specific teaching tasks.
11. Inservice training for teachers in the instructional materials used in class.
12. A resource person in each school readily accessible to teachers for help and advice.
13. An evaluation system to check on process implementation by teachers.
14. Diagnostic testing performed by specialist teachers.
15. Regular meetings with teachers to discuss problems.
16. A specific, high-quality, and yet simple project evaluation design.

The five other projects in the sample involved no more than one-half as many components, and three less than one-fourth as many. The rationale for the total approach to reading improvement is that, in the past, single changes in reading programs seldom led to dramatic improvement in reading achievement, and therefore such improvement is likely to come only if a coordinated series of changes is attempted.

Commercial Reading System   As the backbone of their diagnostic/prescriptive project, three of the projects incorporated a commercial reading system and one developed a reading system of its own. The other two projects relied on informal methods. A reading system provides at a minimum the sequence of reading skills to be taught, diagnostic tests, a mechanism for keeping records of student progress, and an index to commercially available reading materials specifying alternative instructional means for teaching each reading skill defined.

Number of Schools and Grade Levels   The six reading projects in the fieldwork sample differed significantly in the degree of change attempted. One variable has already been mentioned: the complexity of a project measured by the number of changes made in conjunction with diagnosis and prescription. Another variable was the number of schools included in the project. Two projects attempted implementation in an entire school district. One of these districts consisted of over 100 schools and the other of nine schools. A third project attempted implementation in a large number of schools in seven school districts. Three other projects attempted implementation in four schools or less within one district. One last variable was the number of grade levels initially included in the project. One included only primary grades, three included only primary and intermediate grades, and two included kindergarten through twelfth grade. All the projects were in central city school districts.

IMPLEMENTATION STRATEGIES

One of the central premises of the Rand Change-Agent Study was that implementation of educational innovations is best described as a mutually adaptive process, where both the innovation and the institutional setting in which the innovation is being implemented change during the course of implementation in interaction with each other. The implementation strategy in four of the reading projects closely followed this *mutually adaptive* model,[3] since the diagnostic/prescriptive reading innovation was modified as it was implemented to cope with the individual organizational realities of each school in which implementation was attempted. In one of the other projects, the implementation strategy was at the extreme of *coercion*, since the project director used his exceptional authority to literally force all the project teachers into conforming to his highly specified instructional program. Few changes were made in this instructional program during implementation. In the sixth project, the other extreme of a *linear* implementation strategy was used, since the project staff developed a specific diagnostic/prescriptive reading system and then attempted to implement it in the schools through a series of inservice workshops. The innovation was not changed during implementation and the teachers were essentially free to choose what they wanted from the reading system. There was no follow-up into the classrooms or pressure on the teachers to conform to the innovation.

IMPLEMENTATION PROBLEMS

The kinds of modifications to the basic elements of a diagnostic/prescriptive approach to reading made by the projects revealed some of the common problems in implementing this innovation.

---

3   When Rand arrived on site, one of these four reading projects turned out to be only peripherally involved with implementing a diagnostic/prescriptive approach as indicated in the project proposal. Nevertheless, a mutually adaptive strategy was used in implementing the changes attempted.

Reading Teachers   In four out of the five reading projects that made a serious attempt to implement a diagnostic/prescriptive approach,[4] an early decision was made to hire a full-time reading specialist teacher (or other specialist teachers) for each school involved in the project to aid in implementation. Efforts to implement the diagnostic/prescriptive approach thus appeared to have led the projects into making the modification to the basic diagnostic/prescriptive reading innovation of adding a specialist reading teacher. This adaptation was particularly significant because four of the six projects examined were in the Right-to-Read program, where the guidelines issued by the federal program office emphasized that projects should use existing resources as much as possible.

The roles of these reading teachers varied significantly among the projects and among the schools within projects. In some schools the reading teachers were the decision makers regarding project activities in their schools; in most schools they organized any formal inservice training sessions; in some schools they assisted with diagnostic testing and assigning students to groups; in others they managed the reading resource center. In most instances, the reading teachers performed more than one of these functions.

One other important function of the reading teachers was to serve as change agents in their assigned schools. In this role, the reading teachers worked informally with the teachers on a one-to-one basis to interest them in adopting the diagnostic/prescriptive approach and in finding solutions to their individual problems during implementation. The formal inservice training and the tangible elements of the projects generally appeared to have served a far less significant role in changing teacher behavior, since no teacher interviewed in any of the projects had decided and been able to implement the diagnostic/prescriptive approach solely on the basis of the formal inservice training and whatever written instructions were provided. All of the teachers interviewed who had adopted some form of the diagnostic/prescriptive approach had changed either because of working with the reading teacher on an informal one-to-one basis or had been forced into changing by the authority structure of the project. After presentation of the formal elements of a project, the reading teachers typically started in to achieve change by finding one or two teachers who were receptive to change and working with them to implement diagnosis and prescription in their classrooms. As success was achieved, the reading teachers shifted their efforts to other teachers and gradually worked through the school. Sometimes the reading teachers approached teachers with the idea that they team with another teacher who had already made the change to the diagnostic/prescriptive approach. The more successful reading teachers spent

---

4   These four projects included three of the four projects that followed a mutually adaptive implementation strategy and the one project that followed a coercive implementation strategy.

considerable time "mapping" the social structure of the school by listening in the lunchroom, getting to know the teachers on a personal basis, and finding out who was interested in changing. Reading teachers who apparently had been successful in functioning as change agents felt that it took them about two years to change all of the teachers who could be changed. In summary, implementation of the diagnostic/prescriptive approach appeared to occur through a process of infiltration by the project reading teachers into the social structure of the school rather than through formal training activities.

Although performance of the change-agent role was critical to changing the behavior of teachers, many reading teachers apparently had difficulty functioning in this way and were a barrier to implementation of diagnosis and prescription or dropped out of their project. Most of the project reading teachers had formerly been classroom or remedial reading teachers and had not had previous experience in working with teachers. It was difficult for many of these teachers to make the transition to a resource mode—that is, working with teachers instead of with children. No project provided any training in how to function as a reading resource teacher, and thus it was a matter of sink or swim concerning this aspect of their responsibilities. Many sank. For example, in one project only six of the thirteen reading teachers who started were able to make the transition to the reading resource mode, and two of these had previous experience as resource teachers in other subject areas.

Diagnostic Testing   The demands of the diagnostic/prescriptive approach for frequent in-class testing and for record keeping were the elements of the approach that generated the most teacher resistance. "Test, test, test is all we do," was a typical reaction, "It takes valuable time away from teaching." Clearly the test/teach/test style of teaching with detailed record keeping to keep track of student progress is not the way most teachers manage their classrooms now, and they did not readily see which other activities should be displaced for this testing and record keeping.

Testing and record keeping were implemented to a great extent in a project only if performed as an auxiliary service by the project reading or specialist teachers, or by a computerized service provided by the central office. In all such projects, these services were added to the project after it had begun and when it became apparent that without them the tests would not be given and the records would not be kept by the teachers. Providing the teachers with relief from testing and record keeping was the second kind of organizational adaptation to the reading project observed; the indications were that the school districts in which these projects were located planned to continue these services beyond the period of federal support to maintain teacher behavior.

Reading System Adaptations   Another notable kind of adaptation was in the projects (or schools within a project) that attempted to implement a commercial reading system. In all but one of these cases,[5] the schools significantly modified the reading system according to their own perceptions of need. The situation was clearest in the schools that attempted to implement the Wisconsin Design for Reading Skill Development.[6] Only one school in all the projects elected to implement the whole Wisconsin Design available at the time,[7] and even in that case implementation was far from uniform across classrooms. Instead, schools chose to implement one component or another (the "Word Attack" component, for example, or the "Study Skills" component); and, in most cases, they implemented only parts of these components. Teachers' reasons for selecting one component and not others were usually difficult to determine, but were often variations on the themes of either that their students did not need all the skills specified by a reading system or that the highly structured approach to reading instruction required with a reading system is not useful for teaching students more than a small part of what they need to become good readers.

Grade-Level Problems   The reading projects had difficulty adapting to the peculiar characteristics of reading instruction at different grade levels. The two projects that included the high school level failed to have an effect at that level (in one of these projects, the one high school included was dropped in the first year; in the other, only tutorial components partly survived); in the three projects that attempted implementation at the intermediate and primary levels, success was usually greater at primary levels. The general reason why the projects had more difficulty at the higher grade levels was the incompatibility of the diagnostic/prescriptive approach with the organization of the schools at those levels. In the high schools, it was not clear which teachers should implement diagnosis and prescription in their classrooms. Usually it was the English teachers, but they frequently did not consider reading improvement to be their responsibility, had classes in which most of the students did not need reading instruction, did not have access to a wealth of instructional materials coded for reading skills and suitable for high school students, and were usually far less knowledgeable about methods of teaching reading than primary level teachers, one of whose main responsibilities is the teaching of reading. The projects had trouble at the intermediate grade levels for similar reasons, though not to the same degree as at the high school level. Another factor was that high school and intermediate level

---

5   The exception was the project that followed a coercive implementation strategy.

6   "Wisconsin Design" is a shorthand term for the Wisconsin Design for Reading Skill Development, a reading system developed by the Wisconsin Research and Development Center for Cognitive Learning.

7   The Comprehension component of the Wisconsin Design was not available at the time of our visits to the projects.

teachers thought that reading was a job for primary level teachers, notwithstanding exhortations by the projects that reading could and should be taught in all subject matter areas.

Teaching reading at the intermediate and high school levels requires different instructional materials, and perhaps different definitions of reading skills, different diagnostic tests, and different grouping strategies than at the primary levels. The projects did not generally have the resources to meet these realities. The adaptation was generally to drop the higher grade levels from the projects.

Effects of Planning   Although the sample of only six projects is not large enough to draw a firm conclusion, there appeared to be a significant difference between the four Right-to-Read funded projects and the two Title III funded projects in the number and extent of other kinds of adaptations. In one Title III project, the director resigned at the end of the second year over a difference in educational philosophy with the superintendent, staffing problems, and difficulties in working with the schools. After the project director left, a substantial shift was mandated by the superintendent from an informal approach to diagnosis and prescription, to implementing the Wisconsin Design reading system. The shift in project activities was so drastic as to produce an almost entirely new project, except that most of the staff of reading teachers was continued. In the other Title III project, the original main objective of providing reading specialist teachers and resources to the participating schools to assist them in implementing the diagnostic/prescriptive approach was dropped, and effort was shifted to providing tutorial services in the schools and after-hours workshops for volunteer teachers. The four Right-to-Read projects underwent far less severe shifts in the nature of their activities.

The reason why the Right-to-Read projects underwent less severe adaptations appears related to the planning process and organizational structure that Right-to-Read projects were expected to follow. Right-to-Read issued guidelines that *each school* in a project, through the mechanism of a Unit Task Force broadly representative of all school staff, should select its own version of a diagnostic/prescriptive approach to reading. Right-to-Read also provided a so-called "eleven-step planning process kit" to aid the Unit Task Forces in making their selections. The kit included a detailed need assessment procedure.

Although each Right-to-Read project followed the guidelines differently (in two of the four Right-to-Read projects, for example, the participating schools decided jointly on what changes to make in their reading programs), the flexibility provided by school-based decision making, the participation of staff from the schools in decision making, and the overview of project objectives obtained through participation in conducting the needs assessment and filling out the steps in the planning process appeared to overcome some of the problems that appeared in the Title III projects. In contrast, both of the Title III projects were planned by groups outside the schools in which implementation was attempted with no participation by these schools in the planning process. The first exposure of these schools to the project was after implementation began.

In commenting on the Right-to-Read needs, assessment procedure and planning process, one respondent said, "It sets the stage. With needs assessment (and planning procedure), you don't feel as if you're thrown into it" (the diagnostic/prescriptive approach). We interpreted this comment to mean that the needs assessment and planning procedure served the purpose of introducing project staff to the kinds of changes involved in implementing a diagnostic/prescriptive approach to reading and guiding them into initial implementation. The steps in the Right-to-Read needs assessment and planning process are analogous to the procedures of performing diagnosis and prescription in the classroom: First, students' skill needs are assessed, then instructional materials are selected, and so forth.

Contrary to what might be expected, the information that surfaced through the needs assessment and planning processes seldom produced any surprises that led planning group members to select alternatives that departed substantially from trends already underway in the district or in the school or were not in line with their previous experiences. For example, if a parent on the planning team had been involved in organizing tutoring programs, then the reading project had a tutoring program; or if planning group members were interested in diagnostic testing, then major effort was devoted to developing diagnostic tests. In summary, the Right-to-Read planning processes seemed to serve more for the purposes of giving the participants an overview of the change that they were going to attempt and involving them in the process of change than as a means of developing information that affected decisions.

IMPLEMENTED CHANGE

The degree of change implemented in the six diagnostic/prescriptive reading projects varied greatly. The project that followed a coercive implementation strategy was by far the most successful in changing teacher behavior and improving student scores on diagnostic tests. Implementation in this project was complete and uniform across classrooms. But except for one school in another project, which was also highly successful, the overall pattern in the other five projects was piecemeal implementation of change with none of these less successful projects accomplishing substantially more than the others.

Effects on Teachers   The effects on teachers in the highly successful project and the one successful school in another project were substantial but hard to summarize succinctly because different teachers were affected differently. Obvious behavior changes were that the teachers in these successful instances conformed to the scheduling demands of these projects for grouping their students and sending them to other classrooms. Less obvious but probably more significant kinds of changes were indicated by one teacher who said, "As a result of this project, I now see differences in my kids that I did not see before and how to teach to those differences." She was referring to the different reading skill needs that her students could have and how she could individualize instructional activities in her classroom to meet these needs. She indicated that previously she had grouped students in her classroom as to whether they were slow, average, or fast readers based largely on the results of standardized achievement tests. Now she saw that "slow" and "fast" readers might have the same skill deficiencies and needs for learning, and what she could do about it.

Few teachers in any project appeared to have changed their whole approach to teaching, as might be expected to happen in a project concerned with changing the whole structure of a school (such as by the establishment of open classrooms). Most of the teachers interviewed were asked the open-ended question of how the project had affected their teaching in other subject areas, and few replied that a major change had occurred.

Many teachers interviewed in the less successful projects were strongly opposed to their diagnostic/prescriptive project on the grounds that it required too much emphasis on decoding skills when they thought that broader reading goals were more important, such as reading motivation, being able to get the main idea from a paragraph, and thinking critically. "Word attack, word attack, that's all we teach," one project teacher said, "and that's not enough." The generic problem in these instances was that the structure and emphasis of the skills hierarchies used in the reading projects were not compatible with the instructional approaches to reading that some of the teachers had been trained in and had used for years. These were cases where the professionalism of teachers, which is perhaps greater in the area of reading than in other subject matter areas, was a barrier to implementation.

In the project where a coercive implementation strategy was used, the teachers complained that their teaching had become dull and routine but grudgingly acknowledged that the children had greatly benefited. One teacher summarized the situation with a comment that "it's boring for me but it works for the kids." In contrast, the principals were highly enthusiastic.

Diagnosis Without Prescription   Because of unanticipated organizational problems that caused delays, two of the projects failed to reach the stage of providing teachers with access to libraries of skill-referenced reading materials, and, as a consequence, few of these teachers appeared to have made much progress toward establishing skill-oriented instruction in their reading groups. In one of these projects there was a serious teacher strike that disrupted implementation for a year and in the other a serious conflict between the project director and the superintendent that delayed implementation. Without access to a library of skill-referenced materials, either in the classroom or in a resource center in the school, the teachers faced the problem of locating enough skill-referenced materials to keep their reading groups going. They apparently had not been willing or did not have the expertise to assemble their own libraries of materials.

Total Approach Implementation   Except in the one project where implementation was complete, the idea of a total approach to diagnostic/prescriptive reading improvement suffered the same fate as the reading system: Most schools adopted only a few parts of a project's total approach, usually different parts, while other schools implemented almost no changes. Typically, the most successfully implemented component was learning centers, which would often be adopted by teachers even though they made no other changes in their classroom organization or teaching methods. Another common outcome was that parent involvement usually failed when it was tried. There were instances of both success and failure in implementing most other components of a total approach, such as reading resource centers and peer tutoring.

Number of Schools Involved   There was a high negative correlation between the amount of change implemented by a project and the number of schools that were involved, as might be expected in projects as complex as those examined. The most successful project had only two schools, while the two projects with large numbers of schools had little significant classroom change. The other projects were somewhere in the middle on both counts.

Commercial Reading Systems   There was also a correlation between the use of a commercial reading system and the degree of behavioral change: The project that involved the implementation of a whole array of commercial programs in the one school, in a project that implemented the whole Wisconsin Design, achieved the most change. Perhaps the situation was clearest in the project that switched to the implementation of the Wisconsin Design in its third year. The teachers in this project generally reported that it was most useful to them in the third year. Basically, the reason was that the changes expected of them in the third year were more specific.

CONTINUATION

The prognosis for continuation of the six reading projects is mixed. One has two years to go on its grant, three will probably collapse if federal funds are withdrawn, and two will undoubtedly continue.

In both of the projects that will be continued the superintendents strongly support continued implementation and certainly represent the decisive factor in continuation. Although neither project has shown significant gains in reading achievement scores, the superintendents value their projects as a way of defining a reading curriculum for their districts and providing a means of transferring information about students' reading abilities along with them when they move from school to school.

The most successful diagnostic/prescriptive reading project is one of the three that will not be continued next year unless they obtain additional federal funds. The reasons for discontinuance are complex and difficult to sort out as to their relative importance. One is that although the children in the project have shown dramatic gains in reading readiness and word-attack skills, they have not shown gains on reading achievement test scores; and district officials cite this as a reason why they will not support the project for widespread adoption within the district. Another factor is race: The director is white and the district is highly politicized over the black/white issue. Another is the personality of the project director, who is strong-willed, forceful, and not bashful about confronting teachers—qualities that go a long way toward explaining why the project has been so successful but that have also antagonized many people in the district.

CONCLUSIONS

The adaptations and implementation problems in the six reading projects indicate how potent organizational factors were in affecting project outcomes. Theoretically, the high specificity of the diagnostic/prescriptive approach to reading as compared to many other kinds of educational innovations should have facilitated implementation. In fact, four of the six reading projects involved the implementation of packaged reading systems. Nevertheless, in all but one project where a coercive implementation strategy was used, the outcomes were in general piecemeal implementation of change. Teacher resistance to the routine of testing and the emphasis on decoding implicit in diagnostic/prescriptive reading, external events such as a teachers' strike in one project, and the grade-level structure of schools were all factors that in various ways gradually eroded the initial project plans until only marginal changes were implemented.

One of the conclusions from the six reading projects regarding strategy for overcoming these organizational factors is that implementation of the diagnostic/prescriptive approach requires substantial extra resources. Ideally, implementation of the diagnostic/prescriptive approach would require extra resources only during initial implementation—for example, to provide for in-service training—but as teachers learn the procedures involved, become secure in grouping students for reading instruction, and readjust their time allocations to provide the necessary time for testing and record keeping, the amount of extra resources required would diminish. However, school districts often found it necessary to hire reading teachers and to provide auxiliary support to handle testing and record keeping. Therefore, the organizational change implicit in diagnosis and prescription appears to require behavioral changes that teachers cannot or will not easily assimilate as routine behavior. Granted, the sample of projects in the fieldwork was small, which makes generalization precarious, but the evidence strongly suggests that diagnosis and prescription requires extra work that teachers will not often assume and that therefore must be performed through auxiliary means.

Another conclusion regarding implementation strategy is the importance of flexibility in the diagnostic/prescriptive reading innovation and one-on-one support for teachers. Except in the project where a coercive strategy was used, implementation occurred largely through a process of the reading teachers working with individual teachers informally and on a one-to-one basis to find ways of making diagnosis and prescription useful to them. In effect, implementation occurred through a process of adaptation and social interaction rather than formal decision making and training. Formal in-service training, which was provided in all of the projects, had little effect except perhaps to provide teachers with a general introduction to diagnostic/prescriptive methods.

As a final note, these conclusions emphasize the commonalities among the six reading projects studied, which was at the expense of not summarizing the rich variety of events that occurred and important idiosyncracies. For purposes of developing improved implementation strategies, it may be the commonalities among the reading projects that are important but the perspective should not be lost that in reality each project was very different. As the doctor says in T. S. Eliott's play, *The Cocktail Party*, "All cases are unique but very similar to others."

As Board of Education Approved It

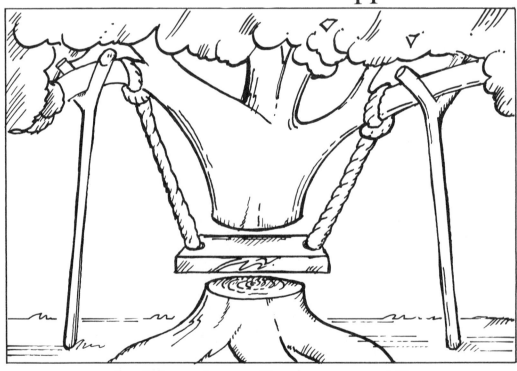

As Teachers Instructed It

PART II

Big Shocks,
Big Programs,
Big Money

And it ought to be remembered that there is
nothing more difficult to take in hand, more
perilous to conduct, or more uncertain in its
success, than to take the lead in the
introduction of a new order of things. The
innovator has for enemies all those who have
done well under the old conditions, and
lukewarm defenders in those who may do well
under the new. This coolness arises partly
from fear of the opponents, who have the laws
on their side, and partly from the incredulity of
men, who do not readily believe in new things
until they have had a long experience of them.

Thus it happens that whenever those who are
hostile have the opportunity to attack they do it
like partisans, whilst the others defend
lukewarmly.

NICCOLO MACHIAVELLI, *The Prince,* 1513

Street-Level Bureaucrats and Institutional Innovation: Implementing Special Education Reform

RICHARD WEATHERLEY AND MICHAEL LIPSKY

In 1972, the Comprehensive Special Education Law of Massachusetts, Chapter 766, was passed by the state legislature.[1] The law was to take effect in September 1974. This measure, hailed as landmark legislation, mandates a significant departure from past practices in the education of children with any kind of physical, emotional, and/or mental handicap. Ours is a study of the first year of implementation of Chapter 766. It is an exercise in analyzing the introduction of innovative policy into public-service bureaucracies that process people on a mass basis.

This chapter focuses on one neglected but highly significant class of implementation contexts—the introduction of innovation into continuing practice. Rather than initiating new programs, providing new subsidies, or calling for new construction, Chapter 766 required adjustments in the behavior of public employees and in the working conditions established for them in their agencies. While we focus on implementation of a statute affecting educational personnel, the class of implementation contexts into which our case study falls includes governmental efforts to change the work requirements not only of teachers but also of police officers, welfare workers, legal-assistance lawyers, lower-court judges, and health workers. These and other public employees intereact with the public and make decisions calling for both individual initiative and considerable routinization. Such public employees share similar work situations.

These "street-level bureaucrats," as we have called them, interact directly with citizens in the course of their jobs and have substantial discretion in the

---

1 Chapter 766 of the Acts of 1972, The Commonwealth of Massachusetts.

execution of their work.[2] For such public workers, personal and organizational resources are chronically and severely limited in relation to the tasks that they are asked to perform. The demand for their services will always be as great as their ability to supply these services. To accomplish their required tasks, street-level bureaucrats must find ways to accommodate the demands placed upon them and confront the reality of resource limitations. They typically do this by routinizing procedures, modifying goals, rationing services, asserting priorities, and limiting or controlling clientele. In other words, they develop practices that permit them in some way to process the work they are required to do. The work of street-level bureaucrats is inherently discretionary. Some influences that might be thought to provide behavioral guidance for them do not actually do much to dictate their behavior. For example, the work objectives for public-service employees are usually vague and contradictory. Moreover, it is difficult to establish or impose valid work-performance measures, and the consumers of services are relatively insignificant as a reference group. Thus street-level bureaucrats are constrained but not directed in their work.

These accommodations and coping mechanisms that they are free to develop form patterns of behavior which become the government program that is "delivered" to the public. In a significant sense, then, street-level bureaucrats *are the policy makers* in their respective work arenas. From this perspective it follows that the study of implementation of policy formulated at the federal or state level requires a twin focus. One must trace the fate of the policy in traditional fashion, from its authoritative articulation through various administrative modifications, to discover the ways this policy affects the context of street-level decision making. At the same time, one must study street-level bureaucrats within their specific work context to discover how their decision making about clients is modified, if at all, by the newly articulated policy. This turns the usual study of implementation on its head. Now the lowest levels of the policy chain are regarded as the makers of policy, and the higher level of decision making is seen as circumscribing, albeit in important ways, the lower-level policy-making context. The relationship between the development and implementation of policy is of necessity problematic since, in a sense, the meaning of policy cannot be known until it is worked out in practice at the street level.[3] Taking these considerations into account, we examine the school

2   This formulation is elaborated in Michael Lipsky, "Toward a Theory of Street-Level Bureaucracy," in Willis D. Hawley and Michael Lipsky, eds., *Theoretical Perspectives on Urban Politics*. Englewood Cliffs, N.J.: Prentice-Hall, 1976, pp. 186-212.

3   The literature on policy implementation is considerable and growing rapidly. For two relatively recent reviews, see Erwin C. Hargrove. *The Missing Link: The Study of the Implementation of Social Policy*. Washington, D.C.: Urban Institute, 1975; and Donald Van Meter and Carl Van Horn, "The Policy Implementation Process: A Conceptual Framework," *Administration and Society* 6, 1974, pp. 445–88.

response to Chapter 766 in the context of the state-level development and articulation of policy.

The impetus for special-education reform in Massachusetts and in other states derives from several related developments. First, university-based special educators have increasingly questioned the efficacy of special classes for many categories of children and have advocated a more generic and less segregated approach. While the issue is still being debated, available evidence suggests that special-needs children do not necessarily learn better in special classes than in regular classes.[4] As one early critic of overreliance on special classes stated:

> It is indeed paradoxical that mentally handicapped children having teachers especially trained, having more money (per capita) spent on their education, and being enrolled in classes with fewer children and a program designed to provide for their unique needs, should be accomplishing the objectives of their education at the same or lower level than similar mentally handicapped children who have not had these advantages and have been forced to remain in the regular grades.[5]

Second, the process whereby children are evaluated, classified, and assigned to special classes has come under attack as being unduly arbitrary, culturally biased, and often motivated more by the desire to get rid of troublesome youngsters than to educate them. For example, a 1970 survey of special-education programs in the Boston schools revealed a number of problems: an absence of uniform policy; failure to provide assessments and services required by state law; widespread misclassification of children of normal intelligence as retarded; use of special classes as dumping grounds, sometimes by rigging results of Stanford-Binet tests to justify exclusion of troublesome children from regular classes; and denial of special services to those in need of them.[6]

---

4 See, for example, Orville G. Johnson, "Special Education for the Mentally Handicapped—A Paradox," *Exceptional Children,* 29, 1962, pp. 62–69; Howard L. Sparks and Leonard S. Blackman, "What Is Special About Special Education Revisited: The Mentally Retarded," *Exceptional Children,* 32, 1965, pp. 242–47; Lloyd M. Dunn, "Special Education for the Mildly Retarded—Is Much of It Justifiable?" *Exceptional Children,* 35, 1968, pp. 5–22; and Stephen M. Lilly, "Special Education: A Teapot in a Tempest," *Exceptional Children,* 37, 1970, pp. 43–49.

For a summary of parent-instigated court challenges to testing, placement procedures, and special-class programming, see Sterling L. Ross, Jr., Henry G. DeYoung, and Julius S. Cohen, "Confrontation: Special Education Placement and the Law," *Exceptional Children,* 38, 1971, pp. 5–12.

A more recent article provides an excellent exposition of mainstreaming, its antecedents, and the difficulties in implementing it: Martin J. Kaufman, Jay Gottlieb, Judith A. Agard, and Maurine B. Kukic, "Mainstreaming: Toward an Explication of the Construct," *Focus on Exceptional Children,* 7, 1975, pp. 1–12.

5 Johnson, "Special Education for the Mentally Handicapped," p. 66.

6 Task Force on Children Out of School. *The Way We Go to School: The Exclusion of Children in Boston.* Boston: Beacon, 1971.

A third concern has been the categorical approach to children requiring special education and the attendant use of labels as an aid to classification.[7] Categorical labels such as "emotionally disturbed," "retarded," "learning disabled," or "brain damaged," it is argued, call attention to a single presumed deficit rather than to the child's developmental potential. Labels stigmatize the child as deviant or deficient without carrying any prescription for remedying the condition. Programs designed in response to such unidimensional labels are frequently themselves unidimensional (also reflecting in part the categorical approach to the training of special educators).[8] Moreover, the categorical approach has led to the accretion of unrelated and frequently conflicting laws, programs, and school-reimbursement· formulas for various categories of children. A history of legislative response to the lobbying efforts of parents organized in categorical interest groups has resulted in the favoring of certain groups over others and the neglect of those who may not fit into a recognized category.

The Massachusetts Comprehensive Special Education Law seeks to provide a "flexible and uniform system of special education opportunities for all children requiring special education."[9] Such children are to be described generically as "children with special needs."[10] The law makes local school districts responsible for the education of all handicapped persons aged three to twenty-one, regardless of the nature or severity of the handicap, and requires the greatest possible integration of handicapped children into regular class settings. This is to be accomplished through in-depth assessment and planning for each handicapped child by an interdisciplinary team, without undue reliance on standardized tests. There are strong requirements for parent involvement and provisions for due process and appeal should a parent be dissatisfied with the outcome. Special-education services are defined broadly to include social and medical services for the child as well as family guidance and counseling for the parents or guardians.

Under prior funding arrangements, the state had paid 100 percent of the costs of institutional and special-school placements but only 50 percent of most in-school services for the various categories of handicapped children. School committees (as local school boards are called in Massachusetts) therefore had faced strong disincentives to the development of local alternatives to institutionalization. Chapter 766 proposed to alter this by requiring school sys-

---

7 For a detailed treatment of school classification, see David L. Kirp, "Schools as Sorters: The Constitutional and Policy Implications of Student Classification," *University of Pennsylvania Law Review*, 121, 1973, pp. 705–797.

8 See Burton Blatt and Frank Garfunkel, *Massachusetts Study of Educational Opportunities for Handicapped and Disadvantaged Children*, Boston: Massachusetts Advisory Council on Education, 1971, esp. pp. 273–284.

9 C. 766§1.

10 C. 766 §9 (1).

tems to pay a share of the cost of institutionalization equal to the average per-pupil cost for children of comparable age within the local jurisdiction. Finally, the law provided for strengthening and decentralizing the state division of special education and defined its responsibilities vis-à-vis local jurisdictions in implementing the law.

The law was intended to produce significant change at all levels of the educational establishment—state, district, individual school, and classroom. Furthermore, it was expected to both alter and add to the work loads of all those responsible for special education. Our intent in studying the implementation of Chapter 766 was to examine the interaction between state-level policy and local implementation, and to observe the development of mechanisms to absorb the added work load and accommodate the resulting stresses, in order to assess these mechanisms' effects on implementation.

METHODOLOGY

The provisions of Chapter 766 took effect in September 1974. During the first year of implementation of the new law, we conducted interviews with school personnel at state and local levels and with a variety of others who played key roles in the passage of the legislation, the development of the regulations, or their implementation.

The major focus of our report is how the law affects the work situations of those at the local level ultimately responsible for its implementation—teachers, counselors, and specialists—and how the adjustments of these personnel to new work requirements affect implementation of the new law. Our concern is the processing of children rather than the content or quality of services and instruction. We studied the process of identification, referral, assessment, and educational-plan development for children with special needs in three school systems. In these three systems, one of the investigators interviewed key officials responsible for special education, attended staff meetings, and reviewed pertinent documents during the 1974–75 school year. A central component of the law is the assessment, by an interdisciplinary team, of children suspected to have special needs. One of the authors observed forty of these assessment meetings, called "core evaluations." All completed records of the 1,097 children evaluated in the three systems were reviewed, under procedures to safeguard confidentiality, for analysis of the salient referral, assessment, and outcome variables. These included the source of, reason for, and date of referral, as well as the ultimate disposition of the case.

Seven elementary schools, three in each of two school systems and one in the third, were selected for more intensive consideration. In these seven schools, personnel playing a role in implementing the law were interviewed, and follow-up interviews were held with teachers of all those children evaluated earlier in the school year. The major purpose of these teacher interviews was to determine what had transpired following the evaluations and development of educational plans for those children.

A comparison of community and school system characteristics is provided in table 4.1.

TABLE 4.1

Community and School Characteristics

	System A	System B	System C
Approximate enrollment	6,000	10,000	11,000
Per-pupil cost	$1,500	$ 1,450	$ 1,100
Pupil-teacher ratio (elementary)	16	15	20
Community median family income	$14,000	$10,000	$11,000
Percent workers professional, technical, managerial in community	45%	39%	22%

Source: Massachusetts Department of Commerce and Development, "City and Town Monograph" series, July 1973. This series is based on 1970 census data and 1971 and 1972 school reports. The statistics have been stated as approximations to discourage identification of the school systems.

The three systems, all in relatively large suburbs of Boston chosen to facilitate comparisons among cases, cannot be considered representative of the more than three hundred local school systems in Massachusetts. However, attendance at numerous meetings with school administrators from throughout the state confirmed to our satisfaction that the experience of these three systems with Chapter 766 has by no means been atypical.

THE IMPLEMENTATION CONTEXT

The response of local systems was conditioned in large measure by what happened at the state level following passage of the law. While many conditions favored successful implementation, some that contributed to local implementation difficulties were the following: poor planning and management by the state division of special education; continued local uncertainty throughout the two-year planning period concerning program requirements and implementation deadlines; the failure to train regular classroom teachers to handle children with special needs; and, perhaps most serious, the failure of the legislature to guarantee adequate funding. These conditions exacerbated workload pressures within the schools, amplified discretion at the local level, and thereby contributed to assertions of unintended priorities in carrying out the law.

The Massachusetts State Department of Education, like most other state departments of education, had long maintained a more or less passive stance toward local systems.[11] This had changed but slightly with the increase of federal funds for education in the 1960s. The state department had a reputation among local administrators as being inefficient, dominated by Boston interests, and, until the advent of Chapter 766, acquiescent to local determination. The state commissioner of education and legislative leaders recognized the need for change in the department's stance. The legislature more than doubled the budget of the Division of Special Education and provided for its decentralization into regional offices.[12] Yet, even the energetic new associate commissioner, Robert Audette, was limited by his own and the division's lack of managerial expertise, his firm commitment to a passive, regulatory role for the division, and the necessity to rely on incumbent staff accustomed to the old laissez-faire style. He was further hampered by a cumbersome process for bringing in new staff and an unrealistically low salary scale. These factors contributed to the recruitment of an enthusiastic but inexperienced staff, seen by local school officials as "anti-school," and the reliance on outside consultant firms.

Considerable time, effort, and money ($146,000) went into the development by an outside consultant of an operations manual for the child-evaluation procedure.[13] The manual, unveiled some ten weeks *after* the beginning of the 1974–75 school year, proved so complex and unwieldy that, in response to vociferous protest, its use was soon made optional. Angry special educators actually considered a mass burning of the manual—nicknamed the "Red Devil" for its bright red cover and onerous contents—on the State House steps. Another manual specifically for administrators was not delivered until three and one-half months after the opening of school.

The two-year delay in implementation—the bill, it will be recalled, was signed into law in July 1972, to take effect as of September 1974—while intended by the legislature for planning and preparation, was not utilized to full advantage. This failure was due in part to uncertainty as to whether full implementation would actually be required in September 1974. Postponement until September 1975, and phased implementation were advocated at various times during the planning period by the governor, the commissioner of education, the Association of School Superintendents, and even House Speaker David Bartley and Representative Michael Daly, the prime sponsors of the bill.

---

11 K. Fred Daniel and Joseph W. Crenshaw, "What Has Been and Should Be the Role of State Education Agencies in the Development and Implementation of Teacher Education Programs (Both Pre- and In-Service)? A Review and Analysis of Literature," Washington, D.C.: U. S. Office of Education, Order #OEC-0-71-3315, 3 Sept. 1971.

12 Muriel L. Cohen, "Massachusetts to Fill 29 Special Education Jobs," *Boston Globe*, 2 Aug. 1973. See also C. 766, §2, for a description of the powers and duties of the Division of Special Education.

13 An internal document of the Massachusetts Division of Special Education, "766 Update," May 1974, lists $146,000 of federal Title V funds as allocated to the child-assessment, or "core-evaluation." process.

Parent and advocacy groups strongly opposed phasing or postponement and threatened to file suit in the event that anything less than full implementation was approved. This debate over phased implementation continued until May 1974, undoubtedly causing many school officials to postpone gearing up until this crucial issue was resolved.

School officials also faced uncertainty about the funding of Chapter 766. While the law provides state support for local special-education costs that exceed a school system's average per-pupil costs, state reimbursement is normally distributed in the November following the school year in which the funds have been expended. Thus, the school system must first raise and expend the funds and then wait for state reimbursement. In the case of Chapter 766, which was likely to increase costs considerably, this procedure would mean a substantial increase in local property taxes to pay for the new and expanded services. Under Massachusetts law, a school committee is autonomous; once it sets the school budget, the town is obliged to raise the necessary revenues. To complicate matters further, estimates of the first-year costs varied from the state department of education's $40 million to local town and school officials' $100 million.[14] In fact, no one knew what the costs would be. Schools could not predict how many children would be referred and evaluated or what specific services these children would require.

While the legislature finally allocated $26 million in advance funding to help the systems finance the initial year of Chapter 766, this only postponed the funding problem. Even prior to enactment of Chapter 766, the legislature had never fully funded the regular state program of aid to education. In the previous year, for example, localities received only 81.2 percent of what they were entitled to under the law.[15] Under Chapter 766, schools could expect to receive full state special-education reimbursements, but, in the absence of greatly increased allocations by the legislature, these funds would be deducted from or "taken off the top" of the regular-education reimbursements. As such an increase in allocations was unlikely, local school officials feared that the total state reimbursements would remain at about the same level but would simply be divided differently, with more going to special-education and less to regular-education programs. Since regular costs would certainly increase, towns would still have to raise property taxes to cover such increases—an unhappy prospect in a state already financing 75 percent of education costs through property taxes, a proportion exceeded by only two states.[16]

If state planning for implementation had been totally misguided or ineffec-

---

14 Mary Thornton, "Unfunded Chapter 766: Who Finally Will Foot the Bill?" *Boston Globe*, 24 Feb. 1974; and James Worsham, "State Says Extra Ch. 766 Cost is $40 M, Not $100 M," *Boston Globe*, 27 Feb. 1974.

15 Editorial, "Paying School Costs," *Boston Globe*, 5 Mar. 1974.

16 Ibid.

tive there would be little point in discussing local-level implementation. Thus, it is particularly important to note that in many ways the circumstances for the implementation of Chapter 766 could be regarded as relatively auspicious, avoiding many of the problems often encountered in policy implementation.[17] First, the law was carefully researched, is clear and concise, and contains detailed, unambiguous regulations.

Second, Chapter 766 had strong constituent support and became in large measure a consumers' bill. Staff of the state legislature's Joint Committee on Education carefully orchestrated a broad-based lobbying effort that evolved into the Coalition for Special Education, an organization of thirty-three consumer and professional groups dedicated to the passage and implementation of this legislation.[18] Initial development of the regulations proceeded with considerable involvement of citizens. The division of special education organized ten task forces composed of parent and professional groups and others interested in the law. Each task force was charged with drafting a section of the regulations. After three full drafts and public hearings held throughout the state, the result was a 107-page document that set forth in clear language the law's requirements. The only opposition to Chapter 766 came from private-school operators who feared a loss of students and revenue if the law were implemented. Public-school administrators supported its intent, although they sometimes argued that Chapter 766 was unnecessary since they were already doing what it would require. For example, one special-education administrator stated in a memorandum to his superintendent, "Indeed, much of what is good in Chapter 766 has long been standard practice in [our town] and elsewhere— not infrequently in the teeth of opposition from the State, which today mandates what yesterday it forbade."

Third, the law provided sufficient resources to increase the bureaucracy's capacity to plan, coordinate, mobilize support for, direct, monitor, and assess implementation. The budget of the division of special education was more than doubled from $350,000 for 1973 to $800,000 for 1974, thereby making available twenty-nine new staff positions.[19] Furthermore, the use of federal funds for contract services provided a means, amply used by the division, to recruit assistance for short-term tasks on short notice.

Finally, several oversight and monitoring mechanisms were established prior

17 On some of the problems of translating legislation into practice mentioned here, see, for example, Edward C. Banfield, "Making a New Federal Program: Model Cities, 1964–1968," in Allan P. Sindler, ed. *Policy and Politics in America.* Boston: Little, Brown, 1973, pp. 124–158. Theodore Lowi. *The End of Liberalism.* New York: Norton, 1969; Martha Derthick. *New Towns In-Town.* Washington, D.C.: Urban Institute, 1972; and Jeffrey L. Pressman and Aaron B. Wildavsky. *Implementation.* Berkeley: Univ. of California Press, 1973.

18 Milton Budoff traces the early development of support for special education in "Engendering Change in Special Education Practices." *Harvard Educational Review,* 45, 1975, pp. 507–526.

19 Cohen, "Massachusetts to Fill 29 Special Education Jobs."

to the scheduled implementation of Chapter 766. A new state agency, the Office for Children, was established to coordinate, monitor, and assess services for children and generally serve as an advocate for their interests. It was assigned oversight responsibility for Chapter 766. Within the Division of Special Education, a Bureau of Child Advocacy was established to process appeals brought by parents under the law. And two private groups, the Massachusetts Advocacy Center and the Coalition for Special Education, jointly announced plans for monitoring compliance in each town. The threat of this monitoring effort helped ensure the compliance of local special-education administrators who often reacted with almost paranoid horror at the thought that an outside group of noneducators would seek to examine their performance.

LOCAL-LEVEL RESPONSES

The major thrust of the Massachusetts Comprehensive Special Education Law, and what makes it truly innovative, is the requirement that children with special needs receive individualized assessment and treatment. This thrust is reflected in a number of provisions: the required assessment of children by interdisciplinary teams with parental involvement; the requirement that a specific educational plan be tailored to the needs of each child; the replacement of generic descriptive labels by behaviorally specific inventories; and the accommodation, insofar as possible, of children with special needs in regular educational settings rather than in segregated classrooms. At the same time, certain provisions of the law are directed toward achieving uniform and nondiscriminatory treatment and comprehensive coverage of all children with special needs. As we will discuss later, these two aims of individualization and comprehensiveness are not entirely compatible in practice.

The requirements of the law created severe problems for local school districts. Extending school responsibility to persons aged three to twenty-one and requiring identification, assessment, and service provision to be accomplished in the first year posed challenges well beyond the capacity of any school system at the time. Special-education administrators began the 1974–75 school year without specific guidelines for constituting assessment teams, evaluating children, or writing educational plans. The regulations stipulated what needed to be done but provided no blueprint for administering the process. Both the division and organized parent groups had taken an adversarial stance toward local schools, and, as a result, administrators feared numerous court suits and appeals, which they believed they would lose. Parents, for the first time, were to be involved in educational planning for their own children, thereby challenging the autonomy of educators. Schools were to provide social, psychological, and medical services that many educators believed to be well beyond the legitimate purview of educational institutions. There was considerable doubt that full state reimbursement would in fact be available to pay for such services, and the likely competition for resources within school systems threatened to exacerbate underlying tensions between regular and special education. Furthermore, each step in implementing the law called for numerous forms to be completed, creating an enormous paperwork burden.

Under Chapter 766, what had formerly been a simple procedure informally worked out by the teacher, the specialist, and perhaps the parents, now became a major team undertaking with elaborate requirements governing each step. The process officially begins with a referral for assessment which may be initiated by a parent, teacher, or other school official, court, or social agency. Before that, however, "all efforts shall be made to meet such children's needs within the context of the services which are part of the regular education program."[20] The referral must document these efforts. Within five days of the referral, a written notice is to be sent to the parents informing them of the types of assessments to be conducted, when the evaluation will begin, and their right to participate in all meetings at which the educational plan is developed. Parents have the right to meet with the evaluation-team chairperson to receive an explanation of the reason and the procedure for the evaluation. The parent must give written consent for the evaluation and its individual components before the assessments may be initiated.

In the case of a full core evaluation, required when it is expected that a child will be placed outside of the regular class for more than 25 percent of the time, at least five assessments must be completed. An administrative representative of the school department must assess the child's educational status. A recent or current teacher must measure "the child's specific behavioral abilities along a developmental continuum, . . . school readiness, functioning or achievement . . . behavioral adjustment, attentional capacity, motor coordination, activity level and patterns, communication skills, memory and social relations with groups, peers, and adults." A physician must conduct a comprehensive health examination. A psychologist must provide an assessment, "including an individually appropriate psychological examination, . . . a developmental and social history, observation of the child in familiar surroundings (such as a classroom), sensory, motor, language, perceptual, attentional, cognitive, affective, attitudinal, self-image, interpersonal, behavioral, interest and vocational factors." A nurse, social worker, guidance counselor, or adjustment counselor must make a home visit and evaluate "pertinent family history and home situation factors." Additional assessments by psychiatric, neurological, learning-disability, speech, hearing, vision, motor, or any other specialists will

---

20 Commonwealth of Massachusetts, Department of Education, "Regulations for the Implementation of Chapter 766 of the Acts of 1972: The Comprehensive Special Education Law," 28 May 1974 (henceforth referred to as "Regulations"), para. 314.0, p. 17.

be carried out if they are considered necessary.[21]

For each assessment, a detailed, written report of the findings must be forwarded to the chairperson of the evaluation team and frequently to the evaluating specialist's supervisor. After the individual assessments are completed, team members may, if they choose, come together in a precore meeting to discuss their findings. Finally, there is another team meeting, with parents in attendance, in which the educational plan is developed. The educational plan must include a specific statement of what the child can and cannot do, his or her learning style, educational goals, and plans for meeting them during the following three, six, and nine months. This entire process, starting from the day the notification letter is mailed to the parents and ending with the completion of the educational plan, is to take no more than thirty days.

These requirements presented school personnel with an enormous increase in their work load in several ways. There were suddenly many more children to be evaluated. Many more individuals had to take part in each evaluation. Educational plans had to be written in much greater detail, completed faster, and circulated to a wider audience. Because team members had different schedules and other responsibilities, getting everyone together for a meeting became a difficult task. An evaluation of a child that might previously have taken two or three people a few hours to complete now took as many as ten to twenty hours for the chairperson and two to six hours for each of the other team members.

From the standpoint of implementation, the chief difficulty presented by Chapter 766 revolved around the tension between the requirements for an individualized approach to educating children and the strong pressures for mass processing created by requirements for comprehensiveness. This tension between individualization, and mass processing is not unique; it is characteristic of many street-level bureaucracies which attempt to reconcile individualized service with high demand relative to resources. Since street-level bureaucracies, particularly schools, may not officially restrict intake, other means must be found to accommodate the work load. Work load pressures in the past were at least partially responsible for many of the abuses that Chapter 766 was intended to correct: special-needs children were subjected to arbitrary assessment, being labeled and dumped into segregated special classes, exclusion, denial of appropriate services, and unnecessary institutionalization. The work load pressures did not disappear with passage of the law. If anything, they increased under the substantial burden of added demands.

School personnel put forth extraordinary efforts to comply with the new

21 The procedures for a full core evaluation are set forth in the "Regulations," para. 320.0, pp. 21–22. An intermediate core evaluation may be given, with the parent's approval, in those cases in which it is expected that the child will *not* be placed outside a regular class more than 25 percent of the time. It differs from the full core evaluation only in that fewer assessments are required. ("Regulations," para. 331.0, p. 34.)

demands. However, under the current system of public education there was simply no way that everything required could be done with the available resources. In the following sections we examine the objectives of the law against the reality of its implementation. The behavior described below indicates the limits of school organization. It does not so much reflect negatively on school personnel as it demonstrates how new demands are accommodated into the work structure of people who consistently must find ways to conserve resources and assert priorities to meet, in some way, the demands of their jobs.

Mainstreaming

Martin J. Kaufman and associates summarize the case for mainstreaming as based on the belief that it will remove stigmas; enhance the social status of special-needs children; facilitate modeling of appropriate behavior by handicapped youngsters; provide a more stimulating and competitive environment; offer a more flexible, cost-effective service in the child's own neighborhood; and be more acceptable to the public, particularly to minority groups.[22]

Chapter 766 requires that, to the maximum extent feasible, children with special needs be placed in regular-education programs, even if for just a small fraction of the school day. If possible, special classes are to be located within regular school facilities.[23] This provision, designed to end the practice of segregating handicapped children, originally evoked fears that special classes would be closed and large numbers of difficult-to-manage children would be returned to regular classrooms.

The specter of hordes of handicapped children being loosed upon regular-class teachers never materialized. To begin with, there were probably not that many children in full-time, self-contained, separate programs. Furthermore, the regulations contained a ''grandfather clause'' whereby all children in special programs as of September 1974 were presumed to be correctly placed unless evidence was presented to the contrary. Data obtained from an official of the state department of education indicate that children were actually shifted from less to more restrictive programs during the first year of implementation. In part, this shift probably reflects increased use of resource rooms. Ironically, by providing separate rooms staffed by specialists to provide special-education services, school systems *decreased* the proportion of fully integrated children by sending them out of the regular classrooms for special help. Table 4.2 shows the percentage of special-needs children in various programs as of October 1974, as implementation was getting under way, and as of October 1975, after implementation.

With regard to mainstreaming, the law's major impact follows from its

22 Kaufman et al., ''Mainstreaming,'' p. 2.
23 ''Regulations,'' para. 502.10 (a), p. 58.

TABLE 4.2

Special-Needs Children by Program Prototype

	October 1974	October 1975
Percent of special-needs children in regular class with support (i.e., no time out)	35.9	19.8
Percent of special-needs children in regular class with up to 25 percent time out	43.9	56.2
Percent of special-needs children in regular class less than 75 percent of the time	20.2	24.0

Source: Data supplied to the author by an official of the Massachusetts State Department of Education.

procedural barriers proscribing the inappropriate assignment of children to self-contained classes. While several instances of active recruitment of children by special-class teachers were noted during the study, such instances were rare. This was true not only because of a lack of space in existing special classes, but also because of a genuine commitment to mainstreaming on the part of special-education administrators and most special-class teachers. Chapter 766 provided special educators the necessary leverage with principals and other administrators to expand and revamp services. There was, however, evidence that a subtle kind of dumping was taking place: there appeared to be a wholesale shifting of responsibility for troublesome children from the regular-class teacher to a specialist or resource-room teacher.

We observed many close working relationships between regular-class teachers and specialists. Specialists would sometimes consult teachers on how to handle particular classroom problems and how best to work with individual children. Some efforts were made to coordinate learning in the regular class with the specialist's intervention program. However, the maintenance of such relationships requires time, which was in short supply. Far more frequently, the teacher had little contact with specialists, had no knowledge of the content of the educational plan, and demonstrated an attitude that the child's learning or behavior problem was the responsibility of someone else, namely, the specialist. Even when specialists sought to work closely with teachers, the pressures of increased case loads and the vastly increased time spent in the assessment process prevented them from doing so. Thus the law, while limiting the segregation of handicapped children, resulted in a further compartmentalization of students needing special services and increased the danger that they might be stigmatized on the basis of their need for help from specialists outside the regular classroom.

More Efficient Identification and Processing

According to estimates from the state department of education, only 50 to 60 percent of children with special needs had been identified and provided services by Massachusetts schools prior to the passage of Chapter 766.[24] The present regulations require local education authorities to undertake a range of activities to identify children in need of special services, although there was no shortage of referrals from teachers and parents. The systems studied varied in the way they translated this requirement into action. System B derived more than half of its referrals from pre- and in-school screening, while screening accounted for but a small fraction of the other two systems' referrals. Furthermore, in all three systems, the kinds of disorders identified through screening were directly related to the specialty of the person doing the screening. For example, System B, which relied much more heavily on speech specialists to conduct screening than the other two systems, referred more than twice as many children for evaluations because of speech problems. In many instances, those doing the screening were actually referring children to themselves. That is, the speech specialist conducting screening would more than likely participate in the core evaluation and eventually treat the child. This overlap of functions suggests that the local systems need to guard not only against failing to identify children in need of special services, but also against unnecessarily recruiting children not in need of special services.

One measure of the relative efficiency of the assessment process is the time required to complete an assessment. The regulations require that the evaluation take place within thirty working days after the parents are informed, or in no more than thirty-five days after the child is referred. Despite substantial differences among the three systems with regard to procedures and staffing, there was surprising uniformity in the time taken to complete assessments. The mean number of months taken to complete the assessments was 6.9 in System A, 7.8 in System B, and 7.9 in System C—all considerably longer than the time permitted under the law and longer than the three months permitted until the plan must be signed by the parent. In Systems B and C, where data were available, only 11.9 percent and 21.2 percent of referrals, respectively, were completed within three months. This is an index of the overwhelming scope of the task confronting the schools.

Equity, Uniformity, and Comprehensive Coverage

Chapter 766 seeks to end arbitrary and discriminatory practices through an individualized approach to the classification and assignment of children with

---

24 Mary Thornton, "Regulations on Special Education to Hike Taxes," *Boston Globe,* 22 Feb. 1974. These estimates, it should be noted, were derived by applying the widely accepted national incidence figures of about 12 percent to the state's school population.

special needs. This is to be accomplished in a way that assures a measure of equity—equal treatment for children with the same needs—as well as responsiveness to parents and teachers. Fiscal constraints and the governance procedures of local school systems impose the additional requirements of accountability, efficiency, and fiscal integrity. These aims constitute conflicting bureaucratic requirements.[25] In the absence of specific guidance from the state department, the three school systems we analyzed pursued different strategies, each of which maximized one or more of these requirements at some sacrifice of the others. The differing approaches to the core-evaluation process taken by the three systems warrant brief description.

System A, with the smallest enrollment, designated a psychologist, a social worker, and a learning-disabilities specialist already on staff as the primary core-evaluation team. Several additional part-time specialists were hired to supplement this team, and existing school-based specialists and teachers were brought in when appropriate. This system has a strong tradition of principal and school autonomy and professionalism. Thus, while the primary team did conduct most of the evaluations in the central district offices, many evaluations were done in the schools, sometimes without the participation of any of the primary-team members. This two-tiered arrangement produced wide disparities among schools in the identification and assessment of children. The team and administrators adopted a largely reactive stance toward evaluation and, for the most part, simply processed referrals coming to them. Personnel at all levels rationalized this reactive posture with the belief that most children with special needs were already being served and that the services provided by the system were superior to those found in most other systems.

System B hired an outside business consultant to design a procedure for central oversight of the work flow. New forms and other required documents were developed for personnel involved at each step of the referral and evaluation process. Central files made it possible to determine which forms were outstanding for any particular child, and follow-up procedures were instituted to assure completion of the process. On the whole, the record-keeping system was excellent. Assessments and educational plans were forwarded to administrative supervisors to ensure central quality control. An aggressive case-finding effort was enhanced by the thorough orientation of teachers and principals. School psychologists were designated as chairpersons of the core-evaluation teams, and to accommodate this added responsibility the number of psychologists was doubled. The procedures adopted by System B tended to be dominated by a concern for completing forms properly and speedily. As a result, assessment meetings were conducted hastily and with a minimum of genuine deliberation.

25 See James Q. Wilson, "The Bureaucracy Problem," *Public Interest*, 6, 1967, pp. 3–9.

In System C, the largest of the three but with the smallest per-pupil expenditure, most evaluations were attended by the special-education administrator or one of the program directors. Their presence assured a high degree of quality control. These administrators viewed their participation as a means of training school-based staff through their example and interactions in the meetings. The evaluations were regarded as belonging to the schools, and the chairpersons of the core-evaluation teams had a much more varied array of backgrounds than chairpersons in the other systems. Whereas in Systems A and B the outcome of an evaluation was usually predetermined, System C held relatively few of the "pre-core" meetings in which team members would meet, usually without the parents, to discuss the assessments and educational plan. As a result, the core meetings in System C tended to be characterized by a great deal of give-and-take, a high level of parent involvement, and genuine group problem solving. The deliberations were longer, with more people involved, and this system conducted a much higher percentage of full-core rather than pre-core evaluations.

One indication of the differences in style among the three systems is shown in a comparison of numbers of persons involved and time spent in the core-evaluation meetings. Of meetings observed, the mean duration was forty-two minutes in System A, fifty in System B, and seventy-four in System C. The mean number of participants was 6 in System A, 5.7 in B, and 9.5 in C. While the three systems developed idiosyncratic procedures for identifying and processing special-needs children, all confronted the same serious problem: no explicitly mandated system of priority in referral, assessment, or provision of services accompanied the requirement for uniform treatment of children with special needs. It seemed as if all children were to be processed at once without official regard to the seriousness of the individual situation; a child with multiple physical and emotional problems was to be processed no sooner than a child with a slight hearing impairment.

In practice all three school systems made unofficial distinctions between routine and complex cases. Routine cases were viewed by school personnel as those in which the completion of the educational-plan form was necessary in order to provide the services of a specialist. In these cases, an implicit decision would be made prior to referral that a service was needed. The evaluation was then viewed as a bureaucratic hurdle to be gotten over as quickly as possible, in some cases even without the supposedly mandatory participation of parents. Many of these meetings took on a contrived, routine character. The more complex cases were those in which the assessment of the child was in fact problematic—there was some disagreement among school personnel regarding the assessment or educational plan, considerable expense to the school system might be involved, or the parents were viewed as potential "troublemakers." Troublesome parents were those thought likely to disrupt the process by complaining, questioning, or rejecting recommendations of professionals; or those whose higher socioeconomic status suggested to school personnel that a threat might be forthcoming. The percentage of complex cases varied considerably among the three school systems. In System C the majority of cases fell into this category, while in systems A and B complex cases constituted perhaps no more than 15 to 25 percent of the referrals.

In addition to making distinctions among kinds of referrals, the three systems employed a variety of unofficial rationing techniques to hold down the number of referrals. First, teachers sometimes failed to refer children despite evidence of problems that should have indicated the need for evaluation. Classroom teachers were deterred by the necessity of completing the forms and justifying their assessment of the problem to the principal and specialists. For some teachers, acknowledgment of a problem they could not handle themselves represented failure. They could look forward to the end of the school year when they would pass the children on to the next teacher in line; consequently, many tended to refer only those who were most troublesome. Second, a principal would occasionally dissuade parents from requesting a core evaluation with assurances that the child was doing fine or that services were already being provided. Third, referrals from teachers were submitted through the principal and/or specialist, and in a number of instances the principal or specialist would simply fail to follow through. Finally, administrators sometimes gave instructions to cut back on referrals. In one of the systems, principals having the largest number of referrals were told by the central administration to curtail evaluations because of the costs of services being recommended.

In general, these rationing practices resulted from unsanctioned, informal categorization of potential referrals. Such categorization reflected the personal priorities of the individuals making the referral decisions. In weighing the relative costs and benefits of referring a child for core evaluation, individuals implicitly appeared to act on several criteria. Concern for the well-being of their children was without question the foremost consideration for the great majority of school personnel. Without such concern, implementation of Chapter 766 would have broken down completely, for in all three school systems administrators and specialists kept the process going by working extraordinarily long hours under constant stress with little hope of catching up, at least during the first year or two.

The institutional rewards system provided another criterion. Some principals believed that they themselves would be at least informally evaluated on the number and handling of referrals. In System B and System C principals were encouraged to refer; in System A they were not.

The degree to which children were creating problems for teachers or other personnel because of their disruptive behavior also affected decisions. Teachers interviewed generally stated that they referred the ''loudest'' children first. This general criterion was supported by an examination of the dates of referral for learning and behavior problems; in Systems B and C, where sufficient data were available, behavior referrals occurred with greatest frequency in the first three months of the school year.

The speed of processing tended to be affected by the position of the person making the referral. In general, parent and principal referrals, while accounting for a relatively small percentage of total referrals, were processed more rapidly than those from teachers.

Finally, the availability of services within the system influenced decisions. In one system, school-based specialists decided informally whether or not a child should be referred on the basis of the presumed solution rather than the presented problem. If they foresaw a need to buy the services of additional specialists, a quick evaluation would be held.

Both systems and individual schools varied in their rate of referral and processing. By the end of June 1975, System A had completed evaluations on approximately 3.8 percent of its students; System B, on 5.5 percent; and System C, on 2.8 percent.[26] Some individual schools in these systems did not refer and evaluate any children, while others processed many. Of the schools in Systems B and C, which had evaluated at least five children, some completed nearly half of the evaluations within the required three-month period, while others completed none. There were also variations in the reasons for referral. Speech problems were the primary referral reason for about 20 percent of children evaluated in System B, only 5 percent in System A, and fewer than 2 percent in System C. While learning referrals were relatively constant across the three systems, ranging from 58.1 to 65.9 percent of referrals, behavior referrals constituted 22.2 percent in System A, 13.6 percent in System B, and 29.2 percent in System C.

Thus, a law and its administrative regulations, intended to produce uniform application of procedures, instead yielded wide variations in application. The chances of a child's being referred, evaluated, and provided with special-education services were associated with presumably extraneous factors: the school system and school attended, the child's disruptiveness in class, his or her age and sex,[27] the aggressiveness and socioeconomic status of the parents, the current availability and cost of services needed, and the presence of particular categories of specialists in the school system.

Parent Involvement and Interdisciplinary Team Assessment

Chapter 766 seeks to regulate arbitrary and inappropriate classification and

---

26 Statewide, systems completed evaluations in a range from 2 percent to 20 percent.

27 The mean age of children evaluated varied from 12.6 years in System A to 7.5 in System B and 10.3 in System C. In all three school systems, males evaluated outnumbered females by between two and three to one.

assignment of children by placing restrictions on the use of standardized tests and by requiring joint assessment and planning by an interdisciplinary team that includes parents. The net effect of these required procedures in the three systems has been greater involvement of parents, more careful assessment of children, and some genuine team decision making. But, at the same time, both teachers and parents have played a secondary role to specialists in the evaluation process.

The impact of parent participation was as much a function of the team's anticipating pressures from parents as it was a response to their actual involvement. In numerous instances parents made substantial contributions to the assessment or planning processes; however, school personnel frequently took actions aimed at placating or avoiding conflict with parents. For example, one of the authors observed administrators in a lengthy meeting developing a defensive strategy for handling an angry mother whose child's referral papers had been lost by school personnel. Their primary concern was not why the referral did not get processed but rather how to absolve themselves of responsibility.

The parent was usually in the position of joining an ongoing group; generally, the core-evaluation team had met as a group during other assessments, and its members worked together on a continuing basis. The parent, in addition, might confront a sometimes unsubtle implication that the child and parent were somehow at fault for creating a problem. This was particularly true when the problem involved disruptive behavior or a learning difficulty of which the nature was not readily apparent. Perhaps defensive about their lack of time, training, and skills to work with special-needs children, some teachers we observed assigned blame to parents and children, and they were frequently joined in this by other personnel. In fact, the deliberations in assessment meetings often revealed an underlying preoccupation with the assignment of blame. Here, for example, the teacher, asked to describe a child's strengths and weaknesses, responds with negatives:

> Academically, he is below grade; he has a short attention span and a severe learning disability, poor handwriting, poor work habits; his desk is disheveled, and he never puts anything away. His oral is better than his written work. He never gives others a chance. He is uncooperative, ignores school rules—due in part to his frustration with learning. He can't stay in his seat. He won't accept pressure. He is interested in smoking, drugs, and alcohol and has a security problem. He has difficulty with all the specialists. He fights. . . .

There were additional factors which put parents at a disadvantage. Often there were status differences between a poor or working-class parent and the middle-class professionals who might dress differently and speak a different language. The use of technical jargon lent an aura of science to the proceedings, while making much of the discussion unintelligible to parents and, frequently, to teachers as well. One psychologist explained test results to a working-class parent in this way: "He is poor in visual-motor tasks. He has come up [improved] on sequencing-objct assembly-completions which may reflect maturation in addition to training—that is, his visual-motor improvement. . . ." In another meeting, a tutor began, reading from a report: "Reading, 2.1 level; comprehensive language skills, good; daily performance, erratic. He is the type of child with learning problems—he has difficulty processing short sounds, auditory sequencing, and so forth. The visual is slightly better than the auditory channel." In another meeting, a teacher and psychologist, trying to convince a reluctant parent that her child should be held back for a year, produced a computer printout showing the child's performance on test scores in comparison with other children the same age. The parent immediately capitulated.

The regulations governing the core-evaluation meeting call for assessments to deal equally with the child's capacities and strengths as well as with deficiencies. However, an assessment was principally the result of someone's concern about deficiencies. Furthermore, the assessment provided official certification that the child had "special needs" that required services over and above those provided for most other children. Most of the core evaluation was devoted to verifying the child's negative functioning through the recitation of test scores, anecdotal information, and observations. The presentation of negative data appeared to serve two functions. First, teachers frequently presented negative data about a child in an apparently defensive strategy aimed at absolving themselves of responsibility for the child's problem. Second, the negative assessment of a child might prepare the way to obtain parents' compliance with whatever plan school officials wished to impose.

Increased Services

While much of the controversy and effort in the first year's operation of Chapter 766 revolved around the assessment process, the ultimate goal of the law is the provision of services. School systems are required to provide whatever services are recommended by the core-evaluation team for an individual child, without being constrained by cost considerations. If appropriate services are unavailable, the school system must develop them or send a child at local expense outside the system where such services may be obtained. Because of its remarkable comprehensiveness we might have expected this provision to break down in practice through informal imposition of cost or referral restrictions. Nonetheless, we may still legitimately inquire into the extent to which the spirit of the provision was honored.

The requirements immediately expanded the range of options for special education and did lead to some expansion and redesigning of special-education services. In some respects, however, the implementation of Chapter 766 actually resulted in a reduction of services, at least during the first year. One problem was the wholesale withdrawal of services to schoolchildren by the departments of welfare, public health, and mental health, the Massachusetts Rehabilitation Commission, and other state agencies. Special-education administrators bitterly complained of instances in which services previously offered to children at little or no cost were now being withdrawn or offered on a fee basis.

Even more demoralizing for school personnel was the reduction of in-school specialist services which resulted from the assignment of these specialists to complete core evaluations. In general, the specialists who were involved in assessment and educational-plan meetings were the same persons who would be called upon to provide the recommended services. These specialists, along with other team members, faced two problems: the sheer volume of new assessments; and the vastly increased time required to test or otherwise evaluate a child, write up the assessment report, attend the team meetings, and write the educational plan. Specialists were caught in a particularly difficult bind. Their contribution was essential to the assessment process. At the same time, a conscientious discharge of these responsibilities meant less time available to work with children and more time spent completing forms. One specialist said, "It just kills me to walk by those kids with them saying, 'Aren't you coming to see us today?'"

The most frequent response to this overwhelming work load burden was to work harder and longer hours completing paperwork at home. The considerable personal strain on those engaged in implementation at the local level was apparent. While additional staff members were hired in all three systems, this increase in numbers was rarely sufficient to meet the increased demand. That the law was carried out as well as it was is due to the dedication of those at the local level whose extra efforts constituted a sizable hidden subsidy to the school system.

However, the magnitude of the work load often forced specialists to shortchange the assessment process. When assessments could not be bypassed, they were routinized. Meetings became cursory. Parent signatures were obtained on blank forms to cut down the time required to get the signed educational plans returned. Educational plans, instead of providing individually tailored programs, were most often little more than road maps routing children to one or more specialists during the school day.

Earlier we discussed the rationing of attention to assessments in response to the overwhelming demand. For the same reason, special educators rationed the services they provided to children. One form of such rationing was that services that in previous years had been offered on an individual, one-to-one basis were now delivered to groups. This practice was rationalized on the grounds that group treatment is more beneficial, which of course it may be. However, it is hardly accidental that this theoretical breakthrough was coincident with the additional burdens placed on special-education personnel by Chapter 766. Also, the number of hours a specialist would see a child per week was reduced. There was increased reliance on student trainees to fill service gaps. And, finally, initiation of services might simply be postponed until later in the school year.

Team members often failed to respond to very obvious service needs voiced by parents, particularly those involving counseling for emotional problems. For example, upon hearing the results of the testing of her child, a mother looked up and said: "You know I have another boy, William. He probably has that same problem, but they didn't give him those tests. I thought he was lazy and thoughtless, but he was afraid to go into third grade. He wanted to go back to second." The teacher responded, "There is nothing wrong with going back to second." This was the end of that discussion.

The relationship between classroom teachers and specialists is also a source of tension. The specialist can provide some relief for the teacher in handling a classroom problem; however, there are costs to the teacher in seeking such help. Classroom teachers resent the added paperwork burden involved in initiating referrals and the amount of time it takes to get specialists' services through the core-evaluation process. They, too, may be intimidated by the specialists' technical jargon. Like parents, they may be unfamiliar with the assessment process and outnumbered in evaluation meetings.

There are several additional factors inherent in the respective situations of specialists and teachers which contribute to this tension. Classroom teachers and specialists have differing perspectives. Teachers often regard special-needs children as contributing to their difficulties at work, whereas specialists regard these children as clients they were specifically trained to assist. Teachers have only one school year during which to accomplish their objectives for individual children or the class as a whole, but specialists can take a longer view. They may work with children over a period of years spanning the children's entire school careers. Thus a problem of some urgency to the teacher may be seen by the specialist as one that may be put off until some time in the future.

Status differences add to the tension. Specialists typically have qualifications as classroom teachers but also have additional education and certification and, in some cases, higher pay. Furthermore, specialists and teachers are responsible to different lines of authority. The classroom teacher is responsible to the principal, while the specialist reports to a program director or division head who is generally located both physically and administratively close to the top of the system's hierarchy.

An additional source of tension is the discrepancy between teachers' expectations and results. Teachers look to the assessment process to provide some relief from disruptive children, but this expectation frequently remains unsatis-

fied. Teachers reported that 58 percent of the children they referred for evaluation exhibited behavior problems. However, only 21 percent of these children
were reported by the teachers to be getting any help either outside the school
system or from the specialist within the system whose job it was to deal with
behavior problems. Responsibility for children is also a source of conflict
between classroom teachers and specialists. Teachers are subject to conflicting
pressures. On the one hand, they may wish to relinquish responsibility for an
individual child whom they view as disruptive. On the other hand, they may
view themselves as having primary responsibility for the child and may resent
intrusion from outsiders. One teacher put it this way:

> The first- and second-grade teachers here had a list of five or six kids who
> ought to be retained. However, the psychologist recommended promotion on
> the basis of IQ tests. Teachers are losing their identity. We used to have
> teacher aides here who were paid $100 a week and that worked fine. Now
> they hire tutors at $6.75 an hour.

Elimination of Labeling

The Chapter 766 requirement to discontinue the use of descriptive labels conflicts with the limited capacity of street-level bureaucracies to classify and
differentially treat clients. Labels function as client-management aids and also
help define worker-client relationships. Many classroom teachers and
specialists were educated in an era when diagnosis ended with the assignment
of a label, which in turn provided the sole basis for placement and treatment.
Such terminology is not easily unlearned. Under the new regulations, there was
some reduction in the use of labels and a very definite shift to individual
behavioral descriptions. However, the use of labels persisted, as is indicated by
the following statements made at assessment meetings:

> The Bender showed her to have an equivalent score of a five-year-old.
> However, I don't think she is a trainable.
> John was getting an awful lot of special help. He used to be, with an IQ
> under 50, according to state law, in a trainable class, but he has been in an
> educable class and has been progressing beyond what one would expect
> based on test scores alone.

Chapter 766's aim to eliminate labels was also foiled by federal requirements
demanding continued use of the traditional designations. Thus, the State Division of Special Education compelled local school systems to report, as they had
in the past, the numbers of and expenditures for children specifically classified
as mentally retarded, physically handicapped, partially seeing, speech-hearing
handicapped, emotionally disturbed, and learning disabled.

Even as old labels persisted, new ones were invented. When a psychologist and counselor were contrasting programs for "LD [learning disabled] kids" and "our kids," the observer asked who "our kids" were. The psychologist replied, "Oh, they used to be called retarded." In another instance one teacher said that she ran a program for "substantially independent" girls. When asked what that meant, she replied, "Well, we used to call it the EMH [educable mentally handicapped] class."

CONCLUSIONS

In September 1974, Massachusetts school systems confronted challenges to their management capabilities and to their deployment of personnel. They were obliged by the commonwealth to identify all pupils with special-education requirements, including those not previously so classified. Moreover, this responsibility extended to a population both younger and older than the population the schools had previously had to serve. The systems were charged with assessing the special needs of children through consultation with a variety of specialists and with the complete involvement of parents. And they were responsible for designing individualized programs appropriate to those needs, regardless of cost. They were expected to do this with virtually no authoritative assertion of priorities and without firm assurance that they would be entirely reimbursed by the state for increased expenditures. Administrators were caught between the requirements to comply with the law, which they took quite seriously although the state's initial monitoring effort was much weaker than had originally been indicated, and the certainty that their school committees would rebel against expenditures that led to increased taxes. While they had the support of parent groups and others actively concerned with special education, school administrators were dubious about this support because these groups tended to be unsympathetic to any approach which implied that a school system would do less than the law required.

Special-education personnel thus experienced pressures to accomplish enormous tasks in a short period of time with no certainty of substantially greater resources. Many school systems had already been moving in the direction indicated by Chapter 766, but now they *had* to accomplish what had previously been a matter of voluntary educational policy. Under the circumstances, special-education personnel had to cope with their new job requirements in ways that would permit an acceptable solution to what theoretically appeared to be impossible demands.

That the systems we studied processed hundreds of children while maintaining the levels of services they did provide is a tribute to the dedication of school personnel and to the coercive, if diffuse, effects of the law. However, in certain respects the new law, by dictating so much, actually dictated very little. Like police officers who are required to enforce so many regulations that they are effectively free to enforce the law selectively, or public-welfare workers who cannot master encylopedic and constantly changing eligibility requirements and so operate with a much smaller set of regulations, special-education personnel had to contrive their own adjustments to the multiple demands they encountered.

While not, for the most part, motivated by a desire to compromise compliance, school personnel had to formulate policies that would balance the new demands against available resources. To this end, school systems, schools, and individuals devised the following variety of coping patterns:

They rationed the number of assessments performed. They neglected to conduct assessments; placed limits on the numbers that were held; and biased the scheduling of assessments in favor of children who were behavior problems, who were not likely to cost the systems money, or who met the needs of school personnel seeking to practice their individual specialties.

They rationed services by reducing the hours of assignment to specialists, by favoring group over individual treatment, and by using specialists-in-training rather than experienced personnel as instructors. They short-circuited bureaucratic requirements for completing forms and for following the procedures mandated and designed to protect the interests of parents. They minimized the potentially time-consuming problem of getting parents to go along with plans by securing prior agreements on recommendations and by fostering deference to professional authority.

In short, they sought to secure their work environment. As individuals, teachers referred (dumped) students who posed the greatest threat to classroom control or recruited those with whom they were trained to work. Collectively, they sought contractual agreements that the new law would not increase their overall responsibilities.

These responses are not unique to special-education personnel but are typical of the coping behaviors of street-level bureaucrats. Chapter 766 placed additional burdens of judgment on roles already highly discretionary.

The patterns of responses developed by educators to the multiple demands placed upon them effectively constituted the policy delivered to the public under the new law. Given the range of possible "solutions" to the demand-resource dilemma faced by Massachusetts educators, the solution found by any single school system was not predictable. One system made qualitatively superior efforts to comply with the law but ranked lowest among the systems studied in the number of assessments completed. The system that screened and assessed the most students was also the most inclinded to routinize the assessment procedures and dilute the quality of service provisions. But, although the pattern of responses varied to some extent, there was a constant need to routinize, ration resources, control uncertainties, and define the task to derive satisfactory solutions to the new demands.

Despite shortcomings in implementation, the new law has contributed to making special education a general concern. It opens the process of categorizing special-needs children to parents and to the scrutiny of special-education interest groups. It articulates far-reaching objectives for school systems, retains local initiative, and forces a confrontation between school systems' responsibilities for general *and* special education. Chapter 766 heralds the day when all students, the quiet as well as the disruptive, the average as well as the exceptional, those who make good use of their potential and those who do not, will be responded to by the schools as individuals. In this respect, the first year of Chapter 766 should be analyzed not only for the ways in which the coping behaviors of school personnel perpetuate routinization of tasks and segmentation of the population. It should also be analyzed to discover which solutions to coping problems are most consistent with preferred educational objectives.

As the Massachusetts schools complete their third year of operation under Chapter 766, the situation has no doubt changed from the time of our field study. We cannot, however, predict that it has improved. The regulations have been somewhat revised to reflect the operating experience of the schools, and the department of education is attempting to audit local school systems' performance. The early crush of assessments we observed during the first year has no doubt subsided. However, we suspect that the pressure on school personnel to complete assessments has simply given way to pressure to implement, monitor, and revise the educational plans written earlier. If so, our analysis would suggest that these same personnel will now be forced to adopt coping mechanisms similar to those we have described as they attempt to deliver the educational services they prescribed earlier. Furthermore, in all likelihood the assessment and treatment routines and practices established under the press of that first hectic year are now firmly entrenched. As for cost considerations, school systems continue to be concerned about expenditures but now try to assign many regular-education items to the special-education budget, since Chapter 766 expenditures have first claim in the state's educational-reimbursement program.

The enactment of federal special-education reform and the likelihood that public pressure on the courts will eventually force nonparticipating states to adopt such reform suggests that close attention be paid to the Massachusetts experience. The Education for All Handicapped Children Act of 1975 (P.L. 94-142) raises the prospect that the kinds of implementation problems that plagued Massachusetts will be repeated across the country. For example, by requiring participating states to undertake more activities than the Congress is likely to subsidize, the federal law appears to set the stage for the same kind of autonomous priority setting by individual communities that characterized the Massachusetts experience. This is perhaps the first lesson of the Massachusetts case. States attempting special-education reform should expect to encounter problems similar to the ones discussed here if funding is uncertain and local communities must bear the brunt of costs.

There are other lessons for the implementation of laws that seek to change practice at the street level. An essential beginning in special-education reform is the careful preparation of local personnel. Training classroom teachers to be better prepared and more confident in handling children with special needs is particularly important. Specialists need training in consultative skills so that they may better support classroom teachers. Unless roles are redefined and personnel prepared to meet new requirements, children will continue to be shunted from one specialist to the next, with no one having responsibility for the whole child.

Second, rather than simply monitoring compliance with case-finding and assessment requirements, state departments of education should emphasize service provision and should exercise leadership in helping local systems establish, expand, and improve services. In Massachusetts, some local school systems were loath to share service innovations with other systems with which they competed for federal grant funds. The spirit of local independence and autonomy, perhaps at its strongest in New England towns, also impeded the kind of sharing and exchange that could have fostered joint solutions to implementation problems. Instead, each system invented its own evaluation-team model and way of controlling the paper flow, and improvised numerous other responses to state requirements. At the federal level, the Bureau of Education for the Handicapped is giving priority to the development and dissemination of practical tools—a model evaluation manual and service prototypes, for example—which will help states get their programs under way. These may prove to be useful guides if they are not overtaken by events.

Third, it is often assumed that parents' interests are secured by parent participation. But our observations indicate that parents may be subjected to strong pressures from school personnel and may acquiesce in decisions not in the best interests of their children, despite the protection of the law. To properly safeguard the rights of children, each assessment team might include a volunteer or a staff member of another agency who would fill the role of child advocate.

Fourth, as implementation is substantially determined by the coping behaviors of those who have to carry out the new law, it would be useful to analyze these behaviors and reward those that most closely conform to preferred public objectives, while discouraging objectionable practices. Bureaucratic coping behaviors cannot be eliminated, but they can be monitored and directed.

Practical men and women charged with carrying out new legislation understandably and correctly seek appropriate responses, clarity in objectives and priorities, and certainty of support. Our analysis has focused on how school personnel respond when these matters are in doubt. But our findings do not mean that social-reform legislation should be limited to mandating only that which street-level personnel can easily accomplish. On the contrary, much would be lost by reducing the scope of legislation to only that which can be readily accommodated. Rather than encouraging concentration of resources on a limited number of children, Chapter 766 cries out for increasing the scope of coverage. Preschoolers and post-high-school minors have now become, by law, the responsibility of school systems. Parents may petition for special services and challenge schools' decisions about children's care. Indeed, the vision of many educators with whom we spoke was that the law would open the way to treating *every* child as deserving individual assessment and an individualized learning plan. This would be particularly true for the brightest students, generally thought to be a neglected group whose ordinary treatment in school provides suboptimal education and nurtures emotional problems. In short, the thrust of Chapter 766 is, if anything, to increase and expand services. But, as usually happens in most street-level bureaucracies, service providers are left to ration what legislatures and policy-making executives will not.

Concentrating too much on issues of coordination and phasing at the state level also misses the mark to some degree. This focus overlooks the role of law in giving legitimacy to conceptions of the social order and in directing people's energies toward objectives even if these objectives cannot be achieved completely in the short run. Thus, one can argue that the Massachusetts legislature was correct in advancing a law with a scope as broad as the needs of the children and young adults who were to be served. It is not at all obvious that the provision of special-education services would have been more extensive or of better quality had the scope of the law been restricted. And one can argue that the parent and advocacy groups were correct in preventing the division of Special Education from asserting priorities: this kind of limitation not only would have contradicted the law but also would have substituted state planning for local responsibility.

The case of special education in Massachusetts provides a sober lesson in how difficult it is to integrate special services for a stigmatized population, particularly when that population is attended by professional specialists, funded through separate channels, championed by people fearful that they will lose hard-won access to decision making, and perceived to cause work-related problems for those responsible for managing the integration. In such a situation the role of law in legitimizing new conceptions of the public order and in mobilizing resources should not be overlooked.

CHAPTER 5

A Solution in Search of a Problem: Comprehensive Change and the Jefferson Experimental Schools

WAYNE J. DOYLE

The criticism of public schools ranges from the charge that schools need to change educational practices drastically to meet the needs of students in a constantly changing society to the charge that schools are straying too far from teaching the basics. In response, many school people have adopted an innovative stance, in some cases expanding the students' school experiences, while in others trying to do more effectively what they are already doing.

An impressive number of nationally discussed and highly publicized innovations have been created to improve schools in the last half of this century.[1] Giacquinta observed that planned change in public schools in the United States is now taken for granted as both necessary and desirable.[2] Yet, despite efforts to introduce preconceived innovations into the public schools, the goal of bringing about fundamental, effective, and lasting change has not been achieved.[3] In the main, results are not encouraging and certainly have failed to blunt the criticism being levelled at public schools.

The Experimental Schools Program (ESP) of the 1970s represents one attempt to introduce broad, effective, and lasting change. It merits consideration because the ESP was touted as a possible alternative to the widespread criticism that past approaches to funding planned change were unsuccessful and also

This chapter leans heavily on a report by Wayne J. Doyle, Janet Christ-Whitzel, Terrill L. Donicht, Donald F. Eixenberger, Robert B. Everhart, James M. McGeever, Douglas R. Pierce, and Robert M. Toepper entitled "The Birth, Nurturance and Transformation of an Educational Reform," an external evaluation of the Jefferson Experimental Schools Program funded by NIE-HEW, Contract No. OEC-0-71-4751, Northwest Regional Educational Laboratory.

1   D. Orlosky and O. Smith, "Educational Change: Its Origins and Characteristics," *Phi Delta Kappan,* Vol. 53, No. 7, March 1972.

2   J. B. Giacquinta, "Status Risk-Taking: A Central Issue in the Initiation and Implementation of Public School Innovations," *Journal of Research and Development in Education,* Vol. 9, No. 1, November 1975.

3   M. Katz. *Class, Bureaucracy and Schools.* New York: Praeger, 1971.

because it represented a fairly large amount of money, especially as originally planned. Some of the reasons that past programs funded by the national government had not succeeded were as follows:

1. People at the local level had not been sufficiently involved in planning which changes they needed and, consequently, they were expected to implement externally imposed changes.
2. The funding period traditionally had not been long enough to facilitate both planning and implementation and hence implementation efforts had been preempted by time spent in a planning and proposal writing.
3. Planned change attempts had been too piecemeal and had little chance of affecting the total system.
4. Too little had been spent to evaluate the effectiveness of programs, to provide feedback to implementers, and to document carefully what was happening in the implementation process at the local level.

The U.S. Office of Education's Experimental Schools Program was designed to depart from these norms and was funded as an approach to change rather than a project aimed at specific problems.

The first section of this chapter assesses the overall impact of ESP, presenting a brief history of its genesis at the national level, discussing the salient conceptual underpinnings of the national ESP, and offering as a point of reference background information on the Jefferson School District (JSD). The next section gives a summary of major events and developments, both within the JSD and between significant district actors and the sponsoring federal agencies—the U.S. Office of Education (USOE) initially and, after August 1972, the National Institute of Education (NIE). No attempt is made to analyze their causes. The final section provides an analysis of the ESP and discusses implications for future practice, especially as related to funding planned change programs in public schools by federal agencies.

OVERALL ASSESSMENT OF ESP

Genesis of ESP

The concept of a federal program to support experimentation in education arose within the U.S. Office of Education as early as 1967. A review of the extant literature on experimental schools was conducted early in 1969, and a task force of the President's Science Advisory Committee was appointed to survey what was being done and to advise what should be done by the federal government in the field of education. Based upon the task force report, legislation was requested by the USOE, and authorization was obtained (without funding) for fiscal year 1970. In February 1970 the Experimental Schools Program was established, and the program became a cornerstone of President Nixon's educational reform message of that year.[4]

The ESP budget for fiscal year 1971 was $12 million, less than half of the amount originally requested. The House had originally allocated $25 million, which might have allowed maximal flexibility to fund promising research efforts.[5] But the Senate allowed only $15 million[6] and that figure was later reduced to $12 million by the USOE under the discretion allowed it by the Congress.

Although the ESP was not activated until December 1970, programs had to become operational in the schools by September 1971. Initially, projects were begun in three school districts, one of which was Jefferson. The three projects involved more than 11,000 students. Each ESP site was funded for five years (initially for thirty months, followed by the final thirty months.) A second competition in March 1971 led to projects in two more districts in September 1972. These five systems were joined in September 1973 by ten rural districts and three street academies, eventually resulting in more than 25,000 students in eighteen districts.

Conceptual Underpinnings of ESP

The major impetus behind the establishment of the program at the federal level came from the failure of many promising educational innovations to produce significant results. Historically, most educational innovations had attempted to change only one or two components within the school system. The architects of ESP, along with many other educators and researchers, rejected the piecemeal approach, and argued that educational innovations might best be implemented through a comprehensive change strategy. Comprehensive change was defined as "accounting for or comprehending virtually all pertinent conditions; e.g., including at a minimum all the significant elements of a formal educational program."[7] Schooling was seen as a total program (not a set of programs), and change was to cover all aspects of the educational system, including not only curriculum, staffing, evaluation, and governance but also consideration and involvement of the community. Comprehensive change was also tied to the notion of "synergistic effort," i.e., that the whole is greater than the sum of its parts. Thus, the first objective

---

4 Deputy Assistant Secretary for Planning, Research and Evaluation (DASPRE), Department of Health, Education and Welfare; Memorandum to B. Martin and J. Blum, Office of Management and Budget. re: release of funds for the Experimental Schools Program, December 29, 1970, p. 3.

5 House of Representatives Hearings Report #16916, March 4, 1970.

6 Senate Report #91-871, May 15, 1970, p. 14.

7 "Proposed Basic Program Information for Phase Two: Experimental Schools" (rough draft documentation, no author, no date), p. 6. Document in NIE files. This definition of comprehensive change, as well as other conceptualizing about ESP, apparently occurred after the program was transferred to NIE in August 1972. It is difficult to determine precisely because some of the documents which are referred to are undated and without other identifying information.

of ESP was to test the viability of a comprehensive approach to change.

A second objective of the ESP was to "identify and test the major policy questions that lend themselves to experimental solution within the context of comprehensive experimentation, as opposed to piecemeal."[8]

A third objective concerned the idea that the Experimental Schools model would enhance the development, refinement, and utilization of an evaluation/documentation methodology sophisticated enough to assess a comprehensive program. The present chapter is limited to an examination of the first concept—the viability of a comprehensive approach to change.

The Jefferson School District Prior to ESP

The Jefferson School District is in the Northwest United States. It encompasses about 19 square miles and 30,000 people with a school enrollment of approximately 8,000 students. There are two high schools, two junior high schools, and nine elementary schools.

At the time the program began, the district had a stable and homogeneous teaching staff (about 350), many of whom had received most or all of their teaching experience in Jefferson. The administrative component was relatively small, and most of them had been with the district since its inception. A notable exception was the superintendent, who had come to the district in 1966, ostensibly to effect change. The typical manner of instruction could be characterized as traditional, but the district had begun to implement innovative programs in the years just prior to ESP.

The district population in 1971 was primarily young, white, working class, and relatively transient. It had a high unemployment rate. The district served as a bedroom community for a predominately blue-collar constituency. The district's partly suburban and partly semirural community was sometimes referred to as "rurban." Few political or social organizations existed, and there was no governmental structure to create any real sense of community. Having no economic center within the area, and faced with low assessed property evaluation, the district relied more heavily on outside sources of funding (state and federal) than nearly all comparably sized districts in the state. Thus, the district had been in the position of actively seeking funds from these sources. In its letter of interest to the Experimental Schools Program, the district reported a five-year history (since the arrival of the new superintendent) of developing innovative programs with federal and state monies.[9] The Experimental Schools Program, with its offer of a five-year, $5 million source of funds, promised a

---

8 "Release of Funds for Experimental Schools Program," Memorandum, Experimental Schools Project, January 8, 1971.

9 Superintendent, Letter of Interest and Addendum, submitted to USOE on January 14, 1971, in response to OE "Call for Letters of Interest."

short-term solution to the district's financial situation, with the potential effect of establishing more long-term efficiency in its operations.

SUMMARY OF MAJOR EVENTS AND DEVELOPMENTS

The Selection of Jefferson

In January 1971 USOE requested potential respondents to submit a "letter of interest" for "operational projects with a major evaluation thrust, based upon a central theme for educational reform that includes a multiple use of promising practices and the products of research in a comprehensive K-12 framework."[10] Respondents were asked to do the following: demonstrate experience with large-scale innovations; demonstrate staff capacity to manage comprehensive experimentation; develop a plan for participation in the design, implementation, and governance of the project; identify a target population for the potential project; demonstrate how the design fulfills the objectives of ESP, which included a primary target population of approximately 2,000 to 5,000 low-income children with a longitudinal K-12 design and a comprehensive approach to the learning environment; show that practice was to be consistent with the central theme; and finally, demonstrate that the cost of operating the project changes could be managed after the experiment without new outside resources.[11]

Districts had thirty days to answer, and 486 organizations responded. An independent selection committee of six educational luminaries selected Jefferson and seven others to receive sixty-day planning grants, $10,000 each, to complete the design of a comprehensive K-12 educational program for 2,000 to 5,000 students to begin in September 1971. The issues that the proposal was to address were spelled out in the same grant award. Along with additional information gathered during site visits, these proposals were used to select the final sites. Another group of eight educators reviewed all eight proposals and recommended that none of the sites be funded on the basis of the proposals as submitted. However, they did recommend that three sites be funded on the contingency that certain programmatic weaknesses be corrected. ESP officials and district representatives deliberated further and a second site visit was conducted to clarify the committee's request. Finally, an operational grant was awarded to all three sites in May 1971.

The Jefferson Plan

In Jefferson's letter of interest, the superintendent had highlighted their suc-

---

10 National ESP Director, "Basic Program Information, Experimental Schools Program," "Call for Letters of Interest," December 28, 1970, p. 1.

11 Ibid.

cessful experiences with sixteen federal projects, cooperation with two universities, participation in the model gifted program in the state, maintenance of an evaluation and research staff, expertise in school management, specialists in media and materials, and more than six years experience in the design, implementation, and governance of various projects. In February 1971 the superintendent learned that a planning grant had been awarded to the district. After the Board of Education accepted the planning grant, sixty days remained to develop and submit a comprehensive plan. The superintendent distributed a "Planning Grant Activities" paper to the sixteen district administrators, four staff members, and ten consultants who were ostensibly to prepare the ESP proposal. The superintendent emphasized that the purpose of the operations grant, when and if awarded, would be to *operate, not to develop,* an experimental schools program.

Enthusiasm for an ESP did not permeate all the significant district actors. The Jefferson Education Association (JEA) was not at all enthusiastic. In general they wanted to maintain the status quo. Even when supporting specific aspects of the project, the teachers association tended to dampen the prospective impact of the proposed changes.[12]

At a retreat in late February for twenty-three district participants (mostly administrators) the superintendent pointed out that the amount of money that could be involved was beyond comprehension and that it was imperative to continue those programs that had built the reputation that made it possible to get the planning grant. He called for the expansion of the existing projects to all schools on Jefferson's west side (that half of the district that was to serve as the target population for ESP). Small group meetings continued after the retreat, and teams traveled to other school districts in the area. However, the actual writing of the draft for the operational proposal was done mainly by the superintendent. Several weeks before the deadline were spent gaining approval and endorsements for the program and preparing the final draft.

Near the end of the planning grant period, over two hundred of the district's administrators and westside certified personnel responded to a ten-question survey about the essential components of the plan. Their reactions to the nine major project goals are presented below:

- Eighty-eight percent favored all students having one small class per day.
- Eighty-five percent favored vocational work experience for all students.
- Eighty-four percent favored use of different sized class groupings ranging from large group instruction to individualization.
- Eighty-one percent supported the idea of eliminating student failure.
- Seventy-five percent favored some form of year-round schooling.
- Sixty-six percent supported individualized instruction by a differentiated

12 "Position paper: JEA Efficiency Models Committee, Project Promise, Phase II," February 25, 1971.

staff for students whose performance was above or below program requirements, and thirty weeks of group instruction by certificated teachers for
the rest of the students.

- All but 24 percent opposed the appointment of master teachers who
  would supervise a differentiated staff.
- All but 18 percent were opposed or had reservations about a four-day week
  with four to five hours of group instruction and sixteen hours of individualized instruction available per day.
- All but 17 percent opposed or had reservations about reduction of the adult-
  pupil ratio to 1:12 through the implementation of differentiated staffing.

In order to obtain the JEA's endorsement, the superintendent and the six
westside principals made presentations on the final draft of the ESP proposal to
a special meeting of all the members. The superintendent modified the differentiated staffing goal by substituting "lead teacher" for "master teacher" and by
stating that noncertificated personnel would be hired in addition to, not in lieu
of, present staff members. He also promised that the final staffing for the
project would be done in cooperation with the JEA. As a result, about 70
percent of the members voted to endorse the ESP proposal.

The complete proposal was mailed to Washington on April 5, 1971. A week
later the superintendent again emphasized to the district board of directors that,
if funded, it would be an important factor in keeping the district solvent. After
a visit by the national experimental schools director, the superintendent was
notified of an operational grant. The budget for the first thirty months of the
ESP was about $2.5 million.

The seeds sown during the genesis of the project were reaped later as insurmountable problems.

Implementation Problems

The project was beset early by serious implementation problems. Building
principals and teachers were not ready to adopt Experimental School Programs,
especially if those programs were not consistent with past practices. First, there
was much less than enthusiastic endorsement by those who were now being
called upon to adopt and implement new programs. The autonomy of various
buildings facilitated resistance to attempts to impose something new from
without (either the district's central office or Washington, 3,000 miles away).
Second, there was much confusion about the concept of comprehensive change
both within Jefferson and at the national level. Third, there was indecision as
to what kind of monitoring role the federal agency should play. Fourth, there
was the problem of equity within the district. Under the grant terms, eastside
schools were not getting "their" share of the monetary pie. Fifth, there was
disagreement on what role the community should play.

Whatever the explanation, the rather obvious fact remained that ESP was being implemented in Jefferson on a piecemeal basis, not comprehensively. Even if comprehensive change was not understood, it was still evident that not even "articulation" was occurring within the district. Principals and teachers were free to choose whatever they felt served their needs and the needs of their students. They could also opt to continue what they had been doing in the past. The superintendent directed the project, and he and his assistant seemed unable or unwilling to grapple with the implementation problems. They were initially successful in setting up budget allotments and procedures. But beyond structuring the fiscal area, central coordination and control were minimal. Perhaps the minimal coordination was unintentional, but it does appear consonant with the decision made as perceived by a central office administrator who commented:

> Well, we never make very clear decisions. You work around people—you let biases die—and you play games—we make little decisions, not any big ones. I know there's a model of getting clear your objectives, gathering information, looking at alternatives, etc., but we don't go by that model. We avoid big decisions.[13]

A December 1971 report from a site visit to Jefferson by USOE officials raised the problem of implementation. Although the project officer reported that USOE was not too greatly concerned that there was no articulation in the first year of development, they were concerned that the district did not see "articulation," i.e., "comprehensive change"—these words were often used interchangeably—as a priority concern.

Three months after that site visit a new project officer pointed out the vulnerability of the comprehensive theme in the Jefferson experience. Excerpts from the report follow:

> The Experimental Schools project in Jefferson is in danger of losing its identity as a K-12 educational experiment. The principal factor accounting for the present situation is the administrative structure that by tradition has allowed the building principal to exercise almost complete control over his school, resulting in questionable districtwide coordination and management on issues critical to the operation of an experimental school project.
> The experimental schools project instead of being a continuous articulated educational experiment appears to be a series of component schools operating a series of component parts, some of which were in operation prior to the experimental schools project designation.[14]

The diagnosis was not new, but the proposed remedy was; rather than

---

13   Fieldnotes from interview, January 17, 1972.
14   Project officer, "Jefferson Trip Report," USOE/ESP internal memorandum, April 3, 1972. Document in NIE files.

suggesting another report or meeting, the OE project officer advocated direct responsibility and control by the superintendent:

> The director of the experimental schools program, in this case the superintendent, must take physical and mental control of the project schools and be perceived as having (taken) such (control) by the building principals.

> This could be a difficult task, since tradition, a very strong element in the Jefferson School District, which has a very small teacher turnover and up from the ranks long-term principals, has dictated that the principal is the controlling factor in the educational movement of the district.

> The major share of the responsibility would have to come from the superintendent, who could serve as a coordinating force by (a) requiring his approval of proposed plans and subsequent modifications prior to operation, and (b) exercising control of experimental school budgets in component form.[15]

A few days after the site report was filed, the superintendent was back in Washington, for several days of talks. When he returned to Jefferson he brought an OE letter that refused authorization to expand the project to more schools during 1972–73, because OE believed that the expansion would detract from efforts to unify the existing project.[16] Further, he brought word of a compromise. The superintendent was not to exercise more control over the project. Nor was an outsider to be brought in as director (also proposed by USOE). Rather, OE staff members were to come to Jefferson in May to assess the situation directly. A retreat was planned to determine the future course of the ESP's management. This summit meeting, subsequently referred to by the superintendent as "Yalta I," created the ESP Cabinet, which became the structure for governance in the JESP.

Governing the JESP

"Governance" refers to the structure and the process of decision making. Although the governance structure of the school system remained simple and stable, the program was required to adopt or conform to the prevailing distribution of power. The superintendent and his central staff enjoyed hegemony over revenue sources and allocations, personnel administration, support services, and the management of transactions across the system's boundaries. Within their individual schools, the principals enjoyed hegemony over curricular, instructional, and pupil custodial activities.

The ESP Cabinet, created under the USOE/ESP impetus to overcome fragmentation and to promote a sense of comprehensiveness, was adapted to some

---

15 Ibid.
16 Rand Corporation, "Change Agent One," cited in *Education, U.S.A.*, Vol. 18, No. 2, September 8, 1975.

exactly opposite ends. The principals developed the cabinet into a tool for protecting and promoting their autonomy as individuals and their solidarity as a group. As more resources became subject to discretionary use, the cabinet became a "garbage can"[17] for the expression of problems, feelings, ideas, and decisions; what was to have been a unifying source became a strong counter-vailing force against governance centralization.

The fiscal resource allocation and control system remained basically un-changed, since the proposed implementation of fiscal accountability techniques was either dropped or postponed to post-project periods. Funds were dispersed and used within the previously existing allocation structure, generally bypas-sing the ESP Cabinet, and in part relieving the district's reliance upon tradi-tional sources of revenue. The JESP financial structure evolved into an unar-ticulated spending program, characterized by a lack of specificity in planning, few attempts to follow the plans once made, and almost no control over the degree to which expenditures had fulfilled project objectives. However, the $5 million did allow the district to make changes, some of which will continue beyond the end of the project, and most of which would not have occurred otherwise.

Thus, the rhetoric and resources of the program were absorbed into the prevailing system. The district's compliance with the funding agency require-ments was largely symbolic. The federal intervention in Jefferson governance did not generate commitment among the administrators to institutional trans-formation, nor did it yield strong systemwide coordination and control. As the temporary intrusion approached an end, there was little promise of a residue of increased governance capacity for dealing with complex and dynamic inter-dependence.

Community Involvement

Community participation has frequently assumed an idealized stance as a cul-tural given in federal educational programs. In the ESP, community and parent participation was a major concern only in planning the program and not in operating it. Initially the program was to be districtwide and, consequently, community participation was to be at the district level. But this idea never really got off the ground because there was no push from the community for changing the schools. Community interest in the ESP had to be fostered, but at the same time the felt need among educators to control such participation was great. Involvement at the district level in the first phase of the program amounted to calling parents to a districtwide meeting and telling them what the ESP would be about—token participation at best.

17   See M. Cohen, J. March, and J. Olsen, "A Garbage Can Model of Organizational Choice," *Adminis-trative Science Quarterly*, Vol. 17, No. 1, March 1972, pp. 1–26.

Federal officials were not satisfied with the district's response. During the latter half of the program, Parent Advisory Councils were formed for each building. Although most of them amounted to no more than forums for information giving, one council did provide an opportunity for community input. But by moving parent participation to the building level, control was consolidated in the hands of the principals, not the central office personnel who had no way of influencing parents. In the latter part of the project, NIE had nothing more to say about community participation.

It should be pointed out, however, that not only did the community never express any discontent with its role, survey results indicated community approval of school operations. The community also continued to support the Jefferson Schools financially by approving bond and tax levies. Their role had not changed, nor had their support for school activities declined.

Curriculum and Instruction in JESP

There was no indication that teachers and administrators were dissatisfied with existing educational conditions in Jefferson or that any of them had advocated major changes in the patterns of curriculum and instruction. Nor was the community dissatisfied. As a result, there was no wholesale, districtwide change in curriculum and instruction. The proposed major emphases of the program—an eleven-month schedule that involved planning of the school program of each student, an extensive staff retraining program, and program decision making based on program effectiveness—were not implemented as rigorously as originally intended.

The components that were implemented widely included individualized instruction (especially on the elementary level and particularly in the mathematics and communications streams); the interim program (intensive programs held between semesters, especially on the secondary level); career education (also on the secondary level); the purchase of new instructional materials on both levels in virtually all program streams; and building remodeling to facilitate the implementation of purchased or locally developed programs.

In general the selection of programs and their degree of use were decided independently by each building, although on the elementary level, several programs were expected to be implemented by all nine elementary schools. On the secondary level, teachers devoted their efforts primarily to the development of course syllabi, especially for the interim programs. The occupational versatility program on the junior high school level and the work experience program on the senior high school level were major efforts in career education. The mathematics departments at all four secondary schools developed laboratories for individualized instruction and participated in the development of sixth and twelfth grade exit examinations emphasizing basic skills.

Individualization of mathematics and communications instruction was the most pervasive curricular change implemented across the district's elementary schools. The type of individualization implemented by the district is best described as variation by rate, i.e., individual students were given new material to learn only after completing previous assignments successfully. The four westside elementary schools increased their individualization by rate during the first half of the project, but by the end had returned to their original practices. The five eastside elementary schools increased their individualization by rate during the third and fourth years of the ESP, but regressed slightly during the final year. The intermediate level (grades 4 through 6) was generally more active than the primary level (grades K through 3) in the implementation of individualization by rate.

The ESP training program was an accumulation of discrete endeavors, often sponsored by individual buildings, aimed primarily at introducing users to curricular programs or instructional materials purchased with ESP funds. It was not a coordinated effort by the district in support of each of the project components. Most of the training occurred on the elementary level.

Project impact on students was mixed. Districtwide cognitive achievement declined (when compared to the 1968 national norms) during the ESP, perhaps due to the disruptive influence of the program. Additionally, there were few significant long-term (four-year) differences between initial entrants and later entrants to the project. On the other hand, some of the project's instructional approaches (e.g., individually prescribed instruction and other individualized instruction) contributed to improved cognitive and/or affective outcomes for some subgroups, particularly for low prior achieving mathematics students. For these students mathematics achievement went up and so did their attitude toward mathematics. High prior achieving students had better achievement and attitude toward math when they received traditional math instruction. Results were not so clear for reading instruction, where the treatments were not as distinct as those in mathematics. Project impact on other areas was more difficult to determine, since career education, personal development, social studies, etc., lacked definitive student impact information. However, as measured by standardized achievement tests, ESP-instituted programs did not have any overall negative effects on student cognitive outcomes, although they did have some positive effects.

None of this is meant to castigate the day-to-day operation of the district. Jefferson operates a relatively efficient traditional educational program, especially in view of available financial resources. But the district was simply not able to operationalize the sort of comprehensive experiment originally proposed by the superintendent. Jefferson lacked both central coordination and subunit loyalty to project goals. Either characteristic probably would have kept the project much closer to its original goals. A myriad of curricular activities were carried on under the rubric of the ESP; however, specific implementation differed from school to school and did not fit the proposal rhetoric closely.

At the conclusion of the project, the district could highlight the following accomplishments in curriculum and instruction:

- Three westside elementary schools had officially espoused the individually guided instruction model of school organization; one eastside elementary school had also moved away from lockstep self-contained classroom organization in mathematics and communications instruction.
- All elementary schools had installed at least one individualized instructional program in either the mathematics or communication stream; five had installed one in each stream.
- All schools had installed arts and crafts, "fifth day," and/or interim programs emphasizing lifetime sports and training for leisure-time activities, thus taking time away from the usual school subjects.
- Work experience and demonstrated facility with basic mathematical operations were made twelfth grade graduation requirements.
- All schools had purchased or developed instructional hard- and software in virtually all curricular areas and had renovated aspects of their physical plants to facilitate the implementation of new programs.
- Curricular decision making had been transferred from the central office to the individual buildings.

Internal Evaluation in JESP

The district formed its own evaluation team to provide timely and relevant information about the program. By the end of the project, evaluation, like the other functions of governance, community relations, and instruction, had returned to a state very similar to that before the ESP.

Evaluation is intertwined with governance. Evaluation was at the mercy of the administrative staff for financial and psychological support. The inability of the evaluation component to gain the support of the cabinet was crucial. Without this support, evaluation was left without a useful or viable mission. It had no clientele who saw its services as useful, and it lacked consistent support from administrators. It was a marginal unit, chasing an elusive program that never existed as envisioned. Brought into existence to fulfill a USOE requirement, it was progressively abandoned as the force of the mandate declined. During the last year of the project, the evaluation unit suddenly found itself more favorably received in the district as it published reports that placed the district's efforts in a more positive light, but there was no evidence that the evaluation unit ever provided information for decision making in the district.

The internal evaluation mission was not well defined at the onset of the project. This was in part a result of the hurried nature of the initiation of the project. But it was also a reflection of the continuing ambiguity of the Jefferson program itself. Internal evaluation was committed to measuring Jefferson's program against the standard of the district's proposal. The evaluation unit hoped that ultimately the individual schools would incorporate evaluation into their operations. But they did not. Just as the proposal was an overlay constructed by the superintendent with little input by principals or teachers, so the internal evaluation was planned with even less input by the principals and teachers. Worse, the internal evaluators were faced with measuring a non-event. Not only did they encounter the resistance normally expected from people who are being assessed, but also the credibility problems in pursuing phenomena with only a paper existence. The dilemma was to become crucial for internal evaluators. They knew that evaluation had somehow to be useful at the building level as well as at the district level if it were to survive the ESP.

In an effort to reverse the project's fragmentation and to expand their own mission, the internal evaluation group proposed the creation of a management information system. The system would have included a cost efficiency ratio useful for centralized decision making and for program evaluation at the school level. But the conceptual scope and the dollar cost were so large that it never moved from a developmental to an operational stage. It is questionable whether such a complex system would have found acceptance or utility in this setting, for it threatened existing units in the district. The system assumed that a comprehensive, thoroughly articulated project would evolve; it proposed to create an information base for centralized decision making in a system rapidly formalizing decentralized decision making; and it sought to impose rationalistic criteria on a system with little agreement about the validity of the criteria.

IMPLICATIONS FOR FUTURE PRACTICE

Our central point about the comprehensive change model is that many of the implementation problems could have been averted if more time and more careful planning had been allotted to them in the beginning stages. A second important point is that there were some strengths in the comprehensive change model.

Potentially Positive Aspects of the Change Model

An average of one million dollars a year for school reform in one district is a substantial increase in financial assistance by a government agency. That money, about one-eighth of the district's total budget, was sufficient to do a lot of things. For example, the money built an internal evaluation unit with the potential to gather information to facilitate decisions. Additionally, the program provided external evaluation—an evaluation team that reported directly to the funding agency and was not responsible to the district in any way.

The Experimental Schools funds helped Jefferson survive a severe financial crunch. Still, the money that was adequate to help Jefferson survive was not enough to help it change. Lots of money doesn't assure change.

The program spanned a five-year period—a sizable slice of time in the annals of government funding for projects in education. Multiyear funding allows recipients more time to plan initially and more time to implement and revise plans. Conversely, less time is spent writing proposals and searching for outside support. The positive effects of innovations are not seen immediately; in fact, the reverse is usually true. Guaranteeing material support for long-range programs of change is a necessary but not a sufficient condition. It promotes the means by which planned change can occur but in no way ensures that the rhetoric will become reality if other social conditions necessary for change to occur are not present.

The comprehensive change model allowed local districts to make decisions about the specific changes that were to occur within predetermined elements of the system. Those people closest to a situation are usually thought to be best able to make decisions about it. Moreover, it also appears to be logical that locals should be better able to identify elements within a system (governance, curriculum, etc.) that need to be changed. But the ESP model denied locals the right to identify the elements to be changed—they could deal only with specific changes within preselected elements. We recommend retaining that part of the change model that calls for local decisions on specific changes within major elements of the system. We also recommend that local decisions be expanded to include selection of major system elements to be changed. It is highly unlikely that change can occur in those aspects of the educational system when the local actors are not in agreement that indeed they should be changed.

The positive aspects of the comprehensive change model that we recommend keeping are (1) adequate funding of planned change programs to allow for planning, implementation, and evaluation activities; (2) multiyear funding to preserve energies for implementation as well as to facilitate measuring the impact of innovations on clients; and (3) retaining local decision making about specific change within major elements but expanding this to include local decisions about which major elements to change within the system.

Conceptual and Operational Problems

Both the local and national levels of the ESP had conceptual and operational problems. The tasks that faced the planners of experimental schools at the national level were monumental. They had to conceptualize systemic, comprehensive change; communicate the idea to others; decide when a potential grantee knew enough about it to merit funding; decide that a reasonable climate for change existed at the client level; decide that the grantee was able to implement an agreed upon plan; and monitor the implementation of all of these plans. Additionally, federal program officers had minimal time to plan and mount the program, insufficient resources to build a staff capable of supervising a program of such complexity and magnitude, limited resources for staff travel to the various sites, almost constant staff turnover, a lack of continuity in priorities by their superordinate policy makers, and the extreme political vulnerability of the NIE in Washington politics.

When those constraints were combined with the forces working against change in Jefferson, they made a successful program of comprehensive change highly unlikely. Some of the more salient constraints at the local level were failure to come to grips with the concept of comprehensive change; lack of support for change among administrators (except the superintendent), among the faculty generally, and certainly among the community; vagueness in the proposal; a general unwillingness to do things that were not reasonably congruent with past practices; a pattern that pushed decision making to the building and classroom level; no involvement in early planning except for the top level; lack of clarity in the role that the federal government would play; and finally, the infeasibility and undesirability of comprehensive change in the Jefferson district.

Limited Time   Although adequate time is usually assumed, that was not the case in Jefferson or in Washington. One of the basic tenets of the comprehensive change strategy was that projects must be funded over a long period of time to allow districts to deal with implementation issues. That logical and laudable concept was completely ignored when the federal program needed to get under way. Very little time was available for federal planners to conceptualize the notion of comprehensive change. The political scene in Washington required that ESP become operational in the schools by the fall of 1971. Consequently, everything was rushed, beginning at the federal level but permeating as well to the local level, since national ESP officials could not provide to others something they did not possess themselves. The press of time had a great deal to do with the course of the program over the next five years. We strongly urge future planners of change programs to treat time as a valuable resource. Time is as valuable in the conceptualizing and planning stages as in the implementation stage.

Conceptualizing Comprehensive Change   Federally funded change programs seldom have a thorough conceptual base prior to their initiation. While it is understandable, since no one knows how to make change happen, the lack of an adequate conceptualization makes success harder to achieve. The Experimental Schools Program had had national conferences and brainstorming sessions and discussion among educational luminaries. But that is not the same thing as analyzing and synthesizing various ideas and pulling them together into a conceptual framework, asking for expert feedback, and revising accordingly. Since comprehensive change was not understood at the national level, it was not understood in Jefferson. Conceptualization never seemed to get past the point that comprehensive change should embrace several educational elements and that articulation should occur. The local district had to take if from there and be guided by this rather inadequate set of guidelines. This kind of sweeping change makes certain assumptions about the character of the system targeted for change.

Gauging the Climate for Change   We contend that it is the responsibility of public funding agencies to learn about local social conditions in the districts that will facilitate or hinder planned change prior to making a funding decision. If, after the government has committed itself to support change, it turns out that conditions are not at all conducive to planned change, then it is politically impossible to cut off the funds. In the absence of data about local social conditions, it is not possible to make responsible decisions about whether planned change can occur at all, what major elements of the school system can or should be changed, or what specific changes within an educational element can or should be made. It is possible to learn whether or not a district has sufficient impetus to change, and it can also be learned if the capacity exists at the local level to implement and manage a change effort. Even with such information, program success is not assured because our knowledge about conditions conducive to change is itself imperfect. Of course, to implement such a radical departure from traditional change models, adequate resources in time, money, and expertise are necessary. Such resources should be available so that gauging conditions prior to funding can become an important part of an intervention change model.

Local Conditions Hindering Change   The Rand Corporation's study of innovative attempts in public schools found that projects that were generated primarily because an opportunity existed to get outside funds did not win the support of teachers and principals, and change was never seriously attempted. It was evident at an early stage that Jefferson was more oriented to opportunism than to problem solving. Early rhetoric in the district stressed augmenting the budget and getting the district through hard fiscal times more than it did curricular reform. The program was really sold to teachers and other school personnel, as well as the board of education, because of the large amount of money rather than because of the merits of the proposal for planned change. In fact, many teachers and principals were not in favor of several aspects of the proposal, although seven out of ten voted in favor of the program. Since there was in Jefferson no problem that called for solutions other than what they were already using, it is no mystery that district practices were changed very little.

Jefferson can be characterized as a solution in search of a problem.[18]

Plans of action are closely related to the need for a problem-solving orientation. But there was great ambiguity surrounding the very idea of comprehensive change. Part of the confusion can be traced to USOE and NIE. It should be pointed out that this was not something peculiar to the Experimental Schools Program; the problem is at least as old as planned change itself. In Jefferson's case, the vagueness of the charge was somewhat intentional because specific change in the district was to emanate from the grass roots. Nevertheless, the issue of comprehensive change was never really resolved. The project proposal contained little more than broad guidelines, which didn't establish ways to make decisions about policy or any methods of conflict resolution. The document was too imprecise to be of any assistance in implementation.

It is therefore recommended that specific strategies for implementing the grand program design should be spelled out in detail before funds are granted. However, this step should not be attempted until the problem or problems to be solved have been clearly conceptualized and the ends to be gained have been agreed to by both federal and local actors. It may not appear logical to be concerned with means (solutions) prior to conceptualizing and defining the problem and agreeing upon the ends to be accomplished, but a great deal of attention to solution must occur prior to actual implementation. Most of the disagreement within the local district and between the local district and the funding agency occurred over means and not over ends.[19] A major source of resistance to change is the risk that implementers must take in assuming new roles.[20] The means through which new programs are operationalized create new relationships and change the roles and statuses of individuals. These changes in the role and status of individuals are the true innovation, not the mere "introduction" of new materials or objects.

Of course, it can be argued that the change rhetoric in proposals should serve only to gain social, psychological, and financial support and, once that is achieved, it has served its purpose. Ample "wiggle room" must be allowed for reformers and implementers to work out the details. We, too, are firm believers in the notion that action informs thinking, and therefore plans must be subject

18 For a fuller treatment of the problems inherent in the solution preceding problem definition, see W. Doyle, "What Is the Problem? What is the Solution?" *Administrators' Notebook*, Vol. XXV, 1976–77, No. 4, and J. Getzels, "Problem Finding," the 343rd Convocation Address, University of Chicago, *The University of Chicago Record*, Vol. VII, No. 9, November 21, 1973. Also J. Getzels, "Problem Finding and Inventiveness of Solutions," *The Journal of Creative Behavior*, Vol. 9, No. 1, First Quarter, 1975.

19 An obvious point which seems to have been overlooked is that not only did Jefferson fail to get agreement on means, but it could not agree on ends either.

20 J. B. Giacquinta, "Status-Risk-Taking: A Central Issue in the Initiation and Implementation of Public School Innovations," *Journal of Research and Development in Education*, Vol. 9, No. 1, November 1975.

to change. At the same time, we argue that plans dealing primarily with ends are insufficient because they have not grappled with issues that are the main source of conflict in the implementation stage. Solutions cannot be laid on implementers without their assent that the solutions at least remotely relate to the problem to be solved. In essence, we are advocating steps which suggest that more resources be devoted to the initial and negotiation stages.

Another necessary condition of planned change is the existence of an initial impetus. Almost every piece of literature on planned change talks about its importance.[21] Only a minimal impetus to change exists when significant local actors are satisfied with what is. Since there was little sense of a felt substantive problem in Jefferson, existing policies, practices, and procedures were broadly accepted. Of course, there were a few people who were not pleased with the status quo, but there was no widespread dissatisfaction—not from the central office, not from the principals, not from the teachers, not from the students, and not from the community. In essence, there was little internal pressure to change and then only from a superintendent who did not sustain any systematic effort to get the Experimental Schools Program implemented. The only external pressure to change came from federal agencies, but after funds were granted, the agencies were not very influential. Consequently, the changes that occurred were mostly structural not behavioral. Past practices dominated the scene. Only the federal agencies (3,000 miles away) were concerned about change. The viability of the model of comprehensive change could not be tested if the local districts were not going to try to change comprehensively. As a consequence, another important part of the climate that is conducive to change was missing—the need and the incentive or desire to change.[22] That part of the district's environment that wanted change to occur—the external funding agency—could be satisfied easily. The Jefferson District already had the money, and, after all, federal agencies were to be around only for five years, not forever.

The federal agencies' minimal influence was aggravated further by confusion over their role in Jefferson. The local clients were not only unsure of what was expected of them in carrying out a comprehensive, systemic mandate for change, they were equally unclear about the roles that the U. S. Office of Education and the National Institute of Education were to play. The signals from Washington were mixed. A general stance of minimal intervention on the part of federal officials came through clearly. However, specific behaviors

---

21 For an extended discussion of the importance of impetus to change, see N. Gross, J. B. Giacquinta, and M. Bernstein. *Implementing Organizational Innovations: A Sociological Analysis of Planned Educational Change.* New York: Basic Books, 1971. Also S. Sarason, *The Creation of Settings and the Future Societies.* San Francisco: Jossey-Bass, 1972.

22 For a treatment of incentives for change, see J. Pincus, "Incentives for Innovation in the Public Schools," *Review of Educational Research,* Winter 1974.

contradicted that. What the district was to do was not clear, but what could not be done was often made quite clear. Consequently, the district's apparent freedom of choice about implementation was often illusory and the dissonance between appearance and reality was frustrating.

Another local condition militating against change was the autonomous nature of the Jefferson district. To implement comprehensive, districtwide planned change, decisions closer to the top seemed necessary. But Jefferson was characterized by decentralized decision making. School building-level autonomy was the norm for curriculum and instruction, not decisions handed down from the central office. The likelihood that principals and teachers would surrender their autonomy was extremely small unless there existed both impetus and incentive to change, which clearly was not the case.

A further complicating factor was that of the perceived "superiority" of the ESP mission.[23] Since school people in Jefferson were not dissatisfied with what they were already doing and since they were not seriously involved in planning the program, it is not surprising that the new program was viewed with alarm. Any change that threatened professional roles or statuses was not going to be welcomed with open arms. The new ESP was usually viewed as a threat, a plan that *someone else* perceived as superior to what they were doing.

Finally, it should be pointed out that not only was planned comprehensive and systemic change not possible in Jefferson's circumstances, but even in the best of circumstances comprehensive, systemic change is a questionable concept. Organizations legitimately seek a state of equilibrium in order to sustain themselves, and broad, sweeping change in the system militates against the achievement of that steady state. Schools can tolerate only so much change and still attend to the business of "keeping" school, and planned change programs should be sensitive to that need. Even when specific but broad changes are determined at the local level, there are limits to what can be changed and how quickly change can occur. If dissatisfaction exists with an ongoing system it is highly unlikely that dissatisfaction pervades top management, middle management, and all the community clienteles, and that it extends to every function, e.g., staffing arrangements, power and authority, instructional procedures, curricula, the outcomes of schooling, and so on. People are reluctant to change those things with which they are satisfied even if new roles, relationships, and statuses are not directly threatening to them.

Several years ago Smith and Keith[24] suggested that gradualism was a viable alternative to grand and sweeping change. Incremental change is possible in most school districts, while grandiose change is not. If change is successful in

---

23 This concept is discussed in S. Sarason. *The Creation of Settings and Future Societies.* San Francisco: Jossey-Bass, 1972.

24 L. Smith and P. Keith. *Anatomy of an Educational Innovation: An Organizational Analysis of an Elementary School.* New York: John Wiley, 1971.

smaller settings, it may touch as many people both inside and outside the district as larger changes. It is unlikely that a sufficient impetus can be mustered to change an entire system, whereas a subsetting may be changed—even several elements within that subsetting—provided a sense of felt need can be created. It is less complex to get agreement on the functional problem, desired ends, and the means by which a solution can be reached if fewer people are involved and their frames of reference are not too dissimilar. Where solutions call for great interdependence, it is easier to coordinate a few people than a lot of people. But just because planned change occurs in a small setting or on a small scale does not mean that it has to be "piecemeal." The emphasis on comprehensiveness could be changed from extensiveness to intensiveness.

National Conditions Hindering Change   Resources for managing and supervising a program of the magnitude of this one were severely limited. The central ESP office staff ranged from three to six professionals. Each site visit was very brief and supervision was thus minimal. Site visits were infrequent and became even more infrequent as funds for staff travel were limited or cut off. These factors proved to be a major constraint on the ability of the federal agency to monitor the program and to support people in the field. This limitation has plagued federally funded educational programs for a long time.

Another constraining factor was the almost constant turnover of the Washington staff, which was a problem for federal officials but even more so for local ones. Stable relationships with people in the field are a must if good rapport is to be developed and maintained. The aspect of change that encounters the most resistance is the establishment of new roles and relationships; the same applies for federal-local relations. Stability, not change, is in order; some amount of predictability must exist if people are to take risks, and changing certainly involves taking risks. Staff turnover is probably related to all of the factors we have discussed here, but it is certainly related to inadequate staffing and constantly changing priorities. Few, if any, federal educational programs have enjoyed consistently high support throughout their careers; program priorities change when personnel change. The shift usually creates a new set of priorities that are imposed on the local educational agencies (LEAs). Confusion, sometimes bordering on chaos, is the result. It was difficult to keep abreast of what the priorities were in experimental schools. Changes at USOE and NIE policy levels, changes at the agency level, and differing expectations of the numerous panels of experts that descended on both the local project and the external evaluation team created undue anxiety and interfered with continuity.

The impotence of NIE is the final point to be made here regarding constraints on change at the federal level. It is extremely difficult to maintain the continuity necessary to deliver a major program if strong political support does not exist. Staff members at NIE kept leaving, priorities were constantly shifting, and the financial base of NIE was uncertain or declining. The NIE was, and still is, quite vulnerable. It is a stepchild of the USOE and has never achieved legitimacy in the eyes of many powerful Washingtonians. Arthur Wise discussed the taming of the NIE in 1976, four years after its birth.[25] He points out that NIE was intended to foster research that would provide dependable knowledge about the process of learning and education. Therefore, the institute was to be dedicated to the improvement of education through research. The protagonists for a research institute understood that they were creating an agency that would foster careful research, the practical applications of which would take time. It has been argued that Congress either misunderstood the mission of NIE or changed its mission, because they transferred several agencies to NIE that already had near-term problem-solving efforts under way; for example, regional educational laboratories and the research and development centers. This inheritance was largely one of developmental or demonstration projects. NIE had to distribute its funds in accordance with existing commitments, equity among competing purposes, and already developed power bases. So much for the so-called research mission of NIE. As a new and not very powerful agency, NIE had to fight for its survival. When the Experimental Schools Program was transferred from OE to NIE, it, too, had to struggle to survive. Much of the energy that could have gone into making ESP a better program was spent in political infighting.

Many of the problems which decreased the likelihood that planned change would occur could have been predicted in advance. Nothing is new about that condition. But the knowledge educators have about barriers to change and about facilitators of change is usually ignored by both local and federal actors. Change cannot be launched successfully at the same time that it is being planned.

SUMMARY

Many factors from the federal and local planners inhibited effective reform in Jefferson. Still, the Experimental Schools Program was functional for the Jefferson School District. It helped the district through a severe financial crisis and permitted individual schools and individual teachers to try some new things as well as to develop their own new curricula. The ESP did not have a deleterious effect upon student outcomes in general, nor did it have an overall positive effect, at least as measured by both internal and external evaluators. The ESP did have intrinsic value for Jefferson in that it served as a lubricant for social

25 A. Wise, "The Taming of the National Institute of Education: A Personal View," *Phi Delta Kappan*, Vol. 58, No. 1, September 1976.

and bureaucratic forces. By and large, Jefferson gained from the experience.

The Jefferson Experimental Schools Program did not serve its stated function as expressed in the grand design. Broad and sweeping change did not occur, nor was it feasible or desirable in this setting.

Was the overall ESP model for inducing planned reform successful? We submit that generally it was not successful in this particular case and have tried to provide empirical support by documenting what did and did not happen. We advanced some explanations. It was held that the ESP model as conceived and articulated was not really tested in Jefferson. We have argued that some aspects of the model were not congruent with the reality of change and suggested that "comprehensiveness" can be compatible with a gradual and incremental approach.

A final point should be made. If meaningful and effective reform is to occur in promoting educational reform at the local level, a broader social and political context than the LEAs and funding agencies must be considered. Those constraints are not within the purview of this chapter; however, to attempt the development of a new collaborative change model without including such variables is to invite major problems.

CHAPTER 6

Parent Participation in School Innovations

R. GARY BRIDGE

Item: In the fall of 1974, the public schools in Kanawha County, West Virginia, were rocked by violence over textbook adoptions. A school was bombed, and six men were arrested, including the protest leader, Rev. Martin Horan. Sheriff's deputies escorted school buses as protests continued. Over 2,000 people protested in Charleston, West Virginia, when 300 books which they believed to be "irreligious and unAmerican" were returned to school reading lists, and sometime later 200 people attended a Ku Klux Klan rally to protest the Kanawha County schools' use of books like *Soul On Ice*. Carl Marburger, in a *New York Times* column, argued that the school board had shown an "astonishing insensitivity to local cultural values," and he viewed their decisions as the equivalent of adopting *Little Black Sambo* in the largely black Newark, New Jersey schools. Marburger advised school boards to permit more parent participation in the selection of textbooks, and he recalled Thomas Jefferson's advice to trust the informed wisdom of the people.[1]

Item: Widespread taxpayer unhappiness over a 26 percent increase in Milwaukee's school taxes led to an attempt to recall the entire fifteen member Board of Education. In Farmingdale, New York, the townspeople rejected the school district's budget by a three-to-one ratio and ousted the incumbent school board members. In East Meadow, New York, several hundred angry parents demonstrated against the district's decision to close an elementary school because of dwindling enrollments. Similar protests were staged in two nearby school districts where declining enrollments forced cutbacks in school services.[2]

---

1 All newspaper articles cited here appeared in the *New York Times*. Reports of the Kanawha County "textbook wars" were published on January 31, 1974, p. 12; October 23, 1974, p. 30; December 11, 1974, p. 22; February 16, 1975, p. 26; and October 24, 1974, p. 41.

2 *New York Times*. December 15, 1974, p. 58; May 23, 1974, p. 44; February 23, 1975, p. 71; and February 10, 1975, p. 103.

CARL A. RUDISILL LIBRARY
LENOIR RHYNE COLLEGE

Item: A local school district's decision to send a small number of black and Puerto Rican children from the Brownsville section of Brooklyn to schools in the largely white Canarsie section touched off picketing at eight elementary schools, and 6,015 of the schools' 9,736 children stayed home from school. A motorcade of over 400 cars crisscrossed the district to drum up support for the boycott; and at its peak, 8,310 children stayed home, and the boycott spread to other Brooklyn schools. A month later, the district rescinded its order and agreed to "phase out" the Brownsville children from the Canarsie schools over the next eight years. Three days later the schools returned to normal, and white parents were reportedly "jubilant" over their victory, while black leaders expressed bitterness.[3]

Item: In Boston, a court-ordered integration plan triggered school boycotts that left only 76 of 1,031 white children in the largely Irish South Boston schools; 150 black students were escorted to school by over 400 policemen. The boycotts spread to East Boston, a largely Italian neighborhood. Senator Edward Kennedy was driven from the speaker's platform by an egg- and tomato-throwing crowd when he tried to calm the fears of several thousand white parents at an anti-busing rally. Attendance in South Boston schools remained below average for much of the term, and many arrests were made when fights broke out.[4]

Item: At a recent convention of the American Association of School Administrators, a panel of superintendents reported feeling overwhelmed by harrassment and the erosion of their authority due to court decisions, legislative mandates, and extreme pressures from parents.[5]

Item: But not all of the news is bad: In Wyckoff, New Jersey, parents and teachers cooperated to think of ways to combat "drug abuse and antisocial behavior" among students; and in New York, school chancellor Irving Anker announced the creation of five to ten special elementary schools which will be based on "themes" decided by the community, and attended by children whose parents have chosen the school.[6]

Schools which try to implement major changes without considering parents' views are very likely to get a quick lesson in the organization of American education. Changes may be mandated from distant points, but they are im-

---

3 *New York Times.* March 2, 1973, p. 39; March 5, 1973, p. 23; March 13, 1973, p. 43; March 31, 1973, p. 39; and April 3, 1973, p. 37.

4 *New York Times.* September 17, 1974, p. 14; September 21, 1974, p. 60; September 10, 1974, p. 1; November 21, 1974, p. 101; and September 26, 1974, p. 6.

5 *New York Times.* March 5, 1974, p. 1.

6 *New York Times.* February 17, 1975, p. 78; and January 6, 1974, p. 61.

plemented at the building level, and parents can make the difference between success and failure in school innovations.

This chapter, which examines the role parents play in the implementation of change at the school building or district level, will consider three issues: (1) What kinds of schooling decisions do normative models suggest parents *should make*? (2) What kinds of schooling decisions do parents *want to make*? and (3) Who seems to be *competent to participate* effectively? In conclusion, some guidelines are offered for the school administrator who wishes to foster parents' constructive rather than destructive participation.

Some Assumptions At the outset, we must clarify four assumptions which are often ignored in discussions of parental involvement in schooling. First, let us acknowledge the truism that the family plays a crucial role in how well a child does in school and how far the child goes in life. Recent input-output studies of schooling effectiveness provide some idea of just how important family background is when it comes to a child's academic achievement. The well known "Coleman Report"[7] and the more recent *A Study of Our Nation's Students*[8] show quite strikingly that family background factors (e.g., socioeconomic status, parents' expectations for the child, family structure) account for more of the unique variance in achievement test scores than do all of the schooling inputs put together (e.g., teacher's level of education, racial composition of the student body, presence of multiple tracks, per pupil expenditures).[9]

Recent demographic models of status attainment, that is, how people attain the social-occupational-income positions they come to occupy in adulthood, provide additional empirical evidence of the importance of family factors. In one basic model,[10] a child's likelihood of attaining a given level of education is highly predictable from a knowledge of just three family background characteristics: (a) father's occupational status, (b) father's education, and (c) number of siblings. The higher the father's occupational status, the more years of

---

7 James S. Coleman, E.Q. Campbell, C.J. Hobson, J. McPartland, A.M. Mood, F.D. Weinfeld, and R.L. York. *Equality of Educational Opportunity*. Washington, D.C.: U.S. Government Printing Office, 1966.

8 G. Mayekse, T. Okada, W.M. Cohen, A.E. Beaton, Jr., and E.C. Whistler. *A Study of Our Nation's Students*. Washington, D.C.: U.S. Government Printing Office, 1973.

9 The Coleman et al. data show that, among northern white students, family background factors accounted for 20 percent of the unique variance in verbal achievement scores, while eleven school facilities and curriculum factors accounted for only three percent of the unique variance, and seven measures of teachers' qualifications accounted for only two percent of the variance. For a review of the literature on input-output studies of schooling effectiveness, see H.A. Averch et al. *How Effective Is Schooling? A Critical Review and Synthesis of Research*. Santa Monica, Calif.: Rand Corporation, 1972.

10 O.D. Duncan et al. *Socioeconomic Status and Achievement*. New York, N.Y.: Seminar Press, 1972.

education he attained, and the fewer number of siblings a person has, the higher the likelihood of attaining a given level of education. By adding in other factors such as sex,[11] race,[12] parents' aspirations and expectations for the child,[13] and so on, we can predict with even greater accuracy the educational level and occupational position that a child will achieve in adulthood.

Why is the family such a powerful determinant of performance all through life? The greater power of the family (relative to the schools) stems from at least three factors: (a) the schools make contact with the child relatively late in life, after basic learning patterns are already formed; (b) the schools spend fewer hours a day in contact with the child, so that if home and school influence were of equal weight, the family's influence would still be greater because there is more of it; and (c) the family and schools are not equally powerful, because schools control only a narrow range of reinforcers. These crude explanations could be refined substantially, but they should suffice to make this important point: *The family makes a significant difference in a child's performance and eventual life chances, and any school innovation aimed at increasing individual performance should build on or redirect the resources of the family.* A major task of the school administrator is to get the school and the home moving in the same direction.[14]

A second truism, which is often ignored, is that "parents" are not a homogeneous body. We talk about "parents," "the community," "the people," or "consumers," but in reality these aggregates are composed of various

11   K.L. Alexander and B.K. Eckland, "Sex Differences in the Education Attainment Process," *American Sociological Review,* Vol. 39, 1974, pp. 668–682.

12   J.N. Porter, "Race, Socialization, and Mobility in Education and Early Occupational Attainment," *American Sociological Review,* Vol. 39, 1974, pp. 303–316; and A.C. Kerckhoff. *Ambition and Attainment.* Washington, D.C.: American Sociological Association, 1974.

13   W.H. Sewell, A.O. Haller, and G.W. Ohlendorf, "The Educational and Early Occupational Status Attainment Process: Replication and Revision," *American Sociological Review,* Vol. 35, 1970, pp. 1014–1027.

14   J.W. Getzels, "Socialization and Education: A Note on Discontinuities," *Teachers College Record,* Vol. 76, No. 2, December 1974, pp. 218–225. Getzels notes that the influences which shape children are labeled *socialization* when they occur in the context of the home, and *education* when they occur in the schools, yet the underlying principles are the same. The arbitrary education vs. socialization dichotomy has blinded us to the role of the "family as educator" and the "school as socializer," according to Getzels. The point of Getzels' observation is that discontinuities between the lessons of the home (particularly with regard to language and value codes) and the lessons of the schools limits the academic performance of some children. For example, B. Bernstein. *Language and Poverty: Perspectives on a Theme.* Chicago, Ill.: Markham, 1970, has shown that lower social class children tend to use only a restricted language code whereas middle-class children use both a restricted and an elaborated code, so they do better in school where elaborated codes are emphasized. One implication of Getzels' argument is that discontinuities between home and school should be reduced by changing the home environment, and this is the assumption underlying programs which aim to teach mothers to interact with their children in ways which foster "cognitive development," e.g., The Mother-Child Verbal Interaction Project headed by Dr. Phyllis Levenstein and the Parent-Child Development Project headed by Dr. Hazel Leler.

clienteles or segments. Among the indicators often used to operationally define clienteles are ethnicity, religion, "intact" vs. single parent families, educational background and income; but the most significant delimiters of clienteles are attitudes and child-rearing values (which of course are correlated with the other indicators). Anyone who has witnessed the intraschool strife that can break out over an innovation like open education ("humanistic learning" to its proponents and "chaos" to its detractors) must surely appreciate the importance of defining clienteles in terms of attitudes and child-rearing values, as well as the easier-to-record indicators like ethnicity, religion, and socioeconomic status. The point is this: *We should recognize that parents are not a homogeneous body, and therefore we must constantly check our generalizations to be sure that we have specified the groups to which these assertions apply.*

A third issue deals with the role that mothers play in family schooling decisions. One might speculate that: (a) mothers are saddled with most of the family's primary involvement with schools, (b) the specialization of labor between mothers and fathers is probably greater in working-class homes than middle-class homes, and (c) middle-class fathers are probably more involved in schooling matters than are working-class fathers. Economists and sociologists are devoting greater attention to task specialization and role differentiation within families[15] and psychologists have long emphasized the special role that mothers play in the genesis of certain psychopathologies.[16]

We do not have a definitive theory of decision making in families, but it seems safe to advise that, when planning for families' constructive participation in school innovations, leaders ought to consider that in most "intact families," *mothers carry the chief responsibility for making day-to-day schooling decisions and processing school information, but when a perceived crisis occurs, or a nonroutinized decision must be made, fathers may be drawn into the picture. Mothers, in short, probably make the family's initial decision to support or resist a school innovation.*

The fourth, and perhaps most important point, is that it is easier to organize parents, particularly lower social class parents, to resist perceived threats than it is to organize them to achieve long-term, positive goals. James Q. Wilson

15 N.W. Bell and E.F. Vogel. *A Modern Introduction to the Family.* New York, N.Y.: Free Press, 1968; B.J. Biddle and E.J. Thomas. *Role Theory: Concepts and Research.* New York, N.Y.: John Wiley, 1966; Hope Jensen Leichter, "Some Perspectives on the Family as Educator," *Teachers College Record,* Vol. 76, No. 2, December 1974, pp. 175–217; Peter R. Moock, "Economic Aspects of the Family as Educator," *Teachers College Record,* Vol. 76, No. 2, December 1974, pp. 266–278; and Talcott Parsons and R.F. Bales. *Family, Socialization and Interaction Process.* Glencoe, Ill.: Free Press, 1955.

16 G. Blanck. *Ego Psychology: Theory and Practice.* New York, N.Y.: Columbia University Press, 1974; J. Bowlby. *Attachment/Separation.* New York, N.Y.: Basic Books, 1969–1973; and H. Guntrip. *Schizoid Phenomena, Object Relations and the Self.* New York, N.Y.: International University Press, 1969.

has made the same argument in his examination of the conditions which facilitate citizen participation in community development organizations. He writes:

> . . . lower-income neighborhoods are more likely to produce collective action in response to threats (real or imagined) than to create opportunities. Because of the private-regarding nature of their attachment to the community, they are likely to collaborate when each person can see a danger to him or to his family in some proposed change; collective action is a way, not of defining and implementing some broad program for the benefit of all, but of giving force to individual objections by adding them together in a collective protest.[17]

Research on group cohesiveness provides several explanations of why parents will band together for resistance where they would not come together to push for a schooling innovation.[18] An individual's inclination to join a parent group results from a number of forces, and among the sources of these pressures are the following:

Anxiety—It has been shown in laboratory studies[19] that affiliative tendencies increase as anxiety increases, especially among first-borns or only children. Affiliative tendencies, in this case, probably reflect the person's desire to compare his or her reactions with those of others who are threatened, and affiliation provides comfort in the face of threats. In short, "misery loves company," especially miserable company.

Reactance—The loss of freedoms or choices motivates the individual to fight for the restoration of those freedoms, unless the lost freedoms are inconsequential, or there are two or more choices which serve the same needs and only one is lost. This proposition, which forms the basis for *reactance theory*,[20] has received support in a substantial number of experiments. Closing a school or dropping a school program would be a prototypical example of a situation in which reactance is evoked.

Group Identification—In general, people are more attracted to others who are similar to themselves; birds of a feather do flock together much more often

---

17 J.Q. Wilson, "Planning and Politics: Citizen Participation in Urban Renewal," in H.B.C. Spiegel, ed. *Citizen Participation in Urban Development*. Washington, D.C.: NTL Institute for Applied Behavioral Science, 1968, pp. 43–60.

18 For an overview of the group cohesiveness literature, see D. Cartwright and A. Zander, eds. *Group Dynamics: Research and Theory*. New York, N.Y.: Harper & Row, 1968; or B.E. Collins and B. Raven, "Group Structure: Attraction, Coalitions, Communications, and Power," in G. Lindzey and E. Aronson, eds. *Handbook of Social Psychology, Volume II*. Reading, Mass.: Addison-Wesley, 1969.

19 S. Schacter. *The Psychology of Affiliation: Experimental Studies of the Sources of Gregariousness*. Stanford, Calif.: Stanford University Press, 1959.

20 J.W. Brehm. *Response to Loss of Freedom: A Theory of Psychological Reactance*. Morristown, N.J.: General Learning Press, 1972; and J.W. Brehm. *A Theory of Psychological Reactance*. New York, N.Y.: Academic Press, 1966.

than opposites attract.[21] When parents' interests are threatened, they have a new basis for feeling similar to each other, and hence parent groups are likely to coalesce. Their shared fate temporarily overrides differences in social class and attitudes, and this mutual interest forms the basis for group resistance to change; but groups of this type usually do not survive long beyond the threat because the basis for group cohesiveness is lost with the passing of the threat or with the satisfaction of their demands.

Clarity of Group Goals—Attraction to a group is highly dependent upon the clarity of the group's *goals* and the degree of agreement about the *methods* for attaining these goals.[22] To parents, the damages that a contested innovation might do are usually easier to grasp than the potential benefits of adopting an innovation. Threats are here and now, in contrast to the future benefits of an innovation which may not succeed. When parents resist a change in school policies, they have a concrete goal—to stop a specific change from occurring at a specific point in time. In contrast, programs which seek to marshal parents' support over sustained periods of time are usually ones that have vague goals, little consensus on means to obtain these goals, and very ambiguous feedback about how well the group is achieving its goals. The newspaper article about parents and teachers combining to combat "drug abuse and antisocial behavior" is probably a good illustration of a program with a poor prognosis.

Thus, both theoretical reasoning and experience suggest that school leaders would be well advised to assume that, in general, *it is easier to organize parents for resistance than assistance.* Now, with this and the other three assumptions in mind, let us consider what normative models of leadership say about involving parents in school innovations.

When Should Parents Participate in Schooling Decisions? The life of every organization, schools included, consists of a steady stream of problems and there are usually several alternative actions which might solve any given problem. Some actions may produce better solutions than others, but usually there is considerable uncertainty about which action is best. To decide which action to take, the school administrator might: (a) act independently or autocratically, (b) consult with group members before deciding, (c) participate as a discussion leader in a group discussion of the problem, or (d) delegate the problem to subordinates.

---

21 For a review of the empirical research on interpersonal attraction, see E. Berscheid and E.H. Walster. *Interpersonal Attraction.* Reading, Mass.: Addison-Wesley, 1969; Z. Rubin. *Liking and Loving.* New York, N.Y.: Holt, Rinehart and Winston, 1973; and G. Levinger and J.D. Snoek. *Attraction in Relationship: A New Look at Interpersonal Attraction.* Morristown, N.J.: General Learning Press, 1972.

22 B.H. Raven and J. Rietsema, "The Effects of Varied Clarity of Group Goals and Group Path upon the Individual and His Relation to His Group," *Human Relations,* Vol. 10, 1957, pp. 29–44.

TABLE 6.1

Basis for Using Autocratic, Group-Based, or Laissez-Faire Decision Methods

HOW IMPORTANT IS . . .		RECOMMENDED ACTION
Acceptance of the decision	Quality of the decision	
High	High	Use guided group discussion methods to help relevant group members reach concensus.
High	Low	Use group discussion methods.
Low	High	Rely on experts or leaders who have the needed information.
Low	Low	Flip a coin or leave decision to laissez-faire methods.

Which method of decision making is best? It all depends on the nature of the problem, and according to Norman R.F. Maier,[23] the important characteristics which define types of problems are: (a) the importance that group *acceptance* plays in making the decision effective, and (b) the importance of the *quality* of the decision. The effectiveness of some solutions depends entirely on the group's acceptance; it does not matter what the decision is as long as the group accepts it. For example, assume that a principal must schedule two teachers to supervise the playground during the two recesses which occur each day. There are a number of ways yard duty might be assigned; each teacher might supervise one of the two recesses each day, or one teacher might take both recesses on a given day and thus only have yard duty every other day. It really does not matter which schedule is adopted, as long as the playground is supervised by someone, and the teachers accept their assignments.

In other cases, the quality of the decision determines how effective the solution will be, and it does not matter much whether the group likes the solution. This is the case when the problem has a technical dimension. For example, a school district temporarily needs some classroom space. Should they build additional classrooms? Lease existing buildings nearby? Bring in portable classrooms or trailers? The students and faculty will simply have to use whatever space is available, but the alternatives facing the administrator will not all lead to equally high quality decisions; there is a technical solution to this problem which can be determined by figuring the financial costs of different actions.

Maier's two dimensions of acceptance and quality create a fourfold decision table (see table 6.1) which can be used to determine which decisions should be handled autocratically by the leader and which should be allocated to group decision processes. But one problem with this model is that it relies upon vague, intuitive definitions of "acceptance" and "quality."

23 Adapted from Norman R.F. Maier. *Psychology in Industry*. Boston, Mass.: Houghton Mifflin, 1965, p. 170.

Victor Vroom and his colleagues[24] have developed and tested a more sophisticated normative model for deciding what problems are best solved by various decision modes. They distinguish between seven different decision methods for group and individual problems:

A1 You make the decision yourself using the information you have available at the time;

A2 You make the decision yourself, but first you obtain the necessary information from group members;

C1 You make the decision, but only after sharing the problem with individual group members and soliciting their ideas;

C2 You make the decision, but first you get the group's collective suggestions;

D1 You delegate the problem to subordinates;

G1 You analyze the problem with group members and together you arrive at a mutually acceptable solution; and,

G2 You act as a chairperson in the group's attempts to analyze and solve the problem, and you accept whatever decision the group consensus dictates.

Before the decision maker can decide among the seven strategies, he or she must diagnose the nature of the problem. To do this, Vroom and Yetton[25] suggest that these questions be answered:

A   As long as parents accept my decision, does it matter which course of action is taken?

B   Do I have enough information to make a high quality decision?

C   Do parents have enough additional information to result in a high quality decision?

D   Do I know exactly what information is needed, who possesses it, and how to collect it?

E   Is acceptance of the decision by parents critical to effective implementation?

F   If I were to make a decision myself, is it certain that it would be accepted by parents?

G   Can parents be trusted to base solutions on organizational considerations?

H   Are parents likely to be in conflict over which decision is preferred?

Using the answers to these questions, the problem can be assigned to one of fourteen categories or problem types, according to the logic shown in table 6.2. This table also identifies the set of acceptable methods the leader can use to solve the problem.

To illustrate the use of this normative model, consider the following: A

24   Adapted from V.H. Vroom and P.S. Yetton. *Leadership and Decision-Making*. Pittsburgh, Pa.: University of Pittsburgh Press, 1973.
25   Ibid.

TABLE 6.2

Acceptable Decision Methods for Solving Fourteen Types of Problems

PROBLEM TYPE	QUESTIONS FOR DIAGNOSING PROBLEM CHARACTERISTICS								ACCEPTABLE DECISION METHODS
	A	B	C	D	E	F	G	H	
1	NO				NO				A1, A2, C1, C2, G2
2	NO				YES	YES			A1, A2, C1, C2, G2
3	NO				YES	NO			G2
4	YES	YES			NO				A1, A2, C1, C2, G2*
5	YES	YES			YES	YES			A1, A2, C1, C2, G2*
6	YES	YES NO	YES	YES	YES	NO	YES		G2
7	YES	YES NO	YES	YES	YES	NO	NO	YES	C2
8	YES	YES NO	YES	YES	YES	NO	NO	NO	C1, C2
9	YES	NO	YES	YES	YES	YES			A2, C1, C2, G2*
10	YES	NO	YES	YES	NO				A2, C1, C2, G2*
11	YES	NO	YES	NO	YES	YES			C2, G2*
12	YES	NO	YES	NO	YES	NO	YES		G2
13	YES	NO	YES	NO	YES	NO	NO		C2
14	YES	NO	YES	NO	NO				C2, G2*

*Assumes that the answer to Question G is YES.

Source: This table is according to the Vroom and Yetton leadership model, in V. H. Vroom and P. S. Yetton, *Leadership and Decision-Making.* Pittsburgh, Pa.: University of Pittsburgh Press, 1973.

school principal wants to decide on which evening of the week to hold parent-teacher association meetings. All teachers are obligated to attend no matter which night is selected, but parents may find some nights better than others, although the principal has no idea which nights they would prefer. Should the principal: (a) pick an evening, or (b) conduct a poll of parents to find out which evening they would prefer? Obviously, parent acceptance is the most important thing here, and the problem would seem to fall in Problem Type Three. Leaving the decision to parents seems like the best idea.

What implications do these normative models hold for school leaders who wish to involve parents in innovations? When combined with our earlier assumptions, the normative models suggest that the decision areas (domains) which are most appropriate for parental participation are:

1. Decisions which require a high degree of active acceptance among parents and/or children.
2. Decisions which cannot be made without information which the parents have.
3. Decisions where immediate action is not required (unless you are willing to involve only a small group of parent representatives).

4. Decisions where the potential solutions are unclear, or the characteristics of the problem are unknown to school administrators.
5. Cases where the innovation poses a threat to family interests (as contrasted with organizing for the long term pursuit of vague educational goals). Acceptance is the key issue here.

These normative models have proven their worth in some industrial settings, but school leaders can criticize them on at least three grounds. First, the usefulness of these decision models depends upon how well we diagnose the characteristics of the problem. School problems are often difficult to categorize, *except* in overdrawn exaggerations of the various problem types. In these cases, it is usually obvious how one should go about solving the problem. In many cases, these models may not produce better decisions than an experienced school leader would produce using his or her own homegrown model of leadership; but if nothing else, they give a structured decision procedure which may keep an administrator from reacting too hastily in a pressure situation.

The first point was that we lack a reliable system for categorizing problem types, so it is difficult to know which decision method to use, and the second point is related to the first: In education we find ourselves with few standards for assessing the effectiveness of our decisions. In industry, profits provide a unidimensional, reliably measured standard for judging the effectiveness of decisions. If it makes money, it is effective. But in education, we lack agreement about tangible output measures, although some evaluators have treated standardized achievement test results as the sole output of schooling. If we lack convenient measures of decision effectiveness, how can we tell if individual, authoritarian decision making is "better" in a given situation than, say, group decision making?

A third factor which limits the generalizability of normative decision models to education is that schools deal with parents in a different manner than management deals with face-to-face workgroups or management teams. We have already argued that parents form different clienteles or interest groups, and often these groups are nascent until some threat triggers their emergence. Without an identifiable group structure, it is difficult to allocate decisions to group discussion methods, as the normative models would sometimes prescribe. And relying on the identifiable parent groups (e.g., the PTA) may not put the school administrator in contact with the clienteles that really matter. (However, there may be ways that the building administrator can overcome this problem of diverse clienteles with no formal leaders, and this will be discussed later.)

Many well-meaning attempts to increase parents' involvement in school decision making fail for one of two reasons: (a) they allow parents to make only trivial decisions which have little impact on anyone, and hence do not attract significant parent participation, or (b) they delegate complete responsibility to individuals or groups who do not have the time, motivation, or information available to make competent decisions. The normative decision models may help us avoid these two extremes, and their routine use may prevent school leaders from short circuiting their normal problem-diagnosis procedures. Formal models tell us what the school administrator *should do* when deciding who will participate in school innovations. Now let us turn to the realities of school organizations, and consider the decisions parents say they *want to make.*

What Decisions Do Parents Wish to Influence?
Parents are more interested in influencing some schooling decisions than others, and different clienteles have different, often conflicting, interests. In what kinds of issues are different parent groups interested? A 1973 sample survey, one of three surveys made of families involved in an education voucher experiment, provides some answers to this question.[26]

1. Parents were most interested in course content decisions; that is, they were more interested in *what* was taught than *how* it was taught. About three quarters of the parents thought they ought to have a voice in curriculum decisions.
2. Parents were least interested in deciding which teachers were hired and fired; only about half of the parents felt this was a valid concern of parents.
3. About three out of five thought parents ought to be consulted in hiring and firing school principals.
4. A similar percentage, 60 percent, thought that parents ought to decide how schools spend their money.
5. The more educated the parent, the more likely he or she was to believe that parents ought to have a say in curriculum and budget matters.

These are very general categories or domains of decision making, but they give us some idea of the priorities that different groups of parents assign to different kinds of decisions.

The annual Gallup Poll of Public Attitudes Toward Education[27] provides another source of information about what concerns the parents of public school

26 The Elementary Education Voucher Demonstration is now in its fourth year of operation in the Alum Rock Union Elementary School District (San Jose, Calif.). This demonstration, which is funded by the National Institute of Education, permits parents to choose programs (mini-schools) for their children from over fifty that are spread across fourteen schools. The mini-schools vary in their emphases and methods, and free busing is provided to children who attend nonneighborhood schools, so that the different mini-schools represent equal cost alternatives for all families. For additional information about the Alum Rock voucher demonstration, see D. Weiler et al. *A Public School Voucher Demonstration: The First Year at Alum Rock.* Santa Monica, Calif.: Rand Corporation, 1974; also see R. Gary Bridge. *Family Choice in Schooling: Parental Decision-Making in the Alum Rock Education Voucher Demonstration.* Santa Monica, Calif.: Rand Corporation, 1974.
27 George H. Gallup. *The Gallup Polls of Attitudes Toward Education, 1969–1973.* Bloomington, Ind.: Phi Delta Kappa, 1973.

children. In the most recent survey,[28] 64 percent of the parents of public school children said they wanted more information about schools, and when asked "What kind of information would be of particular interest?" the most frequent answer was *information about the curriculum*. Topics like "more information about my child," "information about grading," and "information about how parents can become involved in school activities," were ranked 10, 12, 14, respectively, even though one might expect these matters to take precedence over curriculum concerns. Given that curriculum matters are number one on parents' minds, it is easy to see why "textbook wars" have broken out in Kanawha County and elsewhere.

Who Is Competent to Participate?   Not all parents are interested in participating in school decisions, and it is also true that not all parents are well enough informed to participate in school decisions. Recall that group participation is supposed to be the method of choice in two cases, according to the normative models of decision making: (a) when parents' acceptance is the key to success, and (b) when parents have unique information which leaders lack. The unfortunate fact is that "disadvantaged" families are usually the least informed about matters of schooling, and the result is that advantaged clienteles will have the largest impact on school innovations unless extraordinary efforts are made to involve others.[29]

Returning to the three surveys of voucher parents, we find clear evidence that imperfections in parents' information are correlated with ethnicity, socioeconomic status (SES), and time. Briefly summarized, the three annual surveys showed that:

1. The first year of the demonstration, 17 percent of the respondents did not know about the voucher system, even though their children had attended voucher schools for over two months at the time the interviews were conducted. Awareness of the system was greatest among the relatively advantaged segments of the population: higher income families, more educated respondents, and Anglos as opposed to Mexican-Americans. But by the

---

28   George H. Gallup, "Sixth Annual Gallup Poll of Public Attitudes Toward Education," *Phi Delta Kappan,* Vol. 56, 1974, pp. 20–32.

29   The evidence is compelling that lower-class parents are relatively ineffective gatherers of school information. See for example, R. Gary Bridge, "Parental Decision-making in an Education Voucher System," paper presented at the meeting of the American Educational Research Association, Chicago, Ill., April 1974; R. Gary Bridge, "Can Parents Play the Voucher Game?" *American School Board Journal,* 1975; M.L. Kohn. *Class and Conformity: A Study in Values.* Homewood, Ill.: Irwin-Dorsey, 1969; and J.E. Anderson. *The Young Child in the Home: A Survey of Three Thousand American Families.* New York, N.Y.: Appleton-Century, 1936. For a review of the literature on public knowledge about schools, see Dale Mann, "Public Understanding and Education Decision-Making," *Educational Administration,* Vol. 10, 1974, pp. 1–18.

second year of the demonstration, only 3 percent of the respondents were unaware of the voucher system. Disadvantaged families figured out what was going on, but they did it more slowly than others. The problem, however, is that in a dynamic, ever-changing system, parents who take a long time to discover what is happening are going to be at a continual disadvantage.

2. Parents can choose among mini-school programs which are spread across fourteen voucher schools, and free busing is provided to nonneighborhood schools. During the first year of the demonstration, 59 percent of the parents knew about the free busing provision; but by the second year, 83 percent had this information. Again, this data emphasizes the importance of time.

3. Parents may request program transfers for their children at any time during the school year, but only half the parents knew about this rule during the first year of the demonstration. As expected, advantaged families—in this case, middle-class whites, higher income, and better educated households—were best informed; and this pattern has continued to date, although the percentage of parents who know about transfer policies has increased each year and now stands at 79 percent.

Inaccurate information prevents some parents from participating effectively in school innovations, and some leaders have used this as a justification for not involving parents, or at least "difficult to reach" parents. But these inaccuracies are tractable, or what Etzioni[30] calls "actionable." That is, the situation can be changed if the correct school policies are adopted. To identify policies which may be effective, we must first understand why "disadvantaged" parents are the last to learn what is going on in schools, and why they are least interested in participating in school activities. Table 6.3 summarizes some possible explanations and suggests remedial steps that school leaders might take to raise information levels and foster participation. Additional suggestions are offered in the next section.

Some Guidelines for Effective Parent Participation This concluding section offers some guidelines for school administrators who wish to involve parents in constructive changes. On the basis of the evidence and assumptions presented earlier, the following conclusions seem tenable:

1. Parents are not a homogeneous group; they cluster into clienteles which are characterized by a lack of formal leadership and often do not emerge until parents feel threatened by an innovation. In some cases, the "squeaking wheel" approach to decision making may be appropriate—those who gripe,

30 A. Etzioni. *The Active Society: A Theory of Societal and Political Processes.* New York, N.Y.: Free Press, 1968.

TABLE 6.3

Explanations of Parents' Information about Schools and Potential Actions

HYPOTHESES	*POSSIBLE ACTIONS*
1. *"Alienation"* Schools are just one part of the social system and cannot be expected by themselves to change social and economic conditions which lead people to believe, with some justification, that they cannot control their outcomes. Some parents do not seek information about schools or attempt to participate, because they don't believe it would make a difference.[31]	Schools may not be able to change general feelings of powerlessness, but they can concentrate on building feelings on personal efficacy with regard to schooling. *Consistency* is important. Policies should be stated about parents' areas of control.
2. *Information Networks* Different people belong to different information networks, and some of these are poorly connected to the schools.	When possible, identify existing networks and try to insert information into these networks in a systematic way. If new networks are needed, build them so as to parallel the level of parent participation you want to evoke. (See *Guidelines* Section.)
3. *Preferred Sources of Information* Schools tend to rely on the printed word to transmit information, but in some groups—particularly less educated parents—the printed word is not a powerful source of information. More credence is awarded personal, face-to-face communications.[32]	Do not rely solely on school bulletins. Transmit the same information through multiple channels, especially when it is aimed at less educated households. Use the channels which fit the target groups' habits. Personal contacts are especially valued by lower-class parents.[33]
4. *Costs of Interacting with the Schools — Operating Hours* With the exception of special events (and these are usually highly organized events), most school activities occur during the day, largely between 8 AM and 3 PM. Hence, many parents, particularly those who work on an hourly basis or who cannot control their hours, have to pay a high cost to visit the schools.	Consider non-standard hours of operation at scheduled times (not just special occasions).
5. *"Psychic Costs" of Interacting with the Schools* Dealing with unfamiliar people or unfamiliar situations can be stressful and hence will be	Make sure that parents can contact people of their own ethnic or language group when they

31 Melvin Seeman, "On the Meaning of Alienation," *American Sociological Review*, Vol. 24, 1959, pp. 783–791; and Melvin Seeman, "Alienation and Knowledge-seeking," *Social Forces*, Vol. 20, 1972, pp. 3–17.

32 Bridge, *Family Choice in Schooling: Parental Decision-making in the Alum Rock Education Voucher Demonstration, op. cit.*

33 For example, the Lincoln, Nebraska "Parent-a-Week" program asks teachers to telephone one family a week to discuss any schooling concerns they have. See "Parent-a-Week Call Program Builds Community Image," *Nations Schools*, Vol. 93, No. 5, 1974, p. 47.

TABLE 6.3 *(Cont.)*

Explanations of Parents' Information about Schools and Potential Actions

HYPOTHESES	POSSIBLE ACTIONS
avoided whenever possible. Economists refer to these emotional stresses as "psychic costs" of interaction. To many parents, interacting with school personnel is stressful because of differences in ethnicity, language, or social class, and as a result, they minimize their contacts with the schools or limit them to routinized interactions.[34]	approach the schools. This is especially important in the initial stages of contact. A multi-ethnic school ought to have a multi-ethnic staff "out front."
6. *Role Expectations* Many lower class parents do not believe that they have the right to participate in school innovations. They leave all decisions to professional educators. An analogy can be drawn with the way many people handle medical problems; they pick a physician and turn the decisions over to him/her, unlike other people who will pit one physician's diagnosis against another's. People who turn over all decisions to the schools may be very concerned about the outcomes, but they will take what they are given, even if it is not what they would like. Leaders, hearing no disapproval, ordinarily assume that silence is agreement.	The problem cannot be solved by the school alone, but administrators can help the staff and parents to clarify their respective roles. The staff is of particular importance here, for many school personnel enjoy the freedom of not having to deal with parents (except in structured situations); often the attitude that "professionals know best" serves the teacher more than the child. This is a perversion of the concept of professionalism, and it only maintains parents passivity.

get. But this is hardly an adequate method for building support for the sustained, constructive participation of families. In planning for change, school leaders must carefully consider which clienteles will be affected and how they should (or should not) be involved in the design and implementation of the innovation.

2. Leaders at every level of the school hierarchy ought to have clearly articulated, publicly stated policies with regard to the kinds of decisions parents will be asked to make. When will the leader's decision be final? When will it be subject to the formal review of parents? teachers? When will a group decision be final and when will it be advisory only? Unfortunately, many administrators formulate their leadership philosophy while under siege. They answer these policy questions while locked in battles that might have been avoided if expectations had been identified at the outset of the innovation.

The normative models of decision making were introduced in order to show what some organizational theorists think are the important criteria for

34 K.N. Anchor and F.N. Anchor, "School Failure and Parental Involvement in an Ethnically Mixed School: A Survey," *Journal of Community Psychology*, Vol. 2, 1974, pp. 265–267.

deciding whether a problem will be handled autocratically or by group decision. Generally speaking, the assignment of problems to decision modes depends upon two characteristics of the problem: (a) the importance that group *acceptance* plays in making the decision effective, and (b) the importance that the *quality* of the decision plays. Situations in which parent participation is likely to be most effective are those in which: (a) acceptance of the innovation is crucial to success, or (b) the quality of the decision depends upon information that only parents have.

Acceptance is a necessary but insufficient condition for the success of individual-level (as contrasted with group-level) interventions. In some cases, a goal can be achieved by the actions of relatively few people and it does not matter who participates as long as the job gets done. For example, if parents are needed to chaperone a social event, it does not matter who does it as long as the event is properly supervised. In contrast, in individual-level interventions, success depends upon widespread participation. For example, a scheme for improving reading achievement through guided homework exercises will succeed only if individual parents cooperate. The crucial distinction which must be made is between group-level and individual-level interventions. The typical school-parent organizations (e.g., the PTA) are geared only to achieving group-level tasks.

Certainly no one can specify a priori how a local school administrator should handle each and every problem, but the normative models and similar school-related manuals[35] at least provide some guidelines. The important point is that administrators should formulate and communicate a clear policy about what role—if any—parents will play in the decision process.

3. Parents seem to be most concerned about curriculum innovations, where curriculum is broadly defined to include the emphases which are placed on different skills (i.e., *what* is taught) as well as the instructional methods which are used (i.e., *how* it is taught). Perhaps in contrast to most school employees' intuitions, parents are least interested in making personnel decisions, *except* where attacking particular personnel is the only way that parents can influence curriculum decisions or school practices.

4. Parent involvement in school innovations will be most productive when parents know what is demanded of them; hence schools should set clear objectives for parent participation. Programs which have vague goals and vague requirements for parent participation will be rewarded with vague results. Some of the most successful compensatory (or "problem prevention") programs around today are ones which involve mothers and children in learning experiences, usually in the home. One might speculate that these

35 Dale Mann, "A Principal's Handbook for Shared Control in Urban Community Schools," in *The Politics of Administrative Representation*. Lexington, Mass.: Lexington Books, D. C. Heath, 1976.

programs are successful because: (a) the clientele is clear (e.g., families of children who have reading problems), (b) the behaviors demanded of the parents are understood (e.g., read five to ten minutes each evening using prescribed materials and methods), and (c) the goals are clear to the parents and they are easily measured—hence, the child's progress provides feedback which keeps involvement high. Programs like these carry some basic lessons for schools which wish to stimulate parent involvement, and these lessons can be generalized to a broad range of innovations outside of reading.[36]

5. Parents are not equally well informed about schooling matters, and this means that some are more competent than others to participate in school decisions, especially in those situations where the quality of the decision depends upon parents' information (e.g., choosing a program for a child in a system which offers multiple options). But parents' information levels mirror directly the adequacy of the school's information distribution policies, especially in the case of lower class clienteles.

The impact of school information procedures can be improved, in many cases, by observing these two principles:

a. Honor the communication sources that are preferred by different clienteles; don't expect to reach everyone equally well through one channel. In practice this means that school personnel spend more time in face-to-face contact with "hard to reach," poorer families, while permitting middle-class families to rely on printed materials and their own information-seeking skills.

b. Whenever possible, send information through extant neighborhood networks.[37] If new networks are required, try to create networks which parallel the level of participation you want to elicit from parents. If the innovation is focused on a particular age group or grade level (e.g., a reading readiness program), build the network around classrooms (and the teacher becomes a logical point of contact). If the innovation involves a whole school, try an acquaintance network approach where people who are contacted initially agree to call five or six of their friends, and the school keeps a roster so that isolated individuals are not ignored.

36 K. Hoskisson et al., "Assisted Reading and Parent Involvement," *Reading Teacher,* Vol. 27, 1974, pp. 710–714; E.B. DeFranco, "Parent Education as an Aid to Improving Children's Reading," *Adult Leadership,* Vol. 21, 1973, pp. 320–333 and 346; and M.G. Weiser, "Parental Responsibility in the Teaching of Reading," *Young Children,* Vol. 29, 1974, pp. 225–230.

37 See E. Litwak and H. J. Meyer. *School, Family, and Neighborhood; The Theory and Practice of School-Community Relations.* New York, N.Y.: Columbia University Press, 1974; or E. Litwak and H.J. Meyer. *Relations Between School-Community Coordinating Procedures and Reading Achievement.* Stanford, Calif.: Center for Advanced Studies in the Behavioral Sciences, 1966. They describe community-school linkages in terms of eight categories, one of which is the "common messenger" (people who belong to both the school organization and the community). School aides are a primary example of common messengers, and their potential as a source of information (to and from parents) should not be overlooked.

6. Remember that the time frame is important. The fuse on the community bomb is very short when controversial changes are made and one or more parent groups feels that their interests are threatened. On the other hand, it takes considerable time to involve parents—especially lower-class parents—in constructive innovations. In the Alum Rock voucher demonstration, for instance, the relatively disadvantaged segments of the population were the last to learn the rules of the voucher system. Similarly, in southern "freedom of choice" schools, which gave black families access to white schools, the poorer families were the most likely to reject the opportunity;[38] however, in a similar desegregation situation in the north, middle-class parents initiated the integration effort, but poorer families became the mainstay of the movement.[39] The difference between the two situations is in the time frame; in the southern case, the innovation was implemented in less than two years, but in the northern example, the struggle lasted fifteen years.

Summary   Parents can make or break school innovations, and unfortunately they are most often cast in the role of spoilers, since it is easier to organize parents for resistance than assistance. But successful innovations, especially individual-level interventions, require parent involvement, and schools can amplify their impact by mobilizing the resources of the home and paying close attention to the nature and quality of the home-school linkages.

In this chapter, we have considered the circumstances under which parents should be involved in goal setting and school decision making, the kinds of issues that concern parents, and the strategies by which schools can draw out informed parents who can participate effectively in school innovations at the local level. The issues are complex, and this brief chapter cannot be a manual for managing home-school relations; but hopefully it has at least clarified some of the issues and problems that building administrators should consider in dealing with the diverse clienteles that "parents" represent.

---

38 E.A. Weinstein and P.N. Geisel, "Family Decision-making over Desegregation," *Sociometry,* Vol. 25, 1962, pp. 21–29.
39 E. Luchterhand and H.J. Meyer, "Social Class and School Desegregation," *Social Forces,* Vol. 13, 1965, pp. 83–88.

CHAPTER 7

A New Look at Schooling Effects from Programmatic Research and Development

RALPH A. HANSON AND RICHARD E. SCHUTZ

Mainline inquiry over the past decade on the effects of schooling on student learning has painted a dismal picture. Consider the conclusions of Coleman, of Jencks, and of Averch et al.:

> Taking all these results together, one implication stands out above all: That schools bring little influence to bear on a child's achievement that is independent of his background and general social context; and that this very lack of an independent effect means that the inequalities imposed on children by their home, neighborhood, and peer environment are carried along to become the inequalities with which they confront adult life at the end of school. For equality of educational opportunity through the schools must imply a strong effect of schools that is independent of the child's immediate social environment, and that strong independent effect is not present in American Schools.[1]

> Our research has convinced us not only that cognitive inequality does not explain economic inequality to any significant extent, but that educational inequality does not explain cognitive inequality to any significant extent. The amount of schooling an individual gets has some effect on his test performance, but the quality of his schooling makes extraordinarily little difference.[2]

Research has not identified a variant of the existing system that is

---

Work upon which this chapter is based was performed pursuant to contracts with the National Institute of Education. Views expressed, however, do not necessarily reflect the position, policy, or endorsement of that agency.

1   J. S. Coleman et al. *Equality of Educational Opportunity*. Washington, D.C.: Government Printing Office, 1966, p. 325.
2   C. Jencks et al. *Inequality: A Reassessment of the Effect of Family and Schooling in America*. New York: Basic Books, 1972, p. 53.

120

consistently related to students' educational outcomes.[3]

The school community and the research and development community in education have been hard pressed publicly and professionally by these consistent conclusions that educational research has no demonstrable effect on schools and that schools in turn have no demonstrable effects on children.

The conclusions appear to be supported by the data from which they were derived. We do not question the summary findings of Stephens[4] and Dreeben[5] regarding the ineffectiveness of cumulative educational research to the mid-1960s, nor subsequent empirical and analytic work marked by the Equality of Educational Opportunity survey reported by Coleman et al.,[6] or the various responses to it[7] that comprise the mainline tradition. However, the "no effects" finding reflects an inadequate approach for conducting inquiry about schooling rather than the actual impotence of schools as social institutions or the inherent impotence of educational R&D as a scientific/technical endeavor.

LIMITATIONS OF PRIOR RESEARCH ON SCHOOLING EFFECTS

The mainline research on schooling effects is inadequate for a number of reasons:

1. The overall input-output model motivating such research has totally ignored the *operations* of schooling. Instead of looking at data that relate classroom instruction to children's learning, survey studies have tended to rely on more tangential phenomena that were hoped to relate to the outcomes of schooling. This absence of attention to the phenomenon of interest—schooling per se—is reflected in the proxy variables used to "cover" attributes of

---

3   H. A. Averch et al. *How Effective Is Schooling? A Critical Review and Synthesis of Research Findings.* Santa Monica, Calif.: Rand Corporation, 1972, p. 154.

4   J. M. Stephens. *The Process of Schooling: A Psychological Examination.* New York: Holt, Rinehart and Winston, 1967.

5   R. Dreeben. *On What Is Learned in School Reading.* Reading, Mass.: Addison-Wesley, 1968.

6   Coleman. *Equality of Educational Opportunity.*

7   S. Bowles and H. M. Levin. "The Determinants of Scholastic Achievement: An Appraisal of Some Recent Findings." *Journal of Human Resources,* 1968, 3, pp. 3–24.

F. Mosteller and D. P. Moynihan. *On Equality of Educational Opportunity.* New York: Vintage Books, 1972.

W. G. Spady, "The Impact of School Resources on Students," in F. N. Kerlinger, ed. *Review of Research in Education.* Itasca, Ill.: F. E. Peacock, 1973, pp. 135–177.

T. D. Cook, "The Potential and Limitations of Secondary Evaluations," in M. W. Apple, M. J. Subkoviak and H. S. Lufler, Jr., eds. *Educational Evaluation: Analysis and Responsibility.* Berkeley: McCutchan, 1974.

G. W. Mayeske and A. E., Beaton, Jr. *Special Studies of Our Nation's Students.* Washington, D.C.: Government Printing Office, 1975.

G. W. Mayeske et al. *A Study of the Achievement of Our Nation's Students.* Washington, D.C.: Government Printing Office, 1973.

Jencks. *Inequality.*

Averch. *How Effective Is Schooling?*

the phenomenon—years of teacher training, salary of teachers, amount spent on textbooks, and so on. In no way have the elements of schooling been carefully analyzed and operationally represented in these earlier inquiries.

2. The measures of input and output used in mainline schooling effects studies are *not* appropriate. The input measures have generally been of two kinds: socioeconomic status such as race and parental income level; and financial status such as per pupil expenditures and teacher salaries. While both types of measures are of interest in schooling inquiries, they do not measure aspects of schools, teachers, and pupils which are directly relevant to schooling operations. Other variables are more relevant: the specific skills a pupil is learning relative to the instruction a school is providing; teacher practices such as allocation of time to instruction on specified outcomes; procedures used for grouping and placing pupils; materials used in instruction; and school characteristics such as time allocated to various skill areas, use of instructional staff, use of supporting staff, instructional staff time allocated to instructional outcomes, materials used, and management of program implementation.

For the output variables, the situation is even worse. Mainline studies have uncritically accepted and used standardized tests as the sole measure of instructional effects. Standardized achievement tests (and standardized ability tests that have sometimes been used when achievement tests were not feasible) are deliberately and intentionally constructed to be insensitive to differences in schooling operations, so that they can be used "generally." Unless supplemented with measures that are directly instructionally relevant or program specific, standardized tests can be counted upon to yield "no significant differences" in instructional effects.

3. Mainline studies have relied on either large-scale social surveys or secondary analyses of existing school records. Both are inappropriate because they do not (and cannot) provide evidence about the instructional process as it occurs over time. But long-term studies of the schooling process are a burden to schools since they require considerable personnel effort and provide little if any direct benefits to the participants.

4. Another deficiency relates to the units of analysis used in the research. The pupil and school have generally been the only ones used. While these units are appropriate for some questions, the class or instructional group certainly is the most appropriate for others.[8] Data relevant to all these units must be gathered, aggregated appropriately, and analyzed in relation to the matter being investigated.

8 D. E. Wiley and R. D. Bock, "Quasi-Experimentation in Educational Settings: Comment," *School Review*, 1967, 15, pp. 355–367.

5. Conceptual problems in the conduct of mainline research have carried over to the methods for analyzing the data. In the early studies there was heavy reliance on regression/correlation methods. These have more recently given way to extensions of regression/correlation methods such as path analysis and covariance structure analysis combined with rather complex models.[9] While such methods are useful for some questions, the reliance on such statistical analyses reflects conceptual problems in defining variables and relationships rather than the inherent complexity of the phenomena.

6. Several of these conceptual problems are compounded by the use of "snapshot" data only. Understanding schooling effects requires understanding instructional effects: both phenomena occur over considerable time. Therefore, snapshot designs that look only at pupils and schools at one point in time greatly limit the scope of inquiry. A "stop-action" picture can be useful in determining whether or not a runner has crossed the goal line but not how that goal was achieved. The alternative is to obtain longitudinal data within and across school years on pupils, teachers, and schools by program. Such data have not been gathered in the past.

These limitations of earlier mainline inquiry are not critiqued in isolation. Rather, we offer and illustrate an alternative approach—programmatic R&D.

PROGRAMMATIC R&D

This new approach to schooling effects inquiry departs dramatically from prior research efforts. It has its origin in the programmatic educational R&D conducted by the Southwest Regional Laboratory for Educational Research and Development (SWRL) over the past ten years. In simplest terms, this new methodology incorporates the following features:

1. The use of data from natural school environments involving a defined instructional program that operates across a large number of pupils, classes, schools, and districts, and also across years of schooling.

2. A primary set of data gathering components designed specifically for the instructional program involved and linked to both the operation of the program and the projected research.

3. A secondary set of data gathering components that provide information on specific variables required for research purposes. These measures are prepared and distributed to both minimize required effort and maximize information utility.

4. A program information service that provides reports on progress and results to various audiences of current and/or future users. The information service

---

9 W. H. Sewell, R. M. Hauser, and D. L. Featherman, eds. *Schooling and Achievement in American Society*. New York: Academic Press, 1976.

is also an unobtrusive vehicle for gaining source data regarding program implementation and pupil performance without imposing "data collection" requirements for extrinsic purposes.

The prime feature of the methodology is that it incorporates into the natural instructional environment mechanisms that aid the participants (students, teachers, and administrators) as their first and foremost function but that concurrently provide unique data for understanding instruction and schooling. Because all schools have used a common instructional vehicle with known characteristics in their natural environments, the method permits direct examination of the impact of this vehicle as well as attributes other than the instruction on the effects attained. These attributes may include variables from different perspectives and at different levels of specificity, such as teacher grouping practices, class size, student body ethnic-racial composition, instructional time allocation, school/district implementation effort, and so on. The list of possible attributes that may be considered using this approach is as long as the list of possible conjectures of educational researchers.

Measures of the most currently plausible and useful of these attributes are included as part of the instrumentation accompanying a specific program inquiry. The results for a given attribute are determined by relating its variation across users to variation across the program-specific outcome measures, which have been constructed to be very sensitive indicators of changes in program effects.[10] Based on the results of a single investigation of school operations for an academic year, reasonable inferences as to the importance of an attribute (or attributes) can be ascertained.

But how then can these results be expanded into "scientific" generalizations? The process just described will produce results that are applicable to the specific program and user population involved in a given program. But the greatest impact comes from being able to generalize results beyond both these users and this program. This generalization can be obtained via processes such as cross-validation, replication, generalization, and extension. Because the method inherently includes a large number and representative user populations, cross-validation analyses can be carried out within user subgroups. Replication occurs across years with both the same and different users. Generalization occurs when findings from both different programs and different users are confirmed. Extension occurs through the confirmation of findings from lon-

---

10 A detailed discussion of the methods employed in preparing such measures can be found in R. A. Hanson, G. Behr, and B. Meguro, "Domain-Referenced Tests to Support Instructional Programs." Paper presented at the annual meeting of the National Council of Measurement in Education. New York, April 1977.

R. A. Hanson and R. F. McMorris, "Item Formats and Proficiency Estimation in Domain-Referenced Assessment." Technical Memorandum 5-76-02. Los Alamitos, Calif.: SWRL Educational Research and Development, 1976.

gitudinal data on the same users and the introduction of new measurement constraints and use conditions in subsequent inquiry with predictable results.

THE SWRL/GINN KINDERGARTEN PROGRAM INSTALLATION 1972–73 AND 1973–74

The new methodology is best described and understood in the world of practice. The following sections summarize one of the first such inquiries, which centered around use of the SWRL/Ginn Kindergarten Program and was carried out with a large number of schools across the country beginning in the 1972–73 school year.

Context of the Inquiry[11]

The SWRL/Ginn Kindergarten Program grew from a commitment by SWRL in 1965 to provide the resources that would enable schools to reliably teach students to read, beginning in kindergarten, irrespective of the pupil's previous cultural and educational experience and excepting only those individuals with readily identifiable organic disabilities. The R&D from this commitment yielded a number of instructional products currently in use in schools. The Kindergarten Program itself includes two instructional programs: the Instructional Concepts Program (ICP) and the Beginning Reading Program (BRP), and four support programs.

Developing promising educational products is one matter; financing their use is another. Personnel costs constitute the vast bulk of school district budgets. The small sum of discretionary funds (both absolutely and relatively) available to school officials for nonlabor instructional costs is a serious obstacle to rapid, large-scale adoptions of innovations by districts. However, this same labor-intensive characteristic can be a lever for implementing new instructional products if modest financial incentives can be found without attempting to compete with labor costs.

The opportunity to test and demonstrate the effects of product-referenced financial support in education arose through a complex sequence of actions stimulated by the then-Secretary of the Department of Health, Education, and

---

11 This section documents the sequence of events that provided the reason-for-being of the inquiry. Other parts of the history are reported in detail in:

R. A. Hanson and R. E. Schutz, "The Effects of Programmatic R&D on Schooling and the Effects of Schooling on Students: Lessons from the First-Year Installation of the SWRL/Ginn Kindergarten Program." Technical Report 53. Los Alamitos, Calif.: SWRL Educational Research and Development, 1975.

R. A. Hanson and R. E. Schutz, "Instructional Product Implementation and Schooling Effects: Lessons from the Second-Year Installation of the SWRL/Ginn Kindergarten Program." Technical Report 56. Los Alamitos. Calif.: SWRL Educational Research and Development, 1976.

R. A. Hanson, R. E. Schutz, and J. D. Bailey. "Program—Fair Evaluation of Instructional Programs: Initial Results of the Kindergarten Reading Readiness Inquiry." Technical Report 57. Los Alamitos, Calif.: SWRL Educational Research and Development, 1977.

Welfare, Elliot L. Richardson. In the fall of 1970, Secretary Richardson directed that the U.S. Office of Education (USOE) identify "lessons that had resulted from educational R&D during the last 10 years." USOE identified the SWRL Kindergarten Program as one such "lesson" but was not clear as to how the lesson could be put to use. SWRL asked that USOE make available dollar incentives to school districts for a maximum of 25 percent of the Kindergarten Program's material costs for 100 percent of the pupils in the district over a three-year period. By the end of the third year, the product could be in use with 100 percent of the pupils in the district and would be locally self-sustaining. Terrel H. Bell, then a USOE deputy commissioner, allocated $1.3 million to provide these incentives within eighteen states for the 1972–73 school year. The full costs of implementing the program were trivial for the federal government—less than $5 per child for a full-year program. The cost to implement the program for state and local education agencies was nil, since the program involved no personnel, operations, or facilities beyond those currently in place in the participating districts.

Relationships among the government, the educational R&D, and publishing communities were also straightforward despite the scale of the program. The incentive grants for the installation of the program materials and procedures went from USOE to local education agencies, with nominal state agency involvement consistent with standard ESEA Title III arrangements. School districts used their local practices in deciding whether or not to participate with or without the federal incentive. Districts obtained their materials directly from the publisher. USOE informed participating districts that cooperation with SWRL in a quality assurance inquiry would satisfy Title III grant evaluation requirements. Any district could opt to do its own evaluation, and some did. SWRL dealt directly with local education agencies in the quality assurance inquiry, which was supported by the National Institute of Education (NIE) as a regular part of SWRL's program, and kept state education agencies and USOE officials regularly informed. The commercial publisher of the materials, Ginn and Company, provided computer support for the inquiry at no cost.

It is easy to acknowledge rhetorically that the demonstrated improvement of school practice—the goal of educational R&D—requires the collaboration of the schools, academic institutions, private enterprise, and government. This program made that rhetoric a reality. Complex, large-scale, multi-institutional, organizational interactions have received little attention in the "educational change" literature, although on our evidence they are not only feasible but perhaps required.

Design of the Inquiry

The arrangements under which the Kindergarten Program was to be used in 1972–73 provided the first opportunity to test the claim that important instructional outcomes may be reliably attained in a variety of school settings with a wide variety of students through use of a systematically developed educational product system. Previous inquiries have lacked either key elements or data required for such a test. For example, the Coleman Report and National Assessment studies have included elements of the data for such a test but have lacked referents for, or even knowledge of, the instruction being used with students. The science and mathematics curriculum projects of the 1960s included elements of the instructional product system for such a test but lacked data referenced to student outcomes and to specific features of the instruction. The Follow Through Planned Variations study, conducted concurrently with this inquiry, complements the present findings,[12] but the variations involved in that inquiry were "models" of social and/or program change rather than product systems.

From a design perspective, the present inquiry had a number of positive features. The large size of the sample provided sufficient replicability to permit consideration of effects at the state, district, school, and class, as well as the pupil level. A classic research design might have assigned these units randomly to "treatments." Although we did not and could not do that, the study method does provide abundant potential for cross-validating results both within and across years using both cross-sectional and longitudinal data. The recommendation to use the classroom as the primary unit of analyses in instructional research has often been made, but seldom followed; it was used as the major unit of analysis in this inquiry and worked well.

The two-year inquiry is most clearly distinguished from "evaluations," "interventions," "experiments," "demonstrations," "research," or "development" by the operations involved. The methodology was straightforward, and the data collection operations intruded minimally on participating schools. Our measures paralleled the instruction that was conducted. Since each measure related directly to instruction and was useful in program operations, teachers were motivated to help collect the data for their own purposes. A "pretest" was administered to each child at the beginning of the kindergarten year to assess school-relevant proficiency. Then, for both the Instructional Concepts and the Beginning Reading programs, teachers recorded the completion dates and proficiency scores of pupils during the instruction. "Posttests" were administered at the end of instruction (for ICP) and at the end of the school year (for BRP).

This simple instrumentation yielded a massive data base that was obtained on twenty or more occasions during the year, including over 2,000 schools, 100,000 pupils, and 100 "scores" for each pupil. Statisticians will be quick to note that this sample is much larger than necessary. However, the "sample"

---

12 J. A. Stallings and D. H. Kaskowitz, "Follow Through Classroom Observation Evaluation 1972–73." Menlo Park, Calif.: Stanford Research Institute, 1974.

was not created for research purposes, but rather to assist in the implementation of the program. Its research use was adventitious. For example, teachers were asked to complete only a one-page, six-item demographic data questionnaire especially for the quality assurance study. All of the rest of the data collection was accomplished in the natural course of using the program's materials. The complete costs of the evaluation and the research therefore were marginal and nominal. The benefits of the inquiry to teachers were thus direct, immediate, and specific. Schools received instructional management information analyzed and arrayed in separate reports to each participating class, school, district, and state agency. The activity provided the federal government with an efficient and effective means of satisfying the evaluation requirements of categorical programs. For SWRL, the activity provided an opportunity to extend the technology of quality assurance in the context of instruction. For the educational R&D community, the activity provided a rich data base that can be mined extensively in the future.

Inquiry Instrumentation

The Kindergarten Program used in the inquiry was designed to help children learn conceptual skills fundamental to academic achievement (the Instructional Concepts Program) and to master beginning reading skills (the Beginning Reading Program). To illustrate the methodology we focus here on two aspects of the instrumentation: the Beginning Reading Program and the associated quality assurance components.

The Beginning Reading Program provides instructional resources to teach three major skills to kindergarten pupils: to read the one hundred words taught directly in the program; to sound out and read new words composed of word elements taught in the program; to comprehend the material read.

Instructional materials and procedures are presented in ten units, each typically requiring between one to three weeks to complete. After the completion of instruction on each unit, a twenty-item criterion exercise is provided to assess the pupil's learning of letter names, word elements, words, and word attack.

Quality assurance components used to provide the data to be discussed here are:

1. *Entry Survey:* A twenty-two-item, individually administered, program-specific reading readiness measure[13] given during the first month of school.
2. *Unit Report:* Used to record the dates when a teacher began to use a unit, when it was completed, and the scores of pupils on the unit test (criterion exercise).

---

13 P. L. Coker and S. E. Legum, "Design of the Kindergarten Program Entry Survey." Technical Note 2-72-33. Los Alamitos, Calif.: SWRL Educational Research and Development, September 5, 1972.

3. *BRP Assessment:* A set of forty-three items administered to pupils by their teacher at the completion of instruction with the program or at the end of the school year, whichever occurred first. It provides scores on the four major program outcomes.
4. *School Information Sheet:* Basic information on biosocial characteristics of pupils at each participating school (e.g., Title I eligibility, percent of ethnic minorities enrolled, etc.).

Other than providing data on these components through a district coordinator, the program operated without assistance from outside the district. To support program operations, two kinds of reports were provided to users: Status Reports were issued during the year to verify the assignment of class numbers within each district and to provide the coordinator with a summary of the materials received from the district to date; and Summary Reports to describe the data provided by the district in a manner both understandable and useful for everyone involved with the program. These reports, along with interpretive guides for each class, school, and district, were distributed to districts at the end of each school year.

Inquiry Participants

The number of kindergarten program-quality assurance participants using the Beginning Reading Program in the two inquiry years is given in table 7.1. The vast majority of users participated both years.

TABLE 7.1

Number of KP-QA Participants

Year	States	Districts	Schools	Classes	Pupils
1972–73	18	343	2,049	4,503	115,554
1973–74	18	288	1,949	4,268	111,485

The sample's biosocial characteristics are described in table 7.2.

1. The median family income of participating schools was in the $5,000–8,000 range, with 41 percent in the first year and 39 percent in the second year reporting in that category. The school median family incomes of 74 and 73 percent fell in the $5,000 to $12,000 range. Only 10 and 11 percent reported incomes above $12,000. The average income of families in the sample was considerably below the national average.

TABLE 7.2

Description of Participating Classes in Terms of Biosocial Indicators

	Percent 1972–73	Percent 1973–74
Ethnic Group		
Black	17	18
Spanish-surnamed	4	5
Other	78	77
Income Level		
Below $5,000	17	18
5–8,000	41	39
8–12,000	33	34
Above 12,000	10	11
Title I Eligibility		
Yes	54	55
No	46	45
Reading Level		
Below National Norm	44	44
At National Norm	34	33
Above National Norm	22	23
Location		
Inner City	15	16
Urban	37	40
Suburban	38	34
Rural	10	10
Number of Classes	4,023	4,389

2. Schools were described as Black, Spanish-surnamed, or Other, based on whether half or more of the pupils in attendance were from one or more of these ethnic/racial categories. Those described as Black were 17 and 18 percent; as Spanish-surnamed, 4 and 5 percent; and as Other, 78 and 77 percent for the two respective years.
3. Fifty-two and 56 percent of the schools were in either urban or inner city areas. Coupled with the 38 and 34 percent located in suburban areas, a total of over 90 percent of the schools were from metropolitan areas.
4. The schools indicated their prior level of performance relative to national norms on standardized reading tests. About a fourth had been above national reading norm; another third were at the norm; and 44 percent below it. Thus, over three-fourths of the sample were at or below national norms in terms of prior reading performance.

5. Fifty-four and 55 percent of the schools indicated they were eligible for ESEA Title I (poverty level) funding.

Participating schools represented the full range of characteristics of the nation's schools. However, they overrepresented situations that typically display low educational performance patterns. At the very least, the results obtained should not be inflated because of the composition of the sample.

DESCRIPTIVE RESULTS

Entry Survey

The entry survey provides a baseline for academic proficiency prior to kindergarten instruction.[14] Figure 7.1 shows the overall score distributions for pupils, classes, and schools. It clearly displays the normal distribution at each aggregation level. The overall class average proficiency (score category) on this indicator was 58 percent or about 13 of 22 items correct. Individual classes were distributed around this value. Had our intent been to "standardize" the instrument, these data would reflect ideal psychometric characteristics for academic pretests.

It is of interest to note that this same distribution held consistently for classes across biosocial characteristics—ethnic groups, family income, and prior school reading performance. The average proficiency differences that occurred within categories are consistent with expectations based on prior descriptive data on pupils from such categories. For example, slightly higher entry proficiency was found in classes from schools that have higher family income levels, that do not include ethnic minority groups, that are located outside metropolitan areas, that have a history of reading performance at or above the average on norm-referenced measures, and that are not eligible for Title I funds. There is, as would be expected, considerable overlap in the distributions of class proficiency within each category.

The data indicate that the pupils in most classes already had substantial entering skills prior to instruction. However, the proficiency level is low from the perspective of the basic rudimentary skills required for success in reading, mathematics, and the other primary academic subject matters addressed by schools. The classes typically were sufficiently capable to begin kindergarten instruction but had a "lot to learn" in order to accomplish program objectives.

14 Ibid.
   P. L. Coker and S. E. Legum, "An Empirical Test of Semantic Hypotheses Relevant to the Language of Young Children." Technical Memorandum 2-74-07. Los Alamitos, Calif.: SWRL Educational Research and Development, November 30, 1974.
   P. L. Coker, "On the Acquisition of Temporal Terms." Ph.D. dissertation. Irvine, Calif.: University of California Irvine, 1975.

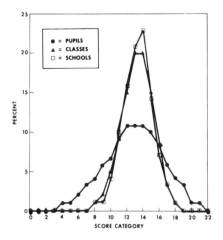

Figure 7.1. Entry survey score distributions

Unit Proficiency and Completion

During BRP instruction, pupils complete a twenty-item test at the end of each of the ten units. These unit tests are scored by teachers and reported on the BRP Record Sheet. Figure 7.2 summarizes the composite results provided by these tests for pupils, classes, and schools. Because the results were so similar for each of the ten units, they were not presented separately. Instead, the raw scores for pupils and the composite averages for classes and schools were used. The distributions of these three measures—pupil raw scores, class composite averages, and school composite averages—are presented. Note for the pupil score distribution, the highest score, 20, is the one most frequently obtained, with 19 being the next most frequently occurring and so on down to a score of 12. Too few pupils obtain scores below 12, 60 percent proficiency, to account for even 1 percent of the total sample. Such a distribution of pupil scores shows the classic pattern associated with instructional mastery. All pupils fall in the range of 60 percent (12 of 20 items correct) to 100 percent (20 of 20 items correct) mastery, with the distribution of the scores being negatively skewed, i.e., the highest scores occur most frequently.

Although the results are not presented here separately for pupils in classes with the various biosocial characteristics referred to earlier, they did prove to be quite similar. Classes with pupils from all of the various biosocial categories showed the same "mastery" pattern on the unit tests. The results showed the average proficiency for all classes was 89 percent, nearly 18 items correct out of 20. This average ranged from 81 percent to 93 percent for classes across the various biosocial categories.

The data on the units completed presented in figure 7.3 show a somewhat different pattern of results. Looking at the results for pupils first, it shows that

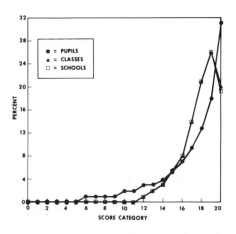

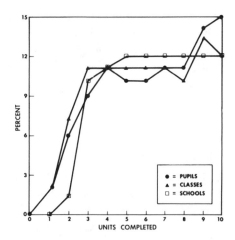

Figure 7.2. BRP unit criterion exercise score distributions

Figure 7.3. BRP unit completion distributions

significant numbers fell into each of the possible unit completion categories—1 to 10. Although more pupils completed all ten units than any other number, only 15 percent of the pupils actually completed 10 units. The distribution tends to resemble a rectangle, with about the same numbers (and percent) of pupils falling into each unit completion category (with the exception of no units completed). More specifically, about 10 percent of the pupils fall into each of the unit completion categories from 2 to 9, with about 2 percent completing one unit and 15 percent completing all ten units.

At the class level, these data indicate that the average class completed six of the ten program units, and they spread out in such a way that the fastest 25 percent (one-fourth) of the classes completed eight or more units and the slowest 25 percent four or fewer units. This reflects tremendous differences across classes in the extent to which they implemented the program with pupils.

This tremendous variability in program units completed for the total set of pupils and classes is also present when classes are divided into biosocial categories. To illustrate, we may consider the results when classes are divided into categories based on the dominant racial ethnic background of pupils. For this biosocial characteristic the categories used are Black, Spanish-surnamed, and Other. Classes were considered to be in a given category when 50 percent of the pupils from the school were from that category. In this case, the data showed classes categorized as Black completed on average 4.8 units, Spanish-surnamed, 5.2 units, and Other, 6.5 units. Considering that completion of a unit of the program represents about three weeks of instruction (give or take a week), such differences are substantial. This same pattern of results is consistent across the other biosocial characteristics—parental income level, prior school reading level, eligibility for Title I funding, and so on. Differences that were often larger than those shown for the ethnic background characteristic existed between classes grouped into the various categories and usually in a manner corresponding to our usual expectations for high and low school achievement.

End-of-Year Proficiency

The effects of the program's instruction were assessed by a test given to pupils at the end of the school year. It provided separate scores on four specific outcomes: Letter Names—identifying written letters given their name orally; Word Elements—identifying written decoding elements given their sounds; Words—identifying written words given orally; and Sentence Reading— reading aloud sentences composed of words taught in the program. Distributions of the scores obtained on each of these outcomes are depicted in figure 7.4 for pupils, classes, and schools.

They show two patterns of results that are readily understood given the way instruction on these outcomes is presented in the program and the previously discussed pattern of unit completion by users. For the letter names outcome especially, but for the word elements outcome and, to a lesser extent, the words outcome, the data approximate the pattern referred to earlier as "mastery." The reader will note that for all three outcomes the highest score was achieved by more pupils than any other score. With letter names, about 82 percent of the pupils obtained the highest possible score, 6 out of 6 correct. The number attaining the next lowest score, 5 out of 6 correct, is the next most frequently attained, and so on. Consequently, the line showing the figure starts near the bottom for low scores and rises very quickly to the top for high scores, i.e., it is very negatively skewed. For the word elements and the words outcomes, both the percentage of pupils obtaining the highest score is lower and the "rise" from low to high scores is more gradual.

The sentence reading outcome shows a second, less common distribution of scores. While the highest score is the one most frequently attained by pupils, the percentage of pupils falling in the successively lower score categories does not decline very rapidly. More specifically, between 8 and 11 percent of the pupils attain each possible score from 0 to 9, with about 19 percent attaining the maximum score of 10.

How can we interpret the different patterns of scores across these outcomes? The most straightforward explanation of these score patterns is in terms of the instructional emphasis given to the outcomes in various units of the program. The letter names and word elements are all introduced in the early units of the program. Because most classes completed four or more units, it is not surprising that very high score patterns were observed on these outcomes.

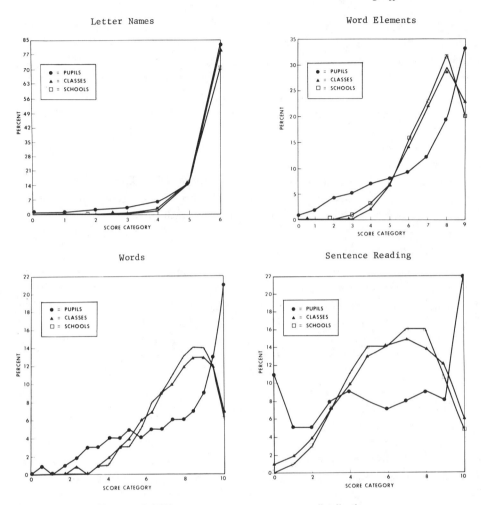

Figure 7.4. BRP assessment outcome score distributions

The introduction of the words tested in the words outcome is also emphasized very heavily in the early units, but new word introductions also occur in the later units of the program. Therefore, the pattern of scores should show more variability for this outcome than on the letter names and word elements. The sentence reading outcome shows by far the greatest variability in outcome scores, which makes sense in terms of the program emphasizing this skill—pupils read sentences more in the later units (those beyond unit 6) than in the earlier ones.

When the average scores of classes in the various biosocial categories were summarized, they showed that all categories of users did score well on the letter names and word elements outcomes; there was little difference between categories traditionally scoring high and low on educational achievement differences. For the words outcome, and, to a greater extent for the sentence reading outcome, there were substantial differences across the biosocial characteristic categories. For example, classes in schools that typically scored above average on standardized tests had an average proficiency of 69.1 and 50.4 on the words and sentence reading outcome, respectively. By way of contrast, classes in schools typically having below average standardized reading test performance had average percentage scores of 51.8 and 29.9 on these two assessment outcomes.

The differences in patterns across both instructional outcome categories and biosocial characteristic categories provide an opportunity to examine the instructional determinants of "disadvantaged" school settings.

Understanding the Results

To help place the inquiry in perspective it is helpful to review the results against the background of findings from earlier studies of schooling effects. Considering only the descriptive data on the pupils, classes, and schools in this inquiry, it is clear that the participants included all of the diverse pupil and school characteristics present in kindergartens. Further, the pupils tended to overrepresent groups that traditionally have low educational achievement. This can be seen in the high proportion of pupils from lower income levels, from ethnic minorities, from ESEA Title I eligible schools, and from schools with poor standardized reading test performance in the study sample as compared to the total national school population.

What proficiencies do these pupils bring to kindergarten? The data from the entry survey show that pupils typically entered schools with considerable proficiency on the concepts and skills needed to begin reading instruction—prereading skills. The level of proficiency they possessed, however, varied widely across classes and schools. Further, the relative level of proficiency for classes varied directly with the biosocial characteristics of the schools and pupils and in a predictable manner. Those schools typically considered "disadvantaged" tended to have lower proficiencies than those considered "advantaged." The results were perfectly consistent across indicators as diverse as parental income level, prior reading performance, racial ethnic background, and school location.

This order of differences corresponds identically to the differences observed and documented in numerous schooling effects surveys and studies, such as Coleman et al.,[15] though the numerical differences provided here reflect more precisely the actual distance between groups in the substance and skills addressed by the Kindergarten Program.

15 Coleman. *Equality of Educational Opportunity.*

The results for the Beginning Reading Program measures made during and after instruction present a mixed set. Those made during instruction show that users in all of the biosocial characteristic categories attained high levels of proficiency on the unit tests for the units they completed. The number of units completed does not display comparable uniformity. Instead, considerable variability exists for classes in the number of units completed. For the total sample of 2,000 classes, one-quarter of the classes completed eight or more units, one-half completed between four and eight units, and one-quarter completed less than four units.

Further, the data show substantial variability in units completed both *across* the various biosocial characteristic categories and also *within* each of the biosocial categories. The average number of units completed by classes in the various biosocial categories corresponds to the crucial pattern observed on the entry survey. The classes in "disadvantaged" settings completed less of the program units than those in the "advantaged" settings with no exceptions. This result is consistent with earlier studies of schooling effects that were based on standardized test results, the National Assessment, and so forth.

As should occur when there are differences in the amount of instruction delivered—units completed—there are differences in proficiency on the program outcomes. This was reflected on the Beginning Reading Program assessment administered at the end of the year. For the letter name and word element outcomes, these differences were reduced because these outcomes receive heaviest instructional emphasis in the earlier program units. Since most classes finished these units, most pupils learned them. This raised the average level of proficiency and reduced the variability that might otherwise have occurred. The average performance of classes on these two outcomes (letter names and word elements) approaches that expected if all classes completed all units and instructional emphasis was equally distributed across all units. For the words outcome, the performance pattern was nearly as "good" as that for the letter names and word element outcomes. More of the words that are tested in it are presented in the later units, however, so the level of performance (proficiency) is somewhat lower. The results for the sentence reading outcome contrast markedly with this pattern. This outcome receives the heaviest instructional emphasis in the later BRP units. Therefore, as expected, both a lower average performance and more variability were observed on this outcome than on the others. Also, the average scores attained by classes within the biosocial characteristic categories differed substantially.

There are two possible explanations for the differences observed in proficiency across classes on the sentence reading outcome of the assessment. The differences could be created by differential instructional completion rates by classes in the various biosocial categories, that is, different groups might do different amounts of studying. But the variability could also be a function of differential ability traits of pupils from different categories. The choice be-tween these two explanations has important educational, scientific, and societal implications. If schooling has an effect on pupils, the first explanation should hold. But if schooling is impotent against biological and social characteristics of pupils, the second explanation should hold. Since educational R&D has heretofore been unable to produce any systematic evidence to support the schooling explanation, the odds overwhelmingly favor the biosocial explana-tion.

These data thus provide a new opportunity to examine the old question of individual differences in pupil learning. All pupils received instruction from the same Beginning Reading Program during the year. At the end of the year, some had learned more than others. Those who learned less tended to be individuals from financially poor, inner city, ethnic minority families, the "educational disadvantaged." But the "disadvantaged" designation only sharpens the problem without pointing to a solution. This is where previous inquiries have stopped, counseling general despair or radical revolution in the face of a massive problem judged to be beyond solution by schools.

All differences in instructional effects have commonly been attributed to noninstructional phenomena. But suppose the same product system, Beginning Reading Program, that was used with all pupils was used differentially with pupils. If the instructional product is indeed effective, it would follow that outcome variability would be created by the manipulable features of instruction rather than being a "fixed" characteristic beyond the influence of schools. The more effective the instructional product and the greater the differential use with categories of individuals, the greater the individual differences among pupils.

If this conjecture were to hold, it would lead to dramatically different impli-cations regarding instruction and schooling than have been drawn from previ-ous research. Rather than concluding that each child must receive unique instruction, it would follow that unique individuals can benefit from instruction with a common product system. Rather than concluding that accountability falls only on pupils and teachers, instructional resources too would be respon-sible for producing results. Rather than concluding that only a total reform can raise schooling from its "miserable status," it would follow that there are more logically and financially available means for strengthening schooling. Other inferences will occur to the reader, who will also have concluded by now that the data do point to the plausibility of this second explanation about the power of (some) schooling effects.

EDUCATIONAL DISADVANTAGE: INSTRUCTIONAL OR INDIVIDUAL?

As a first step, let us consider whether there is a positive relationship between number of units completed and end-of-year proficiency. To simplify, only data on the sentence reading outcome of the end-of-year assessment will be con-

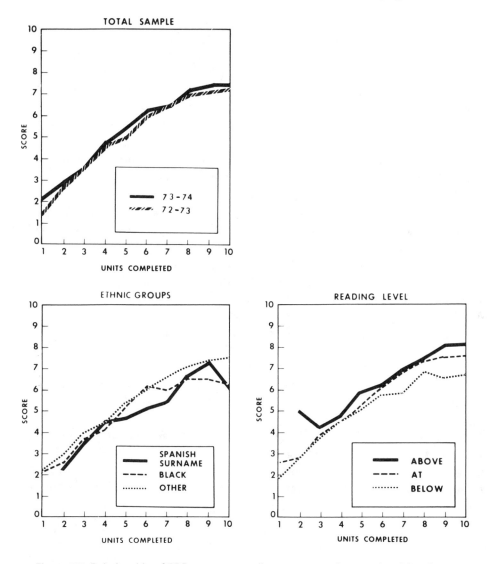

Figure 7.5. Relationship of BRP sentence reading score to units completed for classes

sidered. These data are presented in figure 7.5 for the total sample of classes and for the categories within two of the biosocial characteristics: school reading level and ethnic groups.

To receive credit for the sentence reading outcome a pupil must read *all* words of a sentence correctly. Coupled with the fairly even distribution across the program of instructional emphasis on practice decoding words, reading sight words, and reading sentences aloud, the expectation is that performance on this test should increase as the number of units completed increases. The data for this outcome show very clearly the expected pattern of increase in average score with increasing units completed.

The sensitivity of this sentence reading outcome to the effects of schooling/instruction is remarkable from a technical measurement perspective. It is sensitive to instructional increments at all levels, and the changes in proficiency associated with instructional increments are close to equal. As each additional unit of the program is completed, the average score of classes on the sentence outcome in that unit completion category increases by about one point. Since there are ten units of the program and ten items on the sentence test, the correspondence works out to be quite close.

There is a positive and regular relationship between number of units completed and the end-of-year proficiency for the total sample of classes, but does that cheerful prospect hold within the various biosocial characteristics of users? Figure 7.5 also provides the data on this relationship for two of the biosocial indicators: ethnic groups and reading level. The results show that it holds not only for the total sample, but also for groups below and above the national reading median and for the two ethnic minority pupil groups. Across all categories there continues to be a positive relation between number of units completed and end-of-year proficiency and with comparable levels of proficiency. The latter means, for example, that five units of the program with classes of predominantly Black pupils produces about the same learning as expressed by the sentence outcome score as five units with either minority or non-minority (Other) groups. Proficiency regularly increases as a function of the number of units completed for each characteristic category.

Educational R&D—along with schools in general—has been accused of being unable to do anything to change pupil learning, particularly in the area of reading. These results are important because they support a critical goal of the programmatic R&D: to provide resources for effective instruction across the full range of children found in schools. Approximately equal proficiency increments were registered by all user groups as more units of the program were completed.

Units Completed and Instructional Time

While the data in Figure 7.5 support the expectation that a strong relationship between instruction delivered by teachers and proficiency attained by pupils would exist for our program, it still does not answer two other basic questions raised earlier. More specifically, "Why do certain pupils and classes complete fewer units of the program?" Once again there are two possibilities. One explanation is that certain classes and pupils require more instructional time than others to complete the same amount of instruction. This explanation is the one typically put forth for the slower progress of the disadvantaged, for example, in completing basic skill instruction.

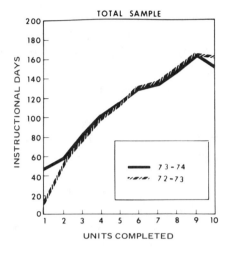

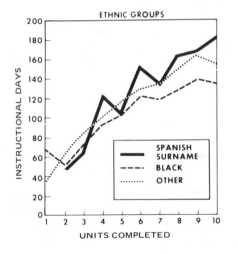

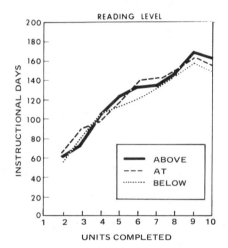

Figure 7.6. Relationship of instructional days to units completed for classes

Another possibility is that the differences in the amount of instruction received is due to differences in the amount of time spent in instruction. This explanation can be examined in this study since data on the amount of instructional time spent (measured in average number of days) by classes completing different numbers of program units were obtained, as depicted in figure 7.6.

The results are presented both for the total set of classes and for the same two biosocial characteristics categories: ethnic groups and reading levels. The results for the total sample show a regular increase in the number of instructional days spent by classes completing more program units.

This relationship was found to hold in both years of the inquiry, which is important in this context because it establishes an operational basis for the differences observed in the amount of the Beginning Reading Program completed by classes. This is perhaps best understood if the relationship had not held. In that case, the expectation is that a parallel line would be found in figure 7.6, i.e., all classes would spend about the same number of instructional days but some would complete more units than others. These data clearly refute that notion by showing clear support for the proposition that the more days (time) spent on instruction the more units completed.

There is, however, another aspect to this proposition, and that is, "Does it hold across the biosocial characteristic categories?"

Classes with predominantly Black pupils and Spanish-surnamed pupils show the same pattern of units completed and instructional days spent as both all Other classes and the total sample of classes. In fact, on the average, these minority classes actually completed the same number of units in fewer instructional days than classes with nonminority pupils.

The same results held up when classes were divided based on the prior school standardized reading performance. Classes in schools that scored above, at, and below the national norms in reading were virtually identical in the number of instructional days they spent to complete the same number of Beginning Reading Program units.

Instruction Received and Entering Proficiency

The preceding result is so important and runs so counter to prior educational findings and speculations that it warrants further examination. Hence, another set of analyses was carried out using the units completed and instructional time data with the results of the entry survey. Classes were divided on the basis of their entry survey score—the average across all pupils in the class on the entry survey test. On this basis, ten groups of classes ordered from low to high and each representing about 10 percent of the total sample, about 500 classes, were designated. For each of these groups, the average number of units completed and number of instructional days spent were calculated. The data on units completed by classes in the various entry survey score categories are shown in figure 7.7.

These data show a clear relationship between class entry survey performance and units completed; when entry survey performance increases, the number of units completed increases.

Examination of the pattern of units completed within the biosocial categories shows this same pattern of increasing units completed with increasing entry survey proficiency. But it also shows that there are real differences in the slopes of the lines for classes in the different biosocial categories. For example,

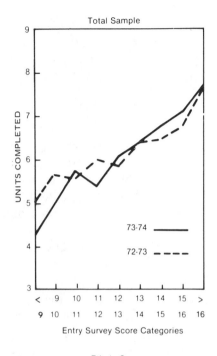

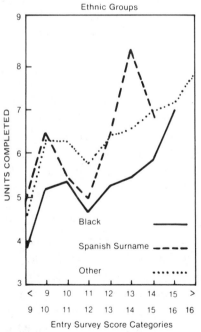

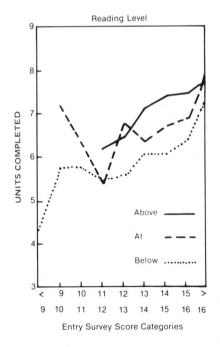

The abscissa labels should be read less than 9, 9 to 10 (read vertically), etc.

Figure 7.7. Relationship of units completed to entry survey score categories for classes

pupils in schools that typically score above the national norms on standardized reading tests tend to complete about two full units more than schools scoring below the national norm, within the same level of children's entering proficiency. This difference is slightly greater than two units for classes in the entry survey categories with means less than 11.0 and slightly less than two units for those with entry survey means greater than 13.0 (see figure 7.7). A similar pattern holds across the ethnic groups and for the income and location groups that are not shown here. In each case, the users in the categories that typically have lower levels of achievement—income of $5,000 or less, inner city, and Black—were disadvantaged by receiving fewer units of instruction on the average than those in typically higher achieving groups—income of $12,000 or more, suburban location, and nonminority pupils—given that they had the *same* entering ability level.

These results suggest the tendency for some children to get *taught* and for others with *equal* entering proficiency who happen to be in different situations to get *caught* instructionally. The most noteworthy aspect of this tendency is that children generally held to be advantaged are those taught, and children alleged to be disadvantaged are those caught. This fact was most clearly illustrated by the school location data which are not given here.[16] Classes in suburban areas tend to complete six and seven units of the program irrespective of the entry level status of pupils. For inner city locations the number of program units completed ranges from 3.2 to 7.9 units, depending upon the entry level status of pupils. This represents substantial differences (over three units) in the amount of instruction delivered, especially to pupils in the lower entry survey categories.

On the basis of these findings, the attainment of educational equality is not nearly so abstract and nebulous an aspiration for the future as it has been in the past. These results suggest that at least some of the factors required to make educational equality a reality are present within schools and need to be exercised. Much can be accomplished simply by ensuring that the decidedly unintended and unintentional disadvantaging results such as implied by these data do not occur.

The data imply that to some extent "advantaging" occurs in identifiable form from year to year as well as within a school year. Figure 7.7 includes comparative data on these relationsips for the overall samples of the two inquiry years. These data show a slight shift in this relationship across the two years, with the 1973–74 classes in the higher entry survey categories completing more units on the average than they did in 1972–73. This may mean "equality" is working from the top down, since those in the lower categories

16 Hanson and Schutz, "Effects of Programmatic R&D on Schooling and Effects of Schooling on Students," 1975.
   Hanson and Schutz, "Instructional Product Implementation and Schooling Effects," 1976.

completed about the same number of units as the 1972–73 classes. Although two years of data represent too little information to completely document a trend, this differential is well worth noting. The pattern may be suggesting another manipulable source—the teacher's decision as to how much to try to teach to whom—that contributes to educational "disadvantage."

If the differences in units completed are related to differences in the days of program use, the relationship between instructional days and entry survey score category also ought to hold. The data in figure 7.8 confirm that this is so. Instructional days increase regularly across the entry survey score categories.

The data in figure 7.8 suggest that the differences in the units completed by the various user groups can best be accounted for by the number of days spent on instruction. Operationally their importance on program instruction and schooling in general is large. For example, in the case of the Black classes as compared to Other classes with the same entry level proficiency, the average *difference* in instructional days ranges from twenty-five to fifty-three days, or between five and ten weeks of instruction. Given that approximately two weeks of instruction are typically required to complete a unit, the importance of this difference in amount of program instruction delivered is clear.

However, this racial ethnic group difference was not the largest observed. The largest difference in units completed occurred when classes were divided into categories by school location. The suburban classes spent an average of seventy more calendar days (fourteen weeks, or almost half of the academic year!) on Beginning Reading Program instruction than did urban and inner city classes, and approximately one-hundred more days than rural classes in corresponding entry survey intervals. On this basis alone, pupils in schools located in different areas can experience a schooling disadvantage equivalent to over one-half a year of reading instruction.

Comparative data for the two years on this relationship are very consistent. The 1973–74 data show classes from the lower entry survey score intervals spent slightly *fewer* days than corresponding classes in 1972—73, whereas classes from the higher entry survey score intervals spent *more* time. Again the implications for clarifying the meaning of educational disadvantage are provocative.

In brief, the data consistently support the explanation that the differences in program performance among the various categories of users result from differences in the number of days spent on instruction rather than from any differential effectiveness of instruction applied to pupils with different biosocial characteristics. The SWRL/Ginn Beginning Reading Program appears to work as efficiently or more efficiently with users in the typically lower-achieving user categories as with other groups. The data indicate that the concept of the "educationally disadvantaged" is a creation of manipulable and manipulated conditions readily under the control of schools rather than a condition resulting from immutable genetic and environmental factors that inherently impede schooling. When teachers teach, pupils learn! The instructional accomplishments of both teachers and pupils under such circumstances deserve better treatment than they have been accorded by earlier research findings on schooling effects.

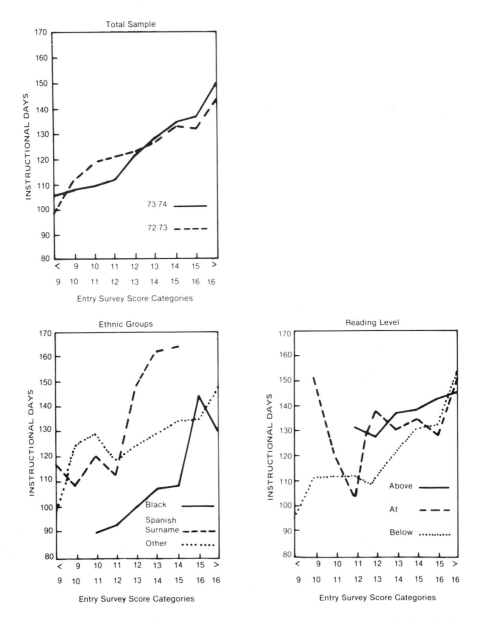

Figure 7.8. Relationship of instructional days to entry survey score categories for classes

MEANING OF INQUIRY FOR SCHOOLS

The results of this inquiry provide evidence that professional advances in education can be achieved through programmatic R&D, which produces useful educational technology and products. The results demonstrate that schools and students (and educational R&D laboratories and centers) have the inherent potential for creditable and credible instructional success. Programmatic R&D in education can provide the necessary wherewithal to realize this potential with important and impressive results for both students and schools. With well-developed instructional products produced by programmatic R&D, alleged biosocial deficiencies of students either prove fictional or readily circumventable. In sum, good R&D makes possible good instruction by schools, which makes possible good performance by students.

The effects of schooling appear not only replicable and reliable but impressive when instruction is supported by well-developed instructional products. An instructional product, like any product, *can* be used poorly; implementation does vary. However, over our two-year measurement period, the results are encouraging. All information regarding the second-year installation indicates increasing implementation success. Schools appeared to use the program during the second year with somewhat greater ease and effectiveness.

More importantly, there is every indication that the results obtained with the Kindergarten Program are under the instructional control of the schools. That is, schools using the program are in position to determine the instructional effects they wish to achieve independent of student and school characteristics. Furthermore, administrators as well as teachers have an accurate picture of the emphasis required on their part to produce these instructional effects.

Overall, there are indications that user groups displaying the lowest levels of proficiency in 1972–73 showed increased effectiveness in the second year of program implementation. These include minority groups, ESEA Title I eligible schools, lower income levels, and urban and inner city locations. However, there are still signs of subtle but distinct means by which children in such settings are treated disadvantageously in instruction. By identifying educational disadvantages in terms of conditions within rather than outside the direct discretion of schools, it should be possible to counter and eliminate the unintended negative consequences of such treatment in the future. In sum, effective instruction and teaching work with all pupils and should be tried more often!

Implications for Change

Attention to educational change has focused on personnel and pocketbook considerations. An alternative approach is provided by the experience and methods of programmatic R&D. In this approach, fundamental and dependable educational changes occur by the transfer of proven means from a context of educational R&D to the schools. This transfer is *not* akin to other laboratory/

real world transfers. The techniques, materials, etc., involved in the present "change effort" were derived from a naturalistic (school and teaching-based) inquiry that involved the schools, rather than from artificial conditions created simply for research purposes. Controlled laboratory experiments, animal studies, and other conventional lines of educationally related inquiry may yield useful information, but they do not yield direct educational change.

There are two methodological parts to the programmatic R&D change paradigm. The first resides in those techniques used to identify the ways schools need to be changed to be more effective. The second is in those techniques used to transfer the means to bring about this change from the R&D context to the school context.

The first aspect of the methodology begins with the central concern of the schools, its instructional program, and works from it to identify the forces influencing those operations. The R&D described here originally involved the development of new research-based instructional programs, their installation and use in schools under natural schooling conditions, and R&D's efforts to make them more effective. The procedures used were neither experimental nor clinical but what Bronfenbrenner,[17] McCall,[18] and other have called "ecologically valid research." Through this process, factors that turned out to be common to all school instructional programs emerged. Once these factors are identified, informational mechanisms designed to alter them can be devised.[19]

The second aspect of the methodology concerns the transfer of the knowledge and technology acquired via the first process back into the control of schools. It is carried out by providing schools with the capability to understand and define the kind of "schooling effects" they wish to achieve. An important element in this process is the notion that school personnel with various areas of responsibilities, such as administration, evaluation, testing, and instruction, be provided with accurate information on pupil learning, i.e., instructional effects throughout schooling operations. This information would define the actions to be taken to improve school operations, and is itself the primary mechanism for change. The conditions and the ways in which schools can obtain such straightforward information are far from clear at this time. Clarifying those conditions should be a challenge both to schools and the R&D community.

One final point about the methodology. This approach does not deny or disregard the necessary contributions of money and people to educational change. It simply ensures that the public gets something for its investment in

17 U. Bronfenbrenner, "The Experimental Ecology of Education," *Educational Researcher,* Vol. 5, No. 9, 1976, pp. 5–15.

18 R. B. McCall, "Challenges to a Science of Developmental Psychology, *Child Development,* Vol. 48, No. 2, 1977, pp. 333–344.

19 G. Behr and R. A. Hanson, "Supporting Program Implementation." Paper presented at the annual meeting of the American Educational Research Association in New York, April 1977.

education and that professionals have the instructional wherewithal to accomplish the public's expected institutional outcomes of schooling in a creditable and credible manner. Further, it does not mean to imply that educational R&D such as that described in this chapter has only direct implications for schools via operational procedures and programs. Rather, it should have a general impact through altering the prevailing conceptions of the "impotence" of schools and the current despair at the prospect of the schools' ability to teach basic skills such as reading.

For example, the described relationship between program units completed and pupil learning, i.e., sentence reading proficiency, and the relationship of instructional units completed to instructional time fit nicely and in some ways extend some of the current theory and practice referred to as "mastery learning." Mastery learning has been referred to by a number of different theorists but most notably by Carroll[20] and Bloom.[21] The basic tenet of mastery learning can be summarized as follows:

> . . . variations in learning and the level of learning of students are determined by the students' learning history and the quality of instruction they receive. Appropriate modifications related to the history of the learners and the quality of instruction can sharply reduce the variation of students and greatly increase their level of learning and their effectiveness in learning in terms of time and effort expended.[22]

The present inquiry provides strong confirmation of the basic relationship implied between learning and instructional time. It also suggests, however, that some of the conceptual models[23] in which this relationship has been embedded may be unnecessarily complex especially in terms of the requirements for the "quality of instruction." Instructional programs using well-developed (and researched) product systems appear to be capable (at least in the areas of basic skills instruction—reading, spelling, composition) of accommodating the full range of pupil instructional needs. Given such instructional resources, the basic relationship between time and learning becomes an operational reality which schools can use in planning and providing schooling effects.

20 J. Carroll, "A model of school learning," *Teachers College Record,* Vol. 64, 1963, pp. 723–733.
21 B. S. Bloom. *Human Characteristics and School Learning.* New York: McGraw-Hill, 1976.
22 Ibid., p. 16.
23 Examples of such models are presented by: W. Cooley and P. Lohnes. *Evaluation Research in Education.* New York: Halsted Press, 1976.
    A. Harnischfeger and D. E. Wiley, "The Teaching-Learning Process in Elementary Schools: A Synoptic View," *Curriculum Inquiry,* Vol. 6, No. 1, 1976, pp. 5–43.

CHAPTER 8

The Nonimplementation of EEP: "All That Money for Business as Usual"[1]

CONSTANCIA WARREN

The New York City schools' Experimental Elementary Programs were, from the very beginning, the result of a compromise. The United Federation of Teachers wanted a continuation and expansion of their More Effective Schools Programs. The MES program began in 1963 as a plan "for saturating ghetto schools with compensatory services,"[2] such as reduced class size and extra staff. MES started in twenty schools, over the opposition of civil rights leaders who objected to the program's location solely in ghetto schools. But MES, when evaluated by the Board of Education and the Center for Urban Education, had proved unsuccessful in raising reading levels.[3] Moreover, the board wanted a program with greater emphasis on the evaluation of experimental efforts, especially those entailing increased staff assistance.

The result of this compromise was EEP, a program that in many ways resembled the MES program. The 1967 contract agreements between the Board of Education and the United Federation of Teachers specified that $10 million would be spent the following year in a series of experimental programs aimed at testing methods to improve the academic achievement of children whose performance fell far below national norms. These programs were designed by a committee from the board, the union, parent associations, and headed by Professor Edmund Gordon of Teachers College, Columbia University.[4] The committee studied innovations in compensatory education across the country, and, in June 1968, submitted its final report to then superintendent of schools, Bernard Donovan, suggesting four models, or combinations of programs, to be

---

1 This is a much revised version of an earlier article, "Organizational Role Conflict and Innovation in Big City Schools: The Case of E.E.P.," prepared with the support of the ERIC Clearinghouse on Urban Education at Teachers College, Columbia University. The author wishes to thank Dr. Edmund Gordon for his assistance in the development of that article.
2 David Rogers. *110 Livingston Street: Politics and Bureaucracy in the New York City School System.* New York, N.Y.: Random House, 1968, p. 197.
3 Ibid., p. 284.
4 This committee became known as the Gordon Committee.

tried in New York City, and recommending the extension of the experiment to four years.[5]

Admonishing the board that extensive planning would be necessary to implement the programs, the committee ended its formal role. During the summer of 1968, eleven schools were selected as sites, but the acrimonious teacher strike of 1968 delayed actual initiation of the programs until January 1969. Thus, while EEP began early in 1969, the first full year of implementation was 1969-70.

The committee recommendations stressed the need for scientific evaluation of the implementation and effectiveness of EEP in raising the achievement levels of students. An interdisciplinary team designed and supervised the evaluation. A research associate was assigned to each school, and was equipped with a variety of methods such as staff interaction analysis, parent surveys, student attitude scales, decision-making analysis, and student achievement tests.[6] The research associates' findings were dismal. The tests showed the children seemed to be achieving no better than before. This failure could not be blamed solely on errors in the design, however. There was much confusion about what EEP was intended to be, in terms of both objectives and specific programs. Many aspects of the design were poorly implemented; others were hardly implemented at all.[7] Nor did the evaluation improve the situation; it remained almost the same in the following two years, though slow progress was made in certain areas. These areas, however, such as the introduction of paraprofessional staff, were those in which the same amount of progress was made in non-EEP schools during that time. Commented Bruce Dollar, one of the evaluators:

> What was most appalling was the way these schools managed to absorb $40 million [over four years] while we searched vainly for signs of implementation. All that money for business as usual.

Why, with all the technical and financial resources available, did EEP fail so miserably? Why were the programs not implemented as designed? While it is true that the 1968 teacher strike created an atmosphere of suspicion and resistance to outside intervention, the strike cannot be blamed for the failure of EEP. Many of the same problems would have occurred without the strike,

5 Among the proposals were: school/community councils, an extended school day, clustered classes, paraprofessionals, individualized instruction, psychoeducational appraisal experts, special classes for children with chronic problems, new classroom staffing patterns, health teams, early diagnosis of learning problems, tutorial clinics, reading resource centers, and formal education beginning at age three. *Final Report of the Committee on Experimental Program to Improve Educational Achievements in Special Service Schools,* June 20, 1968.

6 Field Evaluation Group. *Field Study of the Implementation of the Experimental Elementary Program: 1969–70.* New York, N.Y.: Horace Mann-Lincoln Institute, Teachers College, Columbia University, 1970.

7 Ibid.

although, perhaps with less intensity. MES had met some of the same problems. Wrote one critic at the time:

> Some of the most essential aspects of the More Effective Schools program have not been used: the flexibility, the democracy of staff participation, the freedom to depart from the curriculum in new ways, the research and evaluation process and the interaction with the community. The fault is not with the paper program, but with the people.[8]

Nor was the problem lack of resources. A failing common to efforts in compensatory education was that the funding, while an impressive lump sum, was spread too thinly to have any real effect. But in EEP, $10 million a year divided among eleven schools, even subtracting headquarters personnel costs, gave each school upwards of three-quarters of a million dollars in addition to its regular budget. The problem lay in the lack of implementation, rendering the extensive research and design efforts of the Gordon Committee and its staff virtually useless in many cases.

Essentially, EEP utilized a role change model to foster innovation in an organization with a strong built-in resistance to change—without sufficient sanctions to overcome these barriers. While naiveté about the nature of the organization might be blamed for this lack in the beginning of the experiment, the first evaluation report should have stimulated action in this area. The failure to add support mechanisms once the weaknesses were pointed out cannot be so lightly dismissed. What appears more likely is that neither the administration nor the union wanted EEP to succeed, and they made this clear by not acting forcefully to encourage better implementation.

The Role Change Model   Role, as it is used here, has two aspects: structure and value.

> *Structure* means the *location* of the particular position within the organization in relation to other positions, the *dimensions* or formal requirements of that position, and the *sanctions* available to insure proper enactment of role responsibilities.

> *Value* means the normative expectations for appropriate attitude and behavior of the individuals who fill the positions. These expectations may or may not be articulated, but they belong to the individual who fills the positions, rather than to the position *per se*.[9]

In the hierarchy of the school, there are a wide variety of roles: teacher,

8 Gloria Channon, "The More Effective Schools," *The Urban Review*, February 1967, p. 24.
9 These definitions are an amalgam of definitions of role by different sociologists. See Theodore Sarbin and Ralph Turner, "Role," in the *International Encyclopedia of the Social Sciences*, Vol. 13. New York, N.Y.: Crowell, Collier, and Macmillan, 1962, pp. 546–557.

principal, guidance counselor, student and so forth. In structural terms, each of these roles exists in known relationship to others (location) and carries formal requirements of the behavior of the role occupant relevant to duties to and interaction with the others (dimension). The location of a teacher within the organization of the school, for example, is in fairly specific relation to students, parents, administrators, and colleagues. In addition, outside the school, the teacher may be located in similar networks of relationships to family, social groups, civic groups and the like.

The dimensions of the teacher's role may include teaching, the creation of support for and acceptance of the school in the community, maintenance of rapport with parents, and participation in school activities with other faculty members. Some of these duties may be part of the teacher's role with respect to specific individuals, while others may be part of the teacher's general role in relation to the school environment as a whole. There is inevitably some conflict between the different duties the teacher must fulfill. How the conflict is resolved is shown by the actual behavior of each individual.

Where there is ambivalence for the individual, organizational sanctions can be used to guide his or her actions. Failure to fulfill teaching obligations may result in the loss of the job. Less serious offenses may be met with nonmaterial sanctions in the hope of altering behavior. Nonpunitive sanctions may also be brought to bear in shaping the behavior of the individual. Whatever the sanction applied, the purpose is the same: to insure that role requirements are met.

Within this structure, individual role occupants have sets of expectations about how they will fulfill the obligations of their positions and interact with others in the organization. Many of the expectations of the individuals in the school come under the rubric of professionalism.

> In the professional relationship, . . . the professional dictates what is good or evil for the client, who has no choice but to accede to professional judgment. Here the premise is that, because he lacks the requisite theoretical background, the client cannot diagnose his own needs or discriminate among the range of possibilities for meeting them. Nor is the client considered able to evaluate the caliber of the professional services he receives.[10]

In the schools, professionalism manifests itself in the organizational belief that only administrative and instructional personnel are capable of deciding how best to educate the children. The less educated the parent, the less he or she is respected by the school personnel, and parents of low educational levels are often held in near contempt by school personnel in matters concerning the education of their own children.

In situations of conflict between formal role requirements and the role expec-

10 Ernest Greenwood, "The Elements of Professionalization," in Howard M. Vollmer and Donald L. Mills, eds. *Professionalization*. Englewood Cliffs, N.J.: Prentice-Hall, 1966, p. 12.

tations of the individual, individuals will choose the more comfortable alternative. Thus, in a situation where the formal requirements were less preferred than the individual's expectations, the resulting behavior of the individual would be to act in accordance with his or her own expectations. The application of sanctions either rewarding performance or punishing noncompliance could make behaving in accordance with the formal requirements the more comfortable alternative.

Taken as a whole, role behavior reflects not only the resolution of existing role conflicts, but also a pattern of mutually beneficial relationships for those involved. Were the behavior to cease providing mutual benefit, that individual feeling the loss would perceive a conflict between his or her own expectations and those of others, and would act to alter the situation.

EEP, as a role change model, sought change by the addition of a host of new roles, as well as by altering the locations and dimensions of many of the existing roles. The design, however, was not self-consciously a role-change model, and dealt poorly with the aspects of structural change expected for the proper implementation of EEP. Also, these changes were a challenge to values held by the individuals involved in executing the change. When faced with a conflict between old roles and new, old structures and new, old values and new, most chose the more comfortable path—the one already familiar—rather than the one toward change.

Existing Resistances to Change   In any change effort, it is necessary to recognize the forces within an organization that resist change, and to take these into account in planning for implementation. Those barriers to innovation in the schools are both numerous and formidable. EEP faced the hierarchical structure of the schools, a structure agreed by many to constitute an impediment in any organization. Pressman and Wildavsky, in discussing the difficulties in implementing a program funded by the Economic Development Administration, found that the greater the number of administrative levels through which a change effort must pass between innovator and implementer, the greater the possibility that the original design will be changed, if not subverted outright.

> We are initially surprised because we do not begin to appreciate the number of steps involved, the number of participants whose preferences have to be taken into account, the number of separate decisions that are part of what we think of as a single one. Least of all do we appreciate the geometric growth of interdependencies over time where each negotiation involves a number of participants with decisions to make, whose implications ramify over time.[11]

11 Jeffrey L. Pressman and Aaron B. Wildavsky. *Implementation*. Berkeley, Calif.: University of California Press, 1973, p. 93.

This problem becomes particularly significant when implementation requires the action of those at the bottom of the hierarchy to succeed. Abbott, in discussing the educational hierarchy and its resistance to change, noted that innovations in the schools, if they are to be successful, "almost necessarily originate at the lower levels of the hierarchy."[12] EEP not only originated at the top—it came from outside.

In addition, the hierarchical structure fosters a criss-cross pattern of deference which impedes the risk taking that is involved in altering familiar forms of behavior. The supervisor is responsible for the performance of his or her subordinates (the principal for the teachers, in the case of the school). This makes him reluctant to force change which originated above him upon an unwilling subordinate group, and sets up a tendency to avoid "rocking the boat" which further impedes innovation.

Professionalism, as manifested in the schools, constitutes another built-in resistance to change. The professional's belief that nonprofessionals are incapable of assessing or meeting the needs of the clients limits the variety of individuals considered capable of commenting intelligently on school affairs, and excludes external influences that might challenge existing practices. This impermeability reduces the opportunity for the impetus for change to come from the immediate environment, and isolates the school from comment and criticism which might stimulate change from within before the situation requires outside intervention.[13]

When the model self-contained classroom is combined with an attitude of professional self-sufficiency, the classroom becomes an inviolate sanctuary for the teacher.

> Classrooms are in effect the production departments of the educational enterprise; in them teachers teach. Yet, this role performance is relatively invisible to status equals, or superiors. Children can observe, usually very acutely, the quality of a teacher's execution of her role, but they are not allowed to comment on this, and have few (if any) sanctions to bring to bear.[14]

The classroom teacher expects a certain minimal degree of observation and supervision from the principal, but the principal is higher in organizational status than the teacher. Moreover, "close supervision by a principal . . . might well be viewed by his teachers as an infringement on their professional do-

---

12 Max Abbott, "Hierarchical Impediments to Innovation in Educational Organizations," in Fred Carver and Thomas Sergiovanni, eds. *Organizations and Human Behavior: Focus on Schools.* New York, N.Y.: McGraw-Hill, 1969, p. 47.

13 Everett C. Hughes, "The Social Significance of Professionalization," in Vollmer and Mills, *op. cit.,* p. 64.

14 Matthew B. Miles, "Planned Change and Organizational Health: Figure and Ground," in Carver and Sergiovanni, *op. cit.,* p. 383.

main.''[15] Observation and commentary from equals or inferiors is unwelcome and, in some situations, regarded as spying. In the same way, the principal expects some supervision and advice from his superiors, but not too much, and none from peers or inferiors.

The professional status of teaching was hard fought for, and is, even now, hardly won. The desire for professional status, moreover, is increased by the uncertainty involved in the job of teaching. For a medical doctor or a lawyer, unsatisfactory job performance has more obvious results, and more easily definable causes. For the teacher, it is much more difficult to judge when and if a child has not learned, and why this may be so.

> . . . the difficulty of measuring student learning encourages teachers to try to simplify and narrow their responsibilities by stereotyping and classifying students, by avoiding involvement with the factors outside his or her class that might affect learning, by routinizing student contact, by dismissing the student as a referent group, and by incorporating the student into the organization in the sense that he takes the blame for his nonperformance.[16]

These adaptive mechanisms reduce the willingness of teachers to change their behavior in ways that would require more work and more uncertainty.

The insecure status of the professional educator is heightened by the implication inherent in a change effort that the present course is unsatisfactory. Teachers' unions reinforce this resistance in their likelihood ''to dissent from any needs assessment that puts the blame on their members.''[17] This, combined with the technology of education, which Hawley characterizes as one ''about which knowledge of cause and effect is meager and which must be applied to inputs (students) whose characteristics are complex and unpredictable,''[18] leads to a widespread effort to ''blame the victim'' for failure rather than to ask how changing the nature of the teaching process might be more successful.[19] While the children of the EEP schools had problems which contributed to their learning difficulties, the ''blame the victim'' argument overlooks the children's strengths, protects the incompetent teachers, and, worst of all, reflects the assumption that the students are ''unteachable.''

15 Robert Dreeben and Neal Gross. *The Role Behavior of School Principals.* Cambridge, Mass.: Harvard University Graduate School of Education, 1965.
16 Willis D. Hawley, ''Dealing with Organizational Rigidity in Public Schools: A Theoretical Perspective,'' in Frederick M. Wirt, ed. *The Polity of the School.* Lexington, Mass.: Lexington Books, 1975, p. 193.
17 Dale Mann, ''Synthesis of Case Studies, Part B: Staff Development,'' in Peter W. Greenwood, Dale Mann, and Milbrey Wallin McLaughlin. *Federal Programs Supporting Educational Change, Vol. III: The Process of Change.* Santa Monica, Calif.: Rand Corporation, R-1589/3-HEW, April 1975.
18 Hawley, *op. cit.*, p. 190.
19 The phrase ''blame the victim'' comes from William Ryan. *Blaming the Victim.* New York, N.Y.: Pantheon, 1970.

The problems posed by these barriers were exacerbated when the emotions behind them were intensified by the 1968 teachers' strike, which was seen by many teachers as an assault on their professional status. Efforts to insulate the school from community pressures increased, as did the tendency to see change efforts as a vote of no confidence.

The Fate of EEP as a Role Change Model The role changes that EEP introduced often did involve more work and greater uncertainty, and, without sanctions to support their acceptance, met predictable reluctance on the part of almost everyone concerned. In the case of the school councils, an element of the design viewed as "critical" by the Gordon Committee, the attempt to foster a working relationship with a negatively perceived community was weakened by the lack of successful models to copy. Especially in the new and undefined field of school/community policy making, the lack of guidelines to demonstrate administrative commitment to such a change did not encourage rapport between principals and councils. This allowed principals to continue in their most familiar role—that of running the schools without substantial challenge or advice from "outsiders."

EEP's designers also hoped to change the relationship between principals and teachers, with the principal acting as a conceptual leader in fostering the innovations. To that end, more administrative support personnel were assigned to the EEP schools to free the principal's time. But how was a principal who was trained to be an administrator in the traditional manner supposed to metamorphosize into a "conceptual leader"—a role that involved at the very least more work, if not substantial risk, given the resistance to change? More often than not, this transformation did not occur.

To help teachers deal with the special problems of children in EEP schools, psychoeducational appraisal specialists were assigned to several schools. Many of the teachers had never seen a "psychoeducational appraisal specialist" and had little idea how they were supposed to use these new staff members, or to whom they were responsible, or what they were supposed to be doing. Not only were teachers not prepared for the introduction of various specialists, but they were also reluctant to admit that they needed their assistance, for fear that this might imply an inability to perform their own duties. It comes as no surprise then, that the evaluation reports repeatedly found these specialists, who might have been of valuable assistance, either underused or misused entirely.

If outside specialists were seen as superfluous, they were at least seen as peers. Paraprofessionals and aides were seen as inferiors, who, while they could be of assistance in the classroom in certain specified ways, had no business participating in planning classes and activities, as recommended by the Gordon Committee. Allowing them to do so was admitting that even without specialized training they were capable of making pedagogical judgments. More, the residue of hostility from the 1968 strike left teachers suspicious that paraprofessionals and aides were spying on their performance. Thus, the evaluators found that the aides, the assistants, and the paraprofessionals, while utilized in the classroom, were not always used in the most productive manner, and were completely excluded from planning activities.

The redefinition of the classroom teacher's role was stressed both in the original design and in subsequent evaluation reports.[20] One of the most important changes was the introduction of clustered classes. Formerly, teachers were responsible for one classroom unit of pupils, for whom they made all plans. Under EEP, several teachers were to coordinate their efforts in planning for and teaching clusters of three to five classroom units. This placed teachers in new, but poorly understood, relationships with one another. (One EEP teacher confessed that he was simply told, "This year you will team-teach with X and Y.") Team-teaching not only violated the traditional autonomy of the classroom teacher, but also involved more work in cooperative planning. Rather than changing their behavior as hoped, the teachers found new ways of dividing up the pupils and the subjects; but they never really developed a team relationship.

These are but a few examples of the partial or nonexistent implementation of the EEP proposals. On the whole, when the new roles involved more work and/or more risks, the role occupants chose to resolve the conflict between their old role expectations and the new requirements brought by EEP by acting in a manner as similar to the old roles as possible—i.e., "business as usual."

The Withholding of Support Certainly there were technological problems besetting EEP. Even when children are learning without problems, it is difficult to determine exactly how and why they are learning. When problems occur, it is even more difficult to understand where they originate and how they can be remedied. The 1960s saw investigation into the nature of the difficulties facing children such as those in EEP schools, and the investigations provided a wide variety of results. Even with clear results, however, the problem of designing solutions was a relatively new one, and, for that reason, the staff of the Gordon Committee had scoured the country seeking programs that were helping children with similar problems. Unfortunately, the operationalization of the EEP proposals was largely ignored, or incomplete where it existed at all. Far more of the Gordon Committee's report was devoted to describing the nature and purpose of the innovations, than to explaining how

---

20 *Interim Assessment of the Experimental Elementary Program in the New York City Public Schools: 1970–71.* New York, N.Y.: Horace Mann-Lincoln Institute, Teachers College, Columbia University, 1971, pp. 1–11.

they were to be introduced; and this assumed a system that would have welcomed them, not one with resistances as strong as those encountered.

But the most serious problems facing EEP were political. Because the program was a compromise, because all the parties would have preferred something else, no one was really committed to EEP. This lack of support was visible from the beginning, and undercut the chances for success of the entire venture.

When school district administrative personnel and the principals of the eleven schools were informed of their role in EEP, they were given a digest of the Gordon Committee's recommendations prepared by a deputy superintendent from the central office. There was nothing terribly unusual here—a digest is the most practical way to communicate the contents of a detailed report to a large audience. The problem was that it was never made clear whether only those items discussed in the digest were to be retained from the original plans, or whether the digest covered the plan in its entirety. The resulting confusion as to what EEP really was formed the groundwork for many of the problems that followed. While the confusion may have been unintentional, such digests are a known administrative device to satisfy both those desiring the original plan and those who want modifications.[21] The implementation of those programs mentioned in the digest was undercut by an almost complete lack of enforcing sanctions.

Etzioni categorizes sanctions or support mechanisms in three groups—normative, remunerative, and coercive.[22] Normative support for change originates at levels above that of the individuals expected to implement the change. In discussing the politics of staff development, Mann comments:

> Classroom teachers believe in what they are already doing, not in what any change-oriented project wants them to do. . . . For a project to succeed, then, the people in charge must be firmly convinced of the correctness of what *they* want others to do, and they must project that confidence.[23]

But those in charge were not convinced. Over the recommendation of the Gordon Committee that special expertise was necessary and perhaps should be imported, the direction of EEP was given to the assistant superintendent for elementary education, in addition to her other duties, rather than to an individual chosen specifically for EEP. In the same manner, the coordinators of each of the three EEP "models" were not chosen for demonstrated ability in handling similar programs, but simply because they had risen to a certain level

21 Donald S. Van Meter and Carl E. Van Horn, "The Policy Implementation Process: A Conceptual Framework," *Administration and Society,* March 1975.

22 Amitai Etzioni. *A Comparative Analysis of Complex Organizations.* New York, N.Y.: Free Press, 1961.

23 Mann, *op. cit.,* p. iii–29.

in the administrative hierarchy and were available at the time. While this is not to imply that any of these individuals were incompetent, they were less than wholly committed to EEP, and only accidentally, if at all, suited to the position.

Normative support could also have come from the United Federation of Teachers, who logically stood to gain in the long run if the need for more staff could be established. But given the uneasy peace following the 1968 teachers' strike, the UFT may have perceived that it had more to lose in the near future if it attempted to force EEP on an unwilling rank and file. While rumors of UFT sabotage cannot be documented, their quiet lack of support for a program mandated by their own contract agreements provides ample evidence of their lack of commitment.

Perhaps the pivotal role in sanctioning any change effort in schools is that of the principal. Innovations that are perceived by teachers to be supported by the principal are far more likely to be implemented than those not so seen.[24] Why did the EEP principals not support the proposed changes?

> They (principals) can be offended by . . . projects that appear to usurp their self-arrogated "master teacher" function, by those who try . . . to move teachers away from practices sanctioned by the principals. Change-oriented projects are challenges to authority.[25]

Administrators at the district level were no more eager to move than the principals. Perceiving the lack of support for change from above and the resistance from below, the principals seeing, like so many others, no reason to rock the boat, denied their much needed backing to EEP.

Lacking normative support, EEP might have brought more change if remunerative sanctions for changed teacher behavior had been included. The designers of the project had not expected any sanctions to be necessary, and had not allocated any of the funds to teacher bonuses or the like.

Coercive sanctions were also problematic. Whether the funds were being used appropriately or not, one could not simply take away money from a particular school or individual. Board regulations required justifications for the transfer of budget lines and the UFT contract specified conditions under which staff could be terminated or transferred. Moreover, who exactly was to pay for the errors? What good did it do the community to remove the community-based aides and paraprofessionals because others at higher levels were not implementing the programs? Could one teacher, or even three or four, be blamed for the failure of implementation? Or, at the other extreme, could the whole school be penalized for misusing the resources? Perhaps the most debilitating reality was that the removal of the funds would have meant little to the Board of Education within the larger context. EEP was only a temporary program, while

24 Dreeben and Gross, *op. cit.*
25 Mann, *op. cit.*, p. III-36.

the board was a permanent institution. They had managed without the funds before, would do so again at the end of the four years, and could do so sooner, if necessary.[26]

The lack of sanctions in EEP initially could be attributed to naive optimism. But in the face of evaluations that pointed out the lack of implementation, the failure to add sanctions cannot be written off as simple torpor. Those individuals and groups involved were professionals who knew well the resistances to change in the school system, and who saw them demonstrated repeatedly in EEP. Their choice *not* to act constituted a decision to let EEP die without ever having to call openly for the program's failure.[27]

Conclusion   If the EEP experience can teach us something about implementation, then the four years and $40 million were not totally wasted. "Implementation must not be conceived of as a process that takes place after, and independent of, the design of policy."[28] That is so simple a statement as to seem trivial, yet so broad in its mandate as to seem overwhelming. Nonetheless, money alone cannot bring change, however much the quantity. Innovations must be operationalized, with as much, if not more, attention given to the mechanics of instituting a proposal as to the purpose for its introduction. If possible, the number of decision-making levels between innovator and implementer should be reduced to minimize the chances that a program will be so altered or subverted as to make it useless. Staff development would be helpful in encouraging teachers to change the accepted behavior patterns.

Most difficult, however, is the question of mutual commitment to the proposal. In EEP it appears that almost no one really wanted change, and every party's denial of support slowed progress significantly. For a program to succeed, those involved must want it to succeed, especially where built-in resistances are strong. This mutual commitment constitutes normative sanction for change. In its absence, remunerative or coercive sanctions are weaker substitutes. Without any sanctions, inertia triumphs.

---

26 This is known in the baseball world as the Branch Rickey Rationale. When slugger Ralph Kiner confronted his boss, Rickey, the owner of the perenially cellar-dwelling Pittsburgh Pirates, with a demand for a raise in salary based on his league-leading home run record the previous year, Rickey instead gave him a pay cut, explaining "We could've finished in last place without you."

27 This can be characterized as an example of non-decision making, where those in positions of power did not overtly use their power to destroy a policy they did not want, but instead allowed the existing political bias as institutionalized in current practices to defeat the policy for them. See Peter Bachrach and Morton Baratz, "Two Faces of Power," *American Political Science Review*, Vol. 62, December 1962, pp. 947–952.

28 Pressman and Wildavsky, *op. cit.*, p. 143.

CHAPTER 9

Implementation of ESEA Title I: A Problem of Compliance

MILBREY WALLIN McLAUGHLIN

Ratification of the massive 1965 Elementary and Secondary Education Act (ESEA) caused much excitement and self-congratulation in Washington and throughout the country. ESEA resolved the historical logjam of opposition to federal aid for education, and most legislators were confident that Title I of that Act, which targets over $1 billion annually to "meet the special educational needs of disadvantaged children," would reform the educational services available to the nation's poor children. Reformers expected that Title I would, in the short run, stimulate the development of special programs that would compensate for educational disadvantage, thereby equalizing the academic attainment of poor children and their more advantaged peers. In the long run, it was hoped that this compensatory strategy would "break the cycle of poverty" and equalize lifetime opportunities.

The high expectations which surrounded the passage of Title I were based on a number of assumptions:

1. Schoolmen knew what to do with the new resources and would be able to use them to design and implement special compensatory programs.
2. The infusion of new resources into the nation's local school districts would lead to educational reform *from within* and through the existing system.

Thus, the passage of ESEA Title I embodied not only the high hopes of reformers, but also an implicit challenge to the nation's school system. Title I implied that current practices are inadequate and the schools were given the assignment of *self-renewal*.

However, almost a decade after the passage of Title I, and despite a few more optimistic judgments to the contrary,[1] the general verdict is that educators have not successfully met that challenge—that Title I has "failed" as an instrument of national policy. The evaluations that have contributed to this conclusion

---

1 *N.B.* Ralph W. Tyler, "The Federal Role in Education," *The Public Interest,* No. 34, Winter 1974, pp. 164-187.

have focused on the impact of Title I and have tried to assess the effect of Title I programs on target children. Without exception, these national evaluations have been unable to identify how participation in Title I programs or the expenditure of Title I funds have affected target children.[2] The "conventional wisdom" and the opinions of many legislators are summed up by President Nixon in his 1970 education message to Congress:

> We must stop letting wishes color our judgments about the educational effectiveness of many special compensatory programs when—despite some dramatic and encouraging exceptions—there is growing evidence that most of them are not yet measurably improving the success of poor children in school.

The evidence of these national evaluations of the impact of Title I can be interpreted in a number of ways. Many saw the results of these evaluations as evidence that Coleman was right, that "schools can't work" to overcome the educational disadvantages coincident with poverty. As Alice Rivlin remarked in reference to the *G. E. Tempo* study of Title I:

> [This study] added to the layman's impression that compensatory education doesn't work and led some to believe that "there is nothing we can do through education that will help poor children."[3]

And advocating the redirection of resources allocated to education to other social service areas as a more effective federal investment, Daniel Moynihan commented,

> We had thought (as legislation such as Title I was passed) we knew all that really needed to be known about education in terms of public support, or at the very least that we knew enough to legislate and appropriate with a high order of confidence. . . . We knew what we wanted to do in education and we were enormously confident that what we wanted to do could work. That confidence . . . has eroded. . . . We have learned that things are far more complicated than we thought. The rather simple input-output relations which

2 The major evaluations of Title I have been E.J. Mosback et al. *Analyses of Compensatory Education in Five School Districts: Summary."* Santa Barbara, Calif.: General Electric Co., TEMPO Division, 1968, processed; United States Office of Education. *Education of the Disadvantaged: An Evaluative Report on Title I of the Elementary and Secondary Education Act of 1965, Fiscal Year 1968*. Washington, D.C.: U.S. Government Printing Office, Department of Health, Education, and Welfare, 1970; and Gene V. Glass et al. *Data Analysis of the 1968–1969 Survey of Compensatory Education (Title I)*. Washington, D.C.: United States Office of Education, BESE, 1970.
3 Alice M. Rivlin. *Systematic Thinking for Social Action*. Washington, D.C.: The Brookings Institution, 1971, p. 83.

naively no doubt, but honestly, we had assumed to obtain in education simply, on examination, did not hold up. They are not there.[4]

Others saw the results of Title I evaluations not as evidence that education is ineffective as a social intervention strategy, but as an indication that the existing educational technology was inadequate and underdeveloped. This view led to support for the development of the National Institute of Education on the assumption that many of the shortcomings in educational practice for the disadvantaged could be remedied by concentrating more time and energy on basic research and educational theory development. President Nixon saw the disappointing results of these evaluations in this manner:

> We must stop pretending that we understand the mystery of the learning process, or that we are significantly applying science and technology to the techniques of learning. . . . When educators, school boards and Government officials alike admit that we have a good deal to learn about the way we teach, we will begin to climb the staircase toward genuine reform. . . . The purpose of the National Institute of Education would be to begin the serious, systematic search for new knowledge needed to make educational opportunity truly equal.[5]

There is yet another interpretation, however, that makes judgments about the effectiveness of schooling as an antipoverty strategy, or about the success of existing educational technology, somewhat premature, or at least moot. It is possible that Title I programs, as they have been evaluated, have never existed—that Title I has not yet been implemented as intended by reformers. Thus, the failure of Title I in this instance is not so much a failure of special programs, but a failure of a federal policy to bring about these programs on the local level.

The area between inputs and outputs—the implementation stage—is relatively unexplored in all social service areas, and is only recently beginning to receive attention in the area of education. But evidence exists that makes doubt about the implementation of Title I more than just an academic speculation following from a logical possibility.[6] For example, Wargo and his colleagues at

4 Hearings on HR 33, HR 3606, and other related bills, pp. 7–8.
5 U.S. House of Representatives, 91st Congress, 2nd Session. *Message from the President of the United States on Educational Reform*. March 3, 1970, Document No. 91–267.
6 See, for example Washington Research Project and NAACP Legal Defense and Educational Fund. *Title I of ESEA: Is It Helping Poor Children?* Washington, D.C.: Washington Research Report of the Southern Center for Studies in Public Policy and the NAACP Legal Defense and Educational Fund, 1969; NAACP Legal Defense and Educational Fund. *An Even Chance: A Report on Federal Funds for Indian Children in Public School Districts*. Washington, D.C.: NAACP Legal Defense and Educational Fund, 1971; and National Committee on the Education of Migrant Children. *Wednesday's Children: A Report on Programs Funded under the Migrant Amendment to Title I of the Elementary and Secondary Education Act*. Washington, D.C.: National Committee on the Education of Migrant Children, 1971.

the American Institutes for Research concluded in the most recent comprehensive evaluation of Title I:

> National level data indicated that (a) most states and many LEAs [local educational agencies] have failed to implement their programs in full compliance with existing regulations, guidelines and program criteria; (b) funds and services have been underallocated for academic programs, overallocated for supportive (nonacademic) services, and misallocated to children without critical needs for compensatory services; (c) there is little evidence at the national level that the program has had any positive impact on eligible and participating children.
>
> The national level data that indicate a disregard for Title I regulations, guidelines and program criteria suggest that ESEA Title I has never been implemented nationally as intended by Congress. . . . Full compliance to enacting legislation will be required before the national compensatory education program intended by ESEA Title I can be fairly assessed.[7]
>
> Even as late as June 1971, 37 states (74%) were known to be in noncompliance with the law.[8]

Questions about the implementation (or lack of implementation) of ESEA Title I raise questions about another assumption made by reformers as Title I was passed—that the legislation would be in some sense "self-executing," and federal intent would be translated into local practice through the existing regulations and guidelines. Lawmakers expected that local and state education personnel would comply with the intent and spirit of the new law and that—*ipso jure*—innovative practices for education of the disadvantaged would be designed and implemented. Questions about how Title I dollars are spent once they reach the local level thus involve issues about the ability and inclination of local (or state) officials to *comply* with the law and, as part of that compliance, to establish innovative compensatory programs for poor children.

In this chapter I intend to address the problem of implementation by looking at the notion of compliance—what it assumes and how these assumptions square with the reality of the Title I policy system, particularly the Local Educational Agency (LEA).

Compliance There are at least four factors which are assumed to promote compliance with policy directives. One is the existence of *common goals*. Shared and mutually understood objectives are expected to elicit behavior and activities on the part of subordinates that are comparable to and congruent with the intent of the agency issuing the mandate

---

7 Michael J. Wargo et al. *Further Examination of Exemplary Programs in Educating Disadvantaged Children*. Palo Alto, Calif.: American Institutes for Research, July 1971, pp. 9–10.

8 *Ibid.*, p. 65.

or directive. A second factor thought to foster compliance is the presence of *knowledge*. This notion posits not only the existence of shared and reliable knowledge about means and consequences of alternative courses of action—how to most effectively or efficiently achieve an objective—but also assumes the availability of information or feedback to superiors about the success of subordinates in carrying out policy directives. A third way is by offering *incentives* or disincentives—rewards or penalties contingent upon carrying out prescribed activities. A fourth way that compliance can be brought about is by the exercise of effective *authority*. Authority, as it is used here, denotes a relationship between individuals (or organizational units) of unequal resources. It exists or is effective to the extent that instructions or mandates of the superordinate are followed without eliciting *quid pro quo* sanctions or rewards. That is, authority is a relationship based on the ability to reward or punish, but rewards and sanctions are removed to the background.

These four factors—goals, knowledge, incentives, and authority—are interrelated and interactive; none by itself is sufficient and each can be expected to influence compliance to some extent. In framing expectations about the impact of ESEA Title I on disadvantaged children, reformers anticipated that each of these factors would come into play and thereby ensure the effective implementation of this unprecedented federal initiative. Incentives and authority were the formal mechanisms established to ensure compliance to the intent of the law. ESEA Title I established guïdelines and regulations that were intended to constrain or limit the ways in which an LEA could spend Title I dollars. The legislation outlined sanctions for the misuse or inefficient use of these funds. A complex administrative machinery, which relied on the existence of effective authority, was set up to administer these regulations. In light of the cumulating evidence which raises serious doubts about the implementation of the Act, it is worth looking at each of these elements in turn and asking to what extent it shaped the implementation of Title I.

Common Goals   Reformers assumed that members of the Title I policy system—practitioners and policy makers—shared a common interest and concern for meeting the "special educational needs of disadvantaged children." In the view of most participants in the drafting and passage of ESEA Title I, meeting these needs was the goal of the Act. While participants in the Title I policy system may have shared this overriding concern for the plight of disadvantaged youngsters, it is obvious that they did not all interpret the goals of the legislation in the same way—either at the broad level of formal program objective, or at the practical level of program focus.

For example, there was even no agreement within the Title I policy system regarding the broad categorical goals of the Act. Some legislators and a number of schoolmen (at both the SEA and LEA levels) saw the reform of Title I not in its promise to enhance the educational opportunities available to poor children, but simply in the fact of its ratification. To them, the categorical goal of the legislation—meeting "the special educational needs of disadvantaged children"—was an essentially *symbolic*, not an operational, objective. That is, the categorical language of the legislation was interpreted as a political expedient devised to overcome traditional opposition to federal aid for education. By targeting funds to the individual child, the drafters of the Title I legislation were able to resolve the interest group conflicts (over such issues as race and church/state relations) that had historically blocked federal education measures.[9] Thus, many viewed the categorical goals of the Act as necessary political diplomacy and operationally interpreted Title I as *general aid* to the schools. One participant in the Title I process commented:

> There was never a coherent perception of what Title I was on the Hill. Perkins saw it as general aid; Robert Kennedy saw it as project oriented. Morse saw it as general aid, but not to the degree Perkins did. . . . From the beginning, Title I has been seen as a political device for other things (lawmakers would like) to get done.[10]

Indeed, the use to which local districts have put Title I funds expresses the effective preference of many practitioners to utilize Title I as general aid. This is especially true in large, inner city schools where the financial squeezes caused by rising costs for staff, materials and maintenance have made budget balancing an act of high theater.

Even within the categorical parameters established by the Act, LEA officials have interpreted the broad and ambiguous goals mandated by the legislation in many different ways. As the legislative history of Title I demonstrates, enhancing academic achievement was only one of the objectives articulated for Title I and only one of the many objectives stated by local programs. Local programs have framed goals for their Title I programs in such disparate terms as student health and nutrition, clothing needs, cultural enrichment, socialization skills, and so on. A review of the local and national Title I evaluation evidence implies that the formal goals established for Title I are too vague and global to be operational or measurable. Even when these mandated goals have been viewed as more than symbolic, they have been variously interpreted at the local level and have resulted in programs expressing multiple and diverse objectives, which many see to be at odds with the intent of the law.

The explanation for the ambiguous goals set forth in the Title I legislation is

---

9　See Stephen K. Bailey and Edith K. Mosher. *ESEA: The Office of Education Administers a Law.* Syracuse, N.Y.: Syracuse University Press, 1965; and Philip Meranto. *The Politics of Federal Aid to Education in 1965: A Study in Political Innovation.* Syracuse, N.Y.: Syracuse University Press, 1967.

10　Interview, Staff Assistant to Senate Subcommittee on Education, October 1972.

essentially political. It is rooted in federalism and in the country's traditional belief in pluralism which nowhere has been more cultivated and cherished than in the area of education. These beliefs underlie and foster an ethos of local control of education and concomitant fear of, and resistance to, federal involvement in local school affairs. Drafters of ESEA were painstakingly careful to eliminate any language in the legislation which might anger important educational interest groups and thereby endanger the fragile coalition which had been established to ensure swift passage of President Johnson's landmark education bill. The goals for ESEA Title I were written to allow a maximum amount of latitude and discretion as the program was implemented at the local level. How these vague program objectives would be specifically met, reformers assumed, would be worked out at the implementation stage with the assistance and oversight of USOE. In its regulations, however, USOE made the intent of Title I no more specific than a definition of a Title I project as "an activity, or a set of activities, proposed by a state or local educational agency or the Department of Interior and designed to meet certain of the special educational needs of certain educationally deprived children."

The character of the Title I objectives is also symptomatic of the pervasive federal tendency to conceive and express the goals of social programs in unqualified and idealistic terms. Such goal statements not only generate expectations which are unlikely to be met, but also give scant direction to the people or the organizations who are expected to implement them.[11]

In summary, the shared and operationally intelligible goals which are expected to promote compliance do not seem to exist in the instance of ESEA Title I. Although a few states, such as California and Connecticut, have more narrowly focused the objectives for Title I and the uses to which the monies may be put, most SEAs and LEAs have only overarching and insufficiently specified statements of Title I objectives to guide local activities and against which to measure the success of their efforts.

Knowledge   The knowledge necessary for compliance includes both knowing what to do and receiving feedback about the success or adequacy of the consequent activities. "Knowing what to do" implies not only that the subordinate has adequate tools and technology to carry out a directive, but also that he understands the rules of the game—that he has good information about what it is he is supposed to do.

In 1965, it was widely believed that the failure of disadvantaged children in schools could be remedied by the infusion of more money into special compensatory services. Educators argued and reformers expected that a number of

11 See Martha Derthick. *New Towns in Town.* Washington, D.C.: The Urban Institute, 1972; and Jeffrey L. Pressman and Aaron Wildavsky. *Implementation.* Berkeley, Calif.: University of California Press, 1973.

promising strategies for the education of the disadvantaged existed—if not in fact, at least in the minds of schoolmen (who had been hampered in implementing these ideas only through lack of funds). Francis Keppel expressed this confidence in the ability of schoolmen to translate Title I dollars into effective programs in his testimony before the Senate subcommittee hearings on ESEA in 1965. He presented evidence of "promising strategies" to the committee which he argued showed "heartening results:"

> Better than my words, these surveys show what the schools of our nation will do with the resources made available under Title I of the Elementary Act of 1965.
>
> These are descriptions of the kinds of programs that have already been undertaken by imaginative school systems, by school systems under the support of private foundations and others, to show that the type of programs which could be undertaken by Title I could be effective. I think we have some impressive facts here, sir, some impressive facts that when special attention is paid to a variety of educational problems of children from low-income families, that they can work.[12]

But, in fact, in 1965 schoolmen did not know what to do. At that time, the special and complex problems of the disadvantaged were not well understood and only a handful of LEAs had ongoing compensatory education on the books. Although some schoolmen may have had ideas about compensatory strategies which they hoped might prove effective, there was little reliable knowledge in 1965 about successful compensatory education programs. Title I thus asked schoolmen to launch an activity in what was essentially an uncharted area and to implement successful programs for the very group of children the schools historically had seemed least able to help. Furthermore, the institutional isolation of school districts (and, indeed, schools within districts) meant that what knowledge about promising strategies did exist was not shared or disseminated. One of the most important assumptions underlying the expectations of reformers—that "schoolmen knew what to do"—finds little support in reality. Even assuming clearly specified goal statements, schoolmen had insufficient knowledge to implement the objectives of the program with any large measure of confidence or success.

As even a cursory review and almost any school administrator will suggest, the "rules of the game" in the instance of Title I are vague, often contradictory, fugitive, and involve overlapping and amorphous definitions.

For example, a state or local program manager seeking to determine the meaning of "project area" will find himself confronted with imprecise ter-

---

12 U.S. Congress, Senate Subcommittee on Education. *Hearings on Elementary and Secondary Act of 1965.* 89th Congress, 1st Session, 1969, p. 881.

minology, fuzzy relationships and ambiguous delineations of responsibility within the Title I regulations and guidelines. A recent study concluded:

> There are inconsistencies both within and across various publications. Terms are overlapping and often interchanged in a confusing manner. Examples include (especially within the USOE material) the seemingly random use of "selected attendance areas," "target areas," and "project areas." "Attendance areas" and "attendance units" are also used interchangeably. Additionally, it is sometimes difficult to relate certain terms to their corresponding counterparts in other Title I material.[13]

Furthermore, although federal documents require local agencies to undertake a "needs assessment," the term is never clearly defined. In some publications, only economic need is considered. Other documents refer to educational deficits. And the level of focus is never specified. The regulations do not make it clear whether the needs assessment is to focus on the participating child, the designation of eligible "project areas," or what part the resulting analysis is to play in the design of Title I projects.

At yet another level, a school administrator cannot be sure, in reading the Title I documents, which guidelines are *mandates* and which are merely *suggestions*:

> Requirements of actual Title I projects are a mixture of general and special directives, and "suggestions." The terminology is sometimes precise and sometimes quite the opposite. Many directives in USOE publications contain the verb "should" rather than the legally appropriate "shall" or "must." The case can be made that a phrase such as "resources should be concentrated on those children. . ." (Program Guide No. 44, Sect. 4.2) is more a suggestion than a mandatory regulation.[14]

A multitude of examples can be marshalled to illustrate the confusing and imprecise terminology which describes the parameters of compliant behavior. These inconsistencies and ambiguities do little to clarify the requirements from the federal project manager's or school superintendent's point of view.

Responsible individuals at the local level are not even aided by the existence of a handy guide to the administration and implementation of Title I. A conscientious administrator must possess a small library of federal and state documents if he is to be up-to-date on the latest Title I requirement. The rules and regulations which govern Title I cannot be found in a single publication, but

---

13   Iris C. Rotberg and Alison Wolf. *Compensatory Education: Some Research Issues.* Washington, D.C.: The National Institute of Education, Policy Studies Division, Division of Research, May 1974, Appendix B, p. 7.
14   Ibid., p. 9.

instead must be pulled together from the legislation and subsequent amendments, serial issues of state and federal regulations, and various USOE publications, program letters, and guidelines (many of which are not passed on to
LEAs by the State Educational Agencies [SEAs]).

The fuzzy and confusing language of the regulations, combined with their
inaccessibility, means that school administrators often face their first challenge
in implementing ESEA Title I not in thinking about and planning effective
strategies, but in simply trying to understand the rules of the game.

The information which could permit state or federal officials to assess local
activities is generally not available. National evaluations have discovered that
local educational agencies do not collect the fiscal and outcome data which
would permit assessment of the impact of Title I, and that the mandated project
evaluation scheme has resulted in anecdotal and promotional documents, not in
objective project reports. But LEAs have had little incentive to do more than
produce documents which highlight positive program accomplishments and
obscure or minimize disappointments or failures. The result is an absence of
objective and quantitative information which would allow evaluators, legislators or policy makers to assess the impact of Title I or determine the extent to
which LEAs are complying with the intent of the law.

It seems, then, that the absence of shared and mutually understood goals in
the instance of Title I is matched by a general lack of knowledge about effective
treatments, about the rules of the game and about the activities and accomplishments of local Title I programs.

Incentives and Authority   The major and obvi-
ous incentive contained in ESEA Title I is money—a grant of federal dollars
which, theoretically, is contingent upon local compliance with the Act's rules
and guidelines. The success of this financial incentive in producing compliant
behavior depends on the existence of effective authority to oversee local
choices and activities. How effective is the established authority in the Title I
policy system?

Not very. Neither of the oversight agencies in the Title I policy system—the
SEA and USOE—have enforced program regulations with much rigor, enthusiasm, or success. USOE's ineffectiveness as a monitor of local activities
has multiple causes. A lack of federal muscle became evident very early on in
the dispute between USOE Commissioner Francis Keppel and Chicago's
Mayor Richard Daley. In the first year of the Title I program, Commissioner
Keppel requested that the City of Chicago return Title I money that USOE
judged had been misused. Mayor Daley responded to Keppel's request with
angry phone calls to the White House and to influential members of Congress,
arguing that the commissioner and USOE had overstepped its bounds. Wor-
ried congressmen pressed Keppel to withdraw this request in the interest of

intergovernmental harmony and local control of education. USOE retreated and Keppel left government service.

The Keppel/Daley affair, however, merely served to reinforce the traditionally timid and passive USOE position toward the states and local school districts.[15] In addition, responsibility for the administration of ESEA was given to the understaffed Bureau of Elementary and Secondary Education (BESE) whose definition of the USOE role as "checkwriter" was as much a result of the limitations imposed by day-to-day crises as traditional patterns of relationships.

Nor did the SEAs take up the slack resulting from USOE's laissez-faire administration of Title I—for similar reasons. Title I accounts for but a small portion of the SEA's budget, and the target children a small percentage of state school children. SEAs must deal with LEAs on more far-reaching issues such as accreditation, licensing, school finance and the like. Just as USOE was reluctant to jeopardize its familiar pattern of relationships with states, the SEAs have been generally unwilling to destroy good working relationships with the local districts over issues relating to Title I. Questions of local compliance to Title I guidelines are relatively small potatoes compared to the other day-by-day concerns of the SEA. Bayla White has commented on the general lack of attention paid by most SEAs to local program development and compliance:

> The state is responsible for monitoring local operations to see that they conform to the letter and spirit of the law. . . .
>
> States send out evaluation guidelines or requests for information to the LEAs long after the school year has begun. Since the local projects are already underway, the state is in a very poor position to influence either the evaluation design or the kind of information maintained in the Title I projects. States are required by the Office of Education to supply data on the effect of Title I on student achievement. But most states merely collect whatever test data exist, as opposed to requiring uniform testing or the use of selected tests. The evaluation reports filed by the LEAs reach the state officials long after decisions on project approval for the next year are made.[16]

A further factor contributing to ineffective monitoring and enforcement is the informal professional structure of the educational policy system—from USOE to the LEA. The tenets of "professionalism" within this bureaucratic system are stronger than formal rules or explicit responsibilities. Levine has remarked:

> For reasons ranging from professional doctrine through political peace keep-

15 See, for example Frederick M. Wirt and Michael W. Kirst. *The Political Web of American Schools.* Boston, Mass.: Little Brown, 1973.

16 Bayla F. White, "The Role of Evaluation in Title I Program Management," paper presented at the National Academy of Public Administration Conference on Evaluation in Education Programs, Rockville, Maryland, May 26, 1972, p. 4.

ing, the professionals at any level are reluctant to rock the boat, yet Title I to effect change—must do considerable rocking.[17]

For any or all of these reasons, then, the SEAs do not concern themselves much more than USOE with monitoring and enforcing LEA compliance to Title I guidelines. Consequently, there exists little effective authority, and the responsibility for overseeing the use of Title I funds has slipped between the cracks of the Title I policy system. The result of the effective withdrawal of USOE and the SEAs from overseer roles has been an administrative vacuum in which the determination of Title I policy is left to the very unit supposedly subject to oversight—the LEA. The financial incentive embodied in Title I is not effective because the receipt of federal money is not in fact contingent upon compliant behavior. Consequently, LEAs tend to see ESEA Title I as an entitlement, and implementation of the Act reflects predominantly *local* not *national* interests, goals, and priorities.

Since the authority upon which the incentives depend is essentially nonoperational, the important question then becomes: To what extent is there motivation at the local level to comply with the intent and guidelines of ESEA Title I?

Local Self-Interest Anthony Downs has remarked that bureaucratic officials try to attain their goals rationally. In practical terms, this means that whenever the cost of achieving a particular objective rises in terms of time, money and amount of effort required, bureaucrats generally will seek to attain less of that goal—other things being equal. From a purely cost/benefit point of view, there is generally little incentive for a local school administrator to comply with the letter of the Title I law. That is, the costs involved in complying with Title I guidelines are—in the view of the local school administrator—often greater than the rewards.

Title I dollars are supposed to represent new resources for disadvantaged children. These dollars are not intended to supplant or replace local expenditures, but are expected to provide additional, compensatory resources for the educationally disadvantaged. Title I guidelines require that local base expenditures for target children and other children in the district be comparable and that Title I dollars, consequently, provide *extra* help for target children— "Special Educational Programs." In what Michael Kirst calls the "Byzantine" world of school accounting, however, it is extremely difficult to determine if or in what form Title I dollars reach the target population. It is hard to follow the course and impact of any given dollar of an outside funding source through a school system, particularly in the large school system of the sort receiving Title I money. Typically, school administrators engage in "multi-pocket budget-

17 Robert A. Levine. *Public Planning: Failure and Redirection.* New York, N.Y.: Basic Books, 1972, p. 67.

ing"[18] in an effort to economize resources. When a school district has numerous sources of income, each with different categorical purposes and restrictions attached to its use, it is relatively simple for administrators to use funds available to the district to fund their own priorities and interests, rather than comply with the intent of the suppliers of special funds.

The theoretically restricted or targeted revenues may be allocated first to nominally coincident categorical activities within the school district's normal and existing concerns. This allocation frees the district general funds—or hard money—to fund priorities of particular local concern and interest. In such a situation, it is hard to assess the extent to which external funding sources such as Title I have been "symbolically allocated"—that is, have simply been used to replace local funds that would have normally been used in that way; or to what extent it has been a "catalytic allocation," encouraging additional local expenditures; or to what extent "perfect allocation" has occurred—that is, the restricted funds being added onto existing programs without either reduction in other line item funding, or addition of new line items congruent with local concerns but outside the scope of the restricted aid.[19]

In the absence of guideline enforcement, a large number of local districts tend to see Title I funds as functionally "untied" to categorical goals and thus use them as general aid—*symbolically* allocating this money to special Title I services. There are numerous reasons why this is so. Title I funds represent only a small percentage of an LEAs budget. Many school administrators feel that the hassle involved in the complex bookkeeping and accounting assumed by Title I regulations outweighs the benefits. As one local budget official has commented: "If I were offered a choice between $2 of general aid and $3 of categorical aid, I would choose the general aid. The extra dollar just isn't worth it."

But, even if the accounting and targeting hassles were somehow solved, a large number of school districts would probably continue to use Title I as general aid since, in the view of many school administrators, the fiscal needs of the school district are greater than the "special educational needs of disadvantaged children." Title I is predominantly aimed at high-density urban districts which have fewer resources and a lower tax base than their suburban neighbors. But, at the same time, these districts must meet higher costs in providing educational services—teachers' salaries, building maintenance, ancillary student services and the like. Consequently, these districts respond to these fiscal pressures either by blatantly employing Title I as general aid or by stretching the categorical terms of the Act to its broadest possible interpreta-

---

18 David O. Porter. *The Politics of Budgeting Federal Aid.* Beverly Hills, Calif.: Sage Publications, 1973.
19 This analysis draws heavily on fn. 18.

tion. For example, whether or not a slide projector purchased with Title I funds is used for all children in a school or just for Title I eligible children is, of course, difficult for a federal auditor to determine. Thus, the number of border-line instances in which Title I funds have been used as general aid may never be known. However, the number of "gross" misuses of Title I funds identified by federal auditors indicates that the practice of using ESEA Title I as general aid is fairly widespread: "Misuse of Title I funds is considered 'severe' and when asked if this meant that it was 10-15 percent [DHEW] auditors thought it was substantially greater."[20]

Furthermore, in most school districts there exists no unitary interest group which could exert sufficient pressure in support of the categorical goals of Title I. The parents of poor children generally have little voice or effective power; what influence they might possess is usually overwhelmed by competing interests—of the school board in achieving a balanced budget, of teachers in securing a general salary increase, of property owners in holding down tax increases, and of the superintendent in keeping the entire school organization afloat. In most districts, the intent and operational directives of Title I legislation are eclipsed by more urgent and powerful demands of organizational maintenance or equilibrium. As commentators on decision making in local school districts have noted, the choices and activities of the principal actors in an LEA are typically governed by a "bureaucratic rationality" that is the result of an overriding concern for institutional protection, maintenance, and growth.[21]

But fiscal and administrative obstacles constitute only one set of reasons why LEAs are not inclined to use Title I funds to establish special compensatory programs. Implicit in the passage of Title I was the belief that schools thus far had failed to meet the needs of the target population and that new practices must be devised to accomplish the goals of the Act. But schoolmen did not know what to do to initiate successful programs and the incentives to design and implement innovative strategies are few to nonexistent.

The first step in implementing an innovative strategy is the generation of support within the organizational setting. But there are few individuals within the local school organization who would be eager to assume the additional burdens inherent in developing and implementing new practices, in the absence of additional incentives to do so. Innovation, by definition, requires the acquisi-

---

20 Alan Ginsburg et al. *Title I of ESEA–Problems and Prospects*. Washington, D.C.: Department of Health, Education, and Welfare Paper, *circa* 1970.

21 See, for example, James S. Coleman, "Incentives in Education, Existing and Proposed," unpublished manuscript; Charles E. Bidwell, "The School as a Formal Organization," in James March, ed. *The Handbook of Organizations*. Chicago, Ill.: Rand McNally, 1965, pp. 992–1022; and Joseph B. Giacquinta, "The Process of Organizational Change in Schools," in Fred N. Kerlinger, ed. *Review of Research in Education*, Ithaca, Ill.: F.E. Peacock, 1973, pp. 178–208.

tion of new skills, new organizational procedures, and extra time and work. Except for a dedicated minority who find reward merely in the attempt to provide better services for poor children, there are few compelling reasons for participants to expend greater effort than they are otherwise required to expend. This is what Kenneth B. Clark calls the "Law of Economy of Effort." Certainly, the power of the teachers' unions is now explicitly directed toward conserving the energy and effort of teachers. And, in one large west coast school district, principals were unwilling to remain in Title I schools—let alone initiate new programs. Until this district instituted positive incentives for an administrator to assume and retain a principalship of a Title I school (i.e., year-round schools and salary increments), principals were abandoning Title I schools annually. They saw no reason why they should be saddled with responsibility for the extra aides, volunteers, and paper work that are attached to Title I when their colleagues down the street had to deal only with routine school operations.

Furthermore, the state of knowledge in education and the peculiarities of federal funding practices reinforce the disinclination of school districts to implement new and innovative strategies. The opportunity costs are high when a district elects to launch an innovative program. Inherent in the adoption and implementation of any new strategy is the possibility of failure. A school administrator would like to be confident that a new strategy will work at least as well as the one it replaces, if not predictably better. Unfortunately, no such high order of validity or reliability exists in education. Research in educational treatments does not yield the same order of certainty as does a laboratory experiment. Many administrators, then, elect to maximize the possibility of making effective use of extra Title I dollars by sticking with familiar practices or using the funds to purchase technology (such as audio-visual equipment) to supplement existing programs. The state of the art of knowledge in the area of education also means that a school administrator runs the risk of disruption in the local school setting if a new strategy fails. The visibility of a new strategy means that its failure will be also prominent—thereby generating dissatisfaction among the staff and parents. Consequently, many school administrators, after weighing the possible gains of implementing a new approach against the risk of failure and subsequent organizational fallout, often decide to simply expand or support current practices and their predictable consequences.

And there is no penalty attached to a failure to innovate. Schools operate in a nonmarket setting in which there is no interorganizational competition for the "best product."[22] The school as an organization does not possess "profit maximizing" incentives; in fact, the "survival" of the institution is guaranteed by society. Consequently, within a school district, there is no impelling incen-

---

22 See John Pincus, "Incentives for Innovation in Public Schools," *Review of Educational Research*, No. 44, 1974, pp. 113–144.

tive to implement new practices; instead there are some persuasive reasons not to, insofar as the outcomes of innovation are uncertain and changing bureaucratic patterns require risk and additional (but unrewarded) effort.[23]

There is still another reason why the implementation of effective and innovative compensatory programs is the exception rather than the rule in most school districts: the character of the federal funds themselves. The historical instability of federal interests and initiatives leads most local school officials to view Title I commitments as unstable and the allocations as "soft money." Even though Title I is now more or less institutionalized and the possibility of complete withdrawal of Title I aid remote, the threat of significant and unpredictable reductions in local grants remains and is reinforced each funding cycle. Thus, school administrators are hesitant to invest Title I resources in mainline educational efforts, which, of course, are the activities assessed by national impact evaluations and which, *a priori*, could be expected to result in significant change in the educational opportunities available to disadvantaged youngsters.

Taken together, these factors tend to support the "dynamic conservatism" (Schon), "organizational rigidity" (Hawley), and the "conservative tendency" (Coleman) which are said to characterize bureaucratic organizations generally, and schools particularly.[24] In the instance of ESEA Title I, the result has been the allocation of Title I resources for programs that are (1) more of the same and (2) ancillary to the central educational services of the school. Thus the American Institutes for Research (AIR) finding that "funds and services have been underallocated for academic programs, overallocated for supportive (nonacademic) services, and misallocated to children without critical needs for compensatory services" is not surprising in light of the dominant incentives shaping choices and activities at the local school level and in the absence of effective sanctions to behave otherwise.

Conclusions   No federal program ever succeeds completely and only in the ideal do that of the factors promoting compliance—goals, knowledge, incentives and authority—function perfectly. But the slippage and ineffectiveness of these components in the instance of Title I seem extreme. Admittedly, this analysis has characterized a bit starkly those ele-

---

23 To this point, a number of economists have argued that one of the most important differences between market and non-market allocated goods is the amount or organizational and technological *uncertainty* attendant in the provision of non-market goods. In this view, this is one reason why such goods or services are not provided in a market, or are provided at a level considered sub-optimal. See Henry Levin, "Concepts of Economic Efficiency and Educational Production," paper presented at the Conference on Education as an Industry, sponsored by the National Bureau of Economic Research, New York, June 4–5, 1971.

24 Donald A. Schon. *Beyond the Stable State*. New York, N.Y.: Random House, 1971; Hawley, *op. cit.*; and Coleman, *op. cit.*

ments which could promote local compliance with Title I guidelines. Nonetheless, it seems evident that few of the factors that foster compliant behavior are met in the instance of Title I: Goals and guidelines are unclear, treatments are inadequate or underdeveloped, incentives to design or implement innovative strategies are few; categorical requirements conflict in important ways with local self-interest, and established authority is non-operational or powerless. Thus, the failure of local school districts to implement Title I as intended by law could have been predicted.

ESEA presented a challenge of self-renewal—of reform through and within the existing educational system. But the organizational supports that were necessary to reform did not exist. Innovation or reform is difficult to accomplish in any situation. For example, evaluations of ESEA Title III, the Ford Foundation "Lighthouse" projects, as well as other reports of efforts to implement innovations[25] all demonstrate that attempts to innovate are often *pro forma* and frequently disappointing—even when risk capital is available, organizational commitment and support exists, personal incentives are operant, and goals and treatments are clear and operational. The design and implementation of successful innovation—or reform—in the case of Title I, where none of these incentives or supports are present, would be an astonishing accomplishment. In fact, this analysis raises the possibility that LEAs are being held accountable for something that they probably cannot do, given the present arrangement of policies, resources, incentives, and institutional structures.

But in response to evidence of failure on the part of LEAs to implement Title I, lawmakers have devised further mandates and federal bureaucrats have written additional guidelines. These activities are based on a particularly unrealistic view of administrative behavior. The present analysis suggests that promulgation of additional rules and regulations holds little promise of making Title I more effective or notably improving compliance. The history of Title I demonstrates the limited ability (and interest) of federal or state officials to use the sanctions they already possess. And, rooted as these attitudes are in national traditions of federalism and pluralism, it seems unlikely that they will change. Thus, a continued policy or legislative focus devising "tighter" rules and regulations does not seem to be a fruitful way to stimulate change or compliance.

ESEA Title I is one example of the general and serious problems which attend the conceptualization and implementation of broad-scale federal social

25 Richard O. Carlson, Art Gallaher, Jr., Matthew B. Miles, Roland J. Pellegrin, and Everett M. Rogers. *Change Processes in the Public Schools*. Eugene, Ore.: Center for the Advanced Study of Educational Administration, University of Oregon, 1971; John I. Goodlad et al. *Behind the Classroom Door*. Worthington, Ohio: Charles A. Jones, 1970; Neal C. Gross, Joseph Giacquinta, and Marilyn Bernstein. *Implementing Organizational Innovations: A Sociological Analysis of Planned Educational Change*. New York, N.Y.: Basic Books, 1971; and Louis M. Smith and Pat M. Keith. *Anatomy of Educational Innovation: An Organizational Analysis of an Elementary School*. New York, N.Y.: John Wiley, 1971.

action programs. None of the difficulties which plague Title I are unique. One only need look at the experience of the Community Action Programs (CAP), or Title III of ESEA, or Title VI of the Civil Rights Act to find other cases of similar implementation and compliance problems. But the confluence of so many difficulties and organizational deficiencies in a single program is remarkable and has effectively crippled the Title I program from its inception.

This analysis suggests that the lack of local compliance with the guidelines and objectives of the federal Title I program has multiple and interrelated causes. Educational objectives traditionally are foggy and unspecified; in the instance of Title I, these ill-defined goals existed in an undisciplined political system in which no superordinate, operational, or widely accepted objectives were articulated that could impose some order on an inherently ambiguous situation. It is only slight exaggeration to say that the Title I program (particularly in the early years) gave little direction beyond stating: There is a problem out there with the education of poor kids—do something about it!

But lack of clear goals would not have presented an insurmountable problem if there had existed a competent educational bureaucracy at the federal (or state) level which could have established a set of operational objectives for the program and monitored LEA activities and accomplishments. However, this bureaucratic infrastructure or effective authority did not exist when Title I was passed and, in the absence of incentives to do so, has not subsequently been established.

The powerlessness of the nominal authority in the case of Title I is symptomatic of another difficulty encountered by federal education programs generally. The history of local autonomy in the area of education exacerbates the always difficult process of establishing a workable set of incentives for those at the local level to implement federal initiatives and directives. One of the basic assumptions of this essay (and one which I do not believe is at all heroic) is that local administrators will not comply with program guidelines simply because a distant figure in Washington issues them. If federal programs are to be executed within the intent and spirit of the law, not only must the goals be understood in some rudimentary form, but some set of rewards and sanctions must be available to encourage compliance and punish misuse.

The factors which support compliance—goals, an incentive system, information feedback, reliable knowledge about effective strategies, and effective authority—are interdependent in their functioning. Weakness in any one aspect is likely to undermine the others; in the instance of Title I, each was deficient or unstable in some respect. This interdependency greatly complicates any attempt to understand what went wrong with Title I. In fact, because of the problems encountered in the implementation of this federal policy, it is very hard to conclude much of anything at all about the possible success or failure of Title I projects as antipoverty strategies or about the differential effectiveness of educational programs for the disadvantaged. Instead, the disappointment of Title I must be viewed as a failure of federal policy to stimulate these programs at the local level. Accordingly, one of the major lessons of Title I has to do with organizational incentives and imperatives. These must be acknowledged and met if broad-scale federal initiatives such as Title I are to be implemented at all.

Thus the more immediate, and possibly more difficult, task for federal educational policy makers is not just the identification of more effective educational treatments, but the formulation of incentives which would encourage local districts to establish "special educational programs for the disadvantaged."

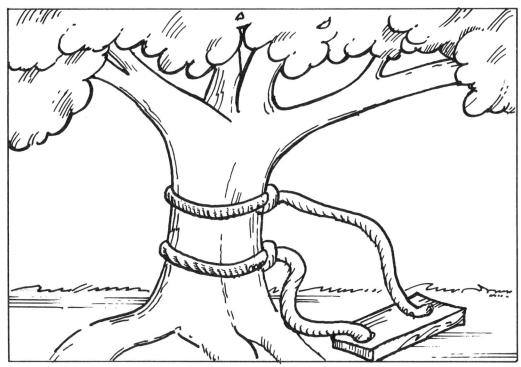

As Educational Specialists Designed It

What the Students Needed !

PART III

What Next?

A president's hardest task is not to do what is
right, but to know what is right.
>LYNDON BAINES JOHNSON, *State of the
>Union Message*, January 4, 1965

CHAPTER 10

Organizational Models of Social Program Implementation

RICHARD F. ELMORE

> All prescripts for action have to
> be simple. Action itself is sim-
> ple, or else it doesn't happen.
>
> —C.P. Snow

> We must understand that organization means delegation, and agencies, and bureaus, and technicians, and that the ideas that can survive delegation, that can be passed on to agencies and bureaus and technicians, incline to be ideas of a certain kind and of a certain simplicity: they give up something of their largeness and modulation and complexity in order to survive. The lively sense of contingency and possibility, and of those exceptions to the rule which may be the beginning of the end of the rule—this sense does not suit well with the impulse of organization.
>
> —Lionel Trilling

> That is not it at all.
> That is not what I meant, at all.
>
> —T.S. Eliot

Over the past decade social reformers have come to feel much like T.S. Eliot's J. Alfred Prufrock: Their accomplishments are a pale reflection of their intentions. The big ideas that have shaped social policy—maximum feasible participation, equality of opportunity, self-sufficiency, compensatory treatment, to name a few—seem to have become caricatures of themselves the moment they ceased to be ideas and began to be translated into action. "That's not what I meant, at all" has become the motto for a whole generation, spawned by Lyndon Johnson's Great Society and tempered by its unraveling.

Concern for the implementation of social programs stems from the recognition that policies cannot be understood in isolation from the means of their

A portion of the work on this article was supported by a grant from the Policy Research and Analysis Division of the National Science Foundation to the Institute of Governmental Research at the University of Washington. Special thanks to David K. Cohen, Harvard Graduate School of Education, who originally suggested that I pursue this idea. Thanks also to Garry Brewer, Dale Mann, Milbrey Wallin McLaughlin, Jerome Murphy, Richard Nelson, Michael Timpane, and Walter Williams for their comments and encouragement.

execution. There is a large collection of carefully documented case studies—in education, manpower, housing, and economic development—all of which point with eerie consistency to the same basic pattern: grand pretensions, faulty execution, puny results.[1] A reasonably broad consensus has developed among analysts of social policy that the inability of government to deliver on its promises derives from a failure to think systematically about the process by which declarations of intent are translated into administrative action. Another way of putting it is that *implementation failures are failures of organization.* Policies are executed by large public organizations. We can't say with much certainty what a policy is or why it is not implemented without knowing a great deal about how these organizations function. As the epigraphs from C. P. Snow and Lionel Trilling suggest, the translation of an idea into action involves certain crucial simplifications. Understanding how organizations work helps us to understand how policies are shaped in the process of implementation.

Implementation analysis requires at least two kinds of knowledge about organizations: how they work internally and how they relate to one another. In the remainder of this chapter I will refer to the former as the "micro-problem" and the latter as the "macro-problem."[2] On the micro level, we expect organizations to operate as units. When policies are implemented, we anticipate that a declaration of purpose will be followed by a set of actions consistent with that purpose. The fact that implementation has become a major problem of public policy suggests that this is not always the case. On the macro level, we know that policy implementation frequently requires the concerted action of more than one organization, each with its own structure, goals, and interests. The success or failure of implementation depends not only on the internal workings of each organization, but on relationships among organizations at different levels of the process.

THE UTILITY OF ORGANIZATIONAL MODELS

If knowledge of organizations is central to the analysis of implementation, then how do we go about putting that knowledge into a form useful for analysis? The single most important feature of organizational theory is its conceptual anarchy. When one looks to the literature on organizations for guidance in the

1 A number of these studies are collected in Walter Williams and Richard F. Elmore, eds. *Social Program Implementation*. New York: Academic Press, 1976. Another collection, which focuses on the role of regulations in the implementation process, is a special number of *Policy Sciences*, Vol. 7, Winter 1976, edited by Francine Rabinovitz, Jeffrey Pressman, and Martin Rein. Two major reviews of the literature on implementation are Donald Van Meter and Carl Van Horn, "The Policy Implementation Process: A Conceptual Framework," *Administration and Society*, Vol. 6, 1974, pp. 445–488; and Erwin Hargrove. *The Missing Link: The Study of the Implementation of Social Policy*. Washington, D.C.: Urban Institute, 1975.

2 I am indebted to Milbrey Wallin McLaughlin and Paul Berman for their development of this distinction in "Macro and Micro Implementation." Santa Monica, Calif.: Rand Corporation, P-5431, May 1975.

analysis of an important practical problem, like implementation, one finds a collection of conflicting and contradictory theories. This diversity of theory is a sure sign that knowledge in the field is "soft." This is not to say that it should be, or ever will be, "hard," but only that it is extremely difficult to use knowledge of this sort as the basis for analysis. Richard Nelson captured this difficulty nicely in his discussion of the intellectual underpinnings of policy analysis. "The problem of making sensible organizational changes," he argues, "is beyond the present capacity of the various organizational analysis traditions." He adds:

> We presently lack [a] . . . normative intellectual structure capable of guiding us effectively regarding organizational choice or modification. . . . We lack even a language that will enable us to list, and talk about, the organizational alternatives in a helpful manner.[3]

So on this point we're stuck. Having established that analysis of the implementation problem requires knowledge of organizations, we find that there is no single, coherent body of organizational theory that will serve as the basis for analysis. There are two ways of coping with this impasse. One is to make a heroic attempt to synthesize all organizational theory into a tidy set of analytical precepts useful in the analysis of implementation. The other is to acquiesce in the present diversity of thought about organizations and try to distill from that diversity a finite number of distinguishable models that can be used to analyze the implementation problem. I've chosen the latter strategy, largely because I believe the former to be impossible. This approach does not speak to Nelson's plea for an "effective normative intellectual structure," since it doesn't result in a single set of prescriptions about how implementation should be organized, but it does speak to his plea for a language that supports the discussion of organizational alternatives.

Those familiar with Graham Allison's analysis of the Cuban missile crisis[4] will recognize that I have cribbed the idea of alternative organizational models directly from him. His was the initial insight, and his is the credit for demonstrating its analytical utility. Readers of Allison will notice, however, that I depart considerably from his treatment. In most instances the differences are attributable to the nature of the subject matter; defense strategy, not surprisingly, raises a considerably different set of problems than the implementation of social programs. It should be sufficient to say that

3 Richard Nelson, "Intellectualizing about the Moon-Ghetto Metaphor: A Study of the Current Malaise of Rational Analysis of Social Problems," *Policy Sciences,* Vol. 5, 1974, p. 398. This article has been expanded into a book, *The Moon and the Ghetto*. New York, N.Y.: Norton, 1977. The book includes a number of case studies demonstrating what Nelson means by analysis of organizational alternatives. His framework differs considerably from the one developed here.

4 Graham Allison. *Essence of Decision: Explaining the Cuban Missile Crisis*. Boston: Little, Brown, 1971.

Allison is not responsible for the use that others make of his ideas.

Viewing the implementation process through a number of different organizational models allows us to be specific about the organizational assumptions we make when we offer prescriptions for improving implementation. Different models, as we will see, lead to quite different perceptions and conclusions. "What we see and judge to be important . . . ," Allison argues, "depends not only on the evidence but also on the 'conceptual lenses' through which we look at the evidence."[5] Policy analysts have, in the past, been fairly casual about specifying the organizational assumptions behind their recommendations. The price for this has been an embarrassingly large gap between the analyst's recommendations and the solutions implemented by administrators.[6] Analysis of organizational alternatives has not been part of the standard repertoire of either analysts or administrators. It is precisely this situation, one suspects, that created the implementation problem in the first place. Forcing analysts and administrators to specify the organizational assumptions underlying their proposals might ultimately drive policy making in the direction of feasible, or implementable, policies.

Some models are basically normative—they're based on strongly held opinions about how organizations ought to operate. Some models are descriptive—they attempt to capture the essential objective attributes of organizations. In some instances it's difficult to distinguish normative from descriptive elements. But in all instances the model is a simplification of reality, not a surrogate for it.[7] Simplification is another name for analysis, since analysis proceeds by isolating the essential elements of a problem and examining their relationships to one another. Simplification, by C. P. Snow's dictum, is also an essential precondition for public action.

I will develop four organizational models representing what I see as the major schools of thought that can be brought to bear on the implementation problem. The *systems management model* is my attempt to capture the organizational assumptions underlying the mainstream, rationalist tradition of policy analysis. Its point of departure is the assumptions of value-maximizing behavior that characterizes microeconomic theory, systems analysis, operations research, and theories of industrial organization. The *bureaucratic process model* represents the sociological view of organizations, updated to include recent research by students of "street-level bureaucracy," which is particularly germane to the analysis of social program implementation. Its point of departure is the assumption that the essential feature of organizations is routinized

---

5 Ibid., p. 2.

6 Ibid., p. 267. See also Arnold Meltsner, "Political Feasibility and Policy Analysis," *Public Administration Review,* November/December 1972, pp. 859–867.

7 This distinction is developed at length in Ralph Strauch, "A Critical Look at Quantitative Methodology," *Policy Analysis*, Vol. 2, 1976, pp. 121–*144*.

behavior. The *organizational development model* represents a relatively recent combination of sociological and psychological theory that focuses on the conflict between the needs of individuals and the demands of organizational life. Finally, the *conflict and bargaining model* represents a tradition of inquiry that addresses the problem of how people with divergent interests coalesce around a common task. It begins from the assumption that conflict, arising out of the pursuit of relative advantage in a bargaining relationship, is the dominant feature of organizational life.

The most important aspect of these models, however, is not that they represent certain established traditions of academic inquiry. As we shall see, their major appeal is that each contains a commonsense explanation for implementation failures. And each explanation emphasizes different features of the implementation process.

The format of the discussion will be the same for each model. I will first present a list of four assumptions that I think captures the essential features of each model. The first assumption states the central principle of the model, the second states the model's view of the distribution of power in organizations, the third states the model's view of organizational decision making, and the fourth gives a thumbnail sketch of the implementation process from the perspective of the model. I will then discuss how these assumptions affect the analyst's perception of the implementation process. In Allison's words, I will develop "a dominant inference pattern" that serves to explain why certain features of the implementation process are more important than others and to predict the consequences of certain administrative actions for the success or failure of implementation efforts. Finally, I will draw some examples from the current case literature on social program implementation that demonstrate the strengths and weakness of each model. This discussion will focus on the distinction between the "micro-problem" (the internal workings of organization) and the "macro-problem" (how organizations relate to one another).

Some readers will no doubt chafe at the idea that highly complex bodies of thoughts about organizational behavior can be reduced to a few simple assumptions, but this is an exercise in the application of theory, not an exercise in theory building. The premium is on the essential insights that each model brings to the problem, not on how to make the theory more elegant or defensible. I have tried mightily to avoid creating straw men. Each model is offered as a legitimate analytical perspective.

MODEL I: IMPLEMENTATION AS SYSTEMS MANAGEMENT

Assumptions

1. Organizations should operate as rational value-maximizers. The essential attribute of rationality is goal-directed behavior; organizations are effective

to the extent that they maximize performance on their central goals and objectives. Each task that an organization performs must contribute to at least one of a set of well-defined objectives that accurately reflect the organization's purpose.

2. Organizations should be structured on the principle of hierarchical control. Responsibility for policy making and overall system performance rests with top management, which in turn allocates specific tasks and performance objectives to subordinate units and monitors their performance.

3. For every task an organization performs there is some optimal allocation of responsibilities among subunits that maximizes the organization's overall performance on its objectives. Decision making in organizations consists of finding this optimum and maintaining it by continually adjusting the internal allocation of responsibilities to changes in the environment.

4. Implementation consists of defining a detailed set of objectives that accurately reflects the intent of a given policy, assigning responsibilities and standards of performance to subunits consistent with these objectives, monitoring system performance, and making internal adjustments that enhance the attainment of the organization's goals. The process is dynamic, not static; the environment continually imposes new demands which require internal adjustments. But implementation is always goal-directed and value-maximizing.

A frequent explanation for failures of implementation is "bad management." We generally mean by this that policies are poorly defined, responsibilities are not clearly assigned, expected outcomes are not specified, and people are not held accountable for their performance. Good management is, of course, the opposite of all these things, and therein lies the crux of the systems management model.

The intellectual roots of the model are diverse: the literature that treats organizations as social systems, microeconomic theories of decision making, theories of management control, and the considerable written record on the use of systems analysis in national defense planning.[8] All these sources share a common normative assumption that effective management proceeds from goal-directed, value-maximizing behavior. All human problem solving proceeds according to the same basic set of operations, beginning from a clearly stated objective, choosing an optimal means of achieving that objective, and

8 Daniel Katz and Robert Kahn. *The Social Psychology of Organizations*. New York: John Wiley, 1966; William Baumol. *Economic Theories and Operations Analysis*. Englewood Cliffs, N.J.: Prentice-Hall, 1972, 3d ed.; Robert Anthony. *Planning and Control Systems: A Framework for Analysis*. Boston: Harvard Graduate School of Business Administration, 1965; C. West Churchman. *The Systems Approach*. New York: Delta, 1968; and Charles Hitch and Roland McKean. *The Economics of Defense in a Nuclear Age*. Cambridge, Mass.: Harvard University Press, 1963.

modifying behavior based on the consequences of that choice.[9] Individuals and organizations can be thought of as problem-solving "systems"—functionally integrated collections of parts that are capable of concerted action around a common purpose. In the individual the controlling and coordinating mechanism is the human mind. In organizations, it is "the management subsystem."

Integration requires control, and control presupposes authority. The management subsystem is "the source of binding pronouncements and the locus of the decision-making process."[10] It provides "a means of insuring role performance, replacing lost members, coordinating the several subsystems of the organization, responding to external changes, and making decisions about how all these things should be accomplished."[11] Through the exercise of hierarchical control, then, the management subsystem makes the organization function as an integrated whole.

The translation of policy into action consists of a deliberate, stepwise process in which goals are elaborated into specific tasks. Robert Anthony's discussion of planning and management control gives a succinct statement of the transition from policy to operations.

> Strategic planning is the process of deciding on objectives, on resources used to obtain these objectives, and on the policies that are to govern acquisition, use and disposition of these resources. . . . Management control is the process by which managers assure that resources are obtained and used effectively and efficiently in the accomplishment of the organization's objectives. . . . [And] operational control is the process of assuring that specific tasks are carried out effectively and efficiently.[12]

These functions are distributed in descending order from the highest to lowest levels of the organization. Taken together, they describe a general set of decision rules for the optimal allocation of resources, tasks, and performance criteria among subunits of an organization.

For all its emphasis on hierarchical control, one would expect that the systems management model would make little or no allowance for the exercise of lower-level discretion by subordinates carrying out policy directives. In fact, this is not quite the case. The problem of subordinate discretion figures prominently in the literature of systems management. Understandably, the issue arose in a very visible way during the initial attempts to apply systems analysis to national defense planning. Defense planners found almost immediately that the ability of the management subsystem to control the performance of subunits

9   Churchman. *The Systems Approach*, p. 6ff.
10   Katz and Kahn. *The Social Psychology of Organizations*, p. 79.
11   Ibid., p. 203. Cf. Churchman. *The Systems Approach*, p. 44.
12   Anthony. *Planning and Control Systems*, pp. 16–18.

was limited by the enormous complexity of the total system. Hence, a great deal hinged on discovering the correct mix of hierarchical control and subordinate discretion. Hitch and McKean call this process "suboptimization," which they define as an "attempt to find optimal (or near optimal) solutions, but to subproblems rather than to the whole problem of the organization in whose welfare or utility we are interested."[13] In organizational terms, suboptimization consists of holding subunits responsible for a certain level of output but giving subunit managers the discretion to decide on the means of achieving that level. In business parlance, these subunits are called "profit centers"; in the public sector they have been called "responsibility centers." Suboptimization provides a means of exercising hierarchical control by focusing on the output of subunits rather than on their technically complex internal operations.

In practice, suboptimization raises some very complex problems: selecting appropriate criteria of subunit performance, accounting for the unintended consequences, or spillovers, of one unit's performance on another's, and choosing the appropriate aggregation of functions for each subunit.[14] But the notion of suboptimization gives the systems management model a degree of flexibility that is not often appreciated by its critics. It is *not* necessary to assume that all organizational decisions are centralized in order to assume that organizations are functionally integrated.[15] If the outputs of delegated decisions are consistent with the overall goals of the organization, then there is room for a certain degree of latitude in the selection of means for achieving those outputs.

13 Hitch and McKean. *The Economics of Defense in a Nuclear Age,* pp. 128–129; also, pp. 396–402. Their choice of the term suboptimization is perhaps unfortunate because to most of us it communicates the meaning "less-than-optimal," which is quite the opposite of the meaning they wish to convey. It is clear from their discussion that they intend the term to mean "optimizing at lower levels." Some writers, however, insist on using the term to mean less-than-optimal. See, e.g., Anthony. *Planning and Control Systems*, p. 35. Two other sources in which the term is used consistently with the meaning of Hitch and McKean are Baumol. *Economic Theories and Operations Analysis*, p. 395n; and Richard Zeckhauser and Elmer Schaefer, "Public Policy and Normative Economic Theory," in Raymond Bauer and Kenneth Gergen, eds. *The Study of Policy Formation*. New York: Free Press, 1968, pp. 73–76. A more recent treatment of suboptimization in policy analysis may be found in E. S. Quade. *Analysis for Public Decisions*. New York: Elsevier, 1975, pp. 95–98.

14 Hitch and McKean. *The Economics of Defense in a Nuclear Age*, p. 129.

15 Nor is it necessary to assume, as Graham Allison does, that a "rational" model of decision making is one that treats all decisions as if they were the product of a single decision maker (Allison. *Essence of Decision*, pp. 3, 28, 36.) Most theories of rational choice encourage this view by using stock phrases like "the decision-maker's problem," "the decision-maker's preference," etc. In organizational terms, though, the important issue is not whether the peculiar fiction of the single, value-maximizing decision maker can be maintained, but whether it is possible to construct a set of organizational controls sufficient to integrate subunits of an organization into a functional whole.

This is a point of difference between Allison's discussion and mine. In his Rational Actor Model (*Essence of Decision*, pp. 10–38), he treats all decisions as the product of a single decision maker, and this makes it very easy to criticize the model. My intention is to demonstrate that there is a substantial body of theory that treats organizations as rational, value-maximizing units, but which does not depend on the fiction of the single decision maker.

A great deal of behavior in organizations can be explained by examining devices of control and compliance. Some are easy to identify, some blend into the subtle social fabric of organizations. One common device is what Herbert Kaufman calls the "preformed decision." He argues that "organizations might disintegrate if each field officer made entirely independent decisions," so organizations develop ways of making decisions for their field officers "in advance of specific situations requiring choice."

> Events and conditions in the field are anticipated as fully as possible, and courses of action [for each set of events and conditions] are described. The field officers then need determine only into what category a particular instance falls; once this determination is made, he then simply follows a series of steps applicable to that category. Within each category, therefore, the decisions are "preformed."[16]

Much of the work of high-level administrators in the implementation process consists of anticipating recurrent problems at lower levels of the system and attempting to program the behavior of subordinates to respond to these problems in standardized ways.

But not all devices of control are so obvious. In a casual aside, Robert Anthony remarks that "the system [of management controls] should be so constructed that actions that operating managers take in their perceived self-interest are also in the best interests of the whole organization."[17] This suggests that an important ingredient of control is to be found in the way people are socialized to organizations. Social psychologists Katz and Kahn observe that all organizations have "maintenance subsystems" for recruitment, indoctrination, socialization, reward, and sanctions that "function to maintain the fabric of interdependent behavior necessary for task accomplishment." These devices are the basis for "standardized patterns of behavior required of persons playing a part in a given functional relationship, regardless of personal wishes or interpersonal obligations irrelevant to the functional relationship."[18] In plain English, this means that organizations often require people to put the requirements of their formal roles above their personal preferences. The effect of this is to enhance the predictability and control of subordinate behavior in much the same way as preformed decisions and suboptimization. The difference is that instead of shaping decisions, it is the decision *makers* who are shaped.

The major appeal of the systems management model is that it can be readily translated into a set of normative prescriptions that policy analysts can use to

16 Herbert Kaufman. *The Forest Ranger: A Study in Administrative Behavior*. Baltimore: Johns Hopkins University Press, 1960, p. 91.
17 Anthony. *Planning and Control Systems*, p. 45.
18 Katz and Kahn. *The Social Psychology of Organizations*, p. 40.

say how the implementation process ought to work. From the model's perspective, there are essentially four ingredients of effective implementation: (1) clearly specified tasks and objectives that accurately reflect the intent of policy; (2) a management plan that allocates tasks and performance standards to sub-units; (3) an objective means of measuring subunit performance; and (4) a system of management controls and social sanctions sufficient to hold subordinates accountable for their performance. Failures of implementation are, by definition, lapses of planning, specification, and control. The analysis of implementation consists of finding, or anticipating, these breakdowns and suggesting how they ought to be remedied.

Analysis is made a good deal easier in this model by virtue of the fact that organizations are assumed to operate as units—there is a single conception of policy that can be traced through the hierarchical structure of an organization. The success or failure of an effort is judged by observing the discrepancy between the policy declaration and subordinate behavior. The analyst focuses on the "clarity, precision, comprehensiveness, and reasonableness of the preliminary policy," on "the technical capacity to implement," and on "the extent to which the actual outputs of the organization have changed in the expected direction after the introduction of the innovation."[19] But in order for this conception of analysis to make any sense in organizational terms, one must first assume that policy makers, administrators, and analysts have a common understanding of policy and have sufficient control of the implementation process to hold subordinates accountable to that understanding.

A great deal would seem to depend, then, on whether organizations can actually be structured on the assumption of the systems management model. The empirical evidence is suggestive, but hardly conclusive. Herbert Kaufman, who has made a career of studying administrative compliance and control, concludes his classic study of the U.S. Forest Service with the observation that "overall performance comes remarkably close to the goals set by the leadership." This was accomplished using a set of management controls and social sanctions that closely approximate the systems management mode. The net result is that, "the Rangers want to do the very things that the Forest Service wants them to do, and are able to do them, because these are the decisions and actions that become second nature to them as a result of years of obedience."[20]

Much the same conclusion is reported by Jeremiah O'Connell in his study of the implementation of a major reorganization of a large insurance company. He sets out to demonstrate the effectiveness of an implementation strategy based on "unilateral" action by top management and on "economic values." The

19 Walter Williams, "Implementation Analysis and Assessment," in Williams and Elmore, eds. *Social Program Implementation*, pp. 281–282.
20 Kaufman. *The Forest Ranger*, pp. 203, 228.

reorganization plan was a pristine example of suboptimization:

> Managers will have line responsibility for the accumulated results every week of a unit composed of seven to ten men. . . . Line responsibility makes each . . . manager accountable for determining the use of his personal time. His record will be the combined record of his agency unit. On this record his performance will be evaluated, he will be recognized, and he will be compensated.

O'Connell argues that the plan had its intended effect of putting "the best resources possible in the most promising markets," hence presumably increasing company profits.[21]

The distinctive feature of both these cases is strong management control in the presence of wide geographical dispersion, which suggests that they must have some relevance to the study of social program implementation. But this is where the distinction between the micro- and macro-problems becomes crucial. No matter how well organized an agency is internally, it might still fail to implement programs successfully if it has to depend on other agencies to execute its decisions. And this is the central problem of social program implementation. In both the examples cited above, the implementing agent is a direct subordinate of management; he is selected, indoctrinated, rewarded, and penalized by the same people who articulate policy. Where more than one agency is involved in the implementation process, the lines of management control are much more blurred. It is not uncommon for implementers of social policy to be responsible to more than one political jurisdiction—to the federal government for a general declaration of policy and to a state or local unit for the myriad of administrative details that determine one's day-to-day survival in a public agency. These jurisdictional boundaries are a permanent fixture of the American federal system; they exist not to enhance the efficiency of social program implementation but to protect the political prerogatives of state and local government. So while the systems management model tells us something about the micro-problem—the antecedents and techniques of internal management control—it says nothing about the macro-problem—what happens when the implementation process extends across jurisdictional boundaries.

As we shall see later, there is also substantial disagreement about the adequacy of the systems management model for representing the micro-problem. In most large public bureaucracies there are a number of factors that undermine hierarchical control, such as routinized behavior that persists in the face of new policies, lack of consensus among superiors and subordinates over organizational goals, and conflict among subunits for the scarce resources of the organi-

---

21 Jeremiah O'Connell. *Managing Organizational Innovation*. Homewood, Ill.: Irwin, 1968, pp. 10, 72, 74, 13.

zation. All of these things tend to undermine the notion of organizations as rational, unitary, value-maximizing units.

Does this mean that the systems management model is of no use in understanding the implementation process? It depends on how one proposes to use the model. For the most part, those who rely on the systems management model don't contend that it gives an accurate description of the implementation process, only that it provides a useful way of thinking about how the process *ought* to work. The distinction is not quite so disingenuous as it sounds. We frequently rely on normative models as guides to action even though we understand perfectly well that they have very little descriptive validity. We do so because they provide useful ways of organizing and simplifying complex problems. In this sense, the test of a model is not whether it accurately represents reality, but whether it has some utility as a problem-solving device. The major utility of the systems management model is that it directs our attention toward the mechanisms that policy makers and high-level administrators have for structuring and controlling the behavior of subordinates.

There is some danger, however, in focusing on the normative utility of the model to the exclusion of its descriptive validity. To say that the model simplifies the implementation process in certain useful ways is not the same as saying that process should be structured around the model. This is a mistake that analysts are particularly prone to make, and it involves a peculiar and obvious circularity. If there is a lack of fit between model and reality, the argument goes, then the model should be used to restructure reality. Only then, the analyst concludes triumphantly, can it be determined whether the model "works" or not. A special form of this argument is that social programs fail because policies are poorly specified and management control is weak. To the extent that we remedy these problems we can predict a higher ratio of successes to failures. The problem with this argument is that the definition of success is internal to the model, and it may or may not be shared by people who are actually part of the process. The systems management model will almost certainly "work" if everyone behaves according to its dictates. If we could make value-maximizers of all organizations, then we could no doubt prove that all organizations are value-maximizers. But the point is that people in organizations who carry out policy don't necessarily share the norms of the model. Sometimes we find it convenient to behave as value-maximizers, sometimes we don't. The distance between the model and reality, in other words, shouldn't necessarily be read as a sign that reality needs reforming. It can also be read as a sign that the model fails to capture certain important elements of the problem.

Another important point about the use of the systems management model is the tendency of analysts to define the implementation process exclusively in terms of the components of the model. To the extent that people act in accordance with the model, they will tend to focus the largest proportion of their effort on the precise specification of policies, on the definition of delegated responsibilities, on the measurement of subunit performance, and on control and compliance procedures. The original policy, whatever it was to start with, becomes these things in the process of implementation. It is no longer a global statement of intent, but a collection of value-maximizing procedures designed to enhance hierarchical control. To see the process exclusively in terms of these elements is to ignore or dismiss as irrelevant all the devices that subordinates have for resisting hierarchical control—and these latter devices may play a very important part in the implementation process. The systems management model has a tendency to make the process appear to be orderly, controllable, and predictable, whether it actually is or not. This is what makes it useful to posit alternative organizational models.

MODEL II: IMPLEMENTATION AS BUREAUCRATIC PROCESS

Assumptions

1. The central attribute of all organizations is routinized behavior; all important behavior in organizations can be explained by examining established routines: regulations, guidelines, budget and planning cycles, clearance procedures, and informal work routines that people develop to simplify and control their jobs. Routines develop slowly over time and represent an accumulated expertise that comes from the repeated performance of a single well-defined task. They are relatively stable and impersonal; they resist change and they can be passed from one generation of employees to the next with minimum disruption.
2. Routinized behavior means that power in organizations is distributed by delegated discretion rather than hierarchical control. The amount of control that any one organizational unit can exercise over another—laterally or hierarchically—is hedged in by the existence of routines. If a routine locates responsibility for a specific task in one unit of an organization, that unit exercises virtually complete control over the execution of that task. Of necessity, some personal discretion is exercised in the performance of organizational routines, but the discretion is circumscribed by the limited scope of the routines themselves. The more elaborate the operating routines of an organization, the more power tends to be dispersed among small units with limited discretion in specific tasks.
3. Organizational changes are, of necessity, changes in operating routines. Consequently, all proposals for change are evaluated in terms of the degree to which they depart from established procedure. Decision making in organizations consists of executing an established routine, making a small discretionary change in a routine, or inventing a new routine to cover a new

responsibility or an unforeseen problem.

4. Policy implementation consists of identifying which of the organization's repertoire of routines needs changing, devising alternative routines that represent the intent of policy, and inducing organizational units to replace old routines with new ones.

We reach instinctively for bureaucratic explanations of implementation failures. "There was a major change in policy," we say, "but the bureaucracy kept right on doing what it did before." Or alternatively, "When the bureaucracy got through with it, the policy didn't look anything like we intended." Lately, bureaucracy has become an all-purpose explanation for everything that is wrong with government. We use terms like "the bureaucracy problem"[22] and "the bureaucratic phenomenon"[23] to describe behavior of public officials that is "inefficient, unresponsive, unfair, ponderous, or confusing."[24]

Bureaucracy has other, less pejorative meanings, of course. For Max Weber, it was a form of government that substituted impersonal, efficient, and routinized authority for that based on personal privilege or divine inspiration. Bureaucracy has also been defined in terms of its objective structural characteristics: size, the nature of its work force, internal criteria of promotion and retention, and proximity to market forces.[25] Bureaucracies share a number of characteristics with organizations in general—hierarchy, division of labor, specialization, etc.—that sometimes lead people to use the terms interchangably.

But none of these broad views captures the specific elements of bureaucracy that affect policy implementation. The problems of implementing policies in bureaucratic settings can be traced to two basic elements: routine and discretion. On the one hand, bureaucratic behavior resists change because it is routinized. But on the other hand, bureaucrats exercise a fair amount of latitude in the performance of their jobs; this discretion is difficult to control by changing policies. Both factors result in unresponsiveness to policy directives, but they seem to lead in opposite directions—the first toward rule-bound behavior, the second toward arbitrary behavior. In fact, they're not nearly as inconsistent as they appear to be. As bureaucracies become more complex, they become more rule-bound because standardized routines are one of the few ways superiors can direct subordinates. Increasing complexity, though, also results in increased delegation of responsibility and, hence, in greater exercise of subordinate discretion. To paraphrase Graham Allison, factored problem-solving leads to fractionated power.[26]

22 James Q. Wilson, "The Bureaucracy Problem," *The Public Interest*, No. 6, Winter 1967, pp. 3–9.
23 Michel Crozier. *The Bureaucratic Phenomenon*. Chicago: University of Chicago Press, 1964.
24 James Q. Wilson. *Varieties of Police Behavior*. New York: Atheneum, 1973, p. 1.
25 Anthony Downs. *Inside Bureaucracy*. Boston: Little Brown, 1966, pp. 24–25.
26 Allison. *Essence of Decision*, p. 80.

In most public service bureaucracies, as we shall see, the nature of the work is such that discretion is concentrated on the bottom of the organization, hedged on all sides by operating routines. This makes it doubly difficult to implement policy. The central focus of the bureaucracy problem, according to James Q. Wilson, is "getting the front-line worker—the teacher, nurse, diplomat, police officer, or welfare worker—to do the right thing." The job of administration is, purely and simply, "controlling discretion."[27]

Bureaucratic routines are of two types—the formal routines by which superiors attempt to control the discretion of subordinates, and the informal routines by which people at all levels of a bureaucracy structure and simplify their work. In the former category are regulations, guidelines, budget and planning cycles, paper-processing and clearance procedures, reporting requirements, and evaluation procedures. In the latter category are the hundreds of rules of thumb, growing out of the day-to-day performance of a job, which provide people with the means of reducing complexity, avoiding trouble, and minimizing uncertainty. Not surprisingly, if you ask a high-level government administrator what implementation means he will probably reply that it consists of translating legislation into regulations and guidelines. In other words, it is the use of formal routines to structure the behavior of subordinates. But if you ask the same question of the front-line worker, the answer is likely to be quite different. In addition to responding to the directives imposed from above, the front-line worker must cope with the immediate pressures of delivering a service, and this requires inventing and learning a completely different set of informal organizational routines. This accounts for the sometimes quizzical, sometimes skeptical look one often gets from teachers, social workers, and others in similar positions when they're asked about the implementation of a policy. "Policy?" they reply, "We're so busy getting the work done we haven't much time to think about policy."

The major consequence of routinized behavior in organizations is the dispersion, even atomization, of power. Every unit at every level of the organization has its own repertoire of routines, firmly rooted in the demands of daily work. Formal procedures, like budgeting and reporting, are intended to enhance hierarchical control and coordination. But the effect of these is hedged in by the fact that most of the actual work, particularly in public service bureaucracies, is done by smaller units with relatively high discretion and their own well-established work routines. Under these circumstances, power tends to become diffused and dispersed among individuals and small units with limited discretion over specific tasks.

The bureaucratic process model, then, traces the effect of routinized behavior, formal and informal, on the execution of policy. The existing routines

---

27 Wilson. *Varieties of Police Behavior*, pp. 2–3, 9, 64ff.

of an organization are taken as given, and the central analytical problem is to discover how a new policy can be made to affect them. The major difference between this view and the systems management model is that the latter assumes that the totality of an organization's resources can be directed toward a single, coherent set of purposes, while the former regards that issue as problematical. Routines are, by their very nature, designed to produce standardized responses to recurring problems. New policies require nonstandard responses. The systems management model assumes that, through the exercise of unitary control, management can direct an organization toward whatever ends it regards as necessary. The bureaucratic process model assumes that the dominant characteristic of organization is resistance to change—not simply inertia (the tendency to move in one direction until deflected by some outside force), but, as Donald Schon observes, "dynamic conservatism"[28] (the tendency to fight to remain the same). In the systems management model one assumes that, given the right set of management controls, subunits of an organization will do what they are told; in the bureaucratic process model, one assumes that they will continue to do what they have been doing until some way is found to make them do otherwise.

In the implementation of social programs the problem of routinized behavior is particularly apparent. New policies must typically travel from one large public bureaucracy to another, and then through several successive layers of the final implementing agency before they reach the point of impact on the client. Whether or not the policy has its intended effect on the client depends in large part on whether the force of existing routine at each level of the process operates with or against the policy.

It is frequently at the final stage of this process—the point of delivery from agency to client—that the forces of routine are most difficult to overcome. This problem is the central concern of students of "street-level bureaucracy." The growth of large public service agencies has created a distinguishable class of bureaucrat—one who shoulders virtually all responsibility for direct contact with clients, who exercises a relatively large degree of discretion over detailed decisions of client treatment, and who therefore has considerable potential impact on clients.[29] From the client's perspective, the street-level bureaucrat *is* the government. Clients seldom, if ever, interact with higher-level administrators; in fact, most public service bureaucracies are deliberately designed to prevent this. Because of the frequency and immediacy of the contact between street-level bureaucrats and their clients, it is usually impossible for higher-level administrators to monitor or control all aspects of their job performance.

28 Donald Schon. *Beyond the Stable State*. New York: Random House, 1971, p. 32.
29 Michael Lipsky, "Toward a Theory of Street-Level Bureaucracy," in Willis Hawley and Michael Lipsky, eds. *Theoretical Perspectives on Urban Politics*. Englewood Cliffs, N.J.: Prentice Hall, 1976, p. 197.

Consequently, a significant distance opens up between the street-level bureaucrat and his superiors. This distance breeds autonomy and discretion at lower levels of the organization. The distinctive quality of street-level bureaucracy is that "discretion increases as one moves down the hierarchy."[30]

But this concentration of discretion at lower levels has a paradoxical quality. For while street-level bureaucrats occupy the most critical position in the delivery process, their working conditions are seldom conducive to the adequate performance of their jobs. More often than not, they find themselves in situations where they lack the organizational and personal resources to perform their jobs adequately, where they are exposed regularly to physical or psychological threat, and where there are conflicting and ambiguous expectations about how they ought to perform their work.[31] Social service delivery jobs are among the most stressful in our society. Street-level bureaucrats are expected to treat clients as individuals, but the high demand for their services forces them to invent routines for mass processing. High-level administrators and policy makers are preoccupied with the way policy is expressed in legislation, regulations, and guidelines. But the major concern for the street-level implementer is how to control the stress and complexity of day-to-day work. Out of this concern grows a whole set of informal routines that students of street-level bureaucracy call "coping mechanisms."

Learning to cope with the stresses of service delivery means learning to rely on simple, standardized sources of information on clients—case histories, employment records, permanent school records, test scores, eligibility forms, etc. It means developing a facility for classifying and labeling people simply and quickly—"an alcoholic parent," "a broken family," "a history of drug abuse," "violence-prone and resistant to authority," "can't hold a job," etc. It means developing one's "faculties of suspicion" in order to spot people who pose a threat either to oneself or to the system one is administering. And it means using the formal procedures of the organization to strike an impersonal distance between oneself, as an individual, and the client.[32] All these mechanisms have the effect of reducing and controlling the stress and uncertainty of daily work, and for this reason they figure prominently in the implementation of social policy. On the other hand, they are not typically included in the policy maker's or the high-level administrator's definition of "policy." More often than not, they're either ignored or regarded as external to the implementation process.

Concentrating on formal declarations of policy at the expense of informal coping routines means that "even the most imaginative manipulations of goals, structure, staff recruitment, training and supervision may . . . represent only

---

30 Wilson. *Varieties of Police Behavior*, p. 7.
31 Hawley and Lipsky. *Theoretical Perspectives on Urban Politics*, pp. 197–198.
32 Ibid., pp. 201ff.

superficial changes . . . rather than the fundamental reforms hoped for."[33] From the perspective of the bureaucratic process model, major shifts in policy have little or no effect until they reach the final transaction between service-giver and client. The elaborate superstructure of regulations, guidelines, and management controls that accompany most social programs tend to have weak and unpredictable effects on the delivery of social services because street-level bureaucrats and their clients develop strong patterns of interaction that are relatively immune to change. Implementation failures, from this point of view, are the result of a failure on the part of policy makers to understand the actual conditions under which social services are delivered.

Empirical evidence demonstrating the effect of organizational routines on the implementation of social policy, while not extensive, is certainly compelling. Probably the first serious attempt to document the street-level effect of a major shift in policy was Miriam Johnson's study of how national manpower policy influences the operation of local employment service offices in California.[34] The employment services is in some respects the archetypal social service delivery system. Initiated and largely funded by the federal government, it is totally administered by the states under broad guidelines from the federal level. The essential transactions of the employment service, however, occur at the street level, where employers and prospective employees are matched. Prior to the mid-1960s the state employment services operated largely as labor exchanges; their purpose was simply to match the best person with the available job. During the mid-sixties, new federal manpower policies emphasized the services' responsibility to undertake remedial programs designed to get the poor and unskilled into the labor market. Then in the early seventies growing skepticism about the services' ability to help the disadvantaged resulted in a shift back to the original conception of the labor exchange. Johnson gives a client's-eye view of what it was like to deal with the employment service in each of these periods.

In the first phase—the labor exchange—the client's transaction with the emploment service was dominated by the impersonal reception line and counter that separated client from bureaucrat. "There was no way for an applicant to bypass the line," Johnson says, because only by waiting in line could the applicant get the required forms.

> The reception line led to the counter, which stood as a rampart, a boundary that defined the combat areas. It protected and defended the public agency from assault and harrassment, from the public it served, from "they"— the enemy.[35]

33 Richard Weatherley, "Toward a Theory of Client Control in Street-Level Bureaucracy," unpublished paper, School of Social Work, University of Washington, 1976, p. 5.
34 Miriam Johnson. *Counter Point: The Changing Employment Service.* Salt Lake City: Olympus, 1973.
35 Ibid., p. 21.

When the California State Employment Service began to respond to the federal mandate to provide services for the disadvantaged, it did so by initiating small, experimental projects rather than attempting wholesale reform of the agency. The employment service workers who participated in these projects were given a great deal of latitude in designing them, and the first things they eliminated were the reception line and the counter. For Johnson, this was evidence that workers were just as oppressed by the routines of the old system as clients.[36] The counter was replaced by more informal, less structured interactions which often took the form of group counseling sessions. But these experimental projects ''had no significant effect on the designers of new manpower programs and delivery systems.''[37] The rest of the employment service seemed largely unaffected by the experimental projects.

With the return to the labor exchange idea in the early seventies, employment service offices looked pretty much the same as they always had, but there was one interesting, seemingly minor difference in operating routines at the local level.

> There was still a counter . . . and there was still a receptionist. . . . [But] on the public side of the counter was something of value, . . . access to the jobs themselves. A Job Information Center was required in all . . . local offices by 1970. . . . The area was open to the public and it was not necessary to be registered for work in order to use the . . . Center. [It] was a self-screening operation in which the office supplied the referral information at the request of the applicant.[38]

It is ironic, after all the bombast and rhetoric of social action in the mid-sixties, that the net effect on the employment service should be something as simple as moving job information from one side of the counter to the other. But the example illustrates both the enormous resilience and importance of operating routines. Experimental projects had very little effect on the day-to-day operations of local offices, and the one change that did occur might easily have been overlooked by an analyst less sensitive to operating routines.

Another important example of street-level response to high-level policy is Weatherley and Lipsky's analysis of the Massachusetts Comprehensive Special Education Law.[39] The law is a carefully conceived effort to put an end to arbitrary and discriminatory treatment of handicapped children by the public school system. Each local school district is required to provide an indi-

---

36 Ibid., pp. 63–64.
37 Ibid., pp. 85–86.
38 Ibid., p. 109.
39 Richard Weatherley and Michael Lipsky, ''Street-Level Bureaucrats and Institutional Innovation: Implementing Special-Education Reform,'' *Harvard Educational Review*, Vol. 47, May 1977, pp. 171–97. (See chapter 4 *infra*.)

vidualized evaluation of a child's needs by a team that includes teachers, specialists, and parents. The evaluation is to result in a plan for each child, outlining the services the school system will offer. If the school system cannot provide the services required, it must pay to have them provided elsewhere. To the extent possible, handicapped children must be included in regular classrooms. And the traditional labels that had stigmatized children with special problems were to be eliminated.

During the first year of its implementation (1974–75), state and local administrators began to discover that the law imposed burdens "well beyond the capacity of any school system."[40] There was a cruel dilemma implicit in the implemented program. On the one hand the law required individualized treatment, but on the other it created such an enormous administrative burden at the local level that educators were forced to develop routines for mass processing.[41] Local educators developed simple decision rules for differentiating more and less difficult cases; the loudest, most disruptive children were referred for evaluation first; children with easily identified, routine problems were processed perfunctorily, while those with more complex problems or "disruptive" parents were treated more circumspectly; teachers and administrators collaborated to reduce referrals when the burden became too heavy.[42] The evaluation conferences, which brought together teachers, specialists, and parents tended to be characterized by largely negative assessments of children, the use of technical jargon, and preoccupation with the assignment of blame, all of which enhanced the position of professionals over parents and made the assessment procedure move more smoothly.[43] The traditional labels for children's problems were eliminated, but new, more euphemistic labels were invented.[44] In other words, routinization at the local level largely undermined the broad purposes of the law.

The basic problem, Weatherley and Lipsky point out, was not that local school personnel were determined to subvert the law. On the contrary, they made great personal sacrifices to make it work. The real problem was that the law reflected absolutely no understanding of how street-level bureaucrats respond to changes in policy and the increased work loads they entail. Faced with a broad legislative mandate and a large, complex new responsibility, local implementers invented operating routines that helped simplify their work but ran counter to the intent of the legislation.

The central importance of routinized behavior is borne out in a number of other studies of schools. One classic account is Philip Jackson's *Life in Class-*

40 Ibid., p. 180.
41 Ibid., p. 182.
42 Ibid., pp. 186–187.
43 Ibid., pp. 189–190.
44 Ibid., pp. 192–193.

rooms.[45] "Learning to live in a classroom," Jackson observes, "involves learning to live in a crowd." Much school behavior consists of crowd control routines that result in "delay, denial, interruption, and social distraction" for students—long lines, bells, whistles, prescribed schedules, and complex and confusing instructions are all part of the daily routine of school.[46] Weikart and Banet, describing their attempt to implement a new educational program, observe that one of the most difficult obstacles they confronted was convincing a school principal to authorize the removal of the bolts that were holding the desks to the classroom floor.[47] Seymour Sarason suggests that the way to make sense of behavior in schools is to observe "programmatic and behavior regularities" as if one were witnessing them for the first time.[48] None of these things is normally included in anyone's definition of educational policy, but they all have an enormous effect on the way schools respond to mandates for change. They are the stuff that makes new policy indistinguishable from old policy after it is implemented.

The major advantage of the bureaucratic process model is that it forces us to contend with the mundane patterns of bureaucratic life and to think about how new policies affect the daily routines of people who deliver social services. Policy makers, analysts, and administrators have a tendency to focus on variables that emphasize control and predictability, often overlooking the factors that undermine control and create anomalies in the implementation process. Bureaucratic routines operate against the grain of many policy changes because they are contrived as buffers against change and uncertainty; they continue to exist precisely because they have an immediate utility to the people who use them in reducing the stress and complexity of work. Failing to account for the force of routine in the implementation of policy leads to serious misperceptions.

Walter Williams argues that most implementation problems grow out of a division of labor between what he calls the "policy and operations spheres."[49] In the policy sphere, people tend to focus on global issues and general shifts in the distribution of power among governmental units. Consequently, when the responsibility for implementation shifts to the operations sphere there is little in the way of useful guidance for implementers. The limited case literature on the role of bureaucratic routines bears out this observation. The unresponsiveness

---

45 Philip Jackson. *Life in Classrooms*. New York: HoH, Rinehart and Winston, 1968.
46 Ibid., pp. 10, 17.
47 David Weikart and Bernard Banet, "Planned Variation from the Perspective of a Model Sponsor," in Walter Williams and Richard F. Elmore, eds. *Social Program Implementation*. New York: Academic Press, 1976, p. 128.
48 Seymour Sarason. *The Culture of the School and the Problem of Change*. Boston: Allyn and Bacon, 1971, p. 63ff.
49 Walter Williams, "Implementation Problems in Federally Funded Programs," in Williams and Elmore, eds. *Social Program Implementation*, pp. 20–23.

of large public bureaucracies to new policy initiatives is more often than not attributable to a failure to connect the "big ideas" of policy makers with the mundane coping mechanisms of implementers.

Unlike the systems management model, the bureaucratic process model does not give any clear-cut prescriptions on how to improve the implementation process. About the only normative advice offered by students of street-level bureaucracy is the rather weak suggestion that "bureaucratic coping behaviors cannot be eliminated, but they can be monitored and directed" by rewarding "those that most closely conform to preferred public objectives [and] discouraging objectionable practices."[50] What this prescription overlooks is the fact that coping routines derive their appeal and resilience from the fact that they are rooted in the immediate demands of work and are, therefore, relatively immune from hierarchical control. Since operating routines are a permanent fixture of bureaucratic life, it seems clear that implementation consists essentially in substituting one set of routines for another. Exactly how this occurs remains obscure, since, as the cases indicate, the results of tampering with bureaucratic routines are usually very unpredictable. The utility of the bureaucratic process model shouldn't hang entirely on its normative power, however, because it provides an enormously useful descriptive insight. It is useful both as a micromodel and a macromodel; in the former case, it allows us to focus on and isolate the patterns that develop in transactions between street-level bureaucrats and their clients, and in the latter case it draws attention to the tenuous formal procedures by which one large organization attempts to influence another. It captures, in other words, a fairly common pattern of implementation failure, where the controls and operating routines generated by one level of government lose their identity as they pass to another.

MODEL III: IMPLEMENTATION AS ORGANIZATIONAL DEVELOPMENT

Assumptions

1. Organizations should function so as to satisfy the basic psychological and social needs of individuals—for autonomy and control over their own work, for participation in decisions affecting them, and for commitment to the purposes of the organization.
2. Organizations should be structured to maximize individual control, participation, and commitment at all levels. Hierarchically structured bureaucracies maximize these things for people in upper levels of the organization at the expense of those in lower levels. Hence, the best organizational structure is one that minimizes hierarchical control and distributes responsibility for decisions among all levels of the organization.

---

50 Weatherley and Lipsky, "Street-Level Bureaucrats and Institutional Innovation," p. 196.

3. Effective decision making in organizations depends on the creation of effective work groups. The quality of interpersonal relations in organizations largely determines the quality of decisions. Effective work groups are characterized by mutual agreement on goals, open communication among individuals, mutual trust and support among group members, full utilization of members' skills, and effective management of conflict. Decision making consists primarily of building consensus and strong interpersonal relations among group members.

4. The implementation process is necessarily one of consensus-building and accommodation between policy makers and implementers. The central problem of implementation is not whether implementers conform to prescribed policy but whether the implementation process results in consensus on goals, individual autonomy, and commitment to policy on the part of those who must carry it out.

Another frequent explanation of implementation failures is that those who implement programs are seldom included in decisions that determine the content of those programs. The closer one gets to the point of delivery in social programs the more frequently one hears the complaint that policy makers and high-level administrators don't listen to service deliverers. What grates most on the sensibilities of teachers, social workers, employment counselors, and the like is the tacit assumption in most policy directives that they are incapable of making independent judgments and decisions—that their behavior must be programmed by someone else. It's difficult for persons who see themselves as competent, self-sufficient adults to be highly committed to policies that place them in the role of passive executor of someone else's will.

The prevailing theories of organization behavior, represented by the systems management and bureaucratic process models, encourage and perpetuate this pathology. Hierarchy, specialization, routine, and control all reinforce the belief that those at the bottom of the organization are less competent decision makers than those at the top. High-level administrators can be trusted to exercise discretion, while those at the bottom must be closely supervised and controlled. Policy is made at the top and implemented at the bottom; implementers must set aside their own views and submit to the superior authority and competence of policy makers and high-level administrators.

Not surprisingly, this view has become increasingly difficult to defend as the work force has become more professionalized and better educated. It's now relatively clear that there are basic conflicts between the individual's need for autonomy, participation, and commitment and the organization's requirement of structure, control, and subordination. Concern for this conflict has led some to posit a "democratic alternative" to established theories of organization.[51]

51   See, e.g., Katz and Kahn. *The Social Psychology of Organizations*, pp. 211ff.

The label we will attach to this alternative is organizational development. There are a number of schools of thought within this tradition, but we will concentrate primarily on the work of Chris Argyris, who has spent an unusually large amount of effort specifying the assumptions on which his view is based.

Argyris takes his point of departure from the observation that what we define as acceptable adult behavior outside organizations directly contradicts what's acceptable inside. On the outside, adults are defined as people who are self-motivating, responsible for their own actions, and honest about emotions and values. Inside organizations, adults are expected to exhibit dependency and passivity toward their superiors; they resort to indirection and avoid taking responsibility as individuals, and they are forced to submerge emotions and values.[52] Resolving this tension requires a fundamentally different kind of organization and a different theory of organizational behavior. Rational or bureaucratic theories of organization stress abstract, systemic properties—structure, technology, outputs—at the expense of the social and psychological needs of individuals.[53] The reasonable alternative is a theory that begins from the needs of individuals rather than the abstract properties of organizations. Such a theory leads "not only to a more humane and democratic system but to a more efficient one."[54]

The essential transactions of organizational life occur in face-to-face contacts among individuals engaged in a common task—work groups. Organizational effectiveness and efficiency depend more than anything else on the quality of interpersonal relations in work groups. Effective work groups are characterized by agreement on goals, open communication, mutual trust and support, full utilization of member skills, and effective management of conflict.[55] The cultivation of these things requires a special kind of skill, which Argyris call "interpersonal competence" to distinguish it from the purely technical competence that comes from the routine performance of a task. Individuals are interpersonally competent when they are able to give and receive feedback in a way that creates minimal defensiveness, give honest expression to their own feelings, values and attitudes, and remain open to new ideas.[56] The trappings of bureaucracy and rational decision making—routines, management controls, objectified accountability—undermine interpersonal competence and group effectiveness, encouraging dependence and

52 Chris Argyris. *Personality and Organization: The Conflict Between System and Individual*. New York: Harper, 1957, p. 53ff.

53 Chris Argyris. *The Applicability of Organizational Sociology*. London: Cambridge University Press, 1972.

54 Warren Bennis. *Organization Development: Its Nature, Origins, and Prospects*. Reading, Mass.: Addison-Wesley, 1969, p. 28.

55 Ibid., p. 2; quoting Douglas McGregor. *The Professional Manager*. New York: McGraw-Hill, 1967.

56 Chris Argyris. *Interpersonal Competence and Organizational Effectiveness*. Homewood, Ill.: Irwin, 1962, p. 42.

passivity while penalizing openness and risk taking. Hence, "the very values that assumed to help make [an organization] effective may actually . . . decrease its effectiveness."[57]

Nowhere in the literature on organizational development is there a simple composite of the well-structured organization. It's fair to infer from the theory, though, that an effective organization would have at least the following features: Most responsibility for decisions would devolve on lower levels of the organization; the focus of organizational activity would be the work group, formed out of people engaged in a common task; and information—statements of purpose, evaluative judgments, and expressions of needed changes—would be readily exchanged without negative social consequences at all levels of the organization. All these features originate from the simple assumption that people are more likely to perform at their highest capacity when they are given maximum control over their own work, maximum participation in decisions affecting them, and hence maximum incentive for commitment to the goals of the group.

The organizational development model gives quite a different picture of the implementation process than either the systems management or bureaucratic process models. In the systems management model, implementation consists of the skillful use of management controls to hold subunits accountable for well-defined standards of performance. In the bureaucratic process model, implementation consists of changing the formal and informal work routines of an organization to conform with a declaration of intent. In both instances, *policy is made at the top and implemented at the bottom*. But in the organizational development model the distinction is much less clear. If major responsibility is actually to devolve on work groups at lower levels of the organization, it makes very little sense to think of policy as flowing from top or bottom. More about this in a moment.

Implementation failures are not the result of poor management control or the persistence of bureaucratic routines, but arise out of a lack of consensus and commitment among implementers. The features of the implementation process that matter most are those that affect individual motivation and interpersonal cooperation, not those that enhance hierarchical control. Success of an implementation effort can be gauged by looking at the extent to which implementers are involved in the formulation of a program, the extent to which they are encouraged to exercise independent judgment in determining their own behavior, and the extent to which they are encouraged to establish strong work groups for mutual support and problem solving.

Empirical evidence on the underlying assumptions of the organizational development model is relatively scarce, but the most important piece of evi-

---

57   Chris Argyris. *Integrating the Individual and the Organization*. New York: John Wiley, 1964, p. 138.

dence in the area of social program implementation comes from a large-scale study done completely outside the organizational development tradition. In 1972, the federal government contracted with the Rand Corporation to conduct a nationwide study of four federally funded education programs, each of which was designed to encourage innovation in the public schools.[58] The programs were administered by different units within the U.S. Office of Education and they used a variety of administrative strategies. Nearly 300 local projects were surveyed, so the potential for variation within and between programs was great. Yet the Rand analysts concluded that overall the "programs had approximately equal effects on project outcomes, despite their different management strategies."[59] They also concluded that "differences between programs explained only a small amount of the variation in implementation outcomes."[60] In short, the federal government's management of the program seemed to have virtually no effect on the success or failure of implementation.

Pursuing this issue further, the Rand group analyzed twenty-nine descriptive case studies of local project implementation, attempting to identify what distinguished successful from unsuccessful attempts at change. The characteristics that emerged from this analysis were things like the existence of a strong local training component, the use of local expertise and technical assistance in project implementation, frequent and regular staff meetings, local development of project materials, and the use of voluntary, highly motivated participants.[61] The significant thing about all these factors is that they are things over which federal administrators have virtually no control. Project success depended primarily on the existence and mobilization of local resources. "Our observations suggest," the analysts concluded, "that it is extremely unrealistic to expect a school district to do something wise with its federal money if it is not already committed to something wise when the funds are first received."[62]

Milbrey McLaughlin, a principal author of the study, looked in detail at a number of projects that were intended to change classroom organization. Discussing the importance of local materials development, she observes that it was "sometimes undertaken because the staff felt they couldn't locate appropriate commercial materials," but she concludes that "the real contribution lay . . . in providing the staff with a sense of involvement and an opportunity to learn by doing." She continues—

58 See chapters 1 through 3 *infra*.
59 Peter W. Greenwood, Dale Mann, and Milbrey Wallin McLaughlin. *Federal Programs Supporting Educational Change, Vol. IV: The Findings in Review*. Santa Monica, Calif.: Rand Corporation, 1975, p. 22.
60 Ibid.; also, pp. 45–47.
61 Greenwood, Mann, and McLaughlin. *Federal Programs Supporting Educational Change, Vol. III: The Process of Change*, p. 39.
62 Ibid., p. 26.

Working together to develop materials . . . gave the staff a sense of "ownership" in the project. It also broke down the traditional isolation of the teacher and provided a sense of professionalism and cooperation not usually available in the school setting. But even more important, development of materials provided an opportunity for users to think through the concepts which underlay the project in practical, operational terms. . . . Although such "reinvention of the wheel" may not appear efficient in the short run, it appears to be a critical part of the individual learning and development necessary to significant change.[63]

Here, in the concrete language of project-level implementation, are the essential elements of the organizational development model: emphasis on individual motivation and commitment (sense of involvement, ownership in the project), the centrality of strong face-to-face work groups (breaking down the traditional isolation of teachers, enhancing professionalism and cooperation), and the explicit criticism of conventional notions of organizational efficiency (the usefulness of reinventing the wheel).

The picture of implementation that emerges from these findings is one in which the ability of policy makers and high-level administrators to manipulate the behavior of implementers using the standard devices of hierarchical control is severely limited. The critical variables are those arising out of individual commitment and motivation. The Rand analysts described the implementation process as "intrinsically" one of "mutual adaptation"; the policy or innovation is shaped by implementers and, likewise, the behavior of implementers is shaped by the policy or innovation.[64] The only way an innovation can become established in an organization, the Rand analysts argue, is for implementers to learn it, shape it, and claim it for their own.

But the full significance of the Rand findings is not adequately expressed by the plausible idea of mutual adaptation. Every defensible view of implementation contains some gesture toward adaptive behavior—in the systems management model, adaptation is a necessary consequence of feedback on the performance of subunits; in the bureaucratic process model, organizational routines evolve slowly over time in response to changing demands. So it's not the notion of adaptive behavior that distinguishes the organizational development model from other perspectives.

The real significance of the organizational development model, and the import of the Rand evidence, is that it effectively turns the entire implementation process on its head. It reverses what we instinctively regard as the "normal" flow of policy, from top to bottom. The message of the model is, quite

---

63 Milbrey Wallin McLaughlin, *infra*, chapter 2.
64 Greenwood, Mann, and McLaughlin. *Federal Programs Supporting Educational Change, Vol. III: The Process of Change*, pp. 3 and 31.

bluntly, that the capacity to implement originates at the bottom of organizations not at the top. In each of the two previous models, the central problem was how policy makers and high-level administrators could shape the behavior of implementers, using the standard devices of hierarchical control. What the organizational development model suggests is that these devices explain almost none of the variation in implementation outcomes. The factors that do affect the behavior of implementers are things that lie outside the domain of direct management control—individual motivation and commitment, and the interaction and mutual support of people in work groups. Hence, the closer one gets to the determinants of effective implementation, the farther one gets away from the factors that policy makers and administrators can manipulate. The result is that, in terms of the effective structure of organizations, *the process of initiating and implementing new policy actually begins at the bottom and ends at the top.* Unless organizations already have those properties that predispose them to change, they are not likely to respond to new policy. But if they have those properties, they are capable of initiating change themselves, without the control of policy makers and administrators. The role of those at the top of the system, then, is necessarily residual; they can provide resources that implementers need to do their work, but they cannot exert direct control over the factors that determine the success or failure of that work.

If one accepts this view, the important business of implementation consists not of developing progressively more sophisticated techniques for managing subordinates' behavior but enhancing the self-starting capacity of the smallest unit. The organizational capacity to accept innovations necessarily precedes the innovations themselves, so one can't expect individuals to respond to new policies unless they are predisposed to do so. But once this predisposition exists, it is no longer practical to think of imposing changes from above. The only conception of implementation that makes sense under these conditions is one that emphasizes consensus-building and accommodation between policy makers and implementers. Mutual adaptation exists not because it is a pleasing or democratic thing to do, but because it is the only way to assure that implementers have a direct, personal stake in the performance of their jobs. This is what the advocates of organizational development mean when they say that more democratic organizations are also more efficient ones.

As a micromodel, organizational development focuses on those aspects of an organization's internal structure that enhance or inhibit the commitment of implementers. The chief determinants of success are the sort of microvariables identified by the Rand analysts: materials development by implementers, strong interpersonal and professional ties among implementers, nonmanipulative support by high-level administrators, and explicit reliance on incentives that elicit individual commitment from implementers rather than those designed to enforce external conformity. To the extent that the implementation process actually becomes these things, it is neither accurate nor useful to think in terms of a single declaration of policy that is translated into subordinate behavior. Policy does not exist in any concrete sense until implementers have shaped it and claimed it for their own; the result is a consensus reflecting the initial intent of policy makers and the independent judgment of implementers.

As a macromodel, organizational development forces us to recognize the extreme limits of one organization's capacity to change the behavior of another. When an agency at one level of government attempts to implement policy through an agency at another level, the implicit assumption is that the former controls factors that are important in determining the performance of the latter. The organizational development model suggests that those factors that have the greatest influence on the success or failure of implementation are precisely the ones over which external agencies have the least control. The maximum that one level of government can do to affect the implementation process is to provide general support that enhances the internal capacity of organizations at another level to respond to the necessity for change, independent of the requirements of specific policies. So, to the extent that the implementation process actually took the shape of the model, the federal government, for example, would invest most of its resources not in enforcing compliance with existing policies, but in assisting state and local agencies to develop an independent capacity to elicit innovative behavior from implementers.

The most powerful criticism of the organizational development model comes, surprisingly, from its strongest supporters. The bias of the model toward consensus, cooperation, and strong interpersonal ties leads us to ignore or downplay the role of conflict in organizations. The model, Warren Bennis argues, "seems most appropriate under conditions of trust, truth, love and collaboration. But what about conditions of war, conflict, dissent, and violence? The fundamental deficiency in models of change associated with organization development," he concludes, is that they "systematically avoid the problem of power, or the *politics* of change."[65] The same criticism may be leveled, to one degree or another, against each of the three models discussed thus far, because none directly confronts the issue of what happens in organizations when control, routine, and consensus fail. There are a wide range of implementation problems that can only be understood as problems of conflict and bargaining.

MODEL IV: IMPLEMENTATION AS CONFLICT AND BARGAINING

Assumptions

1. Organizations are arenas of conflict in which individuals and subunits with

---

65 Bennis. *Organization Development*, p. 77; emphasized in original.

specific interests compete for relative advantage in the exercise of power and the allocation of scarce resources.

2. The distribution of power in organizations in never stable. It depends exclusively on the temporary, situational ability of one individual or unit to mobilize sufficient resources to manipulate the behavior of others. Formal position in the hierarchy of an organization is only one of a multitude of factors that determine the distribution of power. Other factors include specialized knowledge, control of material resources, and the ability to mobilize external political support. Hence, the exercise of power in organizations is only weakly related to their formal structure.

3. Decision making in organizations consists of bargaining within and among organizational units. Bargained decisions are the result of convergence among actors with different preferences and resources. Bargaining does not require that parties agree on a common set of goals, nor does it even require that all parties concur in the outcome of the bargaining process. It only requires that they agree to mutually adjust their behavior in the interest of preserving the bargaining relationship as a means of allocating resources for mutual benefit.

4. Implementation consists of a complex series of bargained decisions reflecting the preferences and resources of participants. Success or failure of implementation cannot be judged by comparing a result against a single declaration of intent, because no single set of purposes can provide an internally consistent statement of the interests of all parties to the bargaining process. Success can only be defined relative to the goals of one party to the bargaining process or in terms of the preservation of the bargaining process itself.

Social programs fail, it is frequently argued, because no single unit of government is sufficiently powerful to force others to conform to a single conception of policy. With each agency pursuing its own interest, implementation does not progress from a single declaration of intent to a result, but is instead characterized by constant conflict over purposes and results and by the pursuit of relative advantage through the use of bargaining. This leads some participants to characterize programs as "failures" and some to characterize them as "successes," based solely on their position in the bargaining process. Conflict and bargaining occur both within and between implementing agencies. Single organizations can be thought of as semipermanent bargaining coalitions, and the process of moving a declaration of policy across levels of government can be understood as bargaining among separate organizations.

Bargaining can be explicit or tacit. We tend to associate the notion of bargaining only with direct confrontations between well-defined adversaries—labor negotiations, arms limitation talks, and peace negotiations, for example. But many forms of bargaining, especially those in implementation, occur without direct communication and with an imperfect understanding by each party of the others' motives and resources.[66] Seen in this light, implementation becomes essentially a series of strategic moves by a number of individual units of government, each seeking to shape the behavior of others to its own ends.

The key to understanding bargaining behavior is recognizing that there is dependency in conflict. Even the strongest adversaries must take account of their opponents' moves when they formulate a bargaining strategy. ''The ability of one participant to gain his ends,'' Schelling observes, ''is dependent to an important degree on the choices or decisions that the other participant will make.'' Furthermore, ''there is a powerful common interest in reaching an outcome that is not enormously destructive of values to both sides.''[67] In implementation, as in all important bargaining problems, parties with strongly divergent interests are locked together by the simple fact that they must preserve the bargaining arena in order to get something of value. Failure to bargain means exclusion from the process by which resources are allocated. But the mutual advantage that accrues to participants in bargaining has little or nothing to do with their ability to agree explicitly on the goals they're pursuing or their means for pursuing them. Mutual advantage results only from the fact that by agreeing to bargain they have preserved their access to something of value to each of them.

Lindblom uses the general term ''partisan mutual adjustment'' to characterize the variety of ways in which individuals with divergent interests coordinate their actions. The common element in all forms of bargaining behavior, he argues, is that ''people can coordinate with each other without someone's coordinating them, without a dominant purpose, and without rules that fully prescribe their relations to each other.''[68] This point is essential for understanding the usefulness of the conflict and bargaining model in the analysis of social program implementation. The model permits us to make conceptual sense of the implementation process without assuming the existence of hierarchical control, without asserting that everyone's behavior is governed by a predictable

---

66 An elegant account of tacit bargaining and coordination is given in Thomas Schelling. *The Strategy of Conflict*. London and New York: Oxford University Press, 1963, p. 53ff.

67 Ibid., pp. 5–6.

68 Charles Lindblom. *The Intelligence of Democracy: Decision Making Through Mutual Adjustment*. New York: Free Press, 1965, p. 3. In the interest of economy of expression, I have taken some liberties with Lindblom's terminology. Lindblom actually develops no less than twelve distinguishable types of partisan mutual adjustment, based on different assumptions about the ability of parties to determine the effect of their actions on others, the level of communication among parties, their ability to use conditional threats, and their ability to elicit behavior using unilateral action (pp. 33–84). I have equated bargaining with partisan mutual adjustment, when in Lindblom's scheme bargaining is one particular type of partisan mutual adjustment involving the use of conditional threats and promises (pp. 71ff.).

set of bureaucratic routines, and without assuming that concerted action can only proceed from consensus and commitment to a common set of purposes. In short, the model provides a distinct alternative to the limiting assumptions of the previous three. Implementation can, and indeed does, proceed in the absence of a mechanism of coordination external to the actors themselves (hierarchical control, routine, or group consensus).

Bargained decisions proceed by convergence, adjustment, and closure among individuals pursuing essentially independent ends. Allison makes this point by saying that "the decisions and actions of governments are . . . political resultants . . . in the sense that what happens is not chosen as a solution to a problem but rather results from compromise, conflict, and confusion of officials with diverse interests and unequal influence."[69] The term resultant, appropriated from physics, emphasizes the idea that decisions are the product of two or more converging forces. The mechanism of convergence depends on what Schelling calls "interdependence of expectations." Parties to the bargaining process must predicate their actions not only on hunches about how others will respond but also on the understanding that others are doing likewise. So bargaining depends as much on shared expectations as it does on concrete actions.

> The outcome is determined by the expectations that each player forms of how the other will play, where each of them knows that their expectations are substantially reciprocal. The players must jointly discover and mutually acquiesce in an outcome or a mode of play that makes the outcome determinate. They must together find "rules of the game" or together suffer the consequences.[70]

In concrete terms, this means that much of the behavior we observe in the implementation process is designed to shape the expectations of other actors. An agency might, for example, put a great deal of effort into developing an elaborate collection of rules and regulations or an elegant system of management controls, knowing full well that it doesn't have the resources to make them binding on other actors. But the *expectation* that the rules *might* be enforced is sufficient to influence the behavior of other actors. The important fact is not whether the rules are enforced or not but the effect of their existence on the outcome of the bargaining process.

The outcomes of bargaining are seldom "optimal" in any objective sense. More often than not, they are simply convenient, temporary points of closure. Asking "what it is that can bring . . . expectations into convergence and bring . . . negotiations to a close," Schelling answers that "it is the intrinsic

---

69 Allison. *Essence of Decision*, p. 162.
70 Schelling. *The Strategy of Conflict*, pp. 106–107.

magnetism of particular outcomes, especially those that enjoy prominence, uniqueness, simplicity, precedent, or some rationale that makes them qualitatively differentiable'' from other alternatives.[71] In other words, the result of bargaining is often not the best, nor even the second or third best, alternative for any party; all parties can, and frequently do, leave the bargaining process dissatisfied with the result. As long as there is an opportunity to resume bargaining, there is seldom a single determinant result—all resolutions are temporary. So one should not expect the mechanisms of bargaining to lead teleologically from a single purpose to a result.

One is tempted to say that the conflict and bargaining model is not a model of organizational behavior at all but a model of what happens when organizations fail. This is a plausible argument. We tend to associate the term organization with a certain threshold of commonality that allows individuals to cooperate around a common set of goals. If this minimum condition isn't met, it seems reasonable to conclude that there is an absence of organization. But sometime ago the theory of organizations took a turn away from this assumption. Cyert and March, dissatisfied with the conventional wisdom of normative economic theory and the sociology of organizations, elaborated an alternative theory, beginning from the premise that organizations are essentially bargaining coalitions.[72] The process of organizational decision making, they argue, involves continuous conflict among subunits over relatively specific purposes that define each subunit's interest in the organization. The overall goals of an organization, they argue, are calculatedly vague and essentially useless as guides to decision making. Hence, organizations are not defined by agreement on overall purposes but only by the process of conflict, bargaining, and coalition-building among subunits. The absence of agreement on overall goals, then, is not a sign of organizational failure but simply a clue directing our attention to the existence of conflict and bargaining as permanent fixtures of organizational life.

The real structure of organizations, then, is to be found in their bargaining processes rather than in their formal hierarchy or operating routines. Notions of top and bottom have very little meaning. Formal position is a source of power, but only one of many, and it does not necessarily carry with it the ability to manipulate the behavior of subordinates. There are innumerable other sources of power—mastery of specialized knowledge, discretionary control over resources, a strong external constituency—all of which can be used to enhance the bargaining position of subordinates relative to superiors, and vice versa. There are no simple rules for determining the distribution of power in

71 Ibid., p. 70; Cf. Lindblom. *The Intelligence of Democracy*, pp. 205–225.
72 Richard Cyert and James March. *A Behavioral Theory of the Firm*. Englewood Cliffs, N.J.: Prentice-Hall, 1963, p. 27.

organizations. Stability, if it exists at all, is the short-term product of bargaining on specific decisions.

This view leads to a considerably different conception of implementation than any of the other models. One understands the process by focusing on conflict among actors, the resources they bring to the bargaining process, and the mechanisms by which they adjust to each others' moves. Most importantly, the distinguishing feature of the conflict and bargaining model is that *it doesn't rest on any assumptions about commonality of purpose*. In each of the previous models, it was possible to say that successful implementation was in some sense dependent on a common conception of policy shared by all participants in the process. In the systems management model, agreement was the product of management control; in the bureaucratic process model, it resulted from incorporation of a new policy into an organization's operating routines; and in the organizational development model, it resulted from consensus among policy makers and implementers. But in the conflict and bargaining model, the outcomes of implementation are temporary bargained solutions—resultants— that reflect no overall agreement on purposes.

This means that success or failure of implementation is largely a relative notion, determined by one's position in the process. Actors who, however temporarily, are capable of asserting their purposes over others will argue that the process is ''successful.'' Those with a disadvantage in the bargaining process will argue that the process is ''unsuccessful.'' It is entirely possible for the process to proceed even though all actors regard it as unsuccessful, because the costs of refusing to bargain may exceed the costs of remaining in a disadvantageous bargaining relationship. Under these circumstances, there is only one objective measure of success or failure, and that is the preservation of the bargaining process itself. So long as all parties agree to bargain, and there is mutual benefit to be gained from bargaining, preservation of the bargaining arena constitutes success. Regardless of the level of conflict in social programs, all actors have an interest in maintaining them as long as they deliver benefits that are not otherwise accessible.

The empirical evidence on conflict and bargaining in social program implementation is abundant. The implementation of federal educational programs provides some of the best examples, because the process occurs in a system where power is radically dispersed across all levels of government. The Elementary and Secondary Education Act of 1965 was intended not simply to increase federal expenditures on education but also to change the operation of state and local educational agencies. Title I of the act was intended to focus attention and resources on educationally disadvantaged children at the local level; Title V was designed to enhance the administrative capability of state educational agencies. In both cases, the pattern of interaction among agencies at different levels of government suggests conflict and bargaining rather than simple progression from a purpose to a result. In its first five years, Title I went from a period of "good working relationships" and "friendly assistance" between the federal government and local agencies, through a stage of aggressive federal enforcement of program guidelines, and eventually back to a relatively passive federal role.

Jerome Murphy demonstrates that the critical element in these shifts was a change in the nature of the bargaining arena in Title I. In the late sixties, civil rights organizations conducted a large-scale study of local abuses of Title I, confirming a widely held suspicion that funds were not being focused on disadvantaged children, and then mounted an aggressive political campaign to force the U.S. Office of Education to take a stronger posture in enforcing program guidelines. After a flurry of enforcement activity, which generated a great deal of political counterpressure from state and local agencies, federal administrators backed away from aggressive enforcement.[73] In other words, federal policy—legislation, regulations, and guidelines—served only as a point of departure for bargaining among implementing agencies. Local implementers designed their actions around expectations about the willingness of federal administrators to enforce the policy. When federal administrators were forced to take a different posture, local administrators responded in part with compliance and in part with counterpressure. The policy actually implemented lies somewhere between the literal requirements of the law and regulations and the interests of local implementers. Another flurry of federal enforcement would alter the situation again.

In the implementation of Title V, the federal government dispensed relatively unrestricted funds to state educational agencies for use in strengthening their administrative capacity. Murphy found that, in the aggregate, Title V did not significantly change the activities or functions of state agencies. The dominant pattern was that "funds were distributed to satisfy the interests of important elements in the organization" and were "expended mainly to meet pressing problems through the simple expansion of existing modes of operation."[74] In other words, the infusion of federal funds simply touched off intraorganizational bargaining in which subunits claimed their share of the bounty and proceeded to use it for their own immediate purposes. In the few cases where significant changes in state agencies did occur, they came "only after strong pressure from outside the organization."[75] As in the case of Title I, it took

---

73   Jerome Murphy, "The Educational Bureaucracies Implement Novel Policy: The Politics of Title I of ESEA, 1965–72," in Alan Sindler, ed. *Policy and Politics in America*. Boston: Little, Brown, 1973, pp. 160–198. See also chapter 9, Milbrey Wallin McLaughlin, *infra*.

74   Jerome Murphy, "Title V of ESEA: The Impact of Discretionary Funds on State Education Bureaucracies," in Williams and Elmore, eds. *Social Program Implementation*, pp. 89 and 91. A more extended treatment of this case is in Jerome Murphy. *State Education Agencies and Discretionary Funds*. Lexington, Mass.: Lexington Books, 1974.

75   Ibid., p. 94.

some shift in the bargaining arena to force a change in the behavior of implementers.

The extremely diffuse and fluid nature of organizational relationships in the field of education has led Karl Weick to characterize educational organizations as "loosely coupled systems."[76] Although conflict and bargaining do not figure prominently in Weick's model, the characteristics of loosely coupled systems that he identifies lead to the same conclusion as the conflict and bargaining model. The lack of structure and determinacy, the absence of teleologically linked events, dispersion of resources and responsibilities, the relative absence of binding regulation—all add up to the kind of system in which concerted action is only possible through tacit or explicit bargaining among relatively independent actors.

The same pattern exists in a number of other studies of social program implementation. Jeffrey Pressman analyzed the effect of a wide variety of federal programs on the city of Oakland and argued that action in urban settings is possible only when "effective bargaining arenas" exist. He attributed the limited impact of federal assistance in Oakland to "the weakness of political institutions and the absence of political leadership," both of which "have combined to limit . . . citizens' effective demands on government and government's willingness and ability to respond."[77] No matter how well organized or skillful federal agencies might be, the success or failure of their efforts depends to a large degree on locally bargained decisions over which they have little or no control. This finding also represents the major conclusion of Pressman and Wildavsky's study of the federal Economic Development Administration's job-creation project in Oakland. The project was intended to increase employment among low-income minorities through capital investments, largely in construction. As it progressed, the complexity of local bargaining relationships increased and the minority employment goal began to recede. Federal administrators substantially overestimated their bargaining position relative to local actors. And the project essentially failed to create any significant minority employment.[78]

In the housing and urban development field, two cases demonstrate essentially the same point. Martha Derthick's classic study of the Department of Housing and Urban Development's New Towns Program concludes that the program failed because federal administrators failed to recognize the limits of their ability to influence local decisions. Programs succeed, she argues, when

76 Karl Weick. "Educational Organizations as Loosely Coupled Systems," *Administrative Science Quarterly,* Vol. 21, 1976, pp. 1–18.

77 Jeffrey Pressman. *Federal Programs and City Politics: The Dynamics of the Aid Process in Oakland.* Berkeley, Calif.: University of California Press, 1975, pp. 14, 143–144.

78 Jeffrey Pressman and Aaron Wildavsky. *Implementation.* Berkeley, Calif.: University of California Press, 1973.

"an adjustment between the federal program and local interests is worked out . . . with the net result that . . . programs are neither 'federal' nor 'local' but a blend of the two."[79]

A much more explosive episode occurred when New York City, in an effort to comply with federal guidelines that accompany low-income housing subsidies, decided to locate a massive public housing project in a middle-class neighborhood of Forest Hills, Queens.[80] The decision touched off a long, heated confrontation between local residents and city, state, and federal administrators. The bargaining was Byzantine in its complexity, and the outcome was a classic example of a bargained decision, or resultant. All the actors converged on a seemingly arbitrary set of figures describing the size and composition of the project; no one was particularly satisfied with the outcome, but it provided a temporary resolution of conflict sufficient to provide the basis for action.

The interesting characteristic of all these cases is that all the participants in the bargaining process stood to gain more from participation than from nonparticipation, even though the result of bargaining was seldom completely in accord with their interests. The payoff for participating in federal programs is access to funds that would not otherwise be available; even when federal regulations run counter to local interests, participation pays for local implementers because it makes them part of the process by which resources are distributed. In some instances, like the Forest Hills housing case, the payoff for participation is the minimization of losses; the residents of Forest Hills stood to gain nothing from the location of a housing project in their neighborhood, but they stood to lose a great deal by refusing to participate in determining the characteristics of that project. Even the strongest adversaries are locked together by the necessity to bargain.

As a micromodel, conflict and bargaining focuses attention on the processes by which organizations form what Pressman called "effective bargaining arenas" in response to policy initiatives. The ability to implement depends on the ability of all parties with a stake in the outcome to form a bargaining relationship. The response of organizations to new policies is to bargain internally over the distribution of resources, responsibilities, and costs. As a macromodel, it defines the central issue as the relative bargaining strength of one unit of government relative to another. Moving a policy from one level to another is never as simple as passing authoritative instructions between agencies; it necessarily involves a test of the willingness of one agency to use its

---

79 Martha Derthick. *New Towns in Town: Why a Federal Program Failed*. Washington, D.C.: Urban Institute, 1972, pp. 97–98. Portions of this study are reprinted in Williams and Elmore. *Social Program Implementation*, pp. 219–239.

80 Mario Cuomo, *Forest Hills Diary: The Crisis of Low-Income Housing* (New York: Random House, 1974), *passim*.

resources to force another to behave in accord with its purposes.

The major criticism of the conflict and bargaining model stems from the fact that the model does not posit an objective definition of success or failure; all statements of success or failure are assertions of relative advantage in the bargaining process. One cannot say that implementation failed because a declaration of intent by one agency of government was not faithfully executed by another. In the typical case, the outcome of implementation is a bargained resultant that needn't satisfy any of the parties. The rationalist critique of this notion is that the model elevates confusion and mindless drift to the level of principle, that it provides an easy excuse for acquiescing in results that satisfy no one, and that it provides no normative basis for improving the implementation process. It is difficult to counter these criticisms, except to say that the failure to understand the intricacies of bargaining may at times be more costly than the failure to posit an objective standard of success. The chief asset of the conflict and bargaining model is not that it provides any clear-cut solutions to implementation problems, as the systems management model does, but that it makes it possible to understand how agencies can engage in concerted action without agreeing on the ends they are pursuing.

CONCLUSION

In closing, two obvious, but obligatory, remarks are in order. The first is that all models are constructs, or ideal types. There is nothing immutable about the distinctions I have drawn here, nor do I make any pretense that the models capture everything that is important about the implementation process. What is useful about the models, I've argued, is that they draw on established traditions of organizational inquiry and they accord with certain commonsense explanations as to why social programs fail. The second observation is that the evidence on social program implementation is skimpy; the cases I've used are intended only to suggest that there is modest empirical support for the assumptions underlying each of the models. This is not to suggest that any of the evidence is very solid or that there is any reason to believe that the evidence favors one model or another. It does suggest that there is a great need for descriptive studies of social program implementation.

The more interesting question is, What use is the notion of alternative models to the analysis of implementation? Granted that certain models highlight certain features of the process while concealing others, what use could one make of this fact? There are a couple of possibilities I would like to suggest briefly. But before I do, there is one possible use of alternative models that comes immediately to mind, about which I am very skeptical. This is the view that the models should be treated as rival hypotheses and that the gradual accumulation of empirical evidence will eventually prove some single model of the process superior to all others. There are two reasons why this is unlikely to happen. First, models contain not only descriptive information but normative information; in spite of empirical evidence that a process operates in a certain way, people can nevertheless persist in the belief that it *ought* to operate in another way. Second, people have the capacity to shape their behavior in response to models; a neat predictive model of an essentially political process, like implementation, invites people to behave in unpredictable ways to achieve their own ends. Given the diversity of opinion reflected in the four models presented here, it seems highly unlikely that the accumulation of evidence will lead to agreement. It will probably just reinforce the disagreement that currently exists. But there are two more promising ideas about the use of alternative models.

The first is that applying different models to the same set of events allows us to distinguish certain features of the implementation process from others. In fact, every implementing agency probably has a set of management controls, a firmly entrenched collection of operating routines, some process for eliciting the involvement of implementers, and a set of internal and external bargaining relationships. The important question is not whether these things exist or not, but how they affect the implementation process. One way of disentangling the effects of these factors is to analyze the same body of evidence from the perspective of several different models. This is the approach taken by Allison in his analysis of the Cuban missile crisis.

The second approach proceeds from the notion that certain kinds of problems are more amenable to solution using one perspective than another. It is conceivable that there are times and settings in which the use of management controls is obviously appropriate, while in other circumstances only bargaining is appropriate. There may be instances in which wholesale delegation of discretion is the obvious course of action to follow, while in others firm control of discretion is necessary. The point is that models can help analysts and decision makers distinguish among different kinds of problems. Using management controls in a system in which power is extremely diffuse, for example, is like using a crescent wrench to turn a Phillips screw. The problem is to understand when certain tools of analysis and strategies of action are likely to pay off and when not.

Neither of these approaches requires that there be complete agreement on the nature of the models or that there be any single model that captures all essential features of the process. All they require is a willingness to treat certain parts of a complex process as analytically separable and to have a high tolerance for ambiguity.

CHAPTER 11

Horses Before Carts: Developing Adaptive Schools and the Limits of Innovation

WILLIS D. HAWLEY

INTRODUCTION

Educators, like other people concerned with bettering themselves and others, are constantly in search of salvation. In recent years the panacea seems to be "change" or, more precisely, innovation. While almost all research on change in public organizations focuses on innovation, the effectiveness of most public organizations, and especially schools, depends less on their willingness to adopt new programs than on their capacity to be adaptive and flexible over time. The argument of this chapter is that the capacity of innovation is highly overrated as a source of improvement in education and that the study of innovation yields too little that would be helpful in improving the schools to warrant the attention we give to it.

Innovation and adaptiveness, while related, are different in important ways. Understanding the former does not provide answers on how to achieve the latter. "Innovations" are invariably conceptualized as products or programs that are to be formulated, adopted, implemented, incorporated, and diffused.

This chapter is, in a sense, a companion to two previous papers on changefulness in public schools. See Willis D. Hawley, "The Possibilities of Nonbureaucratic Organizations," in Hawley and David Rogers, eds. *Improving the Quality of Urban Management*. Beverley Hills, Calif.: Sage Publications, 1974, pp. 371–426; and Willis D. Hawley, "Dealing with Organizational Rigidity in Public Schools: A Theoretical Approach," in Frederick M. Wirt, ed. *The Policy and the School: New Directions in Education Research.* Lexington, Mass.: Lexington Books, D.C. Heath, 1975, pp 187–210.

The "innovativeness" of an organization is defined by its relative speed in achieving one or more of these stages in the process of innovation or by the number of innovations it adopts. Innovations, then, have beginnings and ends. "Adaptiveness" describes the individual or collective behavior of school offi- cials and teachers. "Adaptive people" are creative problem solvers whose behavior is shaped by their diagnosis of problems and resources, both human and technological. Adaptiveness goes beyond reaction to demands, flexibility, or responsiveness to behavior that is aggressively creative, *pro*active, or pro- formist.[1] It requires continual multidirectional changes in behavior.

To be an adaptive school or teacher is akin to being what M.B. Miles and D.G. Lake call "self-renewing." Such an institution (or person) has "the ability to continuously sense and adapt to its external and internal environment in such a manner as to strengthen itself and ultimately fulfill its goal of provid- ing education for children."[2]

This essay reflects a concern that goes beyond the need for adaptive schools, namely, that we have a tendency to define improvements in public policies in terms of new programs, new systems, reorganizations, or more resources. Public policies too often reflect the proverbial triumph of form over substance, of process over product, and of effort over consequence. Social scientists for their part often contribute to all this because we eschew the complex and messy business of studying what happens to the receivers of public policies as a result of their interaction with the services received and those who deliver them. Thus the reforms we advocate often have an otherworldly quality about them that either idealizes the client or neglects the roles government officials actually play. Schools are only one policy arena in which such games are played. While this essay focuses on education, much the same kind of argument could be made about a host of other services including health care, law enforcement, corrections, and welfare programs.

The problem with the emphasis given to educational innovation is not that it is irrelevant. The problem is that the priority given this objective is both out of line with its promise and, more importantly, tends to lead us to put our hopes for improving public policies on doing something new and different rather than on attacking the sources of program or policy failure. In this sense, perhaps less is more.

---

1 This set of ideas follows those of Robert P. Biller, "Adaption Capacity and Organizational Develop- ment," in Frank Marini, ed. *Toward a New Public Administration: The Minnowbrook Perspective.* Scranton, Penn.: Chandler, 1971, p. 113.

2 Matthew B. Miles and D.G. Lake, "Self-Renewal in School Systems: A Strategy for Planned Change," in Goodwin E. Watson, ed. *Concepts for Social Change.* Washington, D.C.: COPED by NTL, NEA, 1967, p. 82.

A number of writers are fond of saying that in education "the more things change, the more they remain the same." We are also advised by those who study the sources of educational innovation that perhaps the most important determinant of the adoption (but not the implementation) of innovation is "exogenous shocks to the system," that is, demands for change by parents, citizen or professional groups, or other governmental agencies. These two observations combined suggest that innovations are often a way of avoiding more fundamental changes. Innovation, I suggest, is often symbolic politics.[3]

In other words, the adoption and *apparent* implementation of new programs can often create the impression that governments are responding to demands for improved performance. Regardless of the innovators' intent, new programs, reorganizations, and the like suggest that the need for change is recognized and is being acted on. Thus the need to keep the pressure on or to create further incentives for change dissipates. The faster schools innovate, the less momentum external demands for change will gather and the less significant will be the perception that school systems require fundamental change. And this is true for both laymen and professionals.

In the pages that follow, I will suggest why innovations don't "work," why adaptiveness promises to increase the effectiveness of schooling, how one might think about conditions that foster adaptiveness, and the implication of these factors for the structure and administration of schools.

DO INNOVATIONS "WORK"?

When educators and researchers invest heavily in achieving or explaining the organizational capacity for innovation, even though they know better, they may come to value innovation for its own sake. This predisposition to see innovation as the key to growth in the effectiveness of public schools is manifest in both the scholarly and professional literature. However, those studies that have sought to assess the consequences of planned innovation raise strong evidence that whether a school is likely to adopt innovations may have little to do with its effectiveness in creating a setting in which learning takes place.[4]

There is considerable consensus, aside from the findings of some short-run case studies, that the research on the consequences of major efforts at educational innovation shows little improvement in rates of student progress—at

---

3 Cf. Murray J. Edelman. *The Symbolic Uses of Politics*. Urbana, Ill.: University of Illinois Press, 1964.

4 Of course, education does not have a corner on unsuccessful innovations. See, for example, Frederick Mosteller, "Comments on 'The Value of Social Experiments,'" in Alice M. Rivlin and P. Michael Timpane, eds. *Planned Variation in Education: Should We Give Up or Try Harder?* Washington, D.C.: The Brookings Institution, 1975, pp. 169–172.

least so far as that progress is measured by cognitive gains.[5] If programs are found to work, the continuity for the child and transferability to other settings are usually weak.

One can, of course, look at a half-empty glass with more sanguine eyes. One very recent study of innovations of the past two decades concludes that they may not have done much good but they have not done any harm.[6] While methodological and conceptual shortcomings in the research on innovation probably result in understating the potential that many of the studied innovations have for increasing the effectiveness of schools,[7] a brief discussion of why the studies have yielded so little evidence that innovations result in substantial improvements in the quality of education should give us some clues as to why adaptiveness should receive more attention.

INNOVATIONS "FAIL" BECAUSE THEY ARE NOT IMPLEMENTED

Students of organizational change agree that it is analytically useful to distinguish between different stages in the innovation process. There are a number of ways the process is described, but the one that appears least complicated and perhaps is most widely utilized is: (1) support or adoption, (2) implementation, and (3) incorporation.

---

5 Almost all the research measures effectiveness in terms of cognitive development. See M.J. Wargo, P.L. Campeau, and G.K. Tallmadge. *Further Examination of Exemplary Programs for Educating Disadvantaged Children*. Palo Alto, Calif.: American Institute for Research, 1971; The Ford Foundation, *A Foundation Goes to School: The Ford Foundation Comprehensive School Improvement Program 1960–1970*. New York: Office of Reports, November 1972; N.L. Gage, ed. *Handbook of Research on Teaching*. Chicago, Ill.: Rand McNally, 1963; J.M. Stephens. *The Process of Schooling*. New York: Holt, Rinehard and Winston, 1967; Robert M.W. Travers. *Second Handbook of Research on Teaching*. Skokie, Ill.: Rand McNally, 1973; Harvey A. Averch et al. *How Effective Is Schooling?: A Critical Review and Synthesis of Research Findings*. Santa Monica, Calif.: Rand Corporation, 1972; Westinghouse Learning Corporation/Ohio University, *The Impact of Head Start: An Evaluation of the Effects of Head Start Experience on Children's Cognitive and Affective Development*. Springfield, Va.: Clearinghouse for Federal Scientific and Technical Information, U.S. Department of Commerce, June 12, 1969; U.S. Office of Education, *Statistical Report Fiscal Year 1968: A Report on the Third Year of Title I Elementary and Secondary Education Act of 1965*. Washington, D.C.: U.S. Government Printing Office, 1970; Gene Glass. *Data Analysis of the 1968–69 Survey of Compensatory Education (Title I), Final Report*. Boulder, Colo.: Laboratory of Educational Research, University of Colorado, August 1970; Milbrey Wallin McLaughlin. *Education and Reform: The Elementary and Secondary Educational Act of 1965, Title I*. Cambridge, Mass.: Ballinger, 1975. Focusing on cognitive development, as most studies do, may also understate the importance of innovations to changing school outcomes. This conclusion is the thrust of the argument offered by Lyn S. Martin and Barbara V. Pavan in their review of the research on the impact of new approaches to teaching and classroom structuring. See Martin and Pavan, "Current Research on Open Space, Nongrading, Vertical Grouping and Teaching," *Phi Delta Kappan*, Vol. 57, January 1976, pp. 310–315.

6 Martin and Pavan, "Current Research."

7 Averch et al. *How Effective Is Schooling?*, p. 151.

There is also agreement that it is substantially easier to achieve adoption of an innovation than to achieve its implementation and incorporation and that the most important reason for this lies in the inability of administrators and other "adopters" to control teacher behavior.

There is considerable evidence that teachers are in a position to resist or modify innovations and that, despite the appearance of adoption by the school system or the school, the proponents of the innovation would not recognize their plan by observing teacher behavior.[8] The most extensive study of the factors associated with innovation concludes that those programs that are implemented are characterized by "mutual adaptation," that is, the adjustment by teachers of characteristics of an innovation so that it meets their needs or their perception of student needs.[9] As Matthew B. Miles has observed, the installation of an innovation in a system is not a mechanical process but a developmental one in which both the innovation and the accepting system are altered.[10] And John Goodlad, after a study of 100 schools in major metropolitan areas, concluded, "much of the so-called educational reform movement has been blunted at the classroom door."[11]

The research shows, then, that teachers play the crucial role in determining whether innovations are implemented and that innovations can be successful only in adaptive settings.

INNOVATION SUCCESS IS CONTEXTUAL

To say that an innovation does not work "on the average" or "overall" is to mask a great deal of information. Some innovations work in some settings but not in others, with some children but not others, and with some teachers but not others.[12] The appropriateness of particular innovations to variations in student characteristics, teachers, values and skills, and parental values and behavior seems to account for some variation in their success. Moreover, the significance of these variables depends on the interactions among them. These presumptions pose enormous problems for large-scale evaluative research, problems that have not been adequately resolved by existing studies.

In their extensive study of the factors that might account for variations in the effectiveness of public schools, Averch and his associates concluded that no variant of school facilities, programs, resources, or personnel significantly

---

8 Cf. Rivlin and Timpane, eds. *Planned Variation in Education,* 1975.

9 Paul Berman and Milbrey Wallin McLaughlin. *Federal Programs Supporting Educational Change, Vol. IV: The Findings in Review.* Santa Monica, Calif.: Rand Corporation, 1974.

10 Matthew B. Miles, ed. *Innovation in Education.* New York: Bureau of Publications, Teachers College, Columbia University, 1964.

11 John I. Goodlad, "The Schools vs. Education," *Saturday Review,* April 19, 1961, p. 60.

12 See Marshall S. Smith, "Evaluation Findings in Head Start Planned Variation," in Rivlin and Timpane, eds. *Planned Variation in Education,* pp. 101–112; and Paul Berman and Milbrey Wallin McLaughlin. *Federal Programs Supporting Educational Change,* Vol. IV.

accounts for variations in student achievements. But they also found that laboratory and small-scale experimental studies—which often come closer than large-scale surveys to resolving the methodological difficulties endemic to educational evaluation—suggest:

> . . . individual methods of presentation appear superior for some tasks and some students but it is still hard to match student characteristics, tasks and types of instruction.
>
> . . . interaction effects seem to exist among various types of (student and teacher) personality, methods of reward, ability to grasp meaningful material, and so on; but these interactions have not been studied in detail.[13]

Innovations for which cognitive gains are reported tend to be characterized by the emphasis they place on improving the capacity of the teachers to match their skills and programs to the stages of affective and cognitive development at which they find individual students. What all of this adds up to, of course, is that innovations that have significant impact on children depend on adaptive behavior by teachers. I will return to the relationship between adaptiveness and school effectiveness later.

Summary

This brief examination of the research on the consequences of educational innovation leads us to several conclusions:

1. Different approaches to research design and execution would probably result in a better record for innovations. It is not clear, however, that improvements in methodology and conceptualization that will allow definitive conclusions in large-scale evaluations are at hand.
2. No single innovation, unless the innovation involves a high degree of individualized instruction, is likely to make a big difference in the performance of aggregates of children (i.e., classes or schools).
3. The crucial determinant of any given innovation's success is the willingness of teachers to employ it and do so creatively and selectively in the context of the needs and abilities of their students.

To the extent that innovations are a manifestation of "the symbolic uses of politics," as I suggested earlier may often be the case, one would not expect innovations or innovative schools to be judged effective in terms of significant impact on changes in student performance.

Thus it appears that we are putting the cart before the horse once again, and it is time to invest at least some of the energy that has gone into developing and evaluating innovation into understanding how to create educational environ-

---

13 Averch et al., *How Effective Is Schooling?*, p. 149.

ments that encourage teachers and school administrators to be adaptive in responding to educational objectives. Only when we achieve that condition can we expect innovations to provide significant benefits to students.

ADAPTIVENESS AND SCHOOL EFFECTIVENESS

Few people will take issue with the notion that schools and teachers should be adaptive. However, the meager resources allocated by either scholars or educational administrators to its attainment suggest that adaptiveness does not have a high priority. Thus there are few hard data that one might employ is assessing the effects of more adaptive school environments on children, and most of what follows rests on theory, observation, and indirect evidence.

For reasons implied above, I take it that the classroom teacher should be our unit of analysis. That is, the relative adaptiveness of schools or school systems depends on the relative adaptiveness of teachers. If such characteristics as what goes on in the community, the superintendent and his staff, the principal's style, student characteristics and norms, organizational arrangements, personal practices, and the like are important to creating adaptive learning situations, it is because these affect the teacher's interactions with students.

While there is substantial disagreement within schools and communities about the specific goals of public education, there appears to be some consensus that the basic concern of formal education should be the learning experience of the student, i.e., the creation of experiences that maximize each student's learning opportunity.[14] There are a myriad of ways that psychologists define learning. A general description that seems to incorporate much of the contemporary research is that of Charles C. Jung, Robert Fox, and Ronald Lippitt:

> Learning is primarily a matter of developing the child's total resources for understanding and dealing creatively with his life and the environment within which he lives. Learning deals with analysis as well as memory, with systems as well as isolated units, with behavior as well as thought process. Divergent as well as convergent thinking is appropriate. Emotions are important along with reason. Clarification of values is as much a part of learning as is the discovery of facts.[15]

To define learning is hard enough; to develop an understanding of its dynamics in the context of social environments, including classrooms, is more difficult. A recent survey of the literature on learning theory concludes that among the questions that existing research and theory leave unanswered are:

14 Cf. Charles C. Jung, Robert Fox, and Ronald Lippitt, "An Orientation and Strategy for Working on Problems of Change in School Systems," in Goodwin E. Watson, ed. *Change in School Systems.* Washington, D.C.: NEA National Training Laboratories, 1967, p. 69.

15 Ibid., p. 69.

1. What are the necessary conditions for learning?
2. What are the roles of practice, of reward and punishment, of stimuli, and of the similarities and differences between them?
3. How do motives influence learning and how are motives themselves learned?
4. What intervening variables can best be used to describe the changes in the organism produced by learning so as to take account of the whole range of possible learning?[16]

It is not surprising, then, that "there is not yet a substantial body of evidence to substantiate a definitive set of desirable teaching behaviors in any one given situation."[17] Moreover, "there is little likelihood that any one given [teaching method] is superior to any other when the overall effects of teaching are appraised."[18]

A recent comprehensive analysis of the research on school effectiveness conducted by the Rand Corporation concludes that, at least as far as cognitive development is concerned, "research has not discovered an educational practice that is consistently effective because no educational practice always 'works' regardless of other aspects of the educational situation."[19]

If any type of educational innovation in recent years can be said to have worked consistently, it is the genre of practices that involve highly individualized instruction. Thus the Rand study cites as representative of other analyses Gordon's conclusions about the relative effectiveness of Title I programs:

> The tightly structured programmed approach including frequent and immediate feedback to the pupil, combined with a tutorial relationship, individual pacing, and somewhat individualized programming are positively associated with accelerated pupil achievement.[20]

The emphasis the Rand team placed on structured and sequenced teaching-learning practices is in large part a function of the fact that most individualized instruction programs subjected to evaluation have been of this sort. There is

16 Winfred F. Hill, "Learning Theory," *Encyclopedia of Education*, 10 vols. New York: Macmillan, 1971, Vol. 5, p. 471.
17 Norma Furst and Russell A. Hill, "Systematic Classroom Observation," *Encyclopedia of Education*, Vol. 2, p. 181. On the same point, see David R. Krathwohl, "Cognitive and Affective Learning," ibid., p. 198; and David W. Ecker, "Affective Learning," ibid., Vol. 1, p. 114.
18 Norman E. Wallen and Robert M.W. Travers, "Analysis and Investigation of Teaching Methods" in N.L. Gage, ed. *Handbook of Research on Teaching*. Skokie, Ill.: Rand McNally, 1963, p. 500. The absence of empirically based theories of instruction is the recurrent theme of over half the articles on teaching collected recently by Ronald Hyman under the title *Contemporary Thought on Teaching*. Englewood Cliffs, N.J.: Prentice-Hall, 1971.
19 Averch et al. *How Effective Is Schooling?*
20 Ibid., p. 119 Cf. also p. 149.

good theoretical reason, backed up by some (weak) empirical evidence, that adaptive behavior on the part of teachers in individualized settings would be more effective than less personalized and flexible approaches to programmed learning.[21]

Being adaptive does not mean "doing your thing" or otherwise behaving without constraint. When it is possible to identify certain teaching methods that work for certain children with respect to certain learning objectives, the application of specific routines is obviously appropriate. But the point is that even in these cases teachers must be willing and able to avoid stereotyping children and assuming that if Joanie learns math in one way, the same teaching strategy will be effective in teaching Joanie reading. Moreover, there may well be tradeoffs between what is called for to achieve cognitive development and the way learning should be structured to achieve a capacity for independent thought, a sense of inquiry, or the ability to relate to others.

Even in the most socially homogeneous communities, the range of student capabilities, needs, and motives will vary significantly in any classroom. This fact, coupled with the state of our knowledge about how children learn, is reason to reemphasize the importance of the teacher to the learning process. In stressing the importance of teachers in integrating cognitive and affective dimensions of learning, David Krathwohl observes:

> Regardless of how materials are organized to facilitate cognitive learning, it is what the teacher does with these materials that determines whether and what kind of learning occurs.[22]

What does all this mean for the organization of schools? If we can agree that children's learning is the central purpose of schools, we can see from the foregoing discussion that achievement of that purpose rests fundamentally with the quality of the teaching that takes place.

Given the complexity, stress, and uncertainty inherent in the teaching process, one might conclude that the effective teacher (vis-à-vis his or her contributions to a pupil's learning) would be intelligent; possess a flexible, open personality; feel comfortable working with others; be able to see causality in multidimensional terms; be able to tolerate ambiguity; and enjoy spontaneous and intimate student-teacher contact.[23] Such characteristics, as I have implied

---

21 One reason the research does not take us very far in this regard is that very few studies actually measure the variation of what teachers actually do in the classroom regardless of the processes they or others say are experienced by students. No large-scale studies, and these have received the most attention, monitor teacher behavior.

22 David R. Krathwohl, "Cognitive and Affective Learning," *Encyclopedia of Education*, Vol. 4, p. 156.

23 Cf. David G. Ryan, *Characteristics of Teachers: Their Description, Comparison and Appraisal.* Washington, D.C.: American Council on Education, 1960; Norman A. Sprinthall, John M. Whitely, and Ralph L. Mosher, "A Study of Teacher Effectiveness," *Journal of Teacher Education,* Vol. 17, Spring 1960, pp. 93–106; and Philip Jackson. *Life in Classrooms.* New York: Holt, Rinehart and Winston, 1968, chap. 4.

earlier, could serve as a definition of adaptiveness.

TOWARD MORE ADAPTIVE SCHOOLS

Utility of Innovation Research Is Limited in Understanding Adaptiveness

At first thought, one might assume that the answers to how adaptiveness could be fostered in schools might be found in the literature on the sources of innovation in public organizations, especially schools. However, there are several reasons why this approach will not take us very far. A brief look at these reasons will not only help distinguish important differences between adaptiveness and innovation but will help to give some context to my later discussion of the factors that influence adaptiveness.

Quality of the Research Research aimed at explaining why some public organizations are more innovative than others is, taken as a whole, something of a bust. While the number of studies being conducted seems to be growing exponentially, basic questions still go un-answered. Most of the research is plagued with methodological and conceptual problems. Many of the conclusions reached are atheoretical, tautological, or they simply beg the question. No study of which I am aware has attempted to explain how differences in the conceptualizations, measurements, and contexts involved might reconcile the various studies. After an extensive review of the literature on educational change, Joseph B. Giaquinta concluded:

> As research designed to test hypotheses derived from theory about organiza-tional change, the quality is poor, and little is contributed to a systematic understanding of organizational change in schools. . . . The literature is basically atheoretical in nature. It contains little work designed to develop and test theories describing the dynamics of the change process or explaining why . . . schools vary in the degree and speed with which they change. Moreover, confidence is not warranted in a number of currently held generalizations about organizational change because the research methods and statistics upon which they are based are inadequate.[24]

And, in any case, those concerned with innovation have not examined the process of incrementalism and adjustment involved in implementation and incorporation except to say that innovations are seldom adopted in their origi-nal form.

---

24 Joseph B. Giacquinta, "The Process of Organizational Change in Schools," in Frederick N. Kerlinger, ed. *Review of Educational Research,* Vol. 1. Itasca, Ill.: F.E. Peacock, 1974, p. 178. Similar conclu-sions are reached by other reviews of the literature; Cf. Berman and McLaughlin. *Federal Programs Supporting Educational Change, Vol. I: A Model of Educational Change.* Santa Monica, Calif.: Rand Corporation, 1974.

Some Differences in the Characteristics of Innova-
tion and Adaptiveness   Innovations are usually defined by researchers (in various ways) as major changes rather than incremental or minor adjustments to existing practices. Adaptiveness could result in great instability and inconsistency for both student and teacher if it meant moving from one distinct pattern of behavior to another.

Innovations are usually introduced with the assumption that they should be implemented systemwide or throughout a school. Indeed, some major studies measure the success of an innovation in terms of how widely it is diffused without altering its characteristics.[25] In other words, in contrast with adaptiveness, innovation is seen as providing a right way to do something rather than an alternative to be adapted to situation, teacher, and student.[26]

A key strategy for advocates of innovation is to convince teachers that great improvements will result from the innovation if it is utilized intact. Not only does this lead to excessive aspiration and in turn invariably to frustration and disillusionment, it also focuses attention on process rather than outcome. Adaptiveness requires not only the rejection of the hope for universalistic solutions but also an emphasis on the behavioral consequences of student-teacher interaction.

Most research on innovation is based on products or teaching strategies that are initiated outside the system being studied. This has led to a belief that innovation depends heavily on "exogenous shocks" to the system.[27] Adaptiveness seems independent of such shocks—at least as experienced by the teacher. Indeed, adaptiveness must be internalized by the teacher and may require some isolation from the threat that usually accompanies "shock to the system."

If, as I suggested, innovation sometimes serves symbolic political purposes, understanding the characteristics of schools that have adopted new programs for such reasons will contribute nothing to understanding the conditions that foster adaptiveness.

Innovations usually require *a* decision by the teacher, and they are by definition temporary. There appears to be some agreement among students of innovation that organizational arrangements that encourage the formulation of new plans are different from those necessary to implement them, which may in turn be different from the structures necessary to achieve incorporation of diffu-

---

25 Berman and McLaughlin. *Federal Programs Supporting Educational Change, Vol. IV: The Findings in Review.* Santa Monica, Calif.: Rand Corporation, 1975.

26 An example is federal programming with respect to innovation in reading. See Miles Myers, "Uncle Sam's Reading Puppeteer," *Learning,* Vol. 4, November 1975, pp. 20–27.

27 Berman and McLaughlin. *Federal Programs Supporting Educational Change, Vol. I*; Cf. Averch et al. *How Effective Is Schooling?*

sion.[28] But adaptiveness involves both formulation and implementation and requires an awareness that no given innovation can be accepted unequivocably. Moreover, most of the research focuses on the formulation and adoption of innovation but ignores later stages, so that the processes by which teachers incorporate and sustain new ideas in their classrooms are not well examined.[29]

Summary   All of this is not to argue that one interested in fostering adaptiveness should ignore the existing research on innovation. But most theorizing about organizational change does not distinguish between innovation and adaptiveness. It is assumed, it seems, that innovative organizations will be adaptive, and vice versa. However, while the latter seems logical, the former does not. As I have suggested, an uncritical and deductive use of findings from these studies would be inappropriate and misleading.

Motivating Adaptive Teaching: A Theoretical Model

People will consider changing their behavior when the change promises to move them closer to their goals. But thinking about changing does not lead to change until some calculation of costs and benefits results in a belief that the benefit of movement toward the goals will be sufficient to warrant the costs.

The innovative process is invariably initiated by persons other than the teacher, and the teacher in effect makes a decision whether to be a spectator or a participant who has no commitments beyond the immediate game. Adaptiveness, on the other hand, involves a decision to be in continual search for new ideas and to maintain considerable flexibility in one's behavior. This decision is, of course, demanding and is likely to be made only if one perceives, on a continuing basis, that there are problems that need solving and that solving the problems will result in some net benefit. From this proposition follows the central dilemma involved in securing adaptive schools: It requires the maintenance of the feeling that one's performance should be better than it is.

Most people are utility maximizers; that is, given their resources, they do things that they perceive will move them closer to the attainment of their objectives. Of course, we often have multiple objectives which may compete and sometimes conflict with each other. In considering changes in patterns of behavior or taking on new responsibilities, we ask whether it will be worth it to change or to otherwise extend ourselves; that is, we weigh the benefits of the new behavior against its costs. This benefit/cost analysis in itself has costs, and

28   Cf. Lloyd A. Rowe and William B. Boise, "Organizational Innovation: Current Research and Evolving Concepts," *Public Administration Review,* Vol. 34, May/June 1974, p. 287; and Giacquinta, "The Process of Organizational Change in Schools."

29   Berman and McLaughlin. *Federal Programs Supporting Educational Change, Vol. I,* p. 8 ff.

for this and other reasons our calculations tend to be superficial, imprecise, and conservative. We, in effect, give more weight to costs than to benefits, in part because we can see the costs clearly since they are in some measure part of our present. It follows, then, that we can encourage people to consider behavior changes either by increasing the clarity and magnitude of the benefits or reducing the perceived costs.

To keep matters reasonably clear, I have spoken of change in terms of the kind of considerations one would undertake in dealing with a specific opportunity or demand for change, for example, the decision to adopt and implement an innovation. The decision to be adaptive also involves the assessment of costs and benefits but—at least in the short run—the promised benefits are less specific and calculable. In addition, one is likely to weigh the costs more heavily because the behavior required is long term and much more complicated than the prospect of adopting a single and relatively well-defined innovation. It should surprise no one, then, that an innovation is easier to attain than a state of adaptiveness.

In any case, a successful organizational strategy for achieving adaptiveness in teacher behavior depends on demonstrating that the benefits exceed the costs and on creating conditions that diminish costs and enhance benefits. Thus an organization must consider three sets of factors for attaining adaptiveness:

1. Factors affecting the perception of a gap between one's performance as a teacher and the objectives one values. This gap depends on both performance and objectives, and the organization might seek to provide information about either or both.
2. Factors affecting costs and the possibilities that these can be minimized. These would include consequences of being adaptive as well as negative sanctions that might be attached to an inability or unwillingness to behave adaptively.
3. Factors affecting benefits, including those that involve material, status, and social rewards as well as those that promote self-esteem or self-actualization.

If an organization can acquire the capacity to affect perceptions in the suggested direction and either reduce costs or increase benefits, or, ideally, reduce costs and increase benefits simultaneously, it will increase the adaptiveness of its members. However, bringing attention to a gap between performance and valued goals without increasing the net benefits one will obtain from adaptiveness will be counterproductive and result in frustration, low morale, defensive behavior, and other unhappy consequences for the children the teacher encounters. In other words, self-awareness and high goals do not necessarily result in better teaching.

Much of the remainder of this chapter examines these three sets of factors in more detail in order to suggest the directions those who seek more adaptive schools might travel. The application of this theoretical framework is confined to the inducement of adaptiveness among teachers.

I will not deal with what causes administrators to favor adaptiveness. I do believe that what I propose about the question of teacher adaptiveness can be employed at any level, though the variables that would be relevant will differ to some extent.

Perceiving a Need for Adaptive Behavior

Adapting one's behavior and staying adaptive depends, as I suggested previously, on the recognition that there is a gap between the goals to which one aspires and one's present capacity to achieve them.

Goal Setting and Adjustment   If goals are to play the role suggested in inducing a predisposition for adaptiveness, they must be explicit, and they must be personalized vis-à-vis students, or at least groups of students. The literature on teacher behavior suggests that while teachers generally aspire to certain idealized objectives such as academic excellence, creativity, and self-esteem for all their students, many find it difficult to sustain a multiplicity of goals, and they tend to narrow their operating objectives to those that appear within reach.

The problem, then, is to create a setting conducive to teachers clarifying their goals and being aware of potential outcomes for their students that they otherwise might not have considered or might have ruled out. This atmosphere can be created by structuring and enriching the interactions teachers have with administrators, peers, parents and students, and professional information (journals, course work, etc.).

Professional Information. I refer here to information about what is going on in other schools or new research that might be relevant to a teacher's general responsibilities and professional interests.[30]

Interaction with Parents and Students. Teachers often shape the goals they have for students without any input from parents or students. It is true, of course, that many parents and children are not very precise or assertive about their hopes, but the capacity to articulate goals can be encouraged, and over time parents and students will learn how to express their aspirations.

Parental and student goal discussions not only help the teacher understand

---

30 The importance of professional involvement of teachers to innovation is found by Ronald G. Corwin, "Innovation in Organizations: The Case of Schools," *Sociology of Education,* Vol. 48, Winter 1975, pp. 1–37.

the values the student is likely to attach to particular learning opportunities, they may also suggest targets the teacher had not considered or had valued inappropriately. This interaction will not occur of its own accord, however. As I implied earlier, many parents do not see themselves as sufficiently knowl- edgeable to question the goals teachers have set for their children. Establishing the notion that such behavior is appropriate and welcome is important, and the demeanor of the teacher, who may also be threatened by such interaction, can determine how parents will behave. Yet unpublished research that Judy Gruber and I conducted in New Haven schools suggests that schools can encourage parental input by establishing parent-teacher councils at the school level, with formal authority to participate constructively in decisions affecting what goes on in the classroom.

Interaction with Peers. A number of writers have pointed to the fact that teachers have little opportunity to interact professionally or to observe their peers and that this contributes to resistance to change.[31] Nevertheless, several studies show that their colleagues are the single most important source of information that teachers have about teaching.[32]

There are at least two requirements for fostering professional interaction among teachers: (1) time and structures that allow it to happen and (2) norms and established processes that reduce the personal costs and establish discus- sion of teaching problems and successes as a professional responsibility.

The contributions that interaction among peers are likely to make to adap- tiveness probably increase proportionately with diversity within the interacting group.[33] At the same time, diversity may also cause work groups to fragment and communication to decline.

Administrators and Goal Setting. As indicated earlier, the clearer one's goals, the greater the likelihood of adaptive behavior. Administrators should therefore be concerned with assisting teachers, individually and collectively, to clarify and prioritize their own objectives and to specify goals for their students. Administrators who take this responsibility seriously will be in a position to facilitate interaction among teachers with similar objectives.

The comparison of the goals of the organization—or of its leadership—to those of a given teacher can be employed as a strategy to induce reconsidera-

---

31 Willis D. Hawley, ''Dealing with Organizational Rigidity in Public Schools: A Theoretical Approach,'' and D.E. Tope, ''Summary of Seminar on Change Processes in Public Schools,'' in Richard O. Carlson, ed. *Change Processes in Public Schools.* Eugene, Ore.: The Center for Advanced Study of Educational Administration, University of Oregon, 1965.

32 This research is reviewed concisely by Ernest House. *The Politics of Educational Innovation.* Berkeley, Calif.: McCutchan, 1974, pp. 70–73.

33 Cf. Jerald Hage and Michael Aiken. *Social Change in Complex Organizations.* New York: Random House, 1970; and Corwin, ''Organizational Innovation: The Case of Schools,'' p. 31.

tion of goals. The adjustment of an individual teacher's objectives can be encouraged by involving that teacher in key decisions concerning how resources are utilized and what curricula are adopted. When such involvement takes the form of group decision making, it is likely to facilitate a willingness to consider new alternative modes of behavior, assuming, of course, that the group is seeking answers as to how the learning environment can be enhanced.

Relating Performance to Goals. The same processes of interaction that facilitate the consideration of alternative objectives and the sharpening of one's purposes also provide information on performance. Exchanges with administrators and peers provide the opportunity for subjective evaluation and interpersonal comparisons. These interactions, as well as those with students and parents and with professional information, encourage self-examination either by (1) raising the possibility that alternative ways of accomplishing certain objectives exist or (2) existing strategies are ineffective.[34]

But the most direct and perhaps most persuasive information on performance should come from objective evaluation of the teachers' contributions to the rate at which children in their classes develop cognitively and affectively. For such evaluation to be motivating, it must have at least two characteristics:

1. It must focus on the goals the teacher values.
2. The teacher must see the measures of performance upon which evaluation is based as adequate and appropriate.

If these two conditions are met, teachers are likely to take evaluations of their performance seriously since the two major rationalizations for dealing with dissonance that evaluation can cause are not available.

One can acquire information about performance from others or one can develop—and school systems can foster—the capacity to acquire the ability to assess themselves. Ronald Lippitt and his associates have argued that to encourage adaptive and innovative behavior, it is useful to:

. . . connect the teacher to the knowledge and methods of the behavioral sciences in order to enable him to conduct a personal research and development process in his classroom. For example, with some professional advice a teacher may administer a series of questionnaires or scientific instruments to his pupils. After analyzing and interpreting these data, he can derive a

---

34 One study of 176 sixth-grade classrooms found that student responses to questionnaires about teacher behavior could be used to change teachers' behavior when the answers brought attention to the fact that teachers' images of what they were doing were different from those of their students. N.L. Gage, Philip J. Runkel, and B.B. Chatteridge, "Changing Behavior Through Feedback from Pupils: An Application of Equilibrium Theory," in W.W. Charters, Jr., and N.L. Gage, eds. *Readings in the Social Psychology of Education.* Boston: Allyn and Bacon, 1963, pp. 173–181.

plan of action or innovation, test it out and evaluate it.[35]

Nonadaptiveness: An Offer One Can't Resist. It is possible that people can be induced to change their behavior, not because they are dissatisfied with their performance or because they accept new goals urged on them by others but because their failure to change will bring about negative sanctions. But the capacity to induce a recognition of the need for adaptiveness in this way has clear limits.

Most of what a teacher does goes unobserved by supervisors or peers who might invoke sanctions. As the literature on innovation clearly shows, teachers enjoy considerable power to resist or substantially modify innovations they are directed to implement. Since it would seem that adherence to new programs or use of new materials is substantially easier to measure than adaptive behavior, the enforcement of demands that teachers adopt the latter is likely to be so great that negative sanctions will not be feared. This also means, of course, that the distribution of positive rewards for adaptiveness is difficult, a point I will return to.

Summary and Comment   This section argues that a predisposition to behave adaptively depends on the recognition that one is not performing to the standards one values. I have argued that, in effect, information-intensive school environments that focus their attention on the possibilities of new goals and/or new processes for achieving old goals foster adaptiveness.[36]

Fostering an awareness that progress toward the fullfillment of one's role expectations is possible is a motivational process similar to that which Argyris and others believe releases and sustains an individual's contribution of psychological energy to the attainment of organizational goals.[37] This process, of course, produces tension, and the stress a person experiences can lead to dysfunctional behavior and not to adaptiveness, depending on the individual's assessment of the relative costs and benefits he will incur in becoming and staying adaptive.

The higher the costs and the lower the benefits, the narrower the gaps should be between perception of one's present performance and one's expectations, so

---

35 Ronald Lippitt et al., "The Teacher as Innovator, Seeker and Sharer of New Practices," in Richard Miller, ed. *Perspectives on Educational Change*. New York: Appleton-Century-Crofts, 1967, p. 309.

36 There is almost unanimous agreement among writers on educational change that information-intensive schools are more likely to be innovative than those in which internal communication, environmental feedback, and knowledge about professional developments are weak. This applies to all stages of the innovation process. Such conclusions, however, rest heavily on research in public organizations other than schools and on the work of various organization theorists. See, for example, Rowe and Boise, "Organizational Innovation: Current Research."

37 Cf. Chris Argyris. *Integrating the Organization and the Individual*. New York: John Wiley, 1964.

that low morale, frustration, passivity, and other forms of counterproductive activity can be avoided. It is difficult to predict how wide the achievement gap should be to induce adaptive behavior; the ability of individuals to deal creatively with tension apparently varies with personality characteristics such as self-esteem, authoritarianism, and assertiveness.

Potential Costs of Adaptiveness

As noted earlier, adaptiveness requires the development of a repertoire of various approaches to teaching, the recurrent assessment of needs and capabilities of individual students, the selective application of techniques on an individual basis, the evaluation of the effectiveness of these techniques, and the reevaluation of one's abilities and the assessment of ways those abilities that need strengthening can be enhanced. The cost involved in achieving and maintaining such behavior can be thought of as technical and psychological.[38] Technical costs are those associated with the development and renewal of the ability to do these things. I use the term "psychological costs" here very loosely to include perceived loss of social esteem, status, and power, loss of self-esteem or self-confidence, frustration, and the like.

Technical Costs   Being adaptive requires the constant gathering and processing of new information. Moreover, since the needs and even the capacities of students change over time, the addition of new skills and the virtual retirement of others will be required.

Creating the rich information field necessary to provide a predisposition toward adaptiveness will reduce some search costs. Most teachers know a lot more about education than they do about other fields. Part of this is caused by time constraints, part of it is due to the fact that norms relating to information sharing are not firmly established, and part of the problem is that formal structures for multiperson problem solving are seldom extant. Administrators and teachers can learn to see themselves as resource people who, once aware of the needs and interests of individual teachers, can refer and provide materials to them. Within schools it seems possible to develop informal experts who acquire a reputation—and thus an incentive—for keeping people informed about their field.

Finally, adaptiveness may, though not necessarily, require new materials with which to work. The literature on educational innovation suggests that the adoption of innovation relates positively to the amount of fiscal resources available, though it may be that it is the *amount* of uncommitted resources

---

38 Other kinds of costs are conceivable but not likely. Being adaptive could result in the loss of material rewards only if performance were tied to rewards and adaptiveness led to decreasing effectiveness. For reasons set out previously, these possibilities are remote.

rather than the total volume of uncommitted resources that is crucial.[39]

The hypothetical relationship between slack in a school system's fiscal resources and willingness to adopt innovations may also apply to the implementation of an innovation; however, empirical evidence is lacking. If such a linkage exists, it is because excess resources allow teachers to try new things that do cost money and to spend less time on scavenging instructional materials, which means that they can move on to thinking about enhancing learning environments.

Potential Psychological Cost   Role Uncertainty. People vary in their ability to tolerate ambiguity, but most of us seek to minimize uncertainty in our relationships with others and in our perception of our responsibilities. The absence of such definition can lead to internal tension and to group conflict.[40] In adaptive organizations, tasks would be various, diffuse, and changing, while goals would often be multiple and general.

Responsibility. Adaptive organizations provide the individual with considerable autonomy but also with considerable responsibility for the attainment of organizational goals. If those working in hierarchical organization do not achieve their objectives, they can always assign their failure to "the system" or to "constraints on my discretion" or directly to the principal. For example, teachers commonly explain the apparent "failure" of students in terms of the students' prior experience, other teachers, or the rigidities of the curriculum, and so on. When teachers play a central role in determining the character of the school and what goes on in the classroom, the "failure" of students to meet the teachers' expectations can be assigned only to students or to themselves. Often teachers feel the students' failure personally.

The willingness to act, particularly to take new initiatives, is related to one's sense of competence.[41] Thus, broadening the scope and depth of one's responsibilities, even if desired by the worker, could result in a conservative approach to work and a sense of impotence. The more serious the individual believes the consequences of possible failure to be, the more likely that he will avoid coming to grips with the problems he faces. This avoidance of responsibility can take many forms. First, it may result in efforts to reduce autonomy by such

---

39 Matthew B. Miles argues that adoption of innovations is related to the availability of material supports. "Innovation in Education: Some Generalizations," in Matthew B. Miles, ed. *Innovation in Education*. New York: Bureau of Publications, Teachers College, Columbia University, 1964, pp. 635–639. See also Rowe and Boise, "Organizational Innovation: Current Research," p. 289.

40 Cf. Neal C. Gross et al. *Explorations in Role Analysis*. New York: John Wiley, 1958; and R.K. Merton, "The Role Set: Problems in Sociological Theory," *British Journal of Sociology*, Vol. 8, 1958, pp. 106–120.

41 Cf. Argyris. *Integrating the Organization and the Individual*; and Victor H. Vroom. *Work and Motivation*. New York: John Wiley, 1964.

means as centralizing authority, establishing standard operating procedures, and insisting on stronger leadership and in loss of professional confidence and self-esteem. Second, the avoidance of responsibility may make the worker focus only on those aspects of the jobs where success is most readily measured,[42] such as securing classroom discipline. This in turn may make quality control trivial and encourage adhering to routine, denying one's feelings, narrowing responsibility and specializing, transferring initiatives to others, and denying personal effectiveness.[43]

The "Problem" of High Aspirations and Identification with the Student. The opportunity to set one's goals, especially when high aspirations are first presented, often results in setting very ambitious targets, and the exhilaration that comes from being given significant responsibility may result in hopes for rapid and significant problem solving. If such high aspirations are disappointed, as they are likely to be, a sense of failure will invariably follow. Adaptiveness requires individual treatment of students, which may lead to a heavy identification with students. Personalization of teaching coupled with excessive aspirations can lead to frustration and anxiety.

Professional Embarrassment. What teachers do in their classrooms is only vaguely known by other teachers. Deviant practices or special interests are generally known, but the nature of interaction with students goes largely unobserved and unreported. Adaptiveness, however, requires considerable interaction, frank discussion of problems, observations by others, and feedback on effectiveness. Though the last of these may never be public knowledge, depending on school policies, adaptiveness will "expose" teacher behavior to the scrutiny of others. Teachers who are least secure about their abilities and those who are in fact less effective may experience professional embarrassment.

Threats to Authority by Parents and Students. Teachers can assert authority and seek control of their classroom by denying the legitimacy of demands of others and by so structuring classroom events that acceptable student behavior is well defined and readily determinable. Adaptiveness requires that teachers grant parents and students the right to suggest objectives and question teaching strategies. This will increase some teachers' sense of vulnerability. Students in adaptive classrooms will see various standards and emphases applied to their peers and should experience less authoritarian behavior. Some students may interpret a teacher's responsiveness to student preferences and the opportunity

---

42 J.D. Thompson. *Organizations in Action.* New York: McGraw-Hill, 1967, pp. 120–122.
43 I.E.P. Menzies, "A Case-study in the Functioning of Social Systems as a Defence Against Anxiety," *Human Relations,* Vol. 13, 1960, pp. 95–121; and Michael Lipsky, "Street Level Bureaucracy and the Analysis of Urban Reform," *Urban Affairs Quarterly,* Vol. 6, 1971, pp. 391–410.

to question why they are asked to do things as a breakdown in authority. Adaptive teachers do, in effect, surrender some power to students.

And it seems likely, at least in the short run, that adaptiveness will undermine methods of student control employed in many so-called traditional classrooms.[44] Of course, if teaching effectiveness reduces disruption and purposeless behavior, adaptiveness will not be costly in this sense. Authority in this case will derive not from position per se but from the contributions teachers make to student development.

Social Disapproval. One of the most pervasive findings in the research on behavior is that the norms of the work group have enormous impact on the willingness of people to try new ideas. Limited evidence suggests that teachers as a group do not reward, and may disapprove of, peers who are innovators,[45] perhaps because innovations can disrupt the relative status of group members and bring about new external demands for changes in the behavior of everyone. Certainly, this negative predisposition is not pervasive, and whether or not it would be applied to adaptiveness is difficult to say. Adaptiveness allows a wide range of behavior to coexist so long as students benefit—which may seem less threatening than innovations.

Loss of Status or Power. The conditions necessary to attain adaptive schools will involve sharing authority, and will, overall, involve a leveling up of status positions of individual teachers. This could mean that some teachers who enjoy special access to resources and information (because of their relations with administrators, contacts outside the school system, or the like) will lose status or power.[46] Department heads, master teachers, area coordinators, and even principals are likely to lose status and power relative to teachers.

---

44 Sieber observes that innovations that help teachers manage their environments, including keeping children under control, are the most readily accepted. S.D. Sieber, ''Organizational Influences on Innovative Roles,'' in T.L. Edel and J.M. Ritchel, eds. *Knowledge Production and Utilization in Educational Administration.* Eugene, Ore.: Center for the Advanced Study of Educational Administration, University of Oregon, 1968.

45 See Edwin M. Bridges, ''The Principal and the Teachers: The Problem of Organizational Change,'' in Richard W. Saxe, ed. *Perspectives on the Changing Role of the Principal.* Springfield, Ill.: Thomas, 1968, pp. 62–63 and the sources cited there.

46 There is some evidence that loss of status or fear thereof is associated with opposition to innovation in schools. M.S. Atwood, ''Small-Scale Administrative Change: Resistance to the Introduction of a High School Guidance Program,'' in Matthew B. Miles, ed. *Innovation in Education;* Richard O. Carlson, ''Unanticipated Consequences in the Use of Programmed Instruction,'' in *Adoption of Educational Innovations*; Lippitt et al., ''The Teacher as Innovator, Seeker and Sharer of New Practices''; and Joseph B. Giacquinta, ''Status Risk and Receptivity to Innovations in Complex Organizations: A Study of Responses of Four Groups of Educators to the Proposed Introduction of Sex Education in Elementary School,'' *Sociology of Education*, Vol. 48, Winter 1975, pp. 38–58.

Potential Benefits of Adaptiveness

            Rewards Deriving from Effectiveness I have previously made a case for the link between adaptive teaching and student learning. As I noted, there are good theoretical reasons to believe this link is strong. A sizable body of school reform literature makes this argument in one way or another,[47] and there is also agreement among many students of school administration that organizational and individual adaptiveness facilitates good teaching. There is, however, only limited systematic evidence—in part because of the small number of schools studied that employ the type of open, collegial structures just described—that this is so.[48] But if, as Robert Schaefer suggests, a teacher is a diagnostician, a "stalker of meaning," and a constant learner, the importance of adaptiveness would be clear.[49]

Teachers benefit in several ways from their own effectiveness: (1) it enhances their self-confidence and self-esteem; (2) it is likely to bring social approval of colleagues; (3) it enhances the prestige of teaching among parents and other "lay persons"; (4) it carries the reward of having achieved a highly valued goal; and (5) it perhaps reduces tension between students and teachers and the likelihood of disruption.

All of this depends, of course, on the teachers awareness of (or faith in) their own success,[50] and others having knowledge of (or belief in) that success. This in turn depends on the nature of the evaluation system and the linkage of incentives to them. I will return to these very complex issues below.

            A Reduction of Interpersonal Conflict over New Ideas Almost all studies dealing with the implementation of innovations stress that group norms suppress the acceptance and use of new ideas.[51] Because adaptiveness requires reduction in status differences and extensive communication and interaction, one might expect the power of social norms and the

---

47 Cf. Averch et al. *How Effective Is Schooling?*, pp. 126–147 and the sources cited there.

48 See Jackson. *Life in Classroom,* chap. 4; Norman A. Sprinthall, John M. Whitely, and Ralph L. Mosher, "A Study of Teacher Effectiveness," *Journal of Teacher Education*, Vol. 17, Spring 1966, pp. 93–106; and Wayne J. Doyle, "Effects of Achieved Status of Leaders on the Productivity of Groups," *Administrative Science Quarterly,* Vol. 16, March 1971, pp. 40–50.

49 See Robert Schaefer. *The School as a Center of Inquiry.* New York: Harper & Row, 1967, p. 57.

50 The literature on innovativeness supports the not surprising notion that innovations have a greater chance of adoption to the extent that potential adapters see them as improving a teacher's chances of achieving valued goals. See, for example, E.M. Rogers and F.F. Shoemaker. *Communication of Innovations.* New York: Free Press, 1971.

51 For example, after reviewing the literature, Ernest House observed that "there is a strong tendency for group values to turn reorientations [innovations] into variations and variations into regular practice" (*The Politics of Educational Innovation,* p. 77). See also Giacquinta, "The Process of Organizational Change in Schools," p. 189.

costs of social disapproval to be lowest in least adaptive schools. But in adaptive schools, group norms will, as I have already suggested, focus on outcome rather than process or behavior. The result of this should be strong norms supporting experimentation and autonomy of style. This in turn should free teachers who value adaptiveness of some of the social disapproval of their deviance in approach. Unlike the innovation process, the success of which is often measured by how widely diffused and incorporated a given idea becomes, adaptiveness makes no such organization-wide demands.

Rewards Deriving from Structural Characteristics of Adaptive Schools   Adaptive schools will be characterized by certain organizational arrangements and leadership styles that I will outline in the next section. These characteristics offer rewarding opportunities over and above their impact on teaching effectiveness. Such opportunities include: (1) access to colleagues and social approval, (2) increases in one's role in decision making, and (3) professional discretion in the development of teaching approaches and classroom management.

Summary   I have argued that to attain adaptiveness in public schools, one must foster conditions that cause teachers to continually specify and reexamine their goals while providing them with evidence about their capacity to meet those objectives. But recognizing that one is falling short of one's goals and being aware that adaptiveness could improve teaching effectiveness will not necessarily cause one to behave adaptively. That commitment depends on the perceived costs and benefits of adaptiveness. I have tried to identify the sources of the costs and benefits and the factors that influence their magnitude.

CONCLUSION: IMPLICATIONS FOR THE ORGANIZATION
AND ADMINISTRATION OF SCHOOLS

There are certain general implications of the foregoing analysis as to how schools might be organized and for general directions that educational administration should take to secure maximum adaptiveness. As before, I have constrained this analysis to the motivational field that teachers experience directly, and the following discussion is also subject to that constraint. Important issues like the roles of school board politics, the impact of superintendents and their staffs, interorganizational competition, the incentives principals have to be adaptive, and the policies of other governments will go untouched here.

The Internal Structure of Adaptive Schools

The available literature suggests that organizational environments that are most effective in motivating people whose jobs require them to deal creatively with uncertainty and to respond flexibly and spontaneously to a variety of problem-solving demands generally provide these people with (1) a role in the development of organizational policies relevant to their work,[52] (2) some autonomy in setting individual goals and substantial freedom in determining the means to achieve those goals,[53] and (3) opportunities for professional interaction.[54]

It follows from these conclusions and from research on the traits of effective teachers[55] that:

1. Adaptive schools should be organized collegially. Key decisions affecting teachers in general should be made democratically or *delegated* by teachers to decision makers.
2. Status differences within the school should be minimized, and formal differentiation of staff authority avoided.[56]

52 Daniel Katz and Robert Kahn. *The Social Psychology of Organizations.* New York: John Wiley, 1966, p. 426; Chris Argyris, "Organizational Effectiveness," *International Encyclopedia of the Social Sciences,* 17 vols. New York: Macmillan and Free Press, 1968, Vol. 11, p. 317 and the sources cited there; and Ronald Havelock. *Planning for Innovation,* pp. 6, 33. It may be noted that participation in the identification of organizational or group objectives and power sharing in general results in greater commitment to the attainment of such goals (Katz and Kahn, p. 332) and to consensus over goals, resulting in organizational effectiveness (Smith and Ari, 1968).

53 Katz and Kahn. *The Social Psychology of Organizations,* p. 362; Robert J. House et al., "Relation of Leader Consideration and Initiating Structure to R and D Subordinates' Satisfaction," *Administrative Science Quarterly,* Vol. 16, March 1971, pp. 19–30; Martin Patchen. *Participation, Achievement and Involvement on the Job.* Englewood Cliffs, N.J.: Prentice-Hall, 1970; Frederick Herzberg. *Work and the Nature of Man.* Cleveland: World Publishing, 1966; and Chris Argyris. *Integrating the Organization and the Individual,* especially chaps. 3, 8, 9. Edwin Bridges has argued that teachers resist innovation because its imposition from "above" is seen as a violation of professional status: "The Principal and the Teachers: The Problem of Organizational Change," in Richard Saxe, ed. *Perspectives on the Changing Role of the Principal.* Springfield, Ill.: Thomas, 1968, p. 63.

54 Donald C. Pelz, "The Innovating Organization: Conditions for Innovation," and Chris Argyris, *Integrating the Organization and the Individual.* Opportunities for interpersonal interaction with coworkers increase job satisfaction (Sawatsky, 1941; Richards and Dobryns, 1957) and, when interaction is related to the attainment of organizational goals, also increases productivity (Bass, 1960, pp. 51–53).

55 Andrew Halpin. *Theory and Research in Administration.* New York: Macmillan, 1966, chap. 4; Arthur F. Corey, "Overview of Factors Affecting the Holding Power of the Teaching Profession," in Timothy M. Stinnett, ed. *The Teacher Dropout.* Itasca, Ill.: F.E. Peacock, 1970, pp. 2–3, 8–9; Philip Jackson. *Life in Classrooms,* chap. 4; Sarason. *The Culture of the School and the Problem of Change.* Boston: Allyn & Bacon, 1970, p. 169.

56 Elizabeth Cohen has found, for example, that equal-status teacher groups allow greater feelings of influence and job satisfaction and provide more chances for rewards from peers: Cohen, "Open-Space Schools: The Opportunity to Become Ambitious," *Sociology of Education,* Vol. 46, Spring 1973, pp. 143–161.

3. Organizational constraints on the individual behavior of teachers should be minimized but, when employed, be tied to linkages between behavior and teaching effectiveness.[57]

Guidelines for Leadership   It should be clear that conventional models of assertive, take-charge leadership are not appropriate to adaptive schools.[58] The leadership role should be that of the facilitator rather than coach or taskmaster. Facilitation of adaptive teaching would include emphasis on the following activities:

1. Attention should be given to goal clarification and specification and the relationship of goals to different teaching approaches.[59]
2. In-service training programs centered on the individual needs of teachers *as they define them* should be provided. Individual needs can, of course, be dealt with in group situations, but decisions by leaders on what people need to learn and the assignment of workers to designated programs will have few consequences for reducing anxiety and psychological stress.
3. Information on new ideas that relate to the goals teachers are pursuing should be provided.
4. The propensity to avoid goal specification and readjustment might be reduced if (a) leaders seek to identify differences in the objectives of individual group members and to raise questions about their compatibility, and (b) leaders foster continual feedback of both subjective and objective information about the capacity of *both* individuals and groups to meet their stated objectives. One relevant norm that leaders can develop in a group is the desirability of self-assessment and recurrent evaluation by peers. Another is the inherent value of individual input, and this norm is particularly important when there is status incongruence in the group. Finally, as Blau suggests, it is possible that organizations can develop ideological commit-

---

57 As I have already implied, research on the structural characteristics of innovative organizations seems to offer up conflicting evidence. Some writers believe, for example, that innovation is facilitated by centralization, and others conclude that decentralization enhances the adoption and implementation of new programs. It may be, as Lippitt and his associates and Shepard imply, that teacher-initiated innovation is more likely in decentralized and less structured schools, while whose in charge of centralized and hierarchical schools are in a better position to impose programs developed elsewhere. Teacher-generated innovation is one aspect of adaptiveness that suggests the importance of autonomy to adaptive teaching. This research is succinctly reviewed by Ronald G. Corwin, "Innovation in Organizations: The Case of Schools," pp. 6–7. Corwin also cites studies showing that innovation is often impeded by formal, hierarchical organizational structures.

58 The literature on innovation suggests that directive leadership is associated with both (1) formal adoption of innovations, and (2) weak implementation and incorporation of the change. See Sieber, "Organizational Influences on Innovative Roles."

59 The importance of this function is emphasized and discussed by Hawley, "Dealing with Organizational Rigidity in Public Schools"; and Giacquinta, "The Process of Organizational Change in Schools," p. 196.

ments to seek out and achieve new goals.[60] This can lead to the view that change is good in itself, but if emphasis is placed on the consequences of the change rather than rewarding changes in processes themselves, this problem may be controllable.

5. Norms encouraging participation in decision making should be fostered, as should the notion that "different" ideas are valuable because they are different. E.P. Hollander, for example, found that in some organizations individuals could build up "idiosyncrasy credits," which facilitated deviant actions, once basic loyalty to the group and its norms had been established.[61]

6. Efforts should be made to clarify the mutual dependence of specific teachers in terms of (a) shared responsibilities for particular students, or (b) the interrelationships between the more general knowledge and experience students have.

7. Regular times should be set aside not only for group decision making but also for informal communication. Such discussions should involve only two or three members, and steps should be taken to rotate the members of such parleys.

8. Leaders should discourage the notion that they have the answer, however attractive it might be to be thought of as the source of wisdom. They should foster, instead, norms that support openness, the right and obligation of each member to observe and comment on the work of others, the distribution of leadership tasks to more than one member of the group, and the desirability of power sharing on an ad hoc basis.

9. As noted earlier, leaders need to manage the levels of tension that result from the identification of what I have called "performance gaps." But how? As Morton Deutsch observes, the results of studies dealing with the effects of tension are not definitive.[62] "The safest generalization seems to be that mild stress often improves group performance and increases cohesiveness, while severe stress often has the opposite effects." What is needed is what James March and Herbert Simon call "optimum stress."[63] The problem, of course, is to predict the point of diminishing returns. Among the factors that might determine how much stress can be dealt with creatively are: (a) the turbulence of the environment, (b) the self-confidence and cohesiveness of the group, (c) commitment to organizational goals by group members, (d) the nature of demands, (e) organizational resources

60 P. Blau. *The Dynamics of Bureaucracy.* Chicago: University of Chicago Press, 1955.

61 E.P. Hollander, "Competence and Conformity in the Acceptance of Influence," *Journal of Abnormal and Social Psychology,* Vol. 61, 1960, pp. 365–369.

62 Morton Deutsch, "Groups: Group Behavior," *International Encyclopedia of the Social Sciences,* Vol 6, p. 272.

63 James G. March and Herbert A. Simon. *Organizations.* New York: John Wiley, 1958, p. 154.

(including teacher skills), and (f) the personalities of individual group members.

The Nature of Evaluation Preceding pages have identified a number of reasons why evaluation of teaching performance is crucial to the attainment and maintenance of adaptiveness in public schools. Evaluation can be thought to have two major purposes: (1) to allow individuals and groups to improve their own performance and (2) to provide information to administrative superiors, policy makers, or clients that can be used to control or to impose change on the organization. Let me refer to the first of these purposes as *internal*, the second as *external*.

Both internal and external evaluations are difficult in school organizations, precisely for the reasons that nonadaptiveness is important:

1. Organizational goals are often multiple and diffuse.
2. Knowledge about the best way to achieve organizational goals is not extensive or definitive.

Evaluation is not only difficult methodologically but it can also have significant costs to the organization. For example, to the extent it poses personal costs, it is likely to reduce risk taking and encourage adherence to familiar ways.[64] My objective is to suggest some guidelines for evaluation in adaptive schools, aimed at maximizing relevant information about teacher performance and minimizing the potential costs such information and its gathering poses.

1. Internal evaluation of individuals seems best carried out and least likely to be resisted if rewards or sanctions are not directly associated with it. Such rewards or penalties are best administered by persons who are not members of the immediate organization or subunit.

    This does not mean that adaptive organizations should not engage in evaluation; rather it means that the internal purposes of such activity should be to develop the capacity of individuals and the group to meet organizational goals. Can evaluation in the absence of formal sanctions induce change or otherwise motivate? The importance of social acceptance by peers and the desire most people seem to have for self-esteem should provide the appropriate leverage if the objectives involved are actually valued by the group or the individual. As noted earlier, the characteristics of adaptive schools are likely to encourage commitment to organizational goals. In any case, evaluation efforts should be individualized or at least

---

64 On this point, with reference to the potentially stifling effect that accountability may have on innovation, see David P. Weikert and Barnard A. Banet, "Model Design Problems in Follow Through," in Rivlin and Timpane, eds. *Planned Variation in Education,* pp. 61–78. Hage and Aiken (*Social Change in Complex Organizations*) argue that conditions increasing the rate of organizational change include lower emphases on the volume and efficiency of production.

tied to readily identified subgroups. Such a strategy would include the identification of individual or team objectives and the specific measures and types of evidence that group members agree are appropriate to know whether objectives they value have been achieved.

2. For purposes here, let me describe external evaluation as having political and administrative components. Political evaluation is aimed at holding the organization accountable for attaining specified objectives. Administrative evaluation, in addition to this function, concerns the control, advancement, or termination of individuals.

    Political evaluation is usually the function of legislative or citizen bodies. It should be concerned solely with group performance—that is, the activity of the nonbureaucratic organization as a whole. The agents of political evaluation may, of course, collect their own data and deal directly with clients. Some of the information so collected may be relevant to assessing individual performance but would not be used externally. Administrators external to the nonbureaucratic work group should share the responsibility for monitoring group behavior.

3. A focus on the group, coupled with reluctance to punish short-run individual failure, may encourage the group itself to be concerned with contributing to goal-related effectiveness of its members. Moreover, there is evidence that individuals draw satisfaction from the success of the group which, in turn, encourages cohesion and collaboration.[65] And, emphasizing group performance in evaluation processes may provide a base from which intergroup competition can be induced. Administrative responsibility for personal evaluation, in effect, screens the individual from environmental threat. There are two reasons why this is important: (a) to encourage the individual to interact with clients and to develop task-related commitments outside the work group; and (b) to facilitate evaluation of individuals over time in order to encourage personal growth and permit a time perspective that can reward adaptiveness in terms of long-term, rather than short-run, impact.

4. As noted earlier, the logic of adaptive schools will be undermined by evaluation that focuses on process rather than the development of students. Product objectives are those derived from organizational goals—as contrasted with various means that might be seen as advancing such goals.

5. If evaluation is to have developmental as well as judgmental purpose, members of the organization must be involved not only in goal setting but also in the specification of performance criteria. Such criteria should ideally be subject to objective verification and should capture the range of organiza-

---

65 D.M. Shaw, "Size of Share in Task and Motivation Groups," *Sociometry, Vol. 23, 1960, pp. 203–208.*

tional goals as well as their relative priority.

These several thoughts only scratch the surface of the difficulties of achieving an effective approach to evaluating adaptive teaching. In general, I have tried to stress the importance of maintaining high levels of feedback to the group and to individuals.

Direct Rewards for Adaptive Teaching   I have noted throughout that the potential motivational value of rewards for performance derives from leader and peer group approval, intrinsic satisfactions involved in achieving valued goals, and experiencing the working conditions necessary to maintaining adaptive organizations. But what is the role of material rewards and career advancement as incentives? Present reward structures in schools do not have much range; there is very limited room for advancement, and neither salary nor leadership roles seem to be closely tied to teaching performance as measured by what happens to students in particular schools or classrooms.

The issue that seems unresolved either by empirical studies[66] or theory is: Assuming one could measure performance, would the motivational value of such things as merit pay and differentiated staffing outweigh the costs with respect to personal conflict, poor communication, and low incentives for sharing skills and ideas? It does appear that ambitious teachers will adopt innovations in order to set themselves apart from others. And this entrepreneurship may result in the premature closure on innovations by other, less aggressive or less confident teachers.[67] How this relates to adaptiveness is uncertain. One possible but problematic way out of this dilemma is to reward people who excel in, and commit themselves to, processes that contribute to the success of others. This approach, however, has the peculiarity of focusing on process rather than product and perhaps rewarding people who are in fact less effective teachers.

Final Comments   Let me conclude by acknowledging two things. First, to secure adaptiveness initially may be thought of as an innovation. On the other hand, moving to a state of adaptiveness is likely to be an evolutionary and incremental process that is not easily packaged, which leads to the second point. Learning to be adaptive is no simple task and requires both the acquisition of technical and interpersonal skills on the one hand and the unlearning of certain behaviors on the other.

---

66 For example, studies disagree on the relative importance of material versus other incentives for inducing teachers to adopt and implement innovations. Cf. Thomas Stephens, "Innovative Teaching Practices: Their Relation to System Norms and Rewards," *Educational Administration Quarterly,* Vol. 10, Winter 1974, pp. 35–43; and Dennis W. Spuck, "Reward Structures in the Public High School," *Educational Administration Quarterly, Ibid., pp. 18–34.*

67 Ernest House. *The Politics of Educational Innovation,* chap. 4.

Following their extensive review of the literature, Harvey A. Averch and his colleagues offer the not very unique conclusion that a noticeable improvement of cognitive and noncognitive student outcomes "*may* require sweeping changes in the organization, structure and conduct of educational experience."[68]

While almost everyone agrees that educational change is necessary, research and policy seem to be guided by one or both of two assumptions: (1) there is one best way to teach particular subjects, and (2) schools that adopt innovations are more likely to be successful than those that do not. I have tried to suggest why these assumptions are misplaced and that before we worry about understanding the innovation process, we need to recognize that it, as well as teaching effectiveness, depends on understanding how schools can be made more adaptive. This recognition should stimulate experimentation and research, and I have attempted to suggest important considerations for both policy makers and students of education changefulness.

Comments
Paul T. Hill

Willis Hawley's chapter identifies some of the chief sources of tension and confusion in American educational policy. His distinction between innovation (the imposition of new inventions in educational services, without serious thought about the needs of the particular students to be served) and adaptation (careful tailoring of services to meet clients' needs and aspirations) is a very useful one. However, I think Hawley's suggestions about how to achieve adaptive education miss the mark. They are based on the assumption that schools will become adaptive if teachers and principals learn to value adaptation. Yet many of the pressures for innovation and against adaptation come from outside the school. Those pressures will not slacken at all in response to the in-school reforms that Hawley suggests.

I would like to achieve two things in my comments. The first is to argue that the concern for innovation pervades the whole educational system and that correctives at the school level are unlikely to succeed. The second is to identify some prerequisites to adaptive education and briefly to suggest the outlines of research that might help bring it about.

Systemic Forces for Innovation
My first theme is that innovation is a deeply rooted preoccupation of the American educational system and that correctives must not stop at the school

---

68   Averch et al., *How Effective Is Schooling?*, p. x (emphasis added).

level but instead address the systemic causes. Hawley has argued very convincingly that services invented at one level are unlikely to be faithfully implemented or effective at another. Unfortunately, such an argument is not enough to discourage inventors from trying to control educational systems so their innovations can be tried. Despite over ten years of unhappy experience with innovation, the pressure to invent new services and to have government mandate their use is undiminished.

The pressure to innovate is partly the result of confusion about the roles of different levels of government in the educational process. Though only local educational agencies deliver educational services, the federal and state governments eagerly assume responsibility for the quality and success of instructional services.

The main federal program for aid to elementary and secondary education, ESEA Title I, is a case in point. Though the legislation permits school districts to use funds in a variety of ways, and less than half the funds are invested in reading instruction, still the U.S. Office of Education relies on reading test-score changes as its criterion for the success of the program. Evaluators have pursued evidence that Title I raises reading test scores in the sincere belief that that alone can justify continuing the federal investment. Many state education agencies have adopted similar positions toward their own compensatory education programs.

Only profound confusion about the roles of higher levels of government could support anyone's believing that a program as diverse and permissive as Title I should be regarded as a machine for producing test-score gains. That belief, however, is consistent with the fact that people at all levels of the educational hierarchy are encouraged to think of themselves essentially as teachers, whose only concern is with the effects of their actions on students. Teachers may regard this as a redundant role for state and federal officials to play, and they are right. But, given the professional backgrounds of federal and state education agency staff, the confusion about roles is easy to understand.

In the ten-year period since the large-scale establishment of federal aid to education, the staffing of the American educational system has changed in a way that reinforces the pressure for innovation. Federal, state, and local education agencies are now dominated by people with advanced training in curriculum design and program evaluation. A major share of all the regulation writing, monitoring, verification, and administration (and a considerable amount of teaching) is now done by people who have or aspire to doctorates from schools of education. Despite differences in the formal roles they occupy, all are primarily interested in affecting the services that schools deliver to students. It should be no surprise that a policy system staffed by such people will be marked by conflict over who is to design and evaluate educational services. To a great extent, educational policy is made through a struggle among potential curriculum innovators, with each trying for autonomy from innovators above and control over innovators below. Would-be innovators seek the support of Congress, the federal and state offices of education, and interest groups to get their inventions mandated into practice. Teachers ultimately control their own classrooms, and generally do not need higher authorities to mandate the services they prefer. But teachers too can become innovators in the negative sense of Hawley's term, if they invent new services without carefully assessing their students' needs. Clearly, adaptive education is not simply teacher-controlled education, and teachers who innovate out of a desire for professional self-expression are just another element of the system's pressure to innovate.

Though the struggle among potential innovators is usually conducted in the languages of educational philosophy and social science theory, the real concern of the participants is to exercise the professional role for which they were trained, i.e., to design and evaluate classroom instructional services. In the long run, the exact nature of services to be delivered is negotiated among the contending innovators, with too little attention to the needs and aspirations of students and their parents.

Even if teachers and principals learned to value adaptive approaches to education, the systemwide pressures for innovation would remain. Schools would still have to struggle for autonomy against "outside innovators." In short, the pressures for innovation would not diminish at all.

Capacities Necessary for Adaptive Education

To conclude, as I have just done, that the system must change is surely one of the most inane actions in the repertoire of policy analysis. Yet it is necessary in the face of Hawley's suggestion that a systemic problem can be treated successfully at the school level, through the careful nurturance of teachers. Such a suggestion implies that the system has the capacity to be adaptive, if only practitioners were properly motivated. I think, to the contrary, that few schools or educational systems have the capacity to be adaptive. The second part of my comment will try to identify some capacities that educational systems must have if they are to provide adaptive education and will suggest lines of research that may make the changes possible.

Improved Accountability Systems   The first such capacity concerns federal and state educational agencies. They must develop a new system of accountability so that schools can be adaptive while giving funding agencies solid assurance that money is being used legally. The second capacity affects federal, state, and local education agencies, all of which need to direct the professional incentives of their administrative staffs away from innovating on classroom instructional services and toward supporting schools' and teachers' efforts to provide adaptive programs. The third capacity affects schools, which need ways of determining their clients' educational needs so that services can be adapted to them.

The first prerequisite is a system of accountability whereby those who deliver educational services can be adaptive to their clients yet assure higher levels of management that funds are used for the general purposes for which they were appropriated. Teachers and local administrators are quite articulate about the negative effects of federal and state regulations that control the time, place, and manner of instruction.

Yet there is another side to the issue. It is that social service programs (in housing, health, etc., as well as education) tend to lose their programmatic character if funding agencies do not make explicit requirements of local practitioners. D.O. Porter has documented the case nicely for school districts' use of federal aid funds.[69] Paul E. Peterson's review of community action agency programs[70] and my own work on the Office of Economic Opportunity (OEO) home-ownership programs[71] conclude that service deliverers become innovators very readily and serve different clients with quite different services than were originally intended. In the OEO experience, service deliverers often became one-person, comprehensive social-service agencies, providing aid of all kinds to people who were identified through patronage or other informal processes. Whatever one thinks of general social work on behalf of needy individuals, that is clearly not the intent of categorical federal or state education programs. (And, likewise, whatever one thinks about whether teachers or administrators should control instruction, teacher sovereignty is no more likely to guarantee adaptive education than is the current system.) Educational programs are not popular enough with Congress and state legislatures to be proof against the inevitable journalistic exposés about the idiosyncratic use of funds by local providers on behalf of a haphazardly selected population.

A new system of accountability—one that permits principals and teachers to be adaptive while assuring higher levels of government that funds are used to provide real educational services to the beneficiaries identified by law—is clearly needed.

There may be no such thing in this country as a strict accountability system for the use of educational funds. But accountability is now attempted, through two basic methods. The first is central management. It uses fiscal monitoring,

---

69 D.O. Porter. *The Politics of Budgeting Federal Aid: Resource Mobilization by Local School Districts*. Beverley Hills, Calif.: Sage Publications, 1973.
70 Paul E. Peterson, "Forms of Representation: Participation of the Poor in the Community Action Program," *American Political Science Review*, June 1970, pp. 491–507.
71 P.T. Hill, "Home Ownership and the Poor," a publication of the Department of Housing and Urban Development's National Housing Subsidy Study, 1973.

on-site verification, and financial sanctions, all conducted by the funding agency. This is approximately the system used by the U.S. Office of Education for ESEA Title I and other programs of assistance for elementary and secondary education. Though simple in conception, the central management method is extremely hard to follow in intergovernmental relations. State education agencies play ambivalent roles in the management of Title I, acting sometimes as agents of the U.S. Office of Education, and other times as protectors of the school districts. And the school districts themselves are too numerous (over 14,000 in Title I) to permit direct management by the Office of Education or the states. As a result, the "direct-management" method has become a loose framework of regulations that require local education agencies to report that they are using funds in specified ways. Reports that are "in compliance" may mask misuse of funds, just as reports "out of compliance" may reflect the efforts of an LEA to meet local needs in just the way that Title I's congressional authors intended. Still, given the size and complexity of the federal system, the current accountability system for federal education programs may be about as effective as it can be.

The second method is accountability by results. This removes funding agencies entirely from the business of monitoring program administration and rewards, or punishes, LEAs and schools solely on their students' achievement gains. This method was so popular in the early 1970s that it came under the kinds of intense critical scrutiny that is usually reserved for front runners in presidential primary races. Critics noted that funding LEAs on the basis of positive results hurts the students most in need (i.e., those whose school systems are serving them least well). Politicians noted the same thing: Michigan's celebrated accountability system was amended when big-city LEAs were about to lose funding. All of which calls into question whether accountability systems based on reading and mathematics achievement test results hold education agencies responsible for the outcomes that the ultimate funding agencies, i.e., Congress and the state education agencies, are really most concerned about. Quite clearly the Michigan legislature was more concerned about keeping Detroit's school system operating than about the niceties of student achievement test results. The same is true of Congress, which has increased support of Title I despite the Office of Education's difficulty in linking Title I spending with students' gains on reading and mathematics achievement tests. Continuing to support educational programs despite poor test results is not a sign of lost political nerve but evidence that the accountability criterion is not exactly what legislators had in mind in the first place.

These two methods of accountability need considerable refinement. In the case of central management, it is time to look seriously at the problems of central management in an intergovernmental context. It is now easy to identify the shortcomings of federal educational management, but for all we know the central management method may already have reached its technical limits. In the case of accountability by results, it is clear that the most commonly used outcome criterion does not reflect legislators' concerns; until such a criterion is devised, accountability by results can only be a slogan. The whole topic of accountability needs a serious review in order to understand the degree to which the two methods outlined above can permit schools to be adaptive while ensuring funding agencies that funds are used properly. A natural topic for such a review would be the potential of hybrid methods, which combine elements of central management, accountability by results, and other techniques. In light of the concern for adaptiveness, one promising "other technique" is accountability through local enforcement whereby local advocacy groups are responsible for the on-site verification that central managers cannot do. Federal and state education programs now contain the seeds of such a management technique in the form of local parent advisory councils, but the technique requires very serious prior research and planning.

Changed Incentives for Administrators   The second prerequisite of adaptive schooling is a change in the structure of professional incentives for educational administrators. As long as educational administrators find true professional fulfillment by competing with teachers for control of classrooms, adaptive education will be impossible.

Such a change in incentives will be hard to bring about without sacrificing the creativity and vigor that have resulted from the increased professionalism of educational managers. The solution is not to hire managers who are less knowledgeable about education but to redefine their roles so that they complement, rather than compete with, teachers and principals.

The federal government is uniquely equipped to provide funds for education programs and to manage and finance very expensive research into learning. On the other hand, the federal government can do very little about the details of the selection and delivery of educational services. The same is true of the states, whose natural role vis-à-vis instructional services may be dissemination and technical assistance (but not innovation!). By elimination, this leaves local practitioners to select and implement services, with specific kinds of help available from federal and state experts. Such a division of roles is so obvious that it must be forthcoming, as administrators adjust to the fact that they are really not deliverers of educational services. For the future, schools of education might add state and federal program management to the research and training agendas of future professionals.

A Way of Assessing Clients' Needs   The third prerequisite for adaptive education is a way for professionals to discover what they must adapt to. A major shortcoming of Hawley's chapter is its assumption that schools can readily discover what their clients' needs are. Consistent with that assumption, Hawley advocates the use of diagnostic-prescriptive instructional strategies, which are based on standard typologies of educational objectives and come packaged with instruments for measuring students' progress. Such techniques do make teachers more aware of their students, but they do not guarantee adaptive schooling. In fact, they establish systems of educational objectives that researchers and teachers, not students or parents, have invented. These objectives may fit local needs and aspirations nicely, but then they may not. Recent efforts to understand parents' aspirations for their children's schooling have shown that parents have strong views but find it difficult to express them. Research about lay participation in school policy making gives a discouraging picture of laymen's ability to make clear and effective presentation of their demands for educational services. Zeigler[72] and others have shown that school boards and other lay advisory groups serve largely to ratify professional choices. More recent research on Title I parent advisory councils suggests that their role, too, is marginal. At best, the councils select from short lists of alternatives formulated by professionals.

The need for a way of discovering parents' and students' aspirations for education is clear. Yet formal decision-making bodies are too intimidating to parents, and standard survey approaches almost always rely on questions formulated in advance by teachers and educational researchers; they may or may not tap the areas of local clients' greatest concern about education.

The best natural device for communicating lay clients' aspirations is a free and functionally perfect market, which allow clients to make an infinite variety of concrete choices. That clearly does not exist in education because reforms like vouchers and free schools offer too few alternatives to permit truly effective market choices. As long as educational services are packaged and delivered by a few large institutions, there will be a need for articulation of clients' aspirations so that adaptive programs can be provided.

If clients cannot spontaneously make a full statement of their goals for education, perhaps some artificial device can facilitate it. Such a device would have to help clients to scan their expectations broadly and to express them in terms that the professionals who run educational institutions can understand.

The National Institute of Education (NIE) has supported a three-year research program to develop a simple method whereby school officials can assess their clients' aspirations for educational services. Early results indicate that parents in particular have different priorities for some educational outcomes than teachers and that some topics that preoccupy teachers do not concern parents at all. Further results in the form of a report by P.J. Blackwell and L.S.

---

72   L. Harmon Zeigler, "The Responsiveness of Public Schools to their Clientele." Report of the Center for the Advanced Study of Educational Administration. Eugene, Ore.: University of Oregon, 1973.

Smith were available in late 1976[73] and that work may point the way toward taking serious account of clients' needs and aspirations and thus help provide agendas for adaptive schooling.

Conclusion

I can only conclude by endorsing Hawley's analysis of the importance of adaptive education; yet I must insist that his prescriptions are too modest. My chief complaint against the analysis is that it looks only within the school for solutions to the school's problems. In so doing, it has failed to recognize the paradox that today's educational policy research can help the schools only if it looks beyond them, to the structure and incentives of the whole educational system.

73   P. J. Blackwell and L. S. Smith, "The Final Report of the NIE Educational Goals Study," unpublished, 1976.

CHAPTER 12

The Decision to Innovate: Career Pursuit as an Incentive for Educational Change

EDWARD W. PAULY

School officials have the power to initiate innovations in the public schools. Most of the time they do not because advocating an innovation is not normally a productive way for school officials to pursue their careers. Typically, school administrators' dependence on civil service tenure and promotion rules, their suspicion of uncertain events, and their reluctance to cope with the complexity of new programs predispose them toward the traditional, rigid patterns of career advancement. Officials know that the established paths for getting and holding a better job in school administration involve specializing in a particular administrative field, doing favors for other officials, keeping one's job "visible" in the organization, and occasionally seeking a transfer to a job with chances for "professional growth." Innovations are not traditionally linked to career advancement because innovation and the bureaucratic job performance demanded of ambitious school administrators are simply not compatible with each other:

- *Innovations increase uncertainty.* The effects of new programs are unknown, and teachers' and parents' reactions to them are unpredictable. Gaining the cooperation of the schools' staff for a new program is difficult because there are few incentives for them to comply with orders from above, especially once each teacher has closed the classroom door. The anxious uncertainty surrounding new programs, which is so difficult for administrators to tolerate or counteract, reflects poorly on all innovations.
- *Innovations multiply the complexities of normal school operations* and impede efforts to achieve a bureaucratic consensus. New programs require new agreements among officials and the revision of old rules and procedures. School officials value the bureaucratic agreements that protect them from loss of authority and status. They are therefore inclined to turn away from innovation proposals that require amendments to the school district's

261

standard operating procedure, or to the unwritten but nonetheless powerful operational code of the local school.

- *Innovations raise doubts about peer recognition,* and therefore threaten officials' rewards. Occasionally, new programs result in benefits to the children who participate in them, but even these infrequent results are not crucial to an official's recognition by his colleagues at district headquarters. The caution, consultation, and discreet behavior exhibited by a "professional" educator (and rewarded by his colleagues) are contradicted by the assertiveness and risk taking required for innovation. As a result, officials view innovation as a threat to their professional recognition and thus to traditional paths to promotion.

The weight of these factors would seem to argue that meaningful innovation would be virtually absent from American public education.

But innovations that have been significant for the educational and professional activities of school districts *do* occur. School districts have recruited untrained local residents who have special skills and tried them as teachers of "problem" children. Mothers on welfare have been trained and employed as preschool tutors and teacher aides. Districts have grouped children of widely differing ages together to encourage teachers to teach in new ways. Teachers have been retrained to use hands-on exercises and games as the basis of instruction instead of lecturing and workbooks. Programs of family life and sex education for retarded students, and bilingual education, both for students of Spanish background and their Anglo classmates, have been begun.[1] In most cases, these innovations were initiated, planned, and implemented by school officials whose jobs and careers are subject to the bureaucratic climate so typically hostile to innovation. Innovations such as these are highly uncertain, complex, and professionally risky for school officials. If the bureaucratic structure of schooling is an important influence on officials' decisions, the question remains: What could cause school administrators to attempt to innovate?

School administrators' decisions reflect a wide variety of concerns, but underneath them all is a common thread of their professional lives: the rational desire to pursue their careers. Because of their shared training and bureaucratic environment, school administrators are typically prompted to base their decisions of this powerful, shared motive. Consequently, decisions both for and against educational innovations depend on the ways officials seek to achieve their career goals.

The great uncertainty and complexity of a school administrator's job make it quite difficult to identify clear goals, or clear methods for goal achievement.

---

1   All of the examples are drawn from the school districts that introduced innovative projects with funds from Section 306 of the Elementary and Secondary Education Act, beginning in 1971. These districts are all included in the empirical analysis of innovation discussed later in this chapter.

These difficulties do not diminish the responsibility of officials for the programs they administer; poor judgments can lead to demotion, or worse. Officials must protect their professional reputations and their bureaucratic responsibilities from the dangers of decisions that threaten their colleagues' jobs or their own reputations. Most important, they come to regard their peers and their environment, the school headquarters itself, as their central concern: peers can understand the officials' problems and give recognition and reward when they are due, and their cooperation is essential to the performance of the officials' duties. The headquarters setting provides the rules and the arena for the school professionals' reward system.

Even for the most altruistic administrators, the opportunities to influence educational decisions increase as they pursue their advancement in the organization. For school administrators trying to do a difficult job in a hostile environment, the strategy of tending to their careers by concentrating on headquarters affairs is the best possible adaptation to the uncertainty, complexity, and the peer-recognition reward system that characterize American public education.

The widespread and persistent impact of this phenomenon is largely due to the role of careerism in school administration. Virtually all school officials are careerists—former teachers who have worked their way up the school district ladder. As a result, they see their present livelihoods, their past accomplishments, and their future opportunities to improve education in terms of a *long progression of jobs* at school headquarters. Career success provides both security and the increased power that comes with gradual promotion up the hierarchy. Not surprisingly, administrators' decisions reflect their common concern for the pursuit of their careers in the school bureaucracy.

The school organization, the peer reward system, and the logic of their careers thus create a common official perspective that is largely independent of an individual administrator's particular preferences or tasks. There is little incentive for administrators to be concerned about things that conflict with the pursuit of their careers, even about the educational failures of the school district's students, to take an extreme case. This case rarely arises, however, for there is a strong tendency for officials to regard educational quality as being quite consistent with their own career success. Lacking contrary evidence, they willingly assume that their careers enhance the setting for good education, though perhaps marginally.

Officials respond to the lessons of their environments and their careers because doing so is *in their interest*, and their response produces a pattern of behavior that can be characterized as *career pursuit*. Career pursuit means being aware not only of one's present job but the one to follow it; valuing the increased discretion that a step up in the hierarchy provides; and recognizing the subtle and tense connections between one's job and the constant assessments of one's peers. And most important, it means acting on these awarenesses. For while position and career do offer benefits that are highly valuable to the people who have chosen school administration, those benefits are not automatically conferred. Taking advantage of the opportunities offered by the school organization requires constant efforts specifically aimed at pursuing one's career. (Not choosing actions and decisions that accord with an official's interest in his job and career would abruptly halt this advancement and might even undermine his job security. Superintendents are rather easily fired, and specialists can sometimes be discharged if their positions are reorganized out of existence. So even administrators uninterested in advancement have incentives to be careerists, as a means to job security.) Throughout the professional life of a school administrator, career pursuit means relying on the advancement motive to untangle personal preferences, professional dilemmas, and ambitions. The career pursuit motive is, as a result, quite important in the lives of school officials.

In most school districts, the bureaucratic situations facing school officials are no invitation to innovation. Yet conditions alone do not make decisions; individuals do. And the central *individual* motivation driving officials' behavior in school districts is the career pursuit motive. Career pursuit influences individual officials despite wide variation in local school district circumstances and great diversity in districts' problems. This chapter argues that whether or not officials choose to advocate an innovation depends on organizational problems and conditions that may make it beneficial, in career terms, for school administrators to innovate. Even though the school district bureaucracy is constitutionally inhospitable to innovation, the problems and opportunities encountered by ambitious school administrators struggling to advance their careers can sometimes stimulate them to embrace innovation as a profitable, if unusual, tactic in their careerist contest. This chapter will show that the likelihood of a school district decision to introduce an innovation depends directly on whether its officials can pursue their careers by advocating the adoption of new programs. It provides evidence that under certain organizational conditions that make it worthwhile for officials to advocate change, the career pursuit motive does cause innovation.

This hypothesis on the source of innovations refutes the presumption that public agencies adopt policies specifically because they are "needed." If school bureaucrats are primarily swayed by career considerations, their decisions to innovate may have little basis in the rational analysis of school district goals, policy alternatives, or students' needs. The importance of this argument to our assessments of public education should be apparent.

INCENTIVES TO ADVOCATE AN INNOVATION

To find out how the drive for career success motivates officials to press for innovation, it is necessary to have an idea of when advocating an innovation will further officials' careers. Since the career system in public education rewards administrators for receiving recognition from their colleagues, it follows that advocating an innovation will further officials' careers only when doing so produces peer recognition. Recognition matters a great deal even when the most competent officials are competing for advancement. This is because there are only tenuous connections between actual competence, competence that is visible to one's peers, and competence that is appreciated by them. *Only the last results in professional recognition.* As a consequence, officials are highly sensitive to the various ways they can seek recognition in their organizations. Most important for this study, they can be counted on to watch out for opportunities for, and obstacles to, recognition that their organization may present to them.

Since the world of school administrators revolves around school headquarters, administrators pay close attention to what goes on there. What happens elsewhere in the school district (in classrooms, for instance) is often too complex and uncertain for them to deal with sensibly. This contributes to the preoccupation with headquarters as well. Administrators' awareness of the headquarters bureaucratic situation is most pronounced when it comes to keeping track of the strategies for gaining recognition and the rules and mechanics of job security and promotion. Promotion in the school bureaucracy depends on the number of job openings and the evaluations of one's colleagues. These requirements of career pursuit are common knowledge to all the officials in each local school district. As a result, officials are constantly concerned with some of the following organizational constraints on their careers:

- How many competitors are there for a given promotion?
- What professional credentials should they have, and what performance expectations should they meet in order to advance?
- Which controversial problems threaten to embroil them in complicated, unrewarding disputes and conflicts?
- How can they assist or help out their administrative colleagues and thus broaden their professional recognition?

All of these concerns are the product of the administrators' attention to the paths they must follow to pursue their careers. Keeping track of these rather mundane, mechanical issues is the careerist's basic bureaucratic tool for coping with the constraints and opportunities affecting career pursuit.

Different officials may face different situations affecting recognition and the mechanics of promotion. Consider the executives of a school district, its superintendent and his immediate associates. Their career concerns are often quite independent of the career problems affecting other staff members, such as curriculum specialists, program directors for special projects, and principals. While superintendents often find it necessary to build a public record of personal attainments that will help them find their next job in another district, principals may pay attention instead to the number of upcoming head-quarters vacancies and the difficulties of being noticed among the ranks of school-level administrators. Some situations in the school organization's environment shape officials' career thinking, no matter what their position. Both executives and staff are affected by the availability of local community support for certain kinds of policies. This is not because administrators commonly attempt to represent community interests, but because established local patterns of support for certain school activities often constrain the menu of professional accomplishments that produce recognition for officials. (For example, high levels of community conflict make it dangerous for administrators to propose an innovation, since it could easily become a focus of hostility and fear.) Taken together, such considerations as these comprise in each local school district a wide range of factors that administrators correctly judge important to their chances for career pursuit.

Since the logic of career ladders is different for top school district executives (superintendents) than for their specialized bureaucratic subordinates, the organizational incentives that matter for these two groups are different. Therefore, the desirability of an innovation will depend on two distinct categories of incentives: those affecting school executives' chances for recognition, and those affecting subordinate staff members' recognition opportunities. In addition, there is an obvious third category of incentives—the external pressures on the whole school organization that may either reward or penalize officials depending on whether their decisions attract community hostility or constituent support. These varying patterns of local support for the school bureaucracy create highly career-relevant incentives for or against innovation.

Since the theory of career pursuit predicts that whether a school district tries an innovation will depend on its officials' ability to gain recognition, it follows that the three kinds of recognition may have a great deal to do with whether it is in the interest of administrators to innovate. The kinds of recognition for careerist behavior that are available to officials determine the likelihood of innovation by motivating them to advocate an innovation, or not. An organizational model can summarize this hypothetical relationship.

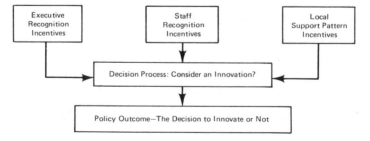

According to this model, the set of career pursuit incentives for each school organization determines whether its officials will decide to innovate. That is, the decision to innovate depends on whether the incentives in a particular school district, taken together, can elicit substantial official support for a proposed innovation. Knowing the organizational situations that reflect career opportunities for officials will therefore help predict when local school districts will decide to innovate. A brief explanation of the career pursuit incentives affecting school officials will help identify the situations that determine officials' innovation decisions.

Executive Incentives

For school district executives (superintendents and their lieutenants), the recognition incentives are generally of two kinds:

- Incentives to build a record of success in order to improve the chances of getting a good position in another school district.
- Incentives to avoid situations of potential conflict over school policies in order to prevent the loss of professional reputation that follows a chaotic administrative situation and the tension accompanying it.

Executives' need to build a record of demonstrated successes stems from the shortness and insecurity of their job tenure,[2] and the fact that former superintendents must always move to another district to find a comparable job (since each district has but one superintendent). (Because only a handful of aides are typically named by each newly appointed superintendent, the outgoing superintendent's aides also often look to other districts for career opportunities. These lieutenants thus also rely on a strong and concrete record of accomplishments in order to pursue their careers.)

Sometimes the normal powers of the district's executive and his lieutenants are inadequate to the task of record building. For example, a newly appointed superintendent may be ignorant of the budgetary devices, union requirements, and subordinates' personalities that frustrate his policies. When the formal authority of the superintendency is not enough to run the school organization effectively, the superintendent can often advance his career in alternative ways—by advocating an innovation that generates publicity, assists him in becoming informed about the school bureaucracy, allows him to hire additional loyal staff people, or meets demands made on him for particular kinds of programs. By starting a new program, the superintendent may quickly be able to show school board members he is accomplishing something, and at the same

---

2 John Merrow, Richard Foster, and Nolan Estes. *The Urban School Superintendent of the Future.* Durant, Okla.: The Southeastern Foundation, 1974, pp. 1, 22–23. See also Richard O. Carlson. *School Superintendents: Careers and Performance.* Columbus, Ohio: Charles E. Merrill, 1972, pp. 1–3 and *passim.*

time learn how the organization works. If he is the author of an innovation, then he is the expert on it—and detailed expertise is a very useful partisan tool. All of these effects of innovating can lead to recognition for a district's executives, but the risks that accompany innovation will typically outweigh the gains unless there are concrete organizational signals that make innovation seem to be the *only* attractive way to build a record of success.

School executives second major recognition concern is avoiding situations of controversy and conflict over school district policies. When school policies become politicized and controversial, high officials are the focus of attention (rather than principals or program specialists), whatever their role in establishing the policy has been.[3] Though school superintendents are the most independent and powerful officials in each school system, their power is delegated to them by their school boards, which tend to measure executive performance according to whether the superintendent appears to be "on top" of school business. His mastery of the situation in the district is constantly, if imperfectly, evaluated. The single occurrence most likely to cause the school board to hesitate in its delegation of power to the superintendent is conflict in any form. Moreover, school boards, in the process of hiring a new superintendent, are careful to investigate the conflict in each applicant's past. As a result, a superintendent's various techniques for pursuing his career while dealing with the district's problems often turn into a strategy for suppressing conflict and appearing to be "in charge." When serious conflicts occur, the career incentives for school executives are to eschew innovation—which, as a threat to established order, is all the more a risky and complex undertaking when the superintendent's position is threatened. Careerist superintendents are considerably more likely to use innovation as a way to bolster their records in the absence of conflict (and to support only as much innovation as will not produce conflict).

Staff Incentives

Two recognition incentives matter most for school district staff members (the specialists and administrators who operate district headquarters and the schools):

- Incentives to differentiate their performance from that of others at their administrative level so colleagues and superiors will recognize their performance.
- Incentives to "cope" with burdensome administrative tasks in order to preserve the professional relationships among colleagues that are the basis for recognition in school systems.

3 Merrow, Foster, and Estes. *Urban School Superintendent,* pp. 7–14, and Robert L. Crain. *The Politics of School Desegregation.* Chicago: Aldine, 1968, pp. 122–130.

Staff members' need for differentiation from their peers stems from the narrowness of career ladders in American education. Ambitious administrators begin their rise from classroom teacher positions, but at each higher administrative level there are far too few available positions to absorb all of them. This is particularly true in school districts with relatively small headquarters staffs.[4] When career ladders are crowded, merely meeting the technical requirements of a job is not enough to merit recognition for competent professional performance. It takes a special, distinguishing accomplishment to be promoted over one's fellows. So, when an official's job doesn't make him look different, he often simply makes his job different. As part of their career pursuit, officials can use their advocacy of an innovation to gain visibility and recognition in the school organization. The dangers of innovating make this approach attractive only when differentiation from the rest of the staff is nearly impossible to attain through the normal channels of specialization and "professional growth." The problem of staff differentiation must be quite severe before officials have enough incentive to adopt an innovation strategy for pursuing their careers.

Burdensome administrative problems can make it impossible or undesirable for staff officials to undertake the professional activities usually needed to obtain recognition. But when demands for coping behavior are high, officials can advance their careers by helping their colleagues deal with the heavy load. Avoiding onerous bureaucratic burdens (when everyone else is sharing them) is not an acceptable strategy for careerist officials depending on peer recognition. If administrative "fire fighting" is the order of the day, then shirking is frowned upon, and service to one's colleagues will generally be remembered and rewarded.[5] Such a situation is a disincentive to innovation; officials advocate an innovation only if they believe their colleagues will not disdain their initiatives.

Local Support Incentives.

Officials feel the impact of local and community support patterns in two ways:

- Incentives to use local and community support to increase the resources and opportunities available to the school organization, so that the officials can be recognized for aiding the professional activities of other district administrators.
- Incentives to avoid provoking latent community conflict that threatens officials' freedom to concentrate on professional and career concerns.

Since the school system depends on its community for funds and for the

---

4 Merrow, Foster, and Estes. *Urban School Superintendent,* pp. 31, 41.
5 Roald F. Campbell et al. *The Organization and Control of American Schools.* Columbus, Ohio: Charles E. Merrill, 1970, pp. 243–246.

definition of education "problems" it is responsible for resolving in the classroom, community support determines the resources and programs that provide opportunities and constraints for careerist officials' activities. School officials can therefore gain recognition by eliciting additional local support for themselves and the other professionals who administer the system.

The availability of local support varies greatly across the nation's 15,000 school districts.[6] In many cases, officials have little opportunity to muster support for more school spending, hiring additional specialized staff, or introducing the most recent "educational technology." In others, officials from principals to superintendents are able to mobilize or shape enough local support so that demands for special programs, new facilities, or extra staff result in the allocation of additional resources. In certain circumstances, proposals for innovation may be good strategies for taking advantage of local support patterns. For instance, when the school district's community is very heterogeneous, groups with special concerns can be effectively mobilized by offers of small, specialized innovative programs. The fragmentation of neighborhoods and civic groups typical of core cities makes the offer of new benefits in the form of special school programs a good tool for building support. In suburbs and rural areas, the more homogeneous and less mobilized support patterns make it difficult to appeal to particular "target" groups for additional support.[7] School districts that depend on city councils for their budget allotments may also be able to use specialized innovations as a way of building support in the context of political competition among council members. Logrolling and vote-trading among city councilmen interested in bringing benefits to their communities can be very helpful to a school district. Officials who advocate innovations that appeal to these elected officials are quite likely to be recognized for aiding their peers. When innovation is a particularly effective strategy for dealing with the community setting of a school district, ambitious officials can accept the risks of innovation in anticipation of the substantial career gains recognition will bring.

Despite the attractiveness of the extra resources the community can supply, school officials are aware of the chance that hostility toward the schools can result when administrators' actions provoke latent community conflicts. When existing community divisions are the source of conflicts in the schools (instead of, say, resistance to some particular school policy, such as desegregation),

6 Ibid., pp. 442–445, 449–450, 457–465. See also Frederick M. Wirt and Michael W. Kirst. *The Political Web of American Schools*. Boston: Little, Brown and Company, 1972, pp. 96–110, 216–221; and Harry L. Summerfield, "The Neighborhood-Based Politics of Education," in Frederick M. Wirt, ed. *The Polity of the School*. Lexington, Mass.: Lexington Books, D.C. Heath and Company, 1975, pp. 172–181.

7 Merrow, Foster, and Estes. *Urban School Superintendent*, p. 25; see also Summerfield in Wirt, *Polity of the School*, *passim*.

then all school officials, not just the executives, suffer. Schools become battle-grounds in such situations, where no decision will be unchallenged and all officials are suspect.[8] Administrative professionalism, with its need for colle-giality and the opportunity to display expertise and seek recognition, becomes impossible. If there are latent or temporarily quiescent hostilities in a locality, school officials sensibly become more wary of the uncertainties and risks of any innovation. When officials try not to provoke underlying conflicts, they are essentially protecting their ability to pursue their careers in the normal ways—without interference from community/distrust and conflict.

Incentives and Students' Needs

The various career pursuit incentives just described have remarkably little to do with the needs of children. The actual outcomes of the schools' many services to their students seem to be quite independent of the various kinds of recogni-tion that ambitious administrators are likely to pursue in their organizations. Yet sometimes incentives can have indirect effects. It is therefore worth con-sidering whether any of the careerist incentives might somehow cue or alert officials to the existence of problems with the school services being given to children—that is, whether these incentives indirectly reflect the needs of stu-dents. The three sets of incentives that stimulate officials to protect their careers (executives avoidance of conflict, staff members coping with bureau-cratic burdens, and all officials avoidance of provoking community hostility) are important because they help officials anticipate negative reactions to their work. In each case, this anticipatory self-protection is quite unrelated to how well or how poorly *current services* are meeting students' needs, so these incentives simply do not tap the question of what these needs actually might be.

Next, consider the incentives that reflect the administrators' opportunities for advancement (executives creating of a record of "success," staff members differentiating themselves from their colleagues, and all officials eliciting extra resources by manipulating local support patterns), and their relationship to students' needs. The crucial determinant of an executive's progress in building a record of accomplishment is whether he is perceived as being "on top" of the school organization. If, for some reason, an executive cannot use established processes such as the budget cycle or teacher contract negotiations to establish this image, he may be inclined to propose an innovation. In this case the importance of the innovation is not that it points out students' needs, but that it

---

8 William L. Boyd, "Community Status and Suburban School Conflict," in Wirt. *Polity of the School*, pp. 103–104: ". . . as the level of conflict in school district policy-making increases, the autonomy and discretion of school administrators is reduced . . . high levels of conflict tend to have a debilitating effect on school officials."

symbolizes the executives' effective management of the school bureaucracy. The value or necessity of the proposed new program is quite incidental to the executive's incentives to propose it.

In the case of careerist staff members, the need to differentiate themselves from their peers may prompt them to question the efficacy of traditional bureaucratic activities for their advancement, given their organization's crowded career ladder. When the usual activities are not likely to produce results, officials may consider advocating an innovation. But, rhetorical posturing to the contrary, school headquarters is generally not staffed with child-centered altruists. There is no more reason to presume an innovation is advocated because it would meet some students' needs than because it is compatible with the training or prior bureaucratic experiences of the officials who proposed it.

Finally, the incentives for officials to elicit extra school resources by taking advantage of local support patterns are primarily related to the availability of extra resources, not to the value of the innovation that may incidentally assist officials in getting the desired support. The innovation is important for its appeal to community members, not necessarily for its value to the students to be served. Thus, for each of the organizational incentives that may sometimes lead to innovation, there is little reason to suspect that the students of a school district are anything other than unnoticed and disregarded when careerist strategies are being planned. If this were not the case, then achievement score gains, for example, would appear on the resumes of candidates for the superintendency. They do not.

Summary of the Argument

The case for predicting school districts' innovation decisions by analyzing their administrators' career incentives has thus far developed several claims.

1. Officials can be expected to advocate innovations when doing so will bring them recognition, because their career success depends on being recognized.
2. The availability of recognition is largely determined by the circumstances of each school organization, because the mechanics of career advancement, the probabilities of promotion, and the constraints and opportunities confronting officials exist within the organization itself. Thus determining the likelihood of innovation often means comparing school organizations with regard to characteristics that influence officials' recognition.
3. For a school executive, career success requires the building of a record of accomplishments, and protecting his career depends on avoiding involvement in conflict. Therefore, knowing when these career incentives make innovation a valuable way for executives to gain recognition makes it possible to predict the likelihood of decisions to innovate.

4. For a staff member, career success requires differentiation from colleagues, and career protection depends on coping acceptably with burdensome administrative tasks. As a result, it is possible to predict when innovation decisions are likely by discovering when these career incentives make innovation an effective way to gain recognition.

5. School officials' career success may sometimes depend on eliciting additional local support for themselves and their colleagues, and the protection of their careers requires not provoking community conflict or hostility. Therefore, an understanding of when local support career incentives make innovation an attractive route to recognition permits the prediction of when a decision to innovate is likely.

6. The career pursuit incentives that can prompt officials to advocate an innovation are not related to the needs of children served by the school district. The motivations that can lead to innovations do not reliably depend on any particular student needs. As a result, the innovation predictions of the career pursuit theory are quite independent of predictions that would be made by the conventional wisdom of "what the school district needs."

Thus far, these claims of the career pursuit theory of innovation have been supported by descriptions of school bureaucracies and by inference. Because of some fortuitous circumstances in the U.S. Office of Education's program to support innovations, it is also possible to test the explanatory power of the theory for an actual case of decision making in a large sample of American school districts.

THE POWER OF CAREER PURSUIT: THE CASE OF SECTION 306

This chapter's explanation of innovation rests on a theory of career pursuit by administrators in local school districts, and on the links in each school organization between careerism and the school system's decision about innovation. The power of this explanation can be tested by analyzing a very concrete set of events. In 1971 each American public school organization had an opportunity to introduce an innovation. Whether or not each local school district decided to innovate will be predicted by relying only on information about the organizational incentives for careerist officials to advocate innovation. The analysis makes use of a clear indication of the decision to innovate, based on the U.S. Office of Education's national competition for innovative proposals to be funded in 1971 under Section 306 in Title III of the Elementary and Secondary Education Act (ESEA)—a competition that provided the data for an empirical test of the power of the career pursuit theory.

The Section 306 program began with the sudden announcement to every school superintendent that the Office of Education would grant approximately $450,000 to each of the local school districts with the best innovations for the school year 1971–72.[9] School districts' proposals had to be filed very quickly. By early 1971 the organizations that had already been initiating or seriously contemplating an innovation were deciding to submit proposals to the Office of Education. They did so very readily because, under 306, a school district with an innovative program did not need to fear restrictive regulations, rigid categorical requirements to demonstrate a "need" for funds, or prohibitive implementation costs (all new costs of the projects were to be covered by the grants). In addition, trivial or deceptive proposals were discouraged—any fancy packaging or "grantsmanship" attempts to get funds without a serious project were too time-consuming to be worth bothering to prepare, and the requirement for school board approval and community involvement raised difficult local political barriers to frivolous applications. The proposals finally submitted by over seven hundred school districts were well developed, vigorously assertive of their own merit, and quite eclectic in the ideas and techniques they advocated. In retrospect, it seems unlikely that school districts that were not already deciding to innovate when the program was announced could assemble credible applications in the short time available to them. Consequently, districts primarily concerned about seeking federal funds instead of pursuing innovation did not attempt to prepare proposals.[10]

As a result, the school organizations initiating innovations for the 1971–72 year were probably the same group that sent proposals to the Section 306 competition. For a federal program to capture so neatly a whole collection of innovation decisions is an unusual, unintentional happening that created a perfect classification of local school districts for analytical purposes. Two kinds of behavior emerged from the decisions of districts to compete for the federal innovation support or not. One, proposing an innovative project, showed that the school organization had advocates for a new program who had

9 The Section 306 program (in Title III, ESEA) was begun abruptly, compared to other similar government money programs. In a departure from the usual pattern of gradual introduction for a new federal policy, section 306 was the product of a congressional compromise during the appropriations process after the ESEA amendments of 1970. After President Nixon's veto of the education appropriations bill for fiscal year 1971, there was little expectation that the new program would receive any money. But when the much-delayed bill became law in November 1970, it included a sum for Section 306. The Office of Education hurriedly announced the program to local school officials on December 10, 1970. The result of the program's odd genesis was a remarkable absence of the anticipatory grantsmanship practiced by some school districts when new money programs are first installed.

The new program was also remarkable for its lack of the usual restrictive "strings" on the recipients of federal funds. The essential criteria for success in the competition were whether a project was innovative, could potentially make a "contribution to the solution of critical education problems" as defined and measured by each locality, and whether the project had local support. Successful proposals were to be awarded about $150,000 yearly, guaranteed in advance for three years; no local funds beyond local per pupil expenditures were required; and post hoc, for-the-record evaluations were to be handled by locally selected professionals, not by officials in Washington.

10 U.S. Office of Education, *Special Programs and Projects: ESEA, Title III, Section 306.* Washington, D.C.: U.S. Department of Health, Education and Welfare, 1972.

worked to secure a decision to innovate. The other, not issuing a proposal, marked the organization as one in which other activities evidently displaced or superseded innovation. The power and accuracy of the career-pursuit predictors of innovation can be analyzed in terms of their ability to assess whether a school district is part of the innovating or the not-innovating groups.

Hypothetical Causes of Innovation

To test the theory, it is necessary to have a set of measures of the organizational factors that stimulate officials to use innovation, instead of some other strategy, in their drive for career success. Because the characteristics of each school organization determine whether officials can be recognized for advocating an innovation, these factors are therefore "cues" for officials to innovate. In order to test the theory's explanatory power, information on these organizational measures of career incentives has been collected for each of the school districts in the sample.[11]

The organizational measures affecting school executives, subordinate staff members, and local support incentives that involve all school officials are briefly described below, along with their hypothetical effects on school officials' incentives to advocate an innovation.

School Executives   The career incentive measures for school executives reflect the drive to build a record of accomplishment, and to avoid entanglement in conflict. The data answer two questions affecting record building, each question yielding a testable hypothesis about innovation.

[12]1. *How many years has the superintendent held his office?* New superintendents typically lack the power and information to meet the demands of the school board and the school organization. An innovation provides the resources to meet those demands and creates an opportunity for the new superintendent to gain recognition. Entrenched superintendents of long experience rarely have to go beyond their formal authority and established information-gathering patterns to be recognized as being successful. Thus, new superintendents would be most likely to innovate.

2. *Does the superintendent have a doctoral degree?* Some superintendents seek success by advertising their community service and local acceptance;

---

11 The sample was constructed to include a broad range of American school districts and to ensure that sufficient "innovating" districts were included to allow for quantitative analysis. A random sample of 813 school districts, stratified by size and drawn by the U.S. Office of Education for a variety of statistical uses, was used in the analysis reported here.

12 Numbers in the left margin refer to the corresponding quantitative estimates in the regression equation presented in table 12.1 below.

others, substantially including those who have taken doctoral degrees, seek it by advertising cosmopolitanism and guild professionalism. For the latter group, merely satisfying local peer demands is insufficient for upward mobility. The necessary national recognition is, however, attainable by using an innovation as a badge of one's special competence. Superintendents relying more on local support for their recognition are not likely to have sought doctoral degrees and probably do not need to take the risks of innovating. Superintendents with doctoral degrees should be more likely to innovate than others.

Executives incentives to avoid entanglement in conflict over the schools may also be relevant to their positions on innovation, as these descriptions of the data indicate.

3. *Is the school district under a court order to desegregate?* The conflicts, pressures, and administrative chaos that are reflected or caused by court-ordered desegregation typically absorb all of the superintendent's time and energy, as well as increasing the chance of conflict over new services or programs. Cautious policies that reduce conflict and do not activate interest groups are most likely to produce recognition for a superintendent in such a situation. Court-ordered desegregation should reduce the likelihood of innovation.

4. *What proportion of the district's schools apparently excludes minorities?* School districts that have substantial minority enrollment are likely to experience conflict; in general, the more desegregation, the more conflict. The district's top executive (rather than principals or the specialized staff) is the focus of the conflict. As conflict over desegregation increases, the incentives to innovate decline. The more schools that exclude minorities, the greater should be the likelihood of innovation.

These pieces of information, each with a corresponding prediction based on school officials' incentives to pursue their careers by innovating, allow us to capture the bureaucratic situation of a school executive deciding whether or not to press for an innovation. Each measure relates to the executive's problem: How much recognition is available to him for advocating an innovation? If the measures accurately explain which school districts decide to innovate and which do not, then there is considerable evidence that an executive's career pursuit problems are in fact at the root of the innovation decision.

Staff Members   The career incentive measures for staff members in school districts reflect the way officials differentiate themselves from one another, and the pressures to spend time coping with low-level administrative tasks. Several different dimensions of the differentiation problem can be measured by answering these three questions.

5. *How many students, on average, attend each school in the district?* Large schools are virtually always highly specialized in their curriculum and administration. When school staff members are specialized, they have difficulty gaining recognition for their more recondite or intangible successes. Highly visible new programs are a good opportunity for these staff members to advance their careers by differentiating themselves, in a highly visible way, from other school specialists. Districts with large schools should therefore be more likely to innovate than others.

6. *How many schools, given the district's enrollment, are there?* Staff differentiation is not only a problem within large schools, but between them, too. When the number of district schools is particularly large (measured by the residual of a regression of schools on district enrollment), there is a "flat" job pyramid: numerous positions in the schools, but few promotions relative to the number of competitors. This flatter than normal job pyramid makes career ladders crowded and thereby increases the pressure on school officials to differentiate themselves by advocating innovation. Districts with numerous schools (relative to their enrollment) should be more likely to innovate than others.

7. *How much recent change in the district's enrollment has there been?* Shrinking districts strongly motivate their officials to differentiate their accomplishments in order to keep their jobs; in the fastest growing districts, promotion is assured without much risk taking. Completely static districts offer no job turnover, making differentiation a moot question. Enrollment drops should increase the likelihood of innovation, while rapid enrollment growth should reduce it; static enrollments should also reduce innovation.

Staff members may also be strongly pressured to adapt their career goals for dealing with low-level administrative tasks. The effect of these adaptations for innovation is measured by two aspects of the staff member's incentive system in the school organization: average class size and number of administrators per student. These measures of staff members' career incentives should show the extent to which recognition is available for officials who advocate innovation. If the organizational situation allows officials to obtain recognition for innovation, then the chances are good that at least some officials will take advantage of the opportunity. However, the data analysis did not show any relationship between the likelihood of innovation and these measures. Perhaps the hypothetical connection between low-level administrative "coping" and a lack of innovation does not exist (or is trivial compared to the staff differentiation incentives); or perhaps the measures are poor representations of the extent of innovation discouraging "coping" tasks.[13]

Local Support   The career incentives created by the patterns of local support for the school system can be measured by examining school officials' opportunities to elicit additional support and the situations in which they must be careful not to provoke community conflict or hostility. Several variables measure officials' chances for gaining new support by manipulating existing support patterns in various ways.

8. *Is the school district fiscally independent of its municipality?* School districts that depend on a local tax-setting board (such as a city council) for their finances have a constant need to build support among the groups whose representatives sit on the board. New and special-purpose programs can be used to bargain with board members; therefore, recognition is quickly given to the school official who suggests and advocates a new program appropriate to the desires of a represented interest group. If the district is fiscally independent, the likelihood of a decision to innovate is less.

9. *Is the school district in a central city?* School districts in cities face severe competition with other public service organizations for funds, while suburbs and rural areas have much less demand for nonschool services and thus less competition. In addition, cities tend to have more heterogeneous populations than other communities. The competition and heterogeneity of cities make new, special programs an attractive way to build support among particular constituency groups.

10. *What proportion of the district's enrollment is minority students?* School districts with no minority enrollment are so racially homogeneous that opportunities for officials to be recognized for proposing special programs to selected students or neighborhoods may be very limited. With higher levels of minority enrollment comes the heterogeneity that creates opportunities for school officials to appeal for support from diverse groups by proposing innovative projects.

The problem of community conflict that might be provoked by a proposed innovation (thus giving officials an incentive not to innovate) has also been measured for school districts in the sample.

11. *Is the school district in a locality to which federal Voting Rights Act examiners have been assigned?* Voting Rights Act examiners have been

---

13   The other variables found to be unrelated to the likelihood of innovation were the age of the superintendent, the proportion of administrators with an advanced degree, the proportion of teachers without a bachelor's degree, the number of administrators per teacher, and the average family income of school district residents.

assigned only to localities with the highest levels of overt discrimination against minorities; such areas are prone to substantial community conflict. Unrest, complaints, and envy are more likely to result than support when a school district proposes new or special programs in a conflictful situation. Therefore, officials cannot advance their careers by advocating innovation in these racially tense communities.

12. *What proportion of eligible blacks in the school district is registered to vote?* The likelihood of severe community hostility and conflict can be expected to increase with the increased participation and involvement of minority citizens; voter registration is one measure of this participation. School officials are able to gain recognition for using innovation to increase local support where the chance for conflict is low. As a result, innovations are most likely where minority registration is low, and the incentives for innovation should decline rapidly with the increased mobilization of minority voters.

These questions are measures of the opportunities and constraints facing school officials in their decisions about whether to seek additional local support for their school organization, and whether innovation is a good way to do so. The recognition they receive depends on their success at gaining resources and avoiding hostility, so their career incentives ought to have a strong impact on their decisions about innovation. If the career pursuit theory is correct about the organizational sources of innovation, then the measured attributes of each school district's local support situation should help accurately to predict the outcome of the innovation decision.

TESTING THE CAREER PURSUIT MODEL

With clear measures of the organizational factors reflecting administrators' career pursuit incentives, it is possible to test the power of the organization politics explanation of innovation. As is true of many empirical tests, this analysis leaves out some conceptual steps in the explanation. For example, the role of individual officials' personal incentives is weighed solely in terms of the organizational measures that have been proposed as being likely to stimulate those incentives. Figure 12.1 displays the relationship of the fully specified theory of innovation to the empirical analysis that tests the theory. The conceptual model, on the left, begins with the interaction of school officials' career pursuit motives with the incentives provided by the organization. Because officials respond directly to the school district's rules, opportunities, and constraints as they pursue their careers, these incentive patterns become very important parameters for officials' actions. Organizational characteristics that can stimulate officials to consider advocating an innovation determine what happens in the decision process (as denoted in the middle on the left side). The

The Organization
Politics Explanation
of Innovation

Testing the Explanation: An Empirical Model
of Career Pursuit and Innovation

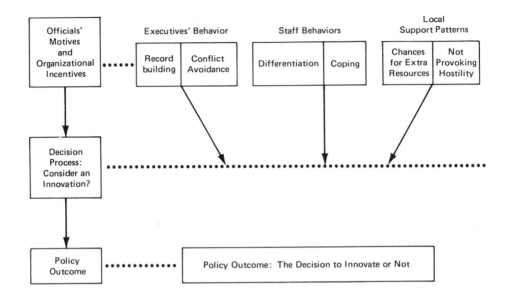

Figure 12.1. Conceptual and empirical models of innovation

result of this process is the decision whether or not to innovate. This is the outcome that the career pursuit theory attempts to predict.

The empirical model above predicts the outcomes of innovation decisions solely in terms of the organizational variables that stimulate officials to consider innovation. The theory of career pursuit is used to make a priori selections of crucial organizational variables. The empirical test of the career pursuit model is essentially a compact representation of this chapter's descriptive and theoretical analysis of what school administrators do and why they do it. What remains clear in both the empirical and the conceptual maps of the theory is that if the organizational stimuli cannot be shown to relate strongly to the innovation decision, the power of the theory must be questioned. While it is not possible to test the organizational incentives theory against a rival explanation here (because of data limitations), it is possible to see how well the organization theory does.

If the measures reflecting officials' career incentives actually predict whether there will be a decision to innovate, then the evidence supports the theory that the school organization determines a district's decisions by influencing the careerist behavior of its officials.[14] Because the career pursuit incentives are not surrogates for officials' notions of the needs of children served by the school district, finding out that strong predictions are made by the career pursuit model tends to displace other explanations. In particular, the claim that innovation is a school district's response to some problem or need on the part of its students becomes highly questionable.

The empirical relationship between school districts' decisions to innovate and the groups of organizational incentive measures has been estimated, using multiple regression techniques. This procedure measures the extent of covariation between the dependent variable (here, innovation decisions) and the predictor variables (the organizational data), and it assesses how much the effects of each predictor variable could have been misestimated.[15]

The results of the regression analysis are shown in table 12.1. Overall, the level of statistical association between the measures of organizational incentives and the decision to innovate is substantial (as well as being significant in a statistical sense).[16]

When the model of career pursuit and innovation was applied to the sample of Section 306 decisions to innovate or not, the following quantitative results were obtained:

1. The predictor variables "explained" a substantial and highly significant portion of the variation among school districts' innovation decisions (this result was confirmed with the use of other estimation techniques, not reported here for reasons of space).
2. The career pursuit variables correctly predicted the innovation decisions of almost 90 percent of the sample districts when discriminant analysis versions of the regression coefficients were applied.
3. Most of the predictor variables proved to be significantly related, with the predicted relationship, to the decision to innovate.

The strength of the career-pursuit variables supports the hypotheses about

---

14 The maintained hypothesis is that innovation decisions depend on a specified set of organizational variables; these are theorized to influence officials' behavior because of the career motivation shared by school administrators. The null hypothesis is that this set of organizational variables has no effect. If (for example) innovation decisions were actually the product of rational official decision making based on an assessment of students' most pressing needs and the availability of resources for several alternative programs, then we would discover that the data would support our null hypothesis. The null hypothesis is therefore a plausible rival hypothesis to hypotheses based on the career pursuit theory. See Carl J. Christ. *Econometric Models and Methods*. New York: John Wiley, 1966.

15 The first criterion is generally called goodness-of-fit; the second refers to the evaluation of the standard errors of the coefficients.

16 A more complete description of the data analysis, sample construction, variables, and a number of statistical issues can be found in the dissertation from which this essay is drawn. See Edward W. Pauly, "The Political Logic of Educational Innovation," Yale University Ph.D. dissertation. Ann Arbor: University Microfilms, 1977.

TABLE 12.1

Regression Analysis of the Decision to Innovate

	Independent Variable	Coefficient	Std. Error	t-stat.
1	Superintendent in office: 0–1 years	.178	.05	3.47 ***
	2–7 years	.086	.04	1.98 **
	8–40 years	−.034	.04	− .75
2	Superintendent has doctorate	.058	.04	1.49 *
3	Desegregation court order	−.186	.06	−3.27 ***
4	Percent schools excluding minorities	.006	.001	6.41 ***
	Baseline (minority data available)	−.072	.09	− .81
5	Students per school	.317	.11	2.96 ***
6	Number of schools, relative to enrollment	.003	.001	2.67 ***
7	Decline in enrollment	.078	.04	2.21 **
	Rapid growth in enrollment	−.055	.07	− .84
8	Fiscal independence	−.065	.03	−1.92 **
9	Central city	.135	.05	2.85 ***
10	Percent minority enrollment	−.060	.04	−1.43 *
	Percent minority enrollment, squared	.011	.01	1.96 **
11	Voting Rights Act examiners	−.173	.13	−1.37 *
12	Black voter registration	−.001	.0004	−2.51 ***
	Black voter registration, squared	.001	.0004	2.63 ***
	Baseline (racial vote data available)	.319	.10	3.29 ***
	Constant	.380		
	R^2	.380		
	F statistic	$F_{(19,459)} = 14.82; p < .001$		

Statistical confidence levels for t-statistics:
(*) $p < .10$ (**) $p < .05$ (***) $p < .01$

Notes: "Baselines" refer to dichotomous variables whose only purpose in the regression equation is to take account of the occasional nonexistence of data for some variables; they have no analytic interpretation. The sample consists of a random sample of school districts (drawn by the U.S. Office of Education and stratified by enrollment size) for which aggregated 1970 Census data are available. Results presented here are consistent with a number of estimates from other sample-selection procedures. N=479.

the impact of officials' career incentives on their innovation decisions. The empirical analysis shows that innovations can be predicted from information about an organization's influence on the careers of its officials. (The 90 percent correct discriminant predictions is a better indicator of statistical association than the R^2 value of .38, because of the artifactual nature of regressions with a dichotomous dependent variable.) The power of these predictions tells a great deal about the behavior of the officials in school organizations. These empirical results strongly support the organizational politics explanation of innovation: the likelihood of innovation increases when school administrators can advance their careers by advocating change.

The Implications of Innovations that Depend on Organizational Politics

These findings have major implications for the ways we think about how educational innovation occurs. One way to see these implications is to imagine how an innovative school district would look, according to the patterns described here. An innovating school district is probably full of ambitious officials working on their pet projects, with each project tailored to gain the support of important colleagues. Each school official is aware of the career consequences of his or her organization's opportunities, its constraints, and its local setting. Out of this professional ferment comes an innovation (or two, or three).

Perhaps it seems surprising, but the picture of an uninnovative school district looks much the same. Its officials are just as likely to be ambitious, but they have decided to pursue their careers by doing their jobs in stable, cautious ways that do not threaten their colleagues or upset their organization. If they were to advocate an innovation, their peer relationships and their jobs would be at risk because of the career constraints facing officials in the uninnovative district. It would be as mistaken to assume that these officials are heartless bureaucrats who ignore students' needs as to assume that innovative officials are primarily concerned about the learning problems of students in their district. In fact, both groups are quite similarly trained and motivated.

It follows directly from this study that if their organization incentives changed dramatically, then our imaginary innovating officials would be completely capable of maintaining the status quo. By the same token, sufficient incentives may encourage a wider range of school officials to advocate an innovation. It all depends on the career interests of school officials and the organizational settings that provide incentives for particular kinds of decisions.

This explanatory model for school districts' innovation decisions can be called an "organizational politics" approach for two reasons. First, the model sees the school organization as exerting powerful influences on the opportunities and constraints facing individual administrators. Because the school bureaucracy is a *system* for resolving the complex, often contradictory interests and values held by people in and around its domain, its functions are essentially political. When it comes to innovation, the hard questions of "who gets what, when, and how"[17] are answered through a political process dominated by the school organization. Second, the model regards the incentives of individual administrators as the central driving force supplying the energies and competence necessary to initiate innovative programs. Initiating an innovation inevitably leads to resistance, high risks, and substantial personal costs for those who press for change, and demands great amounts of energy and expertise. It is a rigorously challenging mission, and an essentially political one.

The process of initiating innovations in school districts is, therefore, domi-

---

17 Lasswell's classic title (Harold D. Lasswell, *Politics: Who Gets What, When, How* (New York: Whittlesey House, 1936).

nated by organizations and by politics. The sources of innovations are the school administrators whose organizations provide the opportunity for them to advocate an innovation and to engage in the political decision-making process that must follow their advocacy. In fact, the empirical analysis presented here was able to produce an explanation of the origins of innovation decisions, using information about officials' incentives that ignored the question of what educational impact the innovation might have. If it will further the careers of school district officials to innovate, they will do so; if it will not, they will support the status quo. The underlying principle here is that *innovations are a product of school organizations rather than of "educational" concerns*. Until we can understand the implications of this pattern of school decision making—for educational innovation and for other pressing educational issues—our attempts to improve the schools are more likely to result in continued frustration than in success.

CHAPTER 13

The User-Driven System and a Modest Proposal

DALE MANN

THE PARADOX OF A USER-DRIVEN, FEDERALLY SUPPORTED SYSTEM

Federal efforts to improve local schools have been hampered by a paradox. Change is whatever the service deliverers—schools and teachers—decide it is to be. The less self-determination is allowed to these ultimate implementers of change, the less total change will result. On the other hand, the federal government has a responsibility to cause improvements in education. We expect the federal government to make change happen even where local authorities— including teachers—may disagree. The decisions of local level actors about what changes should or should not be implemented are legitimate decisions. But so are the decisions of federal level administrators. If delivery level autonomy must be maximized for there to be any change, yet that autonomy vitiates or contradicts federal decisions, and if both sets of actors are making good faith, legitimate decisions, then how can there be a user-driven, federally supported system of school improvement? How can a federally sponsored system be designed that maximizes user self-determination?

A user-driven system of change is indicated from a wide variety of perspectives,[1] but would be successful from the federal perspective only if the users chose to drive in directions endorsed by the national government. More importantly, some users would undoubtedly choose not to go anywhere at all. (Most districts, organizations, and individuals never "choose" in the sense of conscious selection among alternatives, but then neither do they change.) Those most in need of improvement are least likely to participate.[2] Although a

1   In the spirit of Alvin Gouldner, "I have not felt compelled to inundate [these] pages with a sea of footnotes. If the substance and logic of what I say here does not convince, neither will the conventional rituals of scholarship." *The Coming Crisis of Western Sociology*. New York: Harper Torchbooks, 1973, pp. 75–76.
2   It should be noted that the stress on volunteerism in federal programs also leaves untouched those most in need of change. Programs of improvement that employ devices such as "needs-identification" and proposals have already narrowed their clientele to a group that is at least mildly interested in improvement. But the group of schools or local education agencies (LEAs) that will not take those initiatives is in even greater need of assistance. Except for Ed Pauly's work, see chapter 12, *infra*, I am unaware of a single, even descriptive study of that extremely important group.

user-driven system, i.e., a system that maximizes user autonomy, is strongly indicated by recent research, it is also very likely to fail to do what it is supposed to do—make change happen. Any federally sponsored effort to bring about change or improvement should deal with those users who do not wish to improve themselves. How federal purposes (to bring change to those who do and who *don't* welcome it) can be reconciled with a user-driven system (a system that maximizes user self-determination) is the basic paradox for this analysis.

Most federal attempts to foster school improvement have used either a structural or a social-psychological approach. Faced with ninety thousand school buildings and two million teachers, federal programs have concentrated on those parts of the system that are (a) hoped to be determinants of improvement across a range of institutions and (b) easily accessible to intervention. Working on the structural features of schooling (the arrangement of offices, the pattern of regulations and requirements, etc.) is an attempt to deal with diversity by focusing on the generic parts of the system. Citizen councils, administrative decentralization, open classrooms, team teaching, management-by-objectives, and programming-planning-budgeting systems (PPBS) are examples. The central idea has been that if you change organizational arrangements, then those changes will condition or shape subsequent behavior. Structural change is a congenial focus for the federal government because structures can often be modified by affecting the legal or institutional parts of the system (through regulations, reporting requirements, directed grant programs, etc.). But the federal government, no less than any other actor, can do only what it can defend. Local control of local schools is still a powerful amulet against federal incursions. Because structural change is more widely accepted as legitimate, it does not deplete the government's small stock of authority. However, changing individual behavior directly is a lot more assertive, even aggressive, than changing the individual's organizational surroundings with the hope (and unspoken intention) of modifying the individual's behavior. Unfortunately, these "safer," more sanitary structural changes often fail to condition the behavior of people at the delivery level. (One part of the explanation has to do with the loose articulation of units in education or the loose coupling of the parts—pillows absorb huge shocks.)

More recent attempts have moved deeper into the system. These efforts have a (roughly) social-psychological focus. The label is not very satisfactory, but it does recognize that organizations are made up of persons who have their own purposes. The newly classic technique under this rubric is organization development (OD), which, despite the first word in its title, is aimed at changing individual behavior and changing it a lot more immediately than the previously discussed structural mode. Federal efforts designed to encourage, for example, needs assessment, team building, process consultation, and internal research, development, and dissemination (RD&D) capabilities fall under this heading. Of the scores of tenets that describe these techniques, only two need to be noted here.

The first of the OD assumptions is that the person who is to change must recognize the need for that change prior to adopting the new behavior. When the individual to be changed disagrees about the need for a new, improved behavior, the OD approach frequently changes the contingencies of the situation by, for example, making it less threatening, by reducing the amount of changed behavior that is expected, or by reinforcing existing behavior. But, from the perspective of federal policy, there are severe problems with the "felt-need" tenet. First, most school people are at the very least quasi-professionals; they believe in what they are doing. Their current teaching or administrative repertoire represents their best judgment about how to do the murky business of education. Because their current practice is the summary of what they believe desirable and feasible, they are not likely to admit the need to change. Acknowledging a need to change is a negative evaluation of their own performance. Although that is a kind of indictment of self, the social-psychological techniques of change-agentry have no counterpart to the citizen's constitutional privilege against self-incrimination. Second, modifying the change in order to make it more palatable to the person who is to be changed can easily dilute it beyond any federal utility.

The other OD tenet to be considered deals with self-interest. Most psychological approaches stress the individual's self-interest as the sine qua non of behavioral change. Unless the individual's perceived self-interest can be engaged, there will be no change. (How can it be to an individual's self-interest to admit personal or professional inadequacies?) But what happens when self-interest remains persistently at odds with the desired innovation? Federal policy *cannot* be interested in those schools that are marvelously sensitive to client demands, that eagerly search for better ways to teach and learn, that are constantly engaged in self-renewal. Such schools and school systems cannot and should not be the target of federal assistance.[3] The critical test for federal innovation policy is the group that is not interested in change. It is easy to run programs about which there is consensus; it is easy to run programs that do not intend to do anything except to help people do more of what they are already doing. But the federal government should do more than Saint-Exupéry's Little King who was always careful to require only those things that the Little Prince

3   The first year's operation of the Elementary and Secondary Education Act (ESEA) Title I included an incentive feature that gave a bonus to those districts that substantially increased local tax levy expenditures for Title I-eligible children. It quickly became apparent—especially to congressional critics—that only the country's wealthiest school districts had the discretionary resources to increase their own expenditures and thus qualify for the federal bonus. This unintended rich-get-richer feature was quickly eliminated.

would have done anyway. Chester Barnard wrote about four conditions that facilitate the use of authority. He required that the object of authority (1) understand its communication, (2) believe that compliance is good for the organization, (3) believe that compliance is personally beneficial, and (4) actually be able to comply. But since Barnard's conditions are remarkable by their absence, the question is, how can federal policy be conceived so that those people who *don't* understand, and who *don't* believe that an innovation is good for them will nonetheless respond in directions consonant with federal purposes? How can people be brought to do that which they would not otherwise do?

This part of the paradox of a user-driven system that does not satisfy federal purposes could be handled by simply giving up. The retreat from federal purposes that characterizes periods of American government (and some government officials) is motivated in part by the difficulties posed by the paradox. Schools are not, after all, immune from benign neglect. But there may be a more acceptable method than simply copping out. One of the few insights political science has succeeded in elevating to the status of a law declares that the only reliable motive is self-interest. Government works best when it can arrange particular self-interests so that they aggregate to the public good. (Both social psychology and political science use self-interest as a fulcrum for change. The difference is that the political scientist does not expect—and generally does not want—to change the definitions of self-interest that people carry with them. Rather, the political scientist seeks to arrange things so that self-defined self-interest will nonetheless conduce to public interests.)

But how can federal officials in education arrange the self-interests of their partners in the schooling system? How can those people who are to adopt a change—even though they do not want to—come to acknowledge and accept that they should do so? Several methods are represented to a greater or lesser degree in tactics employed by federal programs.

STRATEGIES OF CHANGE

Forcing Change

On rare occasions, there are problems of such compelling importance that their symptoms are proscribed. School attendance, for example, is compelled by the state. Some forms of racial discrimination, in some school settings, can be legally enjoined. Some practices that have formerly been thought to be useful parts of pedagogy are prohibited outright—the harsher forms of corporal punishment for example. The generally aversive sanctions attached to the proscribed behavior must be sufficiently distasteful that the individual acquires a new self-interest in avoiding them. Political scientists define power as requiring someone to do that which he/she would not otherwise do. Although part of this strategy involves denying legitimacy to the old pattern of behavior, under this pure power strategy, what someone *thinks* is less important than what someone *does*. Individuals may persist in disagreement as long as their actions conform to a newly imposed value. Some urban superintendents, for example, have come to care less that some of their principals are racist than that they not act on their beliefs weekdays between 8:30 A.M. and 3:30 P.M.

Buying Change

This is a more common tactic through which the federal government deals with the problem of legitimate disagreement. Agreement can be purchased. It is possible to make the size of an incentive so large that it will swamp (some, but only some) opposition. The reward offered for compliance need not be very large in aggregate federal terms as long as it elicits the intended local response. That is especially the case where local education agencies (LEAs) are over-whelmed with problems and hard pressed for soft money. In that quite common situation school people will respond to practically any program that is pointed at an existing need or that can be bent from its original purposes to serve locally determined purposes. This strategy works by eclipsing the individual's prior self-interest. Because of the size of the new reward, the old self-interest pales. Thus the target of change need not alter his/her orientation to the previous self-interest as long as the superiority of the new one is acknowledged. Buying change has been pilloried as a tactic of "throwing money at social problems" that some people believe does not work. Of course, throwing money at the "problem" of, say, getting a handful of white, male American astronauts to and from the moon worked splendidly. With sufficient patience and cash, the technological or organizational dimensions of social problems can at the very least be ameliorated. The fact that patience and cash are both functions of political will is related to the questions of politics raised by the problem of change. Still, the principle established is that change *can* be purchased and that more changes can be purchased with more money. School reformers may not like the size of the increment and the public may not like the cost, but the strategy is sound.

Persuading Change

This is the heart of the rationalist approach. The notion is that the user/implementer will be so dazzled by the penetrating logic or superior perform-ance of the new thing that it will replace the old thing as the object of the individual's affections. The (unalloyed) promulgation of improved curricula and the lighthouse dissemination of better teaching methods are examples of this strategy. The maintenance of an Educational Resources Information Cen-ters (ERIC) system that makes information about better practice available on user demand is another example. In the persuasion mode the user comes to believe that his/her previously understood self-interest was incorrect—or at least that it was inferior to the benefits associated with the new "persuaded" version.

Manipulating Change

Despite the old saw, "I teach but *you* manipulate," this is a category with great salience to government policy. Few proponents of change operate so purely from a basis of reason that they can resist the temptation to "enlighten" another's self-interest. Manipulation is a process of one person's supplanting another's self-interest until it coincides with the first person's interest— regardless of whether it is "truly" or "actually" to the benefit of the person being manipulated to have acquired a new "self-interest." Obviously, determining the difference between "manipulation" and "persuasion" involves determining "true" self-interests. Manipulation need not go on only through a process of bamboozlement. It can proceed by encouraging someone to identify with a leader, to emulate another, to "fall in line," and so on. The danger in manipulation is in its abuse. Once the manipulator has determined what someone else's "real" self-interest is, then the manipulator quickly comes to feel (often quite passionately) that any or all actions are legitimated by that superior interest. History is so full of sad consequences flowing from that belief that most political scientists believe the individual right of self-determination is virtually inviolable.

Reinforcing Change

A fifth strategy counts on the fact that with or without outside assistance, at any given moment, some districts, some schools, some individuals will be doing something new or different. The initial impetus for that autochthonous (sprung-from-the-ground) change comes from the user. The reinforcement for continuing, intensifying, or extending the change comes from the federal government. Some ESEA projects have, for example, supported the continuation of LEA efforts that had been previously, locally initiated. The Labor Department's Public Works Employment Program gave extra points in its proposal competition to those projects that had been begun with local resources and were only to be completed with federal money. But the requirement in most education programs that federal dollars *not* be used to supplant local dollars attempt to preclude this sort of reinforcement, at least in part to avoid helping the rich get richer and to concentrate assistance on those with the most need. Thus, reinforcing existing change may be antithetical to a basic mission of the federal government.

The success of three of these five strategies rests on altering the individual's definition of self-interest (buying change, persuading change, manipulating change). The strategy of forcing change is indifferent to attitudes, and concentrates only on behavior. The fifth strategy, reinforcement, rests on prior voluntary changes in the definition of self-interest.

The five strategies are not equally available for federal programs, in large part because they vary in the amounts of legitimacy necessary to sanction their use. The forcing technique can be used only where there is substantial social agreement on the goals to be achieved. The attempt to prohibit alcohol abuse is a historic example of the consequences of power that exceeded its legitimacy. The effort to prohibit the use of marijuana is a more contemporary example with similar results. An intermediate case, federal attempts to prohibit some kinds of racial and gender role-identity discrimination, may be used to point out the ways in which some prohibitions that initially overreach the public's consensus are used to educate or to lead the public.

If the legitimacy accorded each strategy is one variable that helps determine the political feasibility of these strategies, the second variable has to do with attitudes versus behavior as a target for change. The attractive thing about changing attitudes is that frequently the resulting behaviors are then voluntarily and cheaply modified.

> When people are subdued by force
> they do not submit in heart.
> They submit because their strength
> is not adequate to resist.
> But when they are subdued by virtue,
> they are pleased in their inner hearts,
> and they submit sincerely.
>
> MENCIUS, *Chinese philosopher, c. 300 B.C.*

Attitude change may be more efficient and more effective, but it is also more difficult to achieve and in some ways demands more legitimation. If, for example, all we aspire to is to get teachers to stop hitting children, that may be achieved by a relatively simple legal injunction or by making the act of hitting a pupil a punishable offense. The infringement of the teacher's person is much less than that which follows from an attempt to change the teacher's behavior by changing the teacher's attitude to a more loving, accepting, humane posture toward children as individuals. The latter has comprehensive, thoroughgoing consequences for the teacher as a person. As an intervention it is much more difficult to legitimate than "simply" proscribing a very particular behavior.

DESIGN SPECIFICATIONS

On her deathbed, Gertrude Stein was supposed to have been asked by her students, "Tell us the answer." She replied, "Tell me the question," and died. The first part of this chapter poses a paradox about the federal role in educational improvement. One consequence of the paradox of a user-driven system is that, although local autonomy should be maximized at the delivery level and although that autonomy may lead to greater achievements in some units, those units (districts, schools, or individuals) will *not* be those most in need of change. A system that only helps the good to get better falls far short of the net improvements that legitimate the federal effort.

If that is the problem, what is the answer? Despite the prudence of the Stein gambit, this part of the discussion suggests a number of features that should characterize a user-driver system. Political science deals with the distribution of values, especially with the clash of legitimately differing values. Because of that, the field is littered with dilemmas that are only partially reconcilable. The features of the user-driven system described below are not a sufficient solution to the basic paradox. They are offered in a spirit of successive approximation. Two rules have been used in selecting these features. (1) What will maximize the prospects for successful change at the service-delivery level (schools and classrooms)? (2) What can reasonably be assumed to be within reach of federal policy makers and program administrators? The features are a sort of factor list. To the extent that each factor can be reflected in policies, regulations, and procedures, the prospects for successful improvement at the service-delivery level should be enhanced. (Most of the features are described as they would apply to an individual.)

Self-Interest

Self-interest is the only reliable motivation: A fundamental task of government is to arrange multiple self-interests so that they aggregate to a larger interest, or, more likely, interests. Thus a user-driven system must capitalize on those moments when its users' self-interests are most clearly engaged.

Survival Self-Interest

Samuel Johnson observed of the prospect of being hanged that it seemed to have a marvelous power to concentrate a person's mind. In a similar fashion, school districts are supposed to respond to exogenous shock.

The cumulative effect of the taxpayers' revolt, declining enrollments, and state constitutional reforms of educational finance has been a greater restructuring of the schooling services than any event since the "baby boom." But that restructuring has been wholly unconsciousness and unsystematized. It is possible that the instinct for survival that accompanies such crises may open districts to assistance, ideas, initiatives from a variety of sources. A user-driven system would use such attention-concentrating crises as cues. The crisis need not be externally generated—internal bureaucratic crises can also be employed, including, for example, those associated with regime changes.

It can also be argued that crises paralyze educational organizations. The vast majority of New York City's nine hundred building principals have done only what was necessary to cope with the dramatic retrenchments forced on them. But a very small group used the fiscal situation as an opportunity to reorganize, redirect, and renegotiate basic aspects of their schools. Most administrators were paralyzed by the fiscal crisis; a few found in the same event the necessary mandate to action. What accounts for the difference? While the answers to that should be pursued at the level of the individual, at both the individual and the organizational level there is probably such a thing as an optimum amount of crisis. Thus, one of the topics that needs attention is what Don Michael has called the "ethical management of crisis." To what extent may federal policy be used to provoke crises in order to stimulate attention to change?

Ambition Self-Interest   The responsiveness of leaders to their clientele has repeatedly been demonstrated to be related to the leader's ambition. For example, a school board member who wants to use her accomplishments with the schools as a platform to run for the city council, and that as a platform to run for the state legislature, and that as a platform to run for the Congress, has a greater personal incentive to be responsive to each constituency than the allegedly "selfless" individual, "above politics," who lacks ambition and who can thus be indifferent to constituency. In addition, public participation in decisions that determine the careers of elites (hiring, firing, promoting, transferring, etc.) has also been found to be related to responsiveness. The ambition of the individual is an aperture that federal policy might exploit by managing the career-enhancing aspects of federal programs (e.g., status, visibility, mobility, identification with federal projects, etc.).

Self-Realization Self-Interest   As professionals, school people want to make a personal contribution to children and to society. They strive to do a better job, to make use of their talents, to realize their potential. This need for self-realization can be harnessed through the same sort of program-design features described elsewhere in this section. (Note: This type of self-interest comes last, not first on this list. Many change-agent efforts have assumed that professionals would rush to embrace that which makes them better professionals. While there has been motion in that direction, it has not been a stampede. And again, the wrong people [in one sense] have moved the farthest.)

Natural Entry Points

A precept in organization change is that naturally occurring apertures for influence should be exploited.

Early Professional Imprinting   Baby ducks relate to any source of early nurturing whether or not it is a duck. If they learn at all, baby birds learn to fly in the first few feet between the edge of the nest and whatever they would otherwise land on. Learning to teach is not quite so Darwinian, but the first days in a classroom do have an imprint on the beginning teacher. The first post as a principal or a superintendent shapes the rest of an administrator's career so powerfully that there is evidence to indicate that many administrators simply repeat whatever they did in their first job as they move through subsequent posts. The apprehension and uncertainty of such moments, combined with the need to perform, create a marvelous opportunity for assistance. The benefits reaped from this tactic have the same sort of premium as the more general pedagogical stress on early childhood education.

Slack Resources   Innovation is also related to the amount of slack resources. Contrary to popular expectations, an organization in which employees straggle in late, take long lunch hours, and go home early is also an institution that has underutilized resources that can be available for new departures. Vestigial offices and redundant staffs are signals of slack resources. Unfortunately, slack resources are more likely to be characteristic of rich schools than poor schools, although that is not always true. Most city schools are an exception. The point is that federal policies designed to facilitate user-driven change should try to exploit slack resources, either by discerning their presence or by providing them.

Second-Circle Emulation .   Peer teaching is a well-known ingredient of effective change. The emulation of other people "in the trenches," "on the firing line," is a credible source of assistance and should be maximized in a user-driven system. But an important caveat needs to be added to this general principle. *Immediate* peers are *not* useful in this capacity. Dissemination and diffusion appear to skip over the adjacent ring of peers and to be effective with a group of like individuals at least once removed. The probable explanation is that first circle peer emulation is too threatening (someone doing a better job while working in the same environment with the same resources is probably a show-off, if not a cheat). It is preferable from the user's point of view to learn from a peer far enough from home so that (a) asking for help can't be interpreted as a self-indictment; so that (b) invidious competition and comparison are reduced; so that (c) the ideas can be changed with impunity; and so that (d) they can be credited to their new user. The general emphasis on linkage networks, especially on a regional or state basis, is consonant with this feature.

The Boundaries of Practice All professionals conduct themselves within a framework of rules, regulations, guidelines, standard operating procedures, and other constraints. While this route to change is a well-worn path for federal programs, it is always open for creative exploitation. An excellent example is the local competency-based teacher education project that arranged to have its teacher competencies written into the license-renewal criteria of an LEA just as the project's federal support was running out.

The informal dimensions of educational organizations also shape behavior, perhaps more powerfully than do the formal boundaries. The sense of camaraderie, of belonging, of turf, and so on, is extremely important. In the past, federal practice has attempted to deal with this by encapsulating change efforts in special purpose projects. While that may nurture the efforts of people inside the project, it also carries the seeds of its own destruction by the larger culture. Still, if the price of the project's entry into the larger system is abandoning the chance of change, then the price is too high. This sort of dilemma needs careful attention, especially from sociologists and anthropologists.

Professional Training The last of the naturally occurring entry points for change is provided by the prerequisite of advanced professional training required for official certification and/or promotion by a variety of jurisdictions. In theory, there should be a multiplier effect from having inculcated the faculties of graduate professional schools with new ideas that are then passed on to students who then become the leaders of institutions. The history of some graduate schools of education (Teachers College among them) demonstrates that, and the intention of teachers' unions and other professional associations to create their own in-service training programs reinforces the idea at the same time that it suggests an aperture for federal support.

Learning Theory Precepts

Several of the practices that characterize the best of teaching and learning are directly relevant to a user-driven system (especially when the individual user is the object of interest). Again, the features that follow should not be read as a counsel of perfection, but rather as a list of desiderata to be maximized where feasible. The challenge to policy management is to determine, discover, or create ways to use these features.

The Participation Hypothesis This is the most empirically established feature of successful behavior-changing efforts. Its basic premise is that as the individual's participation or involvement with an innovation increases, the individual's acceptance of that innovation also increases. The participation hypothesis recurs throughout the social and behavioral sciences. (In political science it illuminates part of the circular rein-forcement between the sense of political efficacy and civic participation; in social psychology it is used to explain the power of peer and group influences; in organizational development it is the basis for many prescriptions about group work.)

Several mechanisms seem to be at work. For one, participation in groups simply makes one more accessible to group influences. Participation shifts the communication encountered by an individual from critical sources to those that are more likely to be supportive of the group. Becoming a participant in a group identifies the participant with the group in the eyes of other people, who modify their expectations accordingly, and those changed expectations then help to shape the behavior of the participant. For the individual, the act of involvement requires the expenditure of some amount of resources—time, concentration, intellectual and emotional expression. Investing personal re-sources is likely to increase one's commitment to the thing being participated in because most people are loath to waste their resources. There is often a sense of loyalty to a group that values the individual enough to have made use of that individual. For both of these reasons, it sometimes happens that in the experi-ence of participation an individual will substitute group for personal judgments rather than disagree with the group. The effect of involvement with urban schools on many advocates of community control is an excellent illustration of the participation hypothesis. Moving from outside to inside the school changed the balance of communication about the school from bad to good; it required previously critical individuals to explain and even defend school actions; it made many people (paraprofessionals especially) reluctant to jeopardize their personal investment through disagreement or dissent; and it flattered them into cooperation. The pejorative label for those outcomes is, of course, cooptation. At the very least, participation can be used to defuse volatile situations; at its most successful it can be used to build support and trust.

Clear Tasks   Situations that are most likely to elicit successful user responses are those that are stated operationally with components, requirements, and actions sharply delineated. Unfortunately, in-novation is by definition murky. Although the *Scientific American* advertises that "in a society that lives by innovation, discovery is our most important product," discoveries are seldom clear even to those who make them. Still, there is a premium on clarity and the federal partner in a user-driven system can help with the translation, operationalization, and communication. The National Institute of Education's (NIE) targeted communications program used this precept by requiring its contractors to analyze the information utilization style of the intended audience before preparing materials designed to be of assistance to that audience.

Early, Frequent Success   The next three speci-
fications deal with a critical area—the process and structure of rewards for
change. In general the task is to design incentives that reinforce behavior that
both the users and the designers regard as desirable. Rewards must be significant (in relation to the effort), and they must be contingent on do-able tasks
where achievement is a realistic expectation. Current federal program management procedures encourage users to propose millennial goals, which, although they cannot be and are not met, are still reinforced by continuation of
project support. Such practices teach users to be cynical about goals, indifferent to *any* achievement level, and disdainful of federal project supervision.

The importance of reinforcement as a management device is paramount.
Tasks in a user-driven system should be divided and sequenced in such a way
that their accomplishment can be the occasion of lots of early rewards. Some
aspects of federal program management (needs assessment procedures, proposal review, progress reporting) might lend themselves to this feature but would
need to be substantially modified. Unfortunately, it is the nature of innovation
that clear, do-able tasks are rare; where they have existed, they have probably
already been done. Still, this is a valid design principle for a user-driven
system.

Nonaversive Feedback   The discussion so far
implies the need for a feedback system from the federal to the user level that
would be nonaversive and realistic. Where the users believe that the life or
death of their projects is determined by an evaluation, they will bias or distort
the evaluation. (Recall the law of self-interest.) While it is understandable and
even praiseworthy that innovative efforts should seek to perpetuate themselves,
that quest obfuscates federal judgments about which programs should be
perpetuated and which not. The introduction of so-called third party evaluators
has not remedied the situation. A second aspect of feedback involves providing
project management with performance assessment data sufficient to inform
their decisions, not about project continuation but about project modification.
The introduction of "documentation and analysis" activities is a step in this
direction. Neither local level project managers nor federal program officers can
trust "evaluation" data to learn about what needs to be done. Thus, in recent
years, NIE has begun to fund "documentation and analysis" efforts that are
separate from evaluation.[4] The results of documentation and analysis efforts

---

4 A feature that is somewhat contrary in spirit to the user-driven system would be the use of an *aversive
threshold.* Some user excursions may be so far afield, so inefficient, or so counterproductive as to
require sanctions beyond initial feedback and subsequent withdrawal of support. A number of prece-
dents exist. New York City regularly publishes a list of its most-wanted parking ticket scofflaws. The
institutional censure list of the American Association of University Professors is an even more assertive
negative sanction. This part of the user-driven system is optional-at-(great)-extra-cost.

can be reported to separate entities within the sponsoring agency and treated as relatively privileged information.

Separating information about short-term project functioning from evaluative information used to determine a project's continuation raises an interesting problem. Suppose that a project gets somewhat off-track and reports that event to a federal program officer, who then struggles dutifully to modify the project in the direction of greater success. Suppose further that the project continues to fail and that its lack of performance eventually becomes manifest through the separate evaluation process. The scenario might then well include one federal employee (the one in possession of the evaluation data and responsible for the project go/no go decision), charging another federal employee (the one with the more realistic documentation data and responsible for the near-term project modification) with having withheld evidence about a failing program that might have been used to make a more timely and fiscally responsible decision about termination. The scenario is a realistic one and points up a critical dilemma: Can the federal government afford to trust the delivery level to make mistakes and, if it can't, how much progress can be expected?

Selective Reinforcement   A central part of the user-driven strategy is the reinforcement of only those user behaviors that appear on the federal agenda. (Obviously, this assumes a federal agenda.) In an operant conditioning laboratory, nonreinforced behavior withers away, but that is an unlikely public prospect, given multipocket budgeting and the 8 to 10 percent federal share of a largely locally funded activity. Nonetheless, federal support should continue to be available only for activities that are consonant with federal purposes. The difference here is no great departure from current practice *except* in the extent of the subsequent user self-determination of means, once the goals are agreed upon. A somewhat greater departure is a more thorough articulation of the federal agenda. Unified and transitively ranked mission statements are not characteristic of large bureaucracies and may even be undesirable if they focus opposition. However, the government has managed to declare several fairly stable priority areas in recent years (e.g., Title I evaluation research, career ed, Teacher Corps). Such declarations can be used as a basis for selective reinforcement.

Sense of Fate Control   Educational achievement is linked to what the learner believes about himself or herself. Where the student believes that success is determined by others (sometimes called an external locus of control), then the student will not try, will fail, and will be confirmed in the self-assessment of inefficacy. The internal/external locus of control has a precise analogy in the subordinate/superordinate hostility and sullen withdrawal that currently afflicts some school district/state education agency (SEA)/federal efforts; the notion of a user-driven system is clearly designed to maximize the beneficial aspects of an internal locus of control.

A User-Monitoring System

One emphasis throughout the user-driver system is on being responsive to locally initiated efforts or at least to situations such as crises or external shocks that are likely to be followed by user receptivity to change. But how, with ninety thousand school buildings and two million teachers, can the federal government become aware of such critical moments? The prospect of a federal intelligence network that would be comprehensive enough and sensitive enough to register such events raises a "big brother" specter. Fortunately, some events leave traces that can easily be registered (strikes, failed bond issues, resignations, promotions, etc.). For the rest, the monitoring system might have to rely on user self-reporting. The point is, however, that in order for the government to act to reinforce or shape change, it must first be aware of the precipitating events, and that is the purpose of the monitoring system.

"Overdesigning"

The arm wrestle that goes on between nominally adopting sites and those innovations that are supposed to change them is well known. The sites are played by King Kong in that struggle, and their power to modify project features is well documented. Given current technology, this phenomenon of partisan mutual adaptation appears to be unavoidable. But a more complete understanding of partisan mutual adaptation would allow us to predict the direction in which projects would change, given certain data about site and process features. That information might then be used, in effect, to "over-design" project features so that their eventual reality would be closer to original intentions than what we now can achieve. The procedure is similar to that of a bridge architect who allows for materials to stress and sag in order that the bridge can settle into place. A few federal programs already provide these grantees with more resources than seems prudent. They do that so that the grantees have enough flexibility to try new things, so that they can concentrate on intended outcomes rather than fiscal management, and so that they have the freedom to fail. The practice of overendowment or redundancy is difficult to defend in public programs although no one objects to redundance or overcapacity in public transportation, especially in jet aircraft.

The Reality of Disjointed Incrementalism

Few things have had a more pernicious effect on federal innovation policy than the projection of a hyperrationalized model of "decision making" or "problem solving" onto the group that is to change or to be changed. People contemplating problems do not solve them by adopting wholesale changes; rather, they avoid them wherever possible. The actions they will take will be enough only to escape the worst consequences, not enough to expunge the source of the difficulty. Race is probably the best example. In a problem-solving mode, one might expect school officials to recognize the problems of racism, to search for alternative solutions, to compare them, and then to select and install that solution with the optimum ratio of benefits to costs. But public action about racism in schooling is neither voluntary nor rational. Only a handful of districts have spontaneously desegregated (White Plains in New York and Berkeley, California, come to mind). Most of the others have waited for court orders, boycotts, or other dramatic difficulties and then have reacted only enough to ameliorate the most egregious and compelling symptoms. ''Problem solving'' is a grossly inaccurate characterization of these events.

The point is not to abandon our aspirations (problem solving) but rather to premise our actions on realistic diagnoses of the behavior of people and institutions (problem avoiding). There is no level or unit of government whose decisions and actions meet tests of academic rationality. If federal policy is to be premised on reality, it should assume a picture of decision making that is much closer to what Lindblom calls ''disjointed incrementalism.'' The following specifications are derived from that body of theory.[5]

Let a Thousand Wheels Be Reinvented   It now seems clear that there are far fewer determinate answers to generic questions in school improvement than had been hoped. The nearly idiosyncratic power of place (recall the ninety thousand public school buildings) has been seriously underestimated. Each site seems compelled—some would say doomed—to a drudging rediscovery of the inadequacy of sleds and rollers and then to a discovery of the usefulness of an axle stuck through a disc. While that may seem horribly inefficient, it should be compared to the situation in which heaps of wheels lie around unused because of the local conviction that ''they won't work here.'' The chief adjustment has to do with shifting federal expectations from isolated though spectacular breakthroughs to net change. The thousand-wheels feature also argues for more patience in program monitoring. The fact that such a policy will seem depressingly atomistic from the national perspective is exactly why the basis for this part of the design specifications of the user-driven system is called *disjointed* incrementalism.

5   See David Braybrooke and Charles E. Lindblom. *A Strategy of Decision: Policy Evaluation as a Social Process,* New York: Free Press, 1963. For an application of the theory to education, see Dale Mann, *Policy Decision-Making in Education: An Introduction to Calculation and Control.* New York: Teachers College Press, 1975.

Marginal Change   Schools, no less than any other social institution, are the product of many, many agreements and compromises, painfully ground out over long periods of time. Moreover, schools are quite successful at many of the tasks handed them (especially considering the resources allowed them). Because of the long-standing sociopolitical reality thus represented, wholesale change or radical transformation is simply not a viable expectation (except in exceedingly rare revolutionary moments). Changes are therefore always incremental; they are calculated from the existing, unchanged base, and they are calibrated in millimeters, not kilometers. Federal policy should recognize that fact by taking into account the state of the local art when deciding whether or not a proposed user departure meets a test of significance. Admittedly, it will be difficult to gain political support for the modest gains implied by an incremental strategy. Surprisingly enough, even congressional audiences of policy elites sometimes need educating about political feasibility. A more accurate appraisal of what is possible should help to avoid the boom-and-bust cycle of support that now follows the overselling and the overreacting between proponents and critics.

Limited Calculation   People use that information which is most convenient—chronologically, geographically, psychically, politically, and economically. They do not make exhaustive searches of a hypothetical universe of alternatives. They do not attempt to determine maximum expected utility on all possible alternatives. A user-driven system would capitalize on these unavoidable limitations by providing technical assistance at the critical junctures described elsewhere in this analysis.

Goals to Means Adjustments   Users can be counted on to behave as everyone behaves. That is, before they decide what sorts of things they want to achieve, they will make a quick inventory of what is available to be used for what purposes. Thus, stated goals will be tailored to available means and not, as in the rational calculus or as in classic economics, the other way around. Since federal means are undoubtedly part of what the users will employ to calculate their goals, the federal government can assist either by making sufficient resources available to support the user's achievement of jointly shared goals or by candidly stating limits on what it believes feasible, given available resources.

A Remedial Orientation   This feature also deals with expectations. Despite rhetoric, very few programs aspire to do much more than make rotten situations somewhat better. While we can quibble over the size of "somewhat," it should be clear that for purposes of honest interlevel relationships in a user-driven system, accurate goal statements are preferable.

Freud said, "Much is won if we succeed in transforming hysterical misery into common unhappiness."

Several of the features of disjointed incrementalism raise questions about how rational, teleological, or goal-oriented people are. While the hyper-rational paradigms of the recent past are not accurate descriptions of people's behavior, that does not mean that people simply emit behavior or that they behave irrationally. The point is that they use a sort of rationality that is overarching or architectonic; that rationality is much more subtle, it reflects more vectors, and it is necessarily more obscure than we have assumed. It has been called a sort of "rough-and-ready guidance rationality" that is not yet adequately captured either in the descriptive models of academics or in the prescriptive models of practitioners.

Successive Approximation   Recent research has demonstrated that the half-life of some project features (as described in the original proposal and then measured from the project's initiation) can be expressed in nano-seconds. Given the facts of project decay (mainly due to partisan mutual adaptation), the design of a user-driven system will need to incorporate many cycles, many iterative stop-and-start attempts to reach a goal. The proverbial frog's halfway jumps to the pond are taken in the spirit of successive approximation. Federal practice ought only to support the early jumps. The use of continuation funding on a short-cycle basis is also in the spirit of successive approximation.

Social Fragmentation   The attempt in the 1960s to build "one-stop shopping centers" in several functional areas of social welfare failed in part because it did not reckon with the range of participants and the range of interests over the range of time necessary to improve a given area. The multiplicity of roles that contributes even to schooling (let alone education) is extraordinary. A user-driven system will need to accommodate and arrange those multiple inputs.

The proposition in this part of the essay is a simple one. Change must incorporate more attention to the users. It is possible to design a system that achieves more of that while not abandoning federal purposes. To the extent that the design specifications outlined here can be satisfied in federal program administration, there will have been a reconciliation of the user-driven system with federal purposes.

A MODEST PROPOSAL

The user-driven system will be matched against the organizational and political realities of the federal government's current project-mediated practices. The concentrated application of the features of the user-driven system should make those activities more effective than might otherwise be the case. Still, this jump of the frog will get only part way to the improvement pond. Schools reflect society and are fundamentally constrained by that society. The problem of student achievement is locked to deeper problems like unemployment, malnutrition, and parenting inadequacies. But even those "deep" problems are caused by bedrock difficulties about income distribution and the persistence of prejudice. Thus, many people have concluded that schools cannot be reformed unless society is reformed (or revolutionized). But the societal brakes on schooling improvement are not the only limit on the prospects for the user-driven system.

The user-driven system also assumes a "project" or "program" vehicle. Since the New Deal, American governments have had a characteristic response to social problems—they have authorized and tried to implement new programs and given those programs to agencies that would "solve" the problem by applying the program. Local governments are as replete with projects as the federal government is with programs. Almost every difficulty has been viewed as something that would yield to a conscious, preplanned, packaged government activity. But there is far less confidence in that assumption than there used to be. Are there not substitutes to project-mediated attempts to make schools better? The remainder of this essay outlines one alternative.

Assume that instead of providing employment for adults, the purpose of federal programs is to improve the learning achievements of children. If it can be accepted that pupil performance is the goal of federal programs,[6] then we might ask what is known about how to cause those performance gains. The answer is, Not much. Averch's dictum states, "Research has not identified a variant of the existing system that is consistently related to students' educational outcomes."[7] Averch's dictum says that there are no universally applicable solutions that may be taken off the shelf and bolted onto the problem of learning. But that does not mean that some practices are not preferable to others under certain conditions or that, in particular circumstances, some techniques are not more effective than others. The point is the particularity of the circumstances. The nearly idiosyncratic power of the site has been one of the points of this essay. The program/project strategy may simply be too gross a technique to accommodate the very finely grained circumstances that spell the difference between success and failure.

If these assumptions are correct, then the problem is (1) how to bypass the project method, and (2) how to concentrate assistance on those things that

---

6 Actually, most programs aspire to improve society by having improved students whose later contributions will enhance personal and social well-being. However, the chain of causality that links those factors is far too attenuated to inform policy decisions.

7 Harvey A. Averch et al. *How Effective Is Schooling? A Critical Review and Synthesis of Research Findings*. Santa Monica, Calif.: Rand Corporation, R-PCSF/RC, March 1972, p. x.

result in student achievement. There is a rather obvious if crass solution—we might buy pupil achievement. We might pay teachers, at least in part, according to how much better than predicted specific groups of students do. Federal programs are already targeted on assistance to rather discrete groups of students, as those students are defined by various learning-related characteristics, for example, age, poverty, physical disadvantage, learning disability, and so on. Teachers with such children would be paid for each point above the predicted level scored by those children.

Components of Plan

- *Identification of target groups.* The federal government would announce which learners, by what defining characteristics, establish the teacher's eligibility.
- *Prediction of achievement.* The amount of gain expected under ordinary circumstances for children in the identified categories would be calculated based on past performance. This may be done at the district level.
- *Setting the rate.* The sponsoring agency would determine how much per child each point of educational achievement above prediction is to be worth (e.g., $7 per point on the Metropolitan Reading Readiness Test for each point above the predicted fifty-first percentile for every left-handed child in a teacher's class).
- *Paying the teacher for the student's performance.* Upon evidence of student performance, the teacher would be paid the indicated amount.

How might such a plan work? Once the principle of paying teachers for causing achievement is established, a number of variations are possible and appear in the following examples.

Example   The federal government is concerned about reading and announces a rate, per point of achievement, that is higher for children in the third grade than in the fourth, higher for children in the second grade than in the third, and highest for first grade children. A number of teachers calculate that, if successful, they might increase their income by 50 percent. They acquire a more vivid interest in in-service education and in alternate methods of teaching reading. Some teachers buy new reading materials on speculation with their own money and train parents in their use. Other teachers split the grants with parents of the achieving children.

Example   The federal government decides to put 20 percent of the money it might otherwise have used to support improvements in schooling for native Americans into an incentive pool. The announcement puts a graduated premium on achievement score gains in reading, mathematics, and written communication in that order, but does not specify the age of the learner. The money is available for learner-achievement gains with the greatest gains rewarded first. In the first two years, tribal councils organize adult learning groups and divide the incentive grant proceeds with those adults whose reading gains make their teachers eligible for the program. After the adult population has been "exploited," elementary and secondary schools begin to have a chance to compete.

            Example   The federal government announces the following schedule for students who score more than one year above their chronologically indicated grade level: $30 for each student previously in the top national quartile; $50 for those in the second quartile; $150 for those in the third; and $300 for those in the bottom. In this case, the incentive grant award goes to the school district, not the teacher. Suburban schools need only a little encouragement to increase their efforts and do so. However, because most of their students were in the low-paying top half, they only break even. After a year they discover that their costs per pupil are high but so is their efficiency. Confident that they can capitalize on economies of scale, and envious of the higher premium attached to lower-achieving students, they recruit some inner-city students into their system.

Several advantages may be argued for such a plan of incentive grants based on gain scores.

1. It premises federal assistance directly and proportionately on improvement in learner performances, not on successful grantsmanship.
2. Some of the best teachers will go where they are most needed (at least as that need is defined by the federal government or by whatever agency defines the target group).
3. Good teaching will be measured in terms of pupil achievement; the best teachers will make a lot of money; schooling productivity will increase.
4. Some teachers will have a "natural" incentive to innovate.
5. Pedagogical questions will be answered at the delivery level, the level closest to the individual learner.
6. Many of the limitations of the project strategy will have been avoided (e.g., superordinate determination; limited-purpose, transient, and exotic activities).
7. As a strategy, the rate is almost infinitely flexible in terms of the characteristics of learner eligibility, the terms of its payment, and the size of that payment. If, for example, a given rate did not elicit sufficient changes in student performance, it might be increased until student performance increased.

There are some equally obvious disadvantages to the use of incentive grants.

1. An incentive grant plan would be hell to implement. Teaching is already codified, bureaucratized, and unionized. In a litigious society, this departure could occupy generations of law firms. The fact that of the country's thousands of school districts, only one chose to experiment with the voucher plan (Alum Rock) does not bode well for an incentive-grant plan.[8] Neither for that matter does the related experience of performance contracting.

2. Many people dislike standardized tests and fear the impoverished professional role in "teaching to the test." But as long as tests are a widely used social (and schooling) hurdle, then learning to do well at tests seems a necessary and desirable skill. In any case, except for some finger pointing, there is not now much pressure to reform tests. If part or all of some teachers' pay were linked to student performance on standardized tests, many teachers would agitate for tests that more adequately, more accurately captured some of subtler properties of the developmental experience.

3. An incentive-grant plan would discriminate among teachers. Their current treatment can be described as equitable, even if not much else can be said about it. Instead of assuming that a teacher's worth is related to longevity in the personnel system, the incentive grant would clearly indicate which teachers are best—at least with various specified learner groups.

4. Incentive grants may resemble "piece work," "commissions," and other commercial but allegedly unprofessional means of remuneration. This objection and the one immediately above will be quite compelling to some people, who should not, therefore, participate. The important thing is that the decision to participate or not should be the prerogative of the classroom teacher, not the union leader.

5. An incentive grant scheme would reduce the role of superordinate and intermediate agencies in determining, managing, and monitoring the means employed in teaching. The granting agency would do several things: determine the target groups most in need of assistance, determine the predicted achievement, set the rate, verify the gains, and write the checks. Still, that activity could be done with less administrative superstructure than now exists in most SEAs and federal agencies. (Some people who might otherwise be unemployed could turn to providing technical assistance, the demand for which would almost certainly jump under an incentive grant plan.)

This modest proposal to premise part or all of some teachers' incomes on the outcomes of their teaching will surely meet a mixed reception. But how satisfied are we with the results of the strategies employed to make change happen

---

8 For example, the California legislature has considered, but never passed, legislation roughly similar to that proposed here. See "The Elementary School Reading Achievement Program," Assembly Bill Number 816, California State Legislature, Sacramento, 1972.

so far? And how interested are we in improving the schooling of children? Depending on how one reads the evidence of the recent past in our efforts at improvement, the prospects of an incentive grant plan will be seen as merely contentious or as possibly hopeful.

CHAPTER 14

The Great Society Did Succeed

SAR A. LEVITAN AND ROBERT TAGGART

President Lyndon Johnson's social welfare philosophy captured the imagination of the country in the mid-1960s and spurred it into action after a decade of lethargy. In Johnson's words, "We have the opportunity to move not only toward the rich society and the powerful society, but upward to the Great Society. The Great Society rests on abundance and liberty for all. It demands an end to poverty and racial injustice."[1] Under the banner of the Great Society, there was a dramatic acceleration of governmental efforts to ensure the well-being of all citizens; to equalize opportunity for minorities and the disadvantaged; to eliminate, or at least mitigate, the social, economic, and legal foundations of inequality and deprivation. Congress moved ahead on a vast range of long-debated social welfare measures and pushed on into uncharted seas. In its 1866 days the Johnson administration moved vigorously to implement these new laws and to fully utilize existing authority. The Warren Court aided this dynamism with sweeping, precedent-setting decisions on a number of critical issues. The public supported this activism, giving Lyndon Johnson in 1964 the largest plurality in history, his Democratic party an overwhelming majority in both Houses of Congress, and his administration high public approval ratings as action got under way.

Yet only eight years after the end of the Johnson administration, the view is widely held that the Great Society failed. The charge is that it exaggerated the capacity of government to change conditions and ineffectively "threw money at problems," overextending the heavy hand of government, pushing the nation too far, too fast, leaving a legacy of inflation, alienation, racial tension, and other lingering ills. The repudiation of the Great Society in the late 1960s was based on a tide of analyses alleging to demonstrate the failures of the Johnson administration's domestic endeavors. There was extensive documentation of the "welfare mess." A crisis in medical care was declared and decried. Scandals and high costs in subsidizing housing were exposed, giving support to theoretical arguments about the inherent ineffectiveness of government intervention. Manpower programs, it was claimed, had little lasting impact on

---

1 Congressional Quarterly, *Congress and the Nation, 1965–1968* (Washington, D. C., 1969), Vol. II, p. 650.

employment and earnings of participants. Doubts were cast on the outcomes of education investments. Urban and racial unrest were blamed on civil rights action and community organization. The economic problems of the 1970s were blamed on economic mismanagement during the 1960s.

A POSITIVE ASSESSMENT

A careful reexamination of the evidence for the complete spectrum of the 1960s social welfare initiatives suggests that the conventional wisdom of the Great Society's failure is wrong. Our own assessments of the Great Society and its legacy, based on analysis of a vast array of program data, evaluations, and related statistics, challenge the widespread negativism toward governmental social welfare efforts.[2] We contend that the findings provide grounds for a sense of accomplishment and hope.

1. *The goals of the Great Society were realistic, if steadily moving, targets for the improvement of the nation.* By concentrating on the small minority of welfare recipients who are cheaters or who shun work, critics have chipped away at the ambitions of the Great Society, and have suggested that those in need somehow deserve their fate. This view ignores the overwhelming majority of welfare recipients who have no other alternatives, workers who either cannot find employment or are locked into low-wage jobs, and the millions of disenfranchised who are seeking only their constitutionally guaranteed rights. Other less strident critics emphasize the difficulties in changing institutions and socioeconomic patterns. No matter how desirable a change may be, it is likely to have unwanted side effects, and the process itself can be an ordeal. Where opportunities and rewards are distributed unequally and unjustifiably, redistribution will obviously affect the previously chosen people. Improvements cannot be accomplished without effort and sacrifice, and the existence of impediments is not proof of unrealistic or unattainable goals.

2. *The social welfare efforts initiated and accelerated in the 1960s moved the nation toward a more just and equitable society.* The claims that these programs were uselessly "throwing dollars at problems," that government intervention cannot change institutions or individuals, or that problems remain intractable are glib rhetoric. The results of government intervention varied, undesirable spillover effects occurred, and the adopted intervention strategies were sometimes ill designed; but progress was almost always made in the desired direction. The gains of blacks and the poor, the two primary target groups of federal efforts, offer the most striking evidence.

---

2   Specific analyses and studies are cited in Sar A. Levitan and Robert Taggart. *The Promise of Greatness* (Cambridge, Mass., 1976), from which this chapter is adapted.

Government programs significantly reduced poverty and alleviated its deprivations. Blacks made major advances in education, employment, income, and rights in the 1960s.

3. *The Great Society's social welfare programs were reasonably efficient, and there was frequently no alternative to active intervention.* The government operates in a fishbowl, so that all its mistakes and excesses are laid bare to the public; similar problems in the private sector are hidden away, leaving the impression of greater efficiency. Criticism of programs is part of the process by which needed or desired changes are engineered, and the discovery of failure is part of a continuing process of improvement.

4. *The negative spillovers of social welfare efforts were often overstated and were usually the unavoidable concomitants of the desired changes.* Examples are legion. Medical care programs were blamed for the inflation in medical costs. Busing was heatedly opposed as inconveniencing the many to help the few. In fact, however, medical costs rose largely because demand was increased suddenly, while supply could respond only slowly. Inflation is unavoidable when reliance is placed on the price mechanism to expand and redistribute resources. Busing to achieve racial balance involves difficulties, but critics have not offered alternatives to integrate the schools. Every program generates problems, but these have usually been manageable.

5. *The benefits of the Great Society programs were more than the sum of their parts, and more than the impact on immediate participants and beneficiaries.* In attacking a specific problem such as unemployment, for instance, there is a whole nexus of variables. On the supply side, consideration must be given to the education and vocational training of the unemployed: their access to jobs, their knowledge of the labor market, and their work attitudes, impediments, and alternatives. On the demand side, the quality and location of jobs must be considered along with their number. Discrimination and hiring standards are also crucial factors. Unemployment might be combated by education and training, better transportation, improved placement services, sticks and carrots to force the unemployed to take jobs, provision of child care, economic development in depressed areas, equal opportunity enforcement, and a variety of other measures. None of these alone is likely to have much impact, but together they can contribute to change, not only in the labor market but in all those dimensions of life so intimately related to work.

6. *There is no reason to fear that modest steps which are positive and constructive in alleviating age-old problems will in some way unleash uncontrollable forces or will undermine the broader welfare of the body politic.* Only dedicated pessimists and gainsayers can doubt our capacity to achieve substantial improvements. And there is no reason to abandon the aim of

providing a minimal level of support for all who remain in need. Progress has been meaningful; it can and must continue. As we enter our third century as a nation, we must reevaluate the recent, as well as distant, past to get not only a realistic understanding of our limitations but also a greater confidence in our potential. We have the power, if we have the will, to forge a greater society and to promote the general welfare.

EVALUATING THE RECORD

Many critics of the Great Society have focused on the least successful attempts at social improvement with their attendant horror stories. There is an opposite temptation to concentrate on and generalize from the areas of accomplishment. The only valid approach is to consider the successes and failures over the entire range of social welfare activities.

Income Support

The expansion of income transfers during the 1965–1975 decade has been criticized from many angles. Aid to Families with Dependent Children—usually called ''welfare''—drew the brunt of criticism. Supplemental Security Income—the reformed system of aid for the aged, blind, and disabled—then came under fire, as did unemployment compensation. Even the previously sacrosanct social security program was questioned. In reality, the Great Society had less impact on the transfer system than on any other social welfare dimension. To blame it for the ''welfare mess'' or for the problems of the social security system is to ignore the complicated factors involved; to associate it with the vast expansion in unemployment compensation in the 1970s or with the difficulties of public assistance for the aged, blind, and disabled is an anachronism. Nonetheless, a major thrust of the Great Society was to provide for the needy. If the programs that attempt to do this are ineffective, then the Great Society's vision must be faulted. Is the transfer system indeed a mess?

Doubts about the soundness of the social security program are, if not groundless, certainly exaggerated. During the 1965–1975 decade benefits were raised substantially in real terms, and the system matured to the point where coverage of workers and benefits to the elderly became nearly universal. The redistributive features of the programs were expanded but social security remained a good insurance buy for most workers.

The system remains secure. Declining birth rates mean fewer workers per beneficiary in the future and may require increased revenues. But this problem is more than a quarter century away, during which time productivity gains should provide the wherewithal for the needed transfers. Government contributions from general revenues are a likely possibility to finance the redistributive aspects of the system. And as a result of past improvements, benefits now meet basic needs and will not have to be raised in real terms as rapidly as in the past.

The veterans' pension and compensation system is an important complement to social security. As World War II veterans age, the proportion of needy veterans receiving benefits not carrying the stigma of welfare will rise.

Unemployment compensation grew at an incredible pace during the recession of the mid-1970s. Benefits and coverage extensions financed out of general revenues increased the transfer, as opposed to the insurance, features of the program. While it helps many nonpoor, unemployment compensation has evolved into a form of aid for the working poor who are frequently subjected to forced idleness but who are shortchanged by the welfare system.

Public assistance benefits for the aged, blind, and disabled were markedly improved over the last decade as the growth of social security and private pensions held down the case load and made reform possible. The Supplemental Security Income program that combined these categorical efforts established a federal floor under benefits and reduced geographic eligibility differences.

Aid to Families with Dependent Children has been the center of controversy. The tripling of case loads and the quadrupling of costs between 1965 and 1972 was alarming to some, as was the subsequent failure to achieve welfare reform. In retrospect, however, the process was neither incomprehensible nor inimical. AFDC benefits were raised substantially to provide most recipients, in combination with in-kind aid, a standard of living approaching the poverty threshold. With liberalized eligibility rules and more attractive benefits, most low-income female-headed families were covered by the welfare umbrella in the early 1970s. Once this had occurred, the momentum of growth slowed.

The welfare explosion did have side effects. No doubt some recipients chose welfare over work as benefits rose above potential earnings. In part, welfare freed mothers from low-paid drudgery to take care of their families. Moreover, the difficulties of placing even the most employable and motivated recipients in jobs paying adequate wages suggested the limited options for the majority of clients. As benefits stabilized in the 1970s, the increase in real wages promised to reduce the attractiveness of welfare to unskilled workers.

The welfare system's bias against families with a male head offered some inducement for nonmarriage or desertion. In cases where AFDC provided a higher or steadier income than male family heads could earn, the costs of broken families had to be balanced against the benefits of improved living standards. The stabilization of real benefits and the rise in real wages should, over time, diminish the inducement to break up homes.

The income support system, including social security, veterans' programs, unemployment insurance, workman's compensation, public assistance for the aged, blind, and disabled, AFDC, and near-cash programs such as food stamps, is incredibly complex. Yet ''messiness'' is inevitable where needs are multifaceted and where goals clash. Concentrating aid on female-headed families yields high target efficiency, since these families have the most severe needs and fewest options, but undesirable results are unavoidable. High marginal tax rates may discourage work, but they also tend to keep down costs and to help the most needy. Benefits may be too high in some areas and too low in others, but on the average they are close to poverty levels and geographic differentials are declining. Most families receiving multiple benefits have severe or special needs.

The income maintenance system is thus functioning reasonably well. The developments that seemed chaotic and dysfunctional have created a system within sight of assuring at least a poverty threshold standard of living for all citizens through a combination of cash and in-kind aid.

Health Care

The Great Society went far toward eliminating the main concern of the aged and a major problem of the poor—health care. Medicare and Medicaid have generally fulfilled President Johnson's promise of assuring the "availability of and accessibility to the best health care for all Americans regardless of age, geography or economic status."[3]

Medicare experienced early difficulties in striving for a balance between assuring adequate services and avoiding overutilization. Problems were associated most frequently with innovations. For instance, extended care was initiated as an alternative to longer hospital stays but became a subsidy for nursing home care until corrective measures were taken. Overly long hospital stays were shortened through a variety of utilization review methods. Perhaps to quell fears that government intervention would mean government control, Medicare may have displayed excessive generosity in considering the desires of doctors and other vested interests. After problems emerged, however, steps were taken to cut the fat from the system.

Medicaid remains an object of much criticism because of its rapid and unexpected growth. The scapegoats were overutilization and inefficiency, but quite clearly the basic cause was the explosion of AFDC. By the early 1970s the momentum of growth had already subsided as the eligible universe was reached and measures were taken to discourage overutilization and waste. Being tied to AFDC, Medicaid shared the geographic inequalities of that system, with even greater disparities resulting from the extension of aid to the medically indigent not on welfare in only some of the states. Yet these inequities were reduced over the years as more openhanded states cut back on frills while the tightfisted ones became more generous.

Medicare and Medicaid contributed to the rapid inflation of health care prices in the late 1960s. But supply did expand and reallocation occurred. The

3   Congressional Quarterly, *Congress and the Nation,* p. 665.

price rises pinched middle-income families and those at the margin of eligibility, and significant inequities were created, providing cogent arguments for a more comprehensive health care system. But with limited resources, those most in need (as defined by individual states) *are* generally being helped. Attempts to blame Medicare and Medicaid for the alleged (and very questionably documented) failure of our health care system are misplaced and even critics must admit these programs' effectiveness in performing their basic missions.

Housing

Low-income housing programs provide obvious benefits to participants. Subsidies reduce the strain on limited budgets, and the shelter is far superior to what participants could otherwise afford. The long waiting lists and low vacancy rates argue that poor people value these programs, notwithstanding the drawbacks associated with project housing.

There are secondary benefits. Publicly assisted units have helped to suburbanize low-income minority families. The courts have used these subsidy programs as a lever for countering residential segregation. Other lesser accomplishments of the programs include increasing the stability and long-term economic status of some families, organizing and delivering services using housing as the nexus, and experimenting with new industrialized construction methods.

Most significantly, however, the housing programs have built new homes for the poor. Construction yields a tangible, lasting product, permitting some control over location and quality. Building specifically for the needy tends to soften the low-rent and low-cost housing market, rather than waiting for the trickle down of increased production resulting from aid to the more affluent. Housing is as good an investment for the government as it is for private individuals in the present inflationary environment; and in a construction slump, increased assisted housing production can provide a needed stimulus to the economy.

The real issue is not the benefits, but rather the costs. Assistance programs are expensive because they house larger numbers of people who cannot afford to contribute much to their maintenance. Subsidized units are more expensive when they are built in high cost areas or according to high standards, or when they are subject to union wage or minority contracting requirements. The government has been bilked at times like any other buyer, but the exposés of the early 1970s exaggerated the extent of such violations. The new housing programs introduced in 1965 and 1968 needed to be refined and administered more carefully and changes were introduced to correct the abuses. A housing allowance, the panacea of the Nixon administration, is certainly worth considering, but the payoffs of direct production should not be ignored in deciding on the best course that should be followed.

Education

Learning is difficult to define or measure and the relationship between educational inputs and outputs is uncertain. Hence, there is little conclusive evidence that intensified efforts on behalf of disadvantaged students have improved their cognitive and social development or that educational gains yield long-run benefits.

The limited and very early evaluations of Head Start indicated that statistically significant improvements in achievement were washed out later when students returned to an "unenriched" environment. Evaluations of Follow-Through suggested that the gains could be sustained, and even more optimistically, that the programs improved with experience. Though these conclusions are all very tenuous, early childhood education is a societywide phenomenon. Given the underlying societal premise that school is worthwhile for younger children, it is sound public policy to concentrate resources on those most in need.

The effectiveness of elementary and secondary education programs for the disadvantaged is equally uncertain. Early studies were not encouraging but more recent findings suggest notable successes. This may reflect the fact that the programs have improved. Compensatory education resources were initially diverted for noneducational purposes and for nondisadvantaged students, but tightened controls have reduced waste and misallocation. Until proven otherwise, there is reason for guarded optimism about the current overall impact of the effort.

Federal aid for higher education can stand on its demonstrated merits. The value of the sheepskin has been documented. The test of success is whether resources are concentrated on those most in need, whether their college attendance has increased, and whether they are able to continue until graduation. By these standards, there has been a high measure of success.

Manpower Services

Training, education, counseling, placement, work experience, and other manpower services can improve the attractiveness of disadvantaged workers to employers and can help open doors to better jobs. Evidence suggests that participants improved their wages and job stability. Further, the value of projected future earnings increments exceeded the average cost of the programs. Society's investment in human resources has been profitable.

Institutional vocational training has been most carefully studied, and the findings indicate beneficial effects despite the usually short duration and a frequent absence of linkages to subsequent jobs. On-the-job training has an even greater payoff as measured by benefit/cost studies because the participant is able to earn while learning and usually is guaranteed employment upon completion of this vocational training.

More intensive remedial efforts such as the Job Corps have had mixed success. The Job Corps has not demonstrated that the average street-hardened youth can be rehabilitated by six or nine months of intensive aid in a specially structured center; the program has shown, however, that at least some will seize the opportunity and benefit substantially. The assertion that the disadvantaged are trapped by their backgrounds or by labor market realities is subject to all-important exceptions and modifications. Many can be helped, and even if the improvements are only moderate, on the average, they are well worth the effort as long as better proven options are unavailable.

Civil Rights

One of the primary aims of the Great Society was finally to secure the fundamental rights of blacks. Along with its impressive legislative record, the administration exerted its leverage in the marketplace and its power as a rule setter while the courts expanded the government's responsibilities and prerogatives. The Nixon and Ford administrations were less forceful, some critics argue. Nevertheless, the stalling points such as employment quotas or busing to end de facto segregation were far different from those of the early 1960s when the rights, rather than the corrective measures, were being debated.

The salutary effects of these civil rights advances were not difficult to ascertain. Black registration and voting increased, with a visible payoff in office holding. Equal employment opportunity efforts had little direct effect in the 1960s, but the screws were tightened considerably in the 1970s. De jure school segregation was largely eliminated and busing to achieve racial balance became widespread despite fervent opposition in some cases and repeated efforts in Congress, with administration prodding, to proscribe busing as a weapon in combating segregation. Fair housing machinery provided legal backing for some victims of discrimination, but little leverage to overcome patterns and practices was included in housing acts or administrative decisions.

While attention was focused on racial issues, there were other areas of advancement. At the beginning of the 1960s, recipients or potential recipients of governmental aid were dependent on the whim and caprice of government bureaucracies. Antipoverty legal efforts established the principle of due process under social welfare programs and pressed the notions of equal protection and welfare as a right, chalking up some noteworthy victories in overturning the man-in-the-house and state residency restrictions.

The neighborhood legal services program was a vital tool in combating poverty, establishing new rights through law reform as well as providing traditional legal aid. Suits on behalf of clients against state and local governments got the program into political hot water. However, since the courts decided most cases in favor of the poor, the neighborhood legal services program was criticized for its effectivness and not for its shortcomings.

Community Action

Maximum feasible participation—an ill-defined and much maligned goal—was a basic approach of the Great Society. The aim was to give minorities and the poor a degree of organizational power in order to change institutions, to protect their interests, and to design innovative strategies to serve themselves. Community action agencies, model cities, concentrated employment projects, neighborhood health centers, and community development corporations, though no more participatory or democratic than other groups in our society, had the express purpose of representing the needs of the poor. In doing so, it was necessary to step on firmly entrenched toes, and this generated antagonism, as did efforts to bring about institutional change. Friction was an inevitable ingredient in the process, and though new community leaders sometimes made a virtue of antagonizing the establishment, conflict was mainly rhetorical. Community groups initiated a number of innovative approaches and were condemned for the waste and high failure rate implicit in experimentation. Yet many of the seeds bore fruit locally and nationally.

The community-based programs defy rigorous assessment because of their diversity, but the more narrowly focused efforts can be compared wtih alternative approaches. Neighborhood health centers, for instance, provided care at roughly the same cost as established institutions. The quality of care was equal, but accessibility and amenability were greater. Health centers used paraprofessionals and took other steps to reach out to those in need, increasing the level of usage. Community development corporations were no more successful in establishing viable businesses in poverty areas than other establishment-run efforts, but the CDC's helped organize the neighborhood and generated short-term employment and income for the poor.

Improving the Status of Blacks

As a result of Great Society civil rights and other initiatives, blacks made very substantial gains on a number of fronts during the 1960s. The purchasing power of the average black family rose by half. The ratio of black to white income increased noticeably. The Great Society's efforts were instrumental in generating advancement. But relative black income fell during the 1971 recession and did not recover subsequently.

Earnings were the primary factor in the income gains made by blacks, although income support and in-kind aid also rose. Blacks moved into more prestigious professional, technical, craft, and secretarial jobs previously closed to them. Earnings rose absolutely and relatively as discrimination declined. Sustained tight labor markets, improved education, manpower programs, and equal employment opportunity efforts all played a role.

The improvements in schooling were dramatic and consequential. Black preschoolers were more likely to enroll than whites, largely because of federally financed early education programs. High school completion increased significantly and compensatory programs provided vital resources to the schools where black youths were concentrated. At the college level, absolute and relative enrollment gains were dramatic, the direct result of government aid programs.

Economic and social progress was not without serious drawbacks. Dependency increased, the black family was buffeted, and already high crime rates accelerated. Without minimizing the negative spillover, there is clear proof that blacks were far better off before the advent of the economic slump than a decade earlier. There is a long way to go to equality and progress has been uneven, but advances have been made.

Fighting Poverty

While the war on poverty was not unconditional, it was more than a mere skirmish. The Economic Opportunity Act programs were only one—and not the primary—front in this assault. The Great Society's economic policies, which combined tight labor markets with structural measures such as minimum wages and manpower programs, helped the employable poor. Welfare, social security, and in-kind aid focused on persons with limited labor market attachment.

The number of poor declined sharply in the 1960s, then leveled off. The early declines were achieved by raising the income of the working poor, and their place was taken by female heads with little opportunity for self-support. The combination of deteriorating labor markets, declining numbers of working poor, and accelerating family breakups caused poverty to level off despite the fact that the government's antipoverty expenditures continued to rise in the 1970s.

The continuance of poverty does not mean government efforts have been ineffective. In 1971, 43 percent of the otherwise poor were lifted out of poverty by income transfers, compared with 30 percent in 1965. In-kind aid and services going to the poor are not included as income in the poverty measurements, yet they cost more than the cash poverty deficit. If victory in the war on poverty means providing the minimal standard of living, then the war has very nearly been won, though some battles remain to be fought.

Achieving Full Employment

The economic setting is a crucial determinant of social welfare policy. The Great Society's expanding efforts could be afforded, despite the drain of the Vietnam war, because of the healthy growth dividend. Manpower development, equal employment opportunity, and economic development efforts worked best in a tight labor market. Inflation and rising unemployment in the 1970s increased needs and at the same time reduced society's ability to pay. A fundamental question is whether economic growth and full employment can be achieved through governmental action.

It is ironic that in the economically troubled 1970s the successes of the 1960s were quickly forgotten and even condemned. The Johnson administration placed highest priority on achieving rapid growth and low unemployment. It succeeded, and prices rose slowly (at least by mid-1970s standards). The Nixon and Ford administrations acted on the premise that added joblessness was necessary to combat inflation and to provide a foundation for measured growth. Unemployment rose precipitously and growth declined, but prices continued to rise rapidly. Common sense would suggest that something was being done right in the 1960s, which was not in the 1970s, and prudence would caution against accepting the claims of policy makers and economists anxious to pass the buck for their own dismal record. Common sense would also question the effectiveness of the strategy of combating inflation by increasing unemployment.

The charge that the Great Society's excesses were the primary cause of the mid-1970s economic difficulties does not square with the facts. Needed restraint was not exercised during the last few years of the Johnson administration and inflationary pressures built up. It is entirely possible that the end-of-the-decade recession could have been moderated or even avoided with more timely action. The Nixon game plan was to let the recession run its course and clamp down on spending. But as the 1972 elections approached, a choice was made to spur the economy. Excessive stimulation and the decontrol of wages and prices led to inflation. The international oil and food crises then continued to push up prices while a combination of governmental restraint and international recession dramatically increased unemployment. The Great Society might be blamed for contributing to the 1969-1971 slump, but subsequent policies have missed the mark far more and, together with international events, must bear the blame for the deepening malaise.

The theoretical basis for shifting blame has always been suspect, suggesting a sophisticated witch hunt more than sound analysis. Apologists for the 1970s recessions have argued that there is a natural rate of unemployment. Demographic changes in the labor market have allegedly raised the potential equilibrium so that unemployment of 5 percent or higher must be accepted. Pushing the aggregate rate below this level in the 1960s, it is claimed, set off a price explosion. The statistical evidence for these assertions is rather shaky at best, and it certainly cannot justify the massive joblessness that prevailed in the mid-1970s. To dismiss structural measures such as manpower training, public employment, and economic developments as if the public policy trade-offs were set in concrete is merely to ensure that they will be. The Great Society's structural programs were not of a scale to change things dramatically, but they were certainly steps forward.

Defeatism about reducing unemployment goes back to the 1950s when similar arguments led to a lengthy period of stagnation. The Great Society demonstrated that a tight labor market could be achieved and maintained for many years. The nation has paid dearly for continuing to ignore this lesson.

Redistributing Income

The money income shares of the highest and lowest quintiles are not much different now than at the outset of the Johnson administration. The aim of the Great Society was not a large-scale redistribution of income, but rather the opening of opportunities for those at the end of the line so that they could gradually pull themselves up. Meanwhile it attempted to provide minimal income, goods, and services for all citizens. From 1960 to 1973, total government social welfare spending rose by 5 percentage points of GNP and needs-based aid by less than 2 percentage points. This was certainly a modest effort at redistribution through direct transfers. The subsequent recesion lowered GNP while raising transfers, but the lower income quintiles lost ground relatively because they were hardest hit by the loss of jobs.

Offsetting the recession-related increase in inequality, federal taxes have become more progressive, leaving the poor in larger proportion of income. The continuing expansion of payroll taxes has been detrimental to the working poor, but the burden was alleviated by raising the tax base more than the tax rate and by altering the benefit formula to make it more redistributive. Tight labor markets are unquestionably the most effective redistributive mechanism. Low unemployment in the 1960s, combined with boosts in the minimum wage, helped those at the end of the labor queue. Conversely, the subsequent recession hurt them most.

Much was made in the late 1960s of the squeeze on middle-income families. The culprit was the slowed growth of real earnings and not redistribution of income. During the Great Society, the gains of the poor were achieved by reducing the share of the rich, but the rich were still better off in absolute terms as aggregate GNP grew rapidly. The Nixon administration claimed to champion the forgotten Americans, but its tax and transfer policies did little to improve their status.

THE CANONS OF GAINSAYERS

A combination of shifting fashions among opinion makers and limited analysis of the facts seems to be responsible for the attacks on the Great Society not only by its opponents, but also by many of its former champions and even its beneficiaries. To assess the effectiveness and value of diverse and complex social welfare endeavors, a judgmental framework is needed. Determinations of statistical significance begin with the articulation of a hypothesis. Using some standard of poof, the evidence may then be tested to ascertain whether contradictions are too frequent to allow acceptance. In assessing performance, one hypothesis would be that a program works, demanding contrary evidence of failure. The converse would be to assume failure and require proof of effectiveness. Different results can be obtained from these different hypotheses when measurements are imprecise and proof equivocal. If clear evidence of success is demanded to discount an assumption of failure, then a positive verdict is unlikely; while if absolute failure must be demonstrated to alter the assumption of success, a more positive judgment is inevitable.

What is the most reasonable hypothesis? A primary consideration must be the danger of drawing the wrong conclusion. Almost all social welfare efforts provide benefits to those who would be worse off without them—extra nutrients, a roof that does not leak, more cash, or preventive health care. To conclude that these goods and services are unnecessary, less important than others which could have been acquired with the same funds, or ineffectively delivered, runs the risk of seriously affecting the welfare of recipients if conclusions are wrong. It may also become the basis for retrenchment or counterproductive change. In evaluating social welfare efforts, the small monetary costs to each citizen must be weighted against the possibly severe losses to particular individuals in need. In considering programs with altruistic goals, the compassionate approach is to assume success until failure is reasonably demonstrated. Critics have frequently stressed economy over compassion.

Questionable Standards

Besides basing judgments on negative hypotheses, critics have applied a number of other questionable standards supportive of their gainsaying. One sure way to support a negative case is to measure the real against the ideal. In support of revenue sharing, for instance, the ideal of a politically accountable and locally adaptable decentralized and decategorized system was compared with the realities of categorical federally run efforts with their inherent administrative complexities. Yet where revenue sharing was tried, it did not significantly alter either adaptability or accountability, while the loss of federal control had some negative consequences.

New and experimental efforts will usually come up wanting when compared to long-standing programs. Most Great Society endeavors got underway in 1965 or later, yet their failure was being trumpeted by the late 1960s on the basis of evidence drawn from the first few years of operation. A longer time period encompassing the evolution of the more successful approaches, the retrenchment of the less successful, as well as the implementation of needed reforms, is required to get an adequate perspective.

Secondary and nonquantifiable goals were frequently ignored, biasing judgments against multipurpose programs. The Great Society efforts usually had multiple aims: to deliver goods and services but also to achieve institutional change, to maximize help for the disadvantaged, and to improve the status of minorities. These were not usually as efficient as programs whose sole purpose was service delivery, but they had more positive spillovers.

While the positive secondary effects of programs frequently were ignored, the negative secondary effects were often in the spotlight. Opponents and threatened interests were quick to seize on incidents of gross failure. Side effects were sometimes taken as proof of failure even when these were part and parcel of achieving the primary aims. For instance, programs redistributing resources by paying for the needs of the poor were blamed for raising prices, while efforts to supply goods and services directly were blamed for competing with alternative sources of supply which had demonstrably failed to provide for the same clients.

Critics applied contradictory standards to social welfare activities. Opponents railed against large or mounting costs as if these inherently demonstrated failure or else stressed the inefficiencies and exaggerated potential savings. Critics of the opposite persuasion focused on what was not being done—target groups who were not being served and benefits which were not adequate to meet minimal standards. The result was a discordant critical chorus of complaints against excessive spending and demands for expanded aid.

Dynamic processes often were ignored in the focus on the problems of the day. Few approaches are right for all seasons and many Great Society initiatives were dependent on rapid economic growth and low unemployment, becoming less effective in subsequent slack labor markets. Some approaches suitable in the early stages of development were inappropriate or unnecessary later. For example, categorical programs staked out new areas and after expansion set the stage for comprehensive reform. These reforms were pushed by emphasizing previous failures when, in fact, they were only feasible because of the successes in building up a foundation through categorical efforts.

Critics tended to use the tools and perspectives of economists, examining the equity and efficiency of existing arrangements, focusing on the pluses and minuses at the margin and implicitly accepting the status quo. Such emphases and methods, presumed to be purely objective and completely rational, were inherently biased. One of the most frequent charges against the Great Society's social welfare programs was their inequity. Geographic disparities and uneven treatment of client groups were inherent in building a system from the ground up. Variations in living conditions and values permitted only gradual standardization. Analysts frequently assumed that inequalities were necessarily inequitable and reprehensible, when in fact they stemmed from a decentralized approach to determing what was equitable.

Great Society programs were also criticized for inefficiencies. If a program aims to change institutions, to experiment with new approaches, or to let a hundred flowers bloom, then it is bound to be inefficient. Change is not an efficient process.

During the Great Society, social analysts and humanists balanced the views of the economists. The latter triumphed in the subsequent years (despite their dismal record in their own area of expertise) because they provided apparent rigorousness and raised the hard-nosed questions consistent with the Nixon and Ford administration philosophies. The result was a deemphasis of nonquantifiable ends, of social and economic change, and of dynamic rather than static analysis.

An Example of Negative Thinking

The critical fallacies are perhaps best illustrated in the critique of the income support system. The performance of welfare programs tended to be measured against an idealized comprehensive system devoid of inequities or inefficiencies, a system in which all those in need would be given cash aid without work disincentives and without any negative spillovers on family stability. Advocates of guaranteed income schemes tended to brush aside fundamental questions of work disincentives, the role of in-kind aid, the difficulties of altering disparities, and many other critical issues. The existing system was contrasted with and found deficient relative to an alternative which was unrealistic and unattainable, as the difficulties of reforming aid for the aged, blind, and disabled demonstrated.

Critics usually ignored constructive processes in their efforts to find fault with the welfare system. Over time, variations among areas were significantly reduced, standards were raised to near the poverty level, and most of the defined universe of need was reached, yet there was little recognition of these achievements in the debate over the welfare mess.

Critics overemphasized the negative spillovers on work and the family. As welfare standards approached or exceeded wages available to potential clients, some chose to stop or reduce work. While some left the labor market, the supply of workers was still excessive and unemployment rates for the unskilled remained at high levels. Although paid labor may have been reduced, it is still a presumption in our society that children are better off with a mother's care and supervision.

The income support programs have been judged by contradictory standards, criticized simultaneously for costing too much and doing too little. Conservative critics focused on in-kind and cash packages which exceeded prevailing wages in some states. Liberal critics focused on the benefits in other states which fell below subsistence levels. These groups joined hands briefly under the banner of welfare reform when conservatives were convinced that the extension of benefits to male heads was the only way to check the growth of

AFDC. When the costs became apparent and growth slowed on its own account, there was a parting of company.

The influence of economists was predominant in the welfare reform debate. The work disincentives issue was argued in terms of trade-offs between lower marginal tax rates, income guarantees, and costs, glossing over the evidence that the 1967 changes which made work more profitable for those on welfare had resulted in almost no increase in work and that training and employment programs for mothers on AFDC accomplished little because jobs were not available. Focusing on the margin where work and welfare overlap, broader realities such as expanding help to increasing numbers of needy and consequent slowing growth were ignored.

Beyond the Welfare State

The "big gun" of critics, wheeled out to shore up weak arguments or when all else fails, is the specter of an all-consuming welfare state. However affluent, the nation cannot afford a continuous expansion of social welfare efforts at the rate of the previous decade. The extrapolation of the 1965–1975 trends led the critics to the inevitable conclusion that the rising welfare expenditures would lead the government to tax employed workers to the poorhouse in order to support idlers. But is such expansion ineluctable or needed?

The social welfare explosion during the previous decade resulted from rapidly rising benefit levels and expanded eligibility. There were millions of deprived persons who qualified for aid. Once they had been helped, the growth momentum slowed. By the mid-1970s, public assistance was reaching almost all the low-income aged, blind, and disabled, as well as most needy female-headed families. Health programs also treated most of the indigent. The food stamp program expanded rapidly to serve an increasing share of the eligible population once standards were liberalized in the early 1970s. After this rapid saturation process, the pressure for expansion eased. There was a distinct leveling off in 1973 and 1974.

Spending accelerated thereafter not because of expanding responsibilities and commitments, but rather because of the severe economic troubles. The combination of rapid inflation and the highest unemployment since the Great Depression forced millions to rely on their social insurance and swelled the number qualifying on the basis of need for in-kind and cash aid. There were no new initiatives on the order of Medicare and Medicaid, assisted housing construction, the war on poverty, or even an old-fashioned WPA-type program. Social welfare expenditures grew because social problems intensified, not because policy makers were openhanded. Real social welfare spending will in all likelihood recede or at least stabilize when the economy recovers.

Once a minimally adequate social welfare system is established, many of the problems which seem so insurmountable dissipate. As in any building process, most of the spillovers occur during early construction and these have already occurred. Many female family heads and disabled males withdrew from the labor force when offered alternative income options, and other low-income families split when welfare provided support for female-headed units. But once welfare levels stabilized in real terms and began to decline relative to earnings, case load growth slowed and the impact upon work and family diminished. Over the long run, rising real earnings and stable or slowly growing welfare standards will increase the attractiveness of work and stable families.

Once a package of aid is provided that guarantees an income above the poverty threshold, improvements in the system should prove easier. Welfare reform floundered in the early 1970s because the costs of establishing an adequate minimum were too great and because some reformers were seeking retrenchment rather than improvement. Eliminating allegedly ineffective approaches proved difficult when their termination would have left former beneficiaries in greater deprivation. Once everyone in need is guaranteed a minimum, it will be easier to substitute one form of aid for another and to concentrate on program performance and effectiveness rather than on dividing too few loaves among the multitudes.

Work disincentives have been a continuing concern, but the problem cannot be attacked until a comprehensive system is in place. Aid to low-income male-headed families, even if packaged so as to maximize work incentives, will still leave some of the less motivated the means to avoid work. If unemployables are provided adequate support, some employables will find ways to qualify. But once the shock effects have been weathered, it will be possible to start improving work incentives without pushing down on the help offered to those who cannot work and to minimize the number of nonworkers by making available attractive jobs.

The choice between public or private provision of goods and services can be more easily resolved once the specter of deprivation is eliminated. As long as welfare standards are inadequate, social insurance programs are pressed into service as transfer mechanisms. Once everyone is above poverty thresholds, the scale and scope of transfer payments can be decided on relative merits rather than on the basis of pressing needs. Similarly the issue of relative versus absolute poverty standards can be addressed directly once a minimum is secured.

Each step we take forward makes the next one easier, while also opening new vistas and opportunities. As President Johnson put it, "The Great Society, is not a safe harbor, a resting place, a final objective, a finished work. It is a challenge constantly renewed, beckoning us toward a destiny where the meaning of our lives matches the marvelous products of our labors."[4]

---

4 Ibid., p. 650.

Index